ANGELA STEIDELE, born in Bruch
and tells historical love stories. Her
*In Men's Clothing: The Daring Life of Catharina Linck alias Anastasius
Rosenstengel* and *Love Story: Adele Schopenhauer and Sibylle Mertens.*
Her 2015 literary debut *Rosenstengel* earned her the Bavarian Book
Prize.

KATY DERBYSHIRE comes from London and has lived in Berlin for
over twenty years. She translates mainly contemporary German fic-
tion, including writers such as Inka Parei, Olga Grjasnowa and Christa
Wolf. Katy's translation of Clemens Meyer's *Bricks and Mortar* was
longlisted for the Man Booker International Prize and earned her the
prestigious Straelen Translation Award. She also co-hosts a monthly
translation lab in Berlin and the bi-monthly live *Dead Ladies Show* and
podcast.

Gentleman Jack

A Biography of Anne Lister:
Regency Landowner, Seducer & Secret Diarist

ANGELA STEIDELE

Translated by Katy Derbyshire

This paperback edition published in 2019

First published in Great Britain in 2018 by Serpent's Tail,
an imprint of Profile Books Ltd
3 Holford Yard
Bevin Way
London
WC1X 9HD

www.serpentstail.com

First published in Germany in 2017 by Matthes & Seitz Berlin as *Anne Lister: Eine
erotische Biographie*

3 5 7 9 10 8 6 4 2

Designed and typeset by Crow Books

Printed and bound in Great Britain by CPI Group (UK) Ltd, Croydon CR0 4YY
The moral right of the author has been asserted.

A CIP record for this book can
be obtained from the British Library

ISBN: 978 1 78816 099 5
eISBN: 978 1 78816 100 8

Contents

Prologue: Deciphering Anne Lister's Diaries ix

Eliza 1791–1810 1

Isabella 1810–1813 19

Mariana 1813–1817 29

'Kallista' 1818–1819 57

Isabella, Mariana and Miss Vallance 1819–1822 69

The Ladies of Llangollen 1822 89

'Frank' 1823 103

Mariana and Isabella 1823–1824 108

Maria 1824–1825 117

Mariana 1825–1826 136

Maria 1826–1827 153

Sibella 1828–1829 161

Vere 1829–1832 168

Ann 1832–1840 186
Neighbours 186
Separation 206
Marriage 212
Honeymoon 218
At Shibden Hall 221
France 242
The Brontës 252
From Halifax to Moscow 257
From Moscow to the Caucasus 269
The Widow 297

John, Muriel, Vivien, Phyllis, Helena, Jill & Angela 304

Epilogue: Reading Anne Lister's Writing 310
Acknowledgements 313
Timeline 315
Bibliography 319
Notes 323
Illustrations and Maps 337

The girls liked me
& had always liked me.
I had never been refused by anyone.
Anne Lister, 13 November 1816

Prologue: Deciphering Anne Lister's Diaries

John Lister was seven years old when his father inherited Shibden Hall. He and his family moved into the old manor house near Halifax in 1854. John grew up amidst whalebones, tiger skins and a stuffed crocodile. Once he had become lord of Shibden Hall, he sifted through the sheaves of old papers, documents and letters left behind by previous generations. He was particularly captivated by the twenty-four 'Diaries & Journals of Mrs Lister'.[1] Their marbled covers were bound in soft calf leather, the thick pages neatly lined with black ink. Nonetheless, the tiny handwriting was hard to read; Anne Lister had used numerous abbreviations, and some parts were even written in a secret code.

What John could decipher fascinated him. Anne Lister had been involved in politics and society and had been the only woman co-founder of the Halifax Literary and Philosophical Society. Her diary was a treasure trove of local history. John Lister published a series of extracts in the *Halifax Guardian* under the headline 'Social and Political Life in Halifax Fifty Years Ago'. There were 121 pieces in all between 1887 and 1892.

What John couldn't decipher tempted him just as much. What might the secret code made up of Greek letters, numerical and invented symbols conceal? He asked a friend, the antiquarian Arthur

Burrell, for help, and he was able to work out the equivalents for 'h' and 'e' on the basis of their frequency of use and their position in the words: Then *halfway down the collection of deeds we found on a scrap of paper these words 'In God is my ...'. We at once saw that the word must be 'hope'; and the* h *and* e *corresponded with my guess. The word 'hope' was in cipher. With these four letters almost certain we began very late at night to find the remaining clues. We finished at 2 am [...]. The part written in cipher – turned out after examination to be entirely unpublishable.*[2] It was *an intimate account of homosexual practices among Miss Lister and her many 'friends'; hardly any one of them escaped her.*[3]

Every entry in Anne Lister's diaries begins with whether and with whom and how often she had sex the previous evening, and whether it was repeated during the night or in the morning. She routinely noted the number and quality of her orgasms and those of her partners. If she woke up alone, she made a note of whether she had masturbated. Burrell found all this *very unsavoury*[4] and advised his friend to burn the diaries immediately. What annoyed him was not only the fact and the sheer number of Anne Lister's female lovers. It was her self-esteem: she too was God's creation. No lesbian self-hatred, no desperation, no tears, no noose. Instead, an early form of gay pride. Anne Lister made no attempt to hide her difference; she flirted with it.

John Lister hesitated to follow his friend's advice. Though there could be no thought of further publication, he did not want to destroy the unique journals. He hid them in a chamber off Anne Lister's bedroom, which she had probably used as a study. He had the wall panelling removed and shelves fitted, then carefully placed the diaries on them and replaced the panels. He had the door to the chamber rendered inconspicuous with more wood panelling. By leaving the window as it was, however, he ensured later owners would notice the room's existence.

After his death, Shibden Hall passed to the Halifax Corporation, which turned the house into a museum. As John Lister had intended,

Anne Lister's diaries were found in their closet – and the coded passages once again aroused curiosity. The municipal librarian Edward
Green tracked down old Arthur Burrell, who handed him the code
but warned him of *what old Halifax scandal knows about Miss Lister*.[5]
The code, which was kept in the safe at Halifax library, was given to
Edward's daughter Muriel Green in the 1930s and to Vivien Ingham
and Phyllis Ramsden in the 1960s, but they had to offer assurance
that *unsuitable material should not be publicised*.[6]

For a century, only a handful of librarians and archivists in Halifax
were aware of what Anne Lister had written down in code. It was
not until the women's liberation movement of the 1970s and 1980s
that the ground was laid for Helena Whitbread (1988 and 1992) and
Jill Liddington (1994, 1998 and 2003) to publish uncensored editions
of her diary. By now five generations of scholars and editors from
Halifax and the surrounding area have spent years deciphering Anne
Lister's handwriting and code, viewing an inexhaustible wealth of
material. I have made grateful use of the transcriptions and editions
of the above-mentioned researchers, particularly Helena Whitbread
and Jill Liddington to whom I owe great respect, and without whose
work this book would not be possible. Although I viewed Anne
Lister's original papers and diaries in the Calderdale archives, I did
not attempt to transcribe any coded passages or new pages myself.
My task was quite different to that of the dedicated Lister scholars; I
wanted to distil Anne Lister's incommensurable day-to-day chronicle and tell the story of her insubordinate life and loves in a single
volume. I have let the diarist herself do the talking to a great extent,
as she was consciously writing down her life: *I am resolved not to let
my life pass without some private memorial that I may hereafter read,
perhaps with a smile, when Time has frozen up the channel of those sentiments which flow so freshly now*.[7]

Eliza

1791–1810

Anne Lister was fourteen or fifteen when she fell in love for the first time. She and Eliza Raine were the same age and in the same class at Manor House School in York. Both were unlike the other girls. Eliza had been born in Madras and had dark skin and black hair. Anne wore threadbare clothing and was subject to a lot of staring and quizzing for being different. *Care despised on my part!*[1] She wanted to learn more than befitted girls, and was called *the Solomon of the school.*[2]

Anne was able to attend this private boarding school thanks to her aunt and godmother, Anne Lister senior, her father Jeremy's youngest sister. His eldest brother, James Lister, was the sole heir to the family seat, Shibden Hall near Halifax, West Yorkshire. James' younger siblings – Joseph and Jeremy, Hannah, Phoebe, Martha and Anne senior – had gone almost empty-handed. Without a dowry, none of the sisters could marry; all four stayed at Shibden Hall with their eldest brother, who also never married. Anne's father, Jeremy, had to take care of his own financial needs. He signed up to the infantry, was sent to Canada and later fought the American rebels in the first battle of the War of Independence in Lexington and Concord, Massachusetts, in 1775. Promoted to the rank of captain, he returned home with the defeated British in 1783. In 1788, aged thirty-five, he

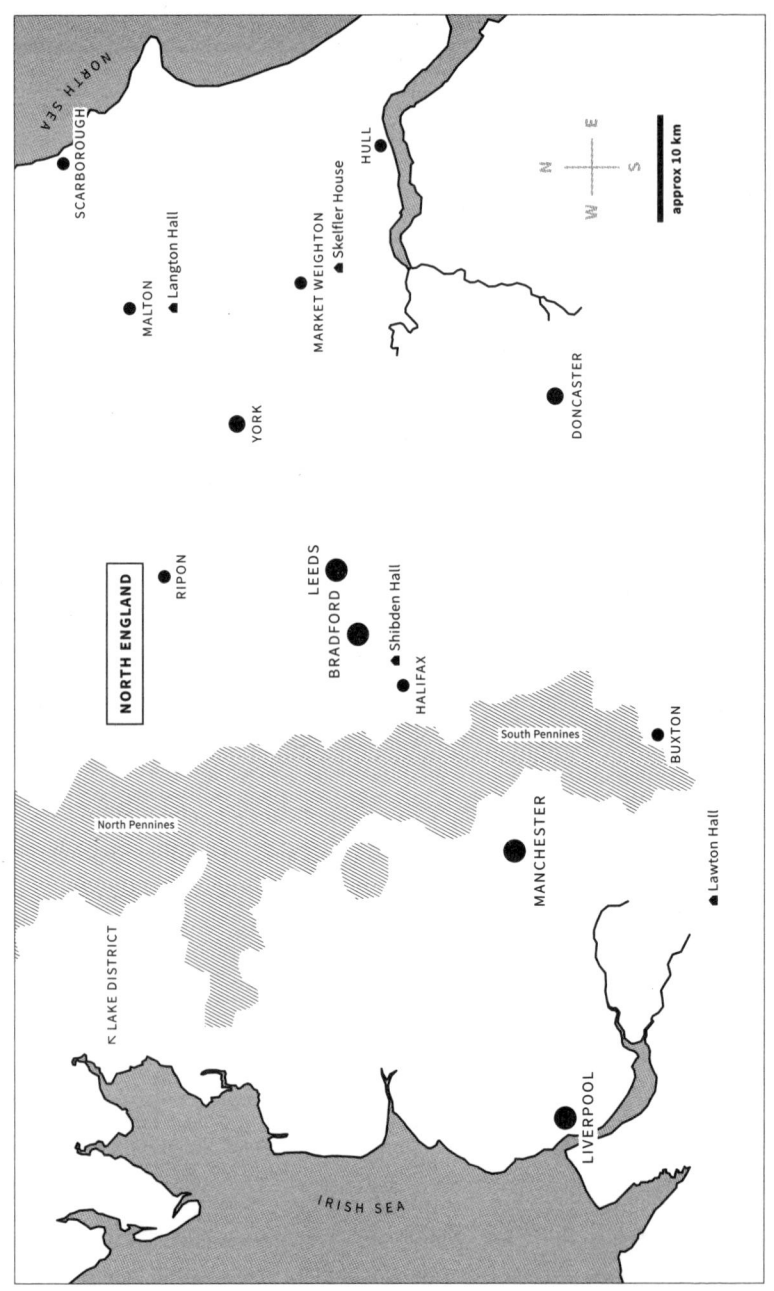

1 Map of northern England, Laura Fronterré.

married eighteen-year-old Rebecca Battle, who was set to receive a modest inheritance. While Jeremy was serving in Ireland in 1789, Rebecca gave birth to her first child, a boy who died shortly afterwards. When she fell pregnant a second time, her sisters-in-law invited her to Halifax, where she had a daughter on 3 April 1791. She was named after her twenty-six-year-old aunt, *she who* [...] *took me on her lap the moment I was born, gave me the first food I ever tasted, lifted me within the pale of Christianity.*[3]

Anne was two when Jeremy used Rebecca's inheritance to buy the modest Skelfler House in Market Weighton, along with the surrounding fields and two leased-out farmyards. Jeremy hoped to live on the income from his property, as his brother James did. Anne spent her early childhood in the rolling landscapes of the Yorkshire Wolds. For the rest of her life, *a good ramble in the Fields* was to be one of her *greatest pleasures.*[4] She later had three brothers, Samuel, John and Jeremy, who also died in infancy, and a sister. When Marian was born in 1798, seven-year-old Anne benefitted too; *my mother had nursed me when my sister was born,* Anne recalled. *She had too much milk. I liked it exceedingly.*[5]

There was no other abundance in the Lister household. Jeremy earned little. When he did have money, he did not spend it wisely, and accustomed to rough army manners, he would argue loudly over domestic matters. In the meantime, his oldest child was growing into an *unmanageable tomboy.*[6] *'Scaped my maid & got away among the workpeople.* [...] *When my mother thought I was safe I was running out in an evening. Saw curious scenes, bad women, etc.*[7] *I was a curious genius and had been so from my cradle,* she wrote of herself, *a very great pickle. Sent to school very early because they could do nothing with me at home.* At that time, girls from the gentry and middle-class families learned to read and write at home and were not sent away to school until at least the age of twelve. Anne, however, started at the Ripon Girls' School run by Mrs Hague and Mrs Chettle in North Yorkshire aged only seven.

GENTLEMAN JACK

Whipped every day, except now & then in the holidays, for two years.[8]
Apart from having *whistled very well,*[9] she claimed to have learned
nothing at the school. *Was always talking to the girls instead of attending
to my book.*[10] Her teachers regarded her as *a singular child, and singularly dressed, but genteel looking, very quick & independent & quite above
telling an untruth.*[11]

Rebecca thought her oldest daughter *a little high flown at times.*[12]
She refused to learn to cook or keep house and left her mother alone
with the maid on washing day. The only domestic chore Anne could
not escape was needlework, as she had to patch and darn her own
clothes. To her mother's chagrin, she would not wear the obligatory
girls' caps and poke bonnets because the protruding brim restricted
her vision. Whenever Anne visited Shibden Hall, Rebecca's letters
enquired with concern as to how her daughter was dressed. Her
Uncle James and Aunt Anne got on better with their wayward niece.
Anne respected James, a quiet bookish man, and her childless godmother treated her niece as the daughter she never had. After a long
stay at Shibden Hall at the age of eleven in 1802, she moved in for
almost a year at the end of August 1803.

Shibden Hall was built in the early fifteenth century and came into the
Lister family's possession via marriage in 1619. The manor house, built
of brick with half-timbered sections and clad in stone, stands just outside Halifax today, in the midst of the Pennines. The old road leading
past Shibden Hall down to Halifax was *so steep, so rugged, and sometimes too so slippery,* that Daniel Defoe thought it *to a town of so much
business as this is, [...] exceeding troublesome and dangerous.*[13]

Halifax had been going through a boom since the eighteenth century, fundamentally changing its landscape and society. Technical
developments such as the spinning jenny and the steam-powered
loom industrialized textile production, which was largely based in the
North and Midlands. Manchester, *this mother of the cotton trade,* could

be spotted from afar by its *thick masses of black smoke and long brick chimneys.*[14] Spreading out from there, entrepreneurs built large mills along the river valleys, in which good English cloth was manufactured. Impoverished villagers flooded into prospering towns like the previously insignificant Halifax to find work, albeit work that paid a pittance. For middle-class factory-owning families, increasing wealth brought with it political influence. As members of the original landed gentry, the Listers held themselves somewhat apart from the new mercantile class, although Anne's second uncle, Joseph, did trade in woollen fabrics, though not too successfully. Thanks to his first wife he owned the large, elegant Northgate House down in Halifax.

As industry spread through the valley, up on the hill at Shibden Hall things were still run in the traditional way. The estate's land, four dozen small fields, none of them larger than five acres, was leased out. A quarry, a small primitive coalmine and a mill brought in additional income, supplemented by dividends from shares in the Turnpike Trust (road tolls) and Calder and Hebble Navigation (canal tolls). Not yet twelve, Anne wrote to her parents about harvesting oats at Shibden Hall and considered the political and socio-historical meaning of *my favourite subject of Farming.*[15] She was taught by the sisters Sarah and Grace Mellin. Aside from that, she took singing lessons twice a week with the organist of the old parish church in Halifax. *I like Music better then* [sic] *Dancing.*[16]

After a year back with her parents and siblings in Market Weighton, where she learned Latin from the local vicar, in 1805 or 1806 Anne was sent to Manor House School in York, which was considered one of the best girls' schools in the area. A boarding school, it occupied the north wing of King's Manor, built as an abbatial palace in the thirteenth century and today housing part of the university. Along with forty other girls, Anne was schooled in reading, writing and arithmetic, geometry, astronomy, geography, history and heraldry. Drawing lessons were given by the artist Joseph Halfpenny, who had published

2 Manor House School, York, 1822, copperplate by Henry Cave.

detailed architectural drawings of York Cathedral, only two minutes' walk from King's Manor. Anne showed greater talent for music. She practised the flute and pianoforte every day and also enjoyed beating the drum.[17]

At school, Anne continued her unusual Latin lessons at her own request, for eight hours a week. Although, as a girl, she could not attend a regular grammar school, she still wanted to learn the language of the sciences like her brothers. *As to what has been said about myself I am perfectly indifferent,* she claimed. *To be thought a little crazy will never give me much uneasiness, so long as I myself feel conscious of mens sana & mens recta.*[18] She did not sleep in the dormitories, but instead shared an attic room with one other girl: Eliza Raine.

For Anne and the other schoolgirls, Eliza may have been the first person they had ever seen from another part of the world. Eliza's father William

Raine had been head surgeon at a hospital in Madras on the southeast coast of India, now Chennai. He and an Indian woman – her name is not documented – had two daughters, Jane and Eliza. Both girls were christened and considered illegitimate but British. They spoke Tamil with their mother and the servants, English with their father and his friends. The latter included William Raine's colleague William Duffin. He and his wife did not have children and grew very fond of the Raine girls. In 1797, Duffin made Raine his successor as Chief Medical Officer in Madras and returned home to York. When William Raine died three years later, William Duffin was executor of his will and brought Eliza and Jane to York. The girls both attended Manor School, with Eliza boarding while Jane moved in with the Duffins at 58 Micklegate. Each of the girls had £4,000 in a London bank account. This capital, which generated enough interest to live on, was to go to them on their marriage or upon reaching the age of twenty-one. Some might have considered them good catches financially – but as illegitimate 'half-castes', they were not accepted by society.

Anne was besotted with Eliza's beauty; thirty years and countless lovers later, she still called her *the most beautiful girl I ever saw*.[19] Anne helped Eliza, who preferred French and drawing, with mathematics. Perhaps it was mere coincidence that the two of them were put in the same room. Or perhaps the staff wanted to set apart two girls who did not really fit in. Whatever the case, Anne and Eliza came to enjoy the isolation of their room. *My conduct & feelings being surely natural to me inasmuch as they were not taught, not fictitious but instinctive.*[20] *I had always had the same turn from infancy* [...]. *I had never varied & no effort on my part had been able to counteract it.*[21]

Eliza and Anne swore to stay united forever. They planned to live together as soon as Eliza came into her inheritance in six years' time. The girls exchanged rings to seal their promise. They were reluctant to be parted in the holidays, the two of them staying with Anne's parents in a rented house in Halifax – *Skelfler is not the neat place that*

1806

Monday August 11th Eliza left us
Had a Letter from her on Wednesday
morning by Mr Ratcliffe the 13th Inst
Wrote to her on Thursday 14th by Mr Lund
Wrote to her again on Sunday 17th put into
the Post office at Leeds on the monday following
that Evening the 18th had a parcel from
her Music Letter & Lavender —
had a Letter Wednesday August 20th
Answered on the 21st
Sunday 24th wrote to ER put into the Post on monday
Wednesday 27th had a Letter from her in answer to two
Friday 28th rec'd a parcel from ER by Mr Lund
Sunday 30th Wrote to ER in answer to ten sheets
by Mr Lund ~ Sunday 7 of September wrote
Tuesday 9th had a Letter from her
Wednesday 10th had a Letter from ER
Friday 12th had a Letter from ER
Thursday 11th wrote to ER in answer to hers of the 10th
Sunday Septbr 14th Wrote to ER by my Uncle &
Aunt I Lister going to Hull on the same
day a short wrote to Miss Hargrave enclosd
with 3 P Handkerchiefs 1 Slip in a parcel
with my Letter to ER in answer to one
from her on Saturday 13th by Mr Vastlet
enclosing me a cornelian Broach —
Monday August 25th 1806 Rode with Mr
Mitchell to Bakup the first time I ever
was out of Yorkshire
Tuesday Sept 16th had a Letter from ER in answer to
mine by my Uncle & Aunt. By the Post they being at Hull
Wednesday rode with Mr Mitchell to Ripley through Elland
Rastrick and Brighouse on that day was the Rastona
at Elland Wednesday Sep 17th 1806

3 First page of Anne Lister's diary, which begins in August 1806 with
a list of letters exchanged with Eliza. West Yorkshire Archive Service,
Calderdale, SH: 7/ML/E/26.

it used to be.[22] By this time, Jeremy had left the army. Eliza was given a friendly welcome by Anne's family. As at Manor School, Anne and Eliza shared a room and a bed at the Listers' house, not only for practical reasons. Early nineteenth-century society was obsessed with virginity, and thought girls were best protected from male seduction by a close female friend, who would engage their hearts and occupy their beds. This parental panic granted girls and women like Anne Lister and Eliza Raine a great many liberties.

After spending the summer holidays together, only Eliza returned to Manor School. Anne is said to have been expelled, although there is no evidence of this. Perhaps Aunt Anne could no longer pay the fees for her niece. Until the girls could meet again, they agreed to write regular letters. To make sure every letter arrived and did not fall into the wrong hands, Anne kept a record of their correspondence. This list was the beginning of her diary.

Monday August 11 Eliza left us. Had a letter from her on Wednesday morning by Mr Ratcliffe. Wrote to her on Thursday 14th by Mr Lund. Wrote to her again on Sunday 17th – put into the Post Office at Leeds on the Monday following – that Evening the 18th had a parcel from her – Music, Letter & Lavender.[23]

Without Eliza, Anne consoled herself with her favourite brother Samuel over *the daily disagreeables that forever beset our unfortunate family.*[24] Anne loved to pit herself against Sam, two years her junior, in 'masculine' arts: chess, fencing with wooden swords, or translating from Latin. She would always win. In the end, though, thirteen-year-old Samuel and eleven-year-old John returned to their boarding school in Bradford. Intending for one of them to inherit Shibden Hall, Uncle James paid their school fees to ensure they got a good education.

Anne received lessons from the Halifax theologian Samuel Knight in the autumn of 1806, learning algebra, rhetoric and classical languages – all subjects befitting a budding gentleman, but not

SH:7/ML/A/8

Halifax — Sunday Feby 21st 1808 —

My dear Eliza

I shall begin with telling you that I cannot say much this week however I will not waste time in making apologies therefore to proceed — I thank you much for your last long Letter which I wish it were in my power to answer more worthily but such pleasure I trust will not always be out of my reach as it has been of late the idea of seeing you so soon can alone reconcile me to it but in this most comfortable thought I find every needful consolation I am glad that you esteem yourself so happily situated and equally so that you think me as affectionate as ever I assure you Eliza I am very steady in my attachments and though not deemed of an affectionate disposition I feel that I can be strongly attached to my dear and kind friend ER — You still give an unfavorable account of your health indeed I cannot get the better of a thousand fears concerning you nor can I forget that tender yet painful anxiety which is to me the greatest proof how much I love you but I see it is in vain to tell of my solicitude since you are so surrounded with society that you have not time to think of your own complaints much less of those of your friend — I daresay M^rs

4 Letter from Anne Lister to Eliza Raine, 21 February 1808. Anne Lister's handwriting was less easy to decipher in her later diaries. West Yorkshire Archive Service, Calderdale, SH: 7/ML/A/8.

a young girl. While practising the Greek alphabet, she occasionally wrote the dates and times in the list of letters to and from Eliza in Greek letters, for instance 'Συνδαι Νοον' for 'Sunday noon'.[25] That October, she wrote her first English note in Greek letters, about her correspondence with Eliza, her studies with Mr Knight and her menstruation.

Anne learned Greek with the New Testament, but as early as 1807, she was studying Demosthenes and a year later Homer, Xenophon and Sophocles; she also read Horace's Latin odes. The Classics interested her not only because they were part of young men's curricula; Anne soon noticed that classical literature exalted in (and laughed at) eroticism and desire in all its forms, without Christian moralising. The translations of her time censored what was considered obscene, so Anne had no other option but to read Greek and Latin poetry in the original. During her reading, she drew up a list[26] of explanations of words such as clitoris, paedophile, eunuch, hermaphrodite and tribade. In Pierre Bayle's *Dictionnaire historique et critique* (1695–1697, published in English in 1738), she came across an entry on Sappho: *You must know that [...] her amorous passion extended even to the persons of her own sex.* According to Lucian, Bayle wrote, *the women of the Isle of Lesbos [...] were very subject to this passion* and Sappho had been made *infamous* by the island's *young maids.*[27] Anne found Bayle's extensive articles *most interesting*[28] and systematically followed his references to Horace, Juvenal and Martial.

The latter wrote two infamous epigrams on women who desire women, for instance on a certain Bassa, who acted chaste and unapproachable in public but secretly fucked women; no other verb would fit the original, in which Bassa penetrates other women with her *prodigiosa Venus,*[29] her *prodigious clitoris.* Anne understood it to be a dildo, something she'd also come across in classical texts.[30] Another of Martial's epigrams deals with a woman named Philaenis,

rougher than a husband's hard-on,
she sticks it to eleven girls a day.
She tucks up her skirt and plays handball,
gets covered in the wrestlers' yellow sand
and easily curls weights that queer guys would find heavy.
Smeared with the dust of the wrestling ring,
she gets worked over hard by her oiled-up trainer;
and she won't eat dinner or recline at the table before she's
thrown up a good six pints of unmixed wine;
which she thinks it's alright to come back to,
once she's wolfed down sixteen rib-eyes.
When she's done with all this, she sates her lust,
she doesn't suck cock – that's not macho enough for her –
instead she absolutely gobbles up girls' middles.
May the gods bring you to your senses, Philaenis,
for thinking it macho to lick cunt.[31]

Nowhere else could a respectable English girl read anything like that in the early nineteenth century. Anne Lister did not let the implicit misogyny of ancient Greece and Rome trouble her. To her, 'Bassa' and 'Philaenis' verified the existence of women who desired women, confirming her own feelings. She used Martial's erotic poetry as intended, reading the books 'with one hand', as Rousseau put it. The margins of several diary entries dealing with her reading of classical texts are annotated with an 'X' for masturbation.[32] Some poems *incurred a cross,*[33] as she called it.

Euphoric from her readings, Anne implored Eliza to learn Latin and Greek as well. She cobbled together a doggerel poem for her (*All hail! thou beauteous charming fair*), singing *amazonian praise* to Eliza as a *poet male*: like the ancient man-less warrior women, she told Eliza

Thy needle, distaff, puddings, and thy pies
Thy much liked cheesecakes and thy curds despise

urging her instead to study grammar and vocabulary, and gain an erotic education from Anacreon, Vergil and Horace: *With these acquirements thou wilt lovers gain.*[34]

Eliza had other matters on her plate. Her sister Jane thought she had found the perfect man in a certain Henry Boulton. He had been in Calcutta, shared Jane's love of India and wanted to return there as soon as possible. Boulton was his father's fourth son and so, like Jeremy Lister, had no hope of an inheritance and had to seek his fortune in the military. Despite her foster father William Duffin's dire warnings, Jane married Boulton in May of 1808 and sailed for India with him.

In her letters to Anne, Eliza vented her rage over men's depravity. Anne responded with an anecdote about Mme Théroigne de Méricourt; this 'Amazon of the French Revolution' had fought to arm women and had made use of her own weapons. She was *a young fanatical girl who would have been one of the finest women in France had she less despised those softer graces and winning charms which she really eminently possessed, insomuch that one young man was so fond of her as to offer marriage upon which she put a pistol to his breast and threatened to shoot him if he ever mentioned the subject again.*[35]

Eliza came to Halifax at the end of that July and helped the Listers to move house. The family could no longer afford their home and had to move to a smaller property on the northern edge of the town. Samuel ridiculed his sister Anne's tiny new room as a *kennel.*[36] Eliza moved into the small space with her, and the two seventeen-year-olds were very happy there, at all times of the day: *felix 8 o'clock* or *felix afternoon,*[37] Anne noted. Inspired by her study of classical languages, she invented her first cipher.

Anne assumed that the loose sheets she used for writing would arouse curiosity. They would not be safe from the eyes of others, even in a locked drawer. If she wanted to write down all her thoughts and experiences without exception, she had to find hiding places in the language or the script she used. Her mother Rebecca had no Latin, but her brother Samuel could have guessed at what lay behind 'felix'. That summer, Anne composed her secret code. Although few people in her immediate surroundings could decipher the Greek letters in which she had written some entries in the past, they still weren't really secure. Anne therefore abandoned the simple phonetic transcription of English words into the Greek alphabet and instead allocated several letters randomly: instead of 'h' she wrote 'θ' (theta), and 'l' became 'δ' (delta).[38] Eliza taught herself the code and used it for her diary as well, which she began to keep at Anne's suggestion.

A little later, Anne perfected her code by adding mathematical symbols and invented characters for individual letters, omitting gaps between the words and also replacing entire words with only one cipher. She was proud of her secret script for *the almost impossibility of its being deciphered & the facility with which I wrote*.[39]

After these happy days in the 'kennel', in September 1808 Anne accompanied Eliza to Scarborough, where her uncle James Raine lived with his wife and four young children. Trips to stay with relatives or friends were the only travel the impecunious young women could undertake. Anne and Eliza spent three weeks in Yorkshire's then most sophisticated coastal resort, the first of its kind. Back in Halifax, Anne introduced Eliza to her piano pupil, Maria Alexander. There was much flirting between the three. In the end, Anne confessed to Maria that she was in love, but didn't say with whom. She might have meant Eliza – or perhaps Maria. As Anne's diary reveals, *after tea at Eliza's instigation I had Miss A on my knee, kissed her.*[40] Did Anne and Eliza let Maria in on their secret? Did Eliza feel so sure of her Anne that she did not begrudge her a flirtation? Or was Anne lying in her diary, and the kiss was not Eliza's suggestion? There is no reason to assume she was

always entirely honest with herself. Embellishment and self-deception
are among the pitfalls, if not the prerequisites, of every diary.

During the spring of 1809, the exchange of letters between Anne
and Eliza grew less regular. That kiss between Anne and her student
seems not to have been without consequences. To her father's annoyance, Anne spent a great deal of time with Maria Alexander and her
lower-class family. As regards her relationship with Eliza, she did not
feel any pangs of guilt. *My mind was the most convenient, capacious
concern possible. It admitted new impressions without crowding or incom-
moding old ones & that all things keep their proper places.*[41] While whispering sweet nothings to Maria Alexander, she versified to Eliza –

> *But fondle thee I must and will*
> *Thou art best loved by me,*
> *For tho' my heart thou wound'st still*
> *No friend have I but thee.*[42]

and practised the rhetoric of love in her rare letters to her first beloved.
In *sweet moonlight,* the murmur of a stream brought to mind *a thousand
pleasing scenes* of Eliza. *Here I turn my eyes to my bed. This I hope after
a few years, which confidence in your affection will shorten, you will share
with me and thus complete my worldly wishes.* Anne sent the page only
half filled. Eliza understood the invitation and wrote below Anne's
lines that she did not know how to pass the time until she could be
united with Anne entirely. *I will always tell thee every thought and every
remnant of desire, and will not my W do the same?*[43] The 'W' stands for
'Welly', a nickname Eliza had given Anne after Arthur Wellesley, 1st
Duke of Wellington, who had conquered India just as Anne had conquered Eliza.

Eliza sensed that something had changed between them. To get
closer to her lover again, she persuaded her foster father William
Duffin to invite Anne to York for the winter concert and ball season

and to bring them out together as debutantes. This prospect was all the more compelling for Anne in her very modest circumstances as she was arguing more than ever with her parents. Her father would not tolerate his now marriageable daughter roaming the streets and fields alone, especially not at the dead of night. Anne had even visited a certain Captain Bourne in his rooms to have him show her his pistols; *those who do not know her judge from this*, wrote a lady from Halifax, with regret, *for she is such a pleasant companion that I myself could have listened to her till I had forgot it.*[44]

Very much looking forward to her stay, Anne announced her arrival for 1 December 1809. *I promise neither to alarm you with sword or pistols or Orpheus like to draw away the very house with music. No flutes, no fifes, no drums shall disturb you on my account, no neighbourhood shall be kept in awe by my skirmishing.* She wrote forthrightly to Eliza about her excitement *to be in the same room with you*, and rejoiced that *soon, very soon I hope to tell you in a more pleasing manner all that better suits my tongue than my pen. I long to impress upon your lips all that real sincerity and warmth of affection which come but frigidly on paper.*[45]

In the first five weeks, Anne and Eliza enjoyed the season in York. The Roman city was considered the capital of the North. While Bradford, Leeds and Manchester grew in industrial significance and size over the coming decades, York remained the historical, cultural, administrative, civic, ecclesiastical and military centre. Visitors flocked from afar to attend its concerts, exhibitions, balls and galas. Anne and Eliza saw the *primadonna assoluta* Angelica Catalani on 22 December, who was then the toast of England, in fact of all Europe. For the first time, Anne Lister got a taste of the big wide world.

At the start of 1810, influenza brought the season crashing to an end. Although she had fallen ill herself, Anne hurried back to Halifax, where the family feared for her brother John's life. She nursed him and shared night watches with Samuel. John died a week later, on 24

January 1810, shortly before his fifteenth birthday. Samuel was now the only male heir to the Listers of Shibden Hall.

Having treated herself with mustard plasters for her infection, Anne returned to Eliza and the Duffins in York. A month later, however, the girls had to part again. After completing her schooling and until marrying, Eliza had to live with a sickly and irritable cousin thirty-five years her senior in Doncaster, according to her father's will. Lady Crawfurd insisted on Eliza coming, as William Raine had granted her a pension of £170 a year if she took in his daughter. She could use the money, as since divorcing her husband she had been living on £130 a year in alimony. Although Eliza had vowed to get along well with her cousin, arguments broke out after only a week. *Constantly teazing it and showing anger, vexation, nay, spite upon me when any thing domestic or otherwise occurred the least contrary to her wish.*[46] Eliza now understood why her sister, who had also had to live with Lady Crawfurd after leaving school, had been in such haste to marry.

Jane's marriage, meanwhile, had failed. As soon as Henry Boulton had set himself up in business in Calcutta with his wife's £4,000, he threw her out on her ear. She returned to England with no money and no chaperone. The journey took her nine months. By the time she set foot on English soil she was pregnant. Had she been raped on the way or had she been forced to prostitute herself? For society, the difference was of as little interest as the injustice Henry Boulton had visited on her. She was the one to be ostracised. Eliza implored Anne to intercede with Mr Duffin on her sister's behalf. In the end he did ensure she could give birth at the home of a friend of his; yet Jane was never to show her face in York again, and Eliza and Anne were told to avoid her.

In her involuntary Doncaster exile, Eliza felt *at times dull for want of your society.* She wrote letter after letter to Anne, begging for at least *brief epistles*[47] from her *dear Lister*, as she now called her 'husband'.

I have felt greatly & deeply disappointed at your forgetfulness of me, Eliza complained; *if you have any consideration for my feelings, answer me by return of post, tell me why I am thus forgotten.*[48] This long and urgent letter elicited the response from Anne that she had not received any post from Eliza. Eliza saw through Anne's lie, but wrote: *when I cease to love you, I cease to live.*[49]

As arranged, Anne arrived for a visit to Doncaster on 30 April 1810. Only four days later, Lady Crawfurd suspected Anne and Eliza of *acting together in some deep plot against her.* Even years later, Lady Crawfurd was to refer to Anne as *the devil incarnate.*[50] Anne abandoned her stay after only a week. *That occurrence believe me dear L has given me more pain than all the accumulation of insults & ungovernable rage directed to myself.*[51] Following an icy silence, Eliza told Lady Crawfurd on 10 May of her *determination of leaving her which she interrupted by saying she was not against it.*[52]

But where was she to go? Back in York, Anne described Eliza's ordeal with Lady Crawfurd to Mr Duffin. In Halifax, she turned to her old teacher Miss Mellin, asking for a place at her school for Eliza, including bed and board. Anne did everything to help Eliza, and at the same time to get rid of her elegantly.

Isabella

1810–1813

While Eliza waited nervously to be delivered from Lady Crawfurd in Doncaster, she had an inkling of the reason behind the sudden paucity of Anne's letters. *Has York, my dear friend, banished me from your recollection? I cannot believe it. Nothing I hope will make you careless of giving me pleasure; you can little know what pain you have given me.*[1] What Eliza apprehensively called 'York' was really named Isabella Norcliffe. She was six years older than Anne and came from a respected wealthy family. Her great passion was for the theatre. Isabella attended every new production and her *talents for the stage are certainly first-rate.*[2] On one occasion she acted out for Anne how the famous Talma had played Hamlet. Isabella's natural habitat, however, was the countryside. 'Tib', as she was nicknamed, was a good horsewoman who could cover the fifteen miles from York to the Norcliffes' country house, Langton Hall, in a morning's ride; she was also expert at driving coaches. Isabella's favourite activity was an early-morning hunt with just her father – *she is the image of her father in everything*[3] – but she also enjoyed larger hunts. *I have taken entirely to coursing, & can think or dream of nothing but horses hares & Greyhounds. [...] I have had no falls yet, & consequently am very courageous.*[4] Like Anne, who slept with a pistol under her pillow, Isabella loved firearms. *Our dispositions harmonize particularly*, Anne noted; *there was a strong natural resemblance between us.*[5]

After Anne first mentioned Isabella in a letter to Eliza, the abandoned lover attempted to gloss over her jealousy. *I am delighted to hear you have got so pleasant a companion as Miss Norcliffe; I never doubted of your making friends wherever you went.*[6] *I think me worthy of your attachment & kindness*, she stressed, adding: *I suppose you sometimes think of me & kindly wish me every good.*[7] Eliza's flattery no longer elicited wild oaths of love from Anne, however. Eliza's next move was to remind Anne that *the day may come when I can at least offer a more substantial proof of gratitude than mere words.*[8] Yet neither the allusions to their sexual relationship nor her £4,000 prompted Anne to join Eliza in lamenting their physical separation; she felt *so happy, so gay & so cheerful*[9] in York, where she commuted between the Duffins' house on Micklegate and the home of the Norcliffes at Petergate, by the minster.

The Duffins – both well into their sixties – liked Anne and took her along to their summer house in Nunmonkton outside York at the end of May 1810. With the group at the Red House was the unmarried Mary Jane Marsh, a woman in her early thirties who was the sickly Mrs Duffin's companion and Mr Duffin's mistress. Eliza soon joined the party too. The moment she received word to come to the school from Miss Mellin, she sent her belongings to Halifax under a rain of curses from Lady Crawfurd, and went straight to her foster parents and her lover. Anne, however, was bothered by Eliza's downcast mood, of which she was partly the cause. *Nothing more surprises me than that any person of sound judgment, and solid sense should be ill tempered. A bad disposition [...] is more frequently brought upon ourselves by bad habit and too weak an opposition to the worst of our passions, than inflicted upon us by nature; a malady, which most can prevent, and all can cure.*[10]

When the time came for Anne to return to her parents in Halifax, she asked the ever cheerful Isabella to meet her on her way through

5 *Mrs Duffin in York*, watercolour by Mary Ellen Best from: *The World of Mary Ellen Best* by Caroline Davidson (Chatto & Windus, 1986)

York. Delighted, Isabella set aside a whole day for Anne. The two of them went up Clifford's Tower, York's medieval ruin, and exchanged intimacies. Anne let Isabella know she had been telling Eliza all about her. Isabella confessed to Anne that *she had seen the only man who could make her happy.* Remembering that day years later, Anne commented: *How little did Isabel think what would afterwards happen.*[11]

Eliza had barely returned to York with the Duffins when Isabella Norcliffe paid a surprise call at the house on Micklegate to get to know Anne's intimate friend. Immediately after their meeting, Isabella wrote to Anne: *It was with difficulty I kept my countenance when I met her; the remembrance of the conversations you had had together about me rushed so forcibly into my mind, that I could think of nothing else; however I had sufficient command of myself not to let it be seen […]. As you may imagine our conversation was chiefly about you, and her opinion so perfectly coincided with my own, that I could not help thinking her a very sensible discerning girl.*[12]

Eliza in turn gave Anne a detailed report of the meeting as soon as she arrived in Halifax. *We spent the day together charming away the hours in talking of you,* Anne wrote to Isabella of the occasion. *You had so often caused the conscious blush, and taught her a strange variety of sensations for which she was unable as perhaps unwilling to account. How in the world do you manage? For you have certainly the art, whether happy I know not, of working wonders in some people. To tell you the truth, you have been ever present to Eliza in 'Midnight Slumbers and in waking dreams'. I can only laugh that she who would sit for hours moping in a quiet corner hearing and observing all without one single utterance of a sound, should thus on a sudden find such magic in a word or look from you. Indeed, Isabella, you are in some things the oddest girl I ever knew. In this instance you rather pass the powers of my comprehension: do, therefore, explain the arcana of those manners which render you to some at once so singular and so enchanting* [...]. *After what Eliza tells me of you I love you ten times more.*[13] Such sophisticated rhetorical advances rather overawed Isabella. She was reluctant to meet Anne's request to write to her, *being perfectly convinced that my letters are incapable of affording either amusement or instruction to any human being and more particularly to yourself who are so much my superior in everything.*[14] Yet Anne did not give up. *I have known you but a short time. I love you God knows how well and how sincerely,* she wrote to her. *Tell me, as you promised, every secret thought, nor fear to confide in my bosom whatever you dare trust to your own. Write to me, Isabella, as you would talk to me* [...]. *Tell me, in short, anything and everything but that your letters are never worth the expense of postage to one who fondly dotes on that which Isabella does.*[15]

Anne wrote to Isabella from her kennel, having moved back in with her parents. Eliza took rented rooms in the neighbourhood and regularly came for dinner. There was some tension in the air. On 14 August, Eliza wrote in her diary: *Dear L & I had a reconciliation,* only to note two days later: *L & I had a difference which happily was made up before the conclusion of the day but left me exceedingly ill.* The next day, Anne made up for everything. *My husband came to me & finally a happy reunion was accomplished.*[16]

The fact that Anne preferred to visit Eliza rather than helping in the parental household led to *all jealousies & broils about so often going to see her.*[17] Anne did not mention the *unpleasant scenes at Home*[18] in her letters to Isabella, nor her difficult relationship with Eliza. Although she favoured long walks, she wrote to her new horsewoman friend about the *very spirited (little) horse* her father had bought her, which was *quite as much as I can manage. The moment one mounts it begins prancing and capering, and as I am not a very steady cowardly scientific rider I dare say like Homer's heroes I shall lick the dust.*[19] She failed to mention her studies of mathematics and Greek with Mr Knight in her letters to Isabella, who had no interest in academic matters, claiming *I trust I shall not on my emission smell so strong of the lamp as to be at all ungrateful to the delicate olfactory nerves of my darling Isabella. Believe me I pray most fervently that I may never be deservedly ranked among that odious class of animals commonly called Learned Ladies.*[20]

In January 1811, Anne contracted scarlet fever. Eliza nursed her lover and requested medical advice from William Duffin in York. When the convalescent wrote to thank him in February, the Duffins invited Anne to stay, but not Eliza. Anne was only too glad to turn her back on Halifax, her parents and Eliza, and returned to live in York in April 1811, under the care of Miss Marsh. She *is really a mother to me.*[21] Above all, though, she enjoyed her reunion with Isabella. *I love the darling Girl with all my heart.*[22]

The two became a couple that spring. Anne's wooing had had the desired effect on Isabella, and York society encouraged their closeness. Now twenty, Anne Lister was regarded as a very sensible woman. She led an exemplary life and preached to her friends *I hope you will take a long walk every day get up early in a morning and go to bed regularly at an early hour.*[23] The twenty-six-year-old Isabella was told by her:

6 *Isabella Norcliffe (far left) and her family in Langton Hall,*
watercolour by Mary Ellen Best from: *The World of Mary Ellen Best* by
Caroline Davidson (Chatto & Windus, 1986)

*Heaven has given you much more than falls to the common lot of mortals.
Put out your talents to interest, and you will soon be rich.*[24] Anne even
advised Isabella to be prudent about her eating, as she *ate heartily and
drank freely*[25] and treated pains of all kinds with a slug of brandy. *There
are more who die from eating too much, than too little,*[26] wrote Anne, for
whom two meals a day sufficed – a late breakfast and dinner in the
late afternoon. Nor did she allow herself *all the freedom of a man*[27]
like Isabella, who was even more boyish than Anne and often cursed
– albeit in such an original manner that Anne wanted to make a list
of her swear words. Aside from that, not being suspected of relationships with men, Anne seemed to Miss Marsh to be *the saving of Isabella*,
which Anne herself considered *to flatter me too* much.[28]

Meanwhile, Eliza was being taught to dance the quadrille by Anne's father in Halifax and went on spending time with the Listers; *your mother last night would not pay you the compliment of saying she felt yr loss, upon which we had a good-humoured quarrel.*[29] She even took tea alone with Samuel, as Aunt Mary, the second wife of Uncle Joseph of Northgate House, was quick to report to her niece in York. *I get quite attached to him, he is so like you and his temper is benevolent and amiable,*[30] Eliza wrote to Anne. Mainly to escape the *disagreeable work at home,*[31] Samuel, the Listers' only remaining son and the heir to Shibden Hall, was considering signing up to the military as his father had. *Your mother is really dejected about Sam, they often quarrel about his taste for the army, they think oppositely as you may imagine, the Lad is more and more eager and his Mother as much so miserable.*[32] Rebecca did not get her way. In the autumn of 1812, Samuel Lister gave Eliza Raine a lock of his hair, sailed for Ireland and reported for duty with the 84th Regiment in Fermoy, near Cork. He sent best wishes to Eliza in every letter to his sister Anne.

His decision made Anne aware of the limitations placed upon her as a woman. She could neither study nor take up a profession and she depended on invitations from benevolent strangers to evade her depressing home life. *Never till this moment did I feel a wish to be freed from that petticoat slavery that but ill subdues a mind superior to its tyranny. But alas! discontent were folly, and to murmur would be to arraign the decrees of Heaven which gave the fiat. Sometimes I could envy you, if it were not impious and unjust,*[33] she wrote to her brother. Being his older sister, she did not skimp on unasked-for advice. *Pray be punctual and attentive in writing to them all* – meaning their better-off uncles and aunts at Shibden Hall and Northgate House – *this is the best way of insinuation into their good graces.*[34] *By all means keep a journal. Whatever trouble this plan may give you at first, count it as nothing, when compared with the delight and, satisfaction, which it will always afford your friends, and, at some future period, yourself. Though*

writing is irksome, and perhaps difficult whilst we are unaccustomed to it,
yet practice will soon gain us a facility, which will amply compensate the
trouble, and mortification of acquiring it. [...] Let me advise you to finish
your notation of the events of the day, every night, before you go to bed.[35]

No diary of Anne's has survived from these years. The first notes
we have of hers, ten loose, closely written sheets, end in February
1810. She is likely to have kept to this method, as we have a further
loose sheet from March 1813 that is clearly out of context. Her diaries
survive in full only from 1816 on.

So we have little evidence of the first years of Anne and Isabella's relationship. From later comments, we can conclude that they were happy
to begin with. In May 1812, still living with the Duffins in York, Anne
wrote to her brother that she and Isabella were inseparable, spent whole
days together and went to the theatre in the evenings. In October 1812,
Anne visited Isabella for the first time at Langton Hall near Malton,
which remains to this day a sleepy hamlet in the Yorkshire Wolds.
Isabella's father had just had the family's country home expensively
refurbished. Anne had never stayed anywhere as elegant before.

For the last two weeks of the visit, they were joined by Isabella's
most intimate friend, Mariana Belcombe, who *made the last fortnight*
of our stay there doubly interesting. On 1 December 1812, a jaunty
Isabella, her sister Charlotte, Mariana Belcombe and Anne took the
Norcliffes' coach to their house at Petergate in York, laughing and
giggling into the evening. *The first night, much to the merriment of our*
party, we all crammed ourselves (in two beds tho') into the same room.[36]
Anne went on joking with her new friend Mariana for two weeks in
York while Isabella visited relatives in the countryside. Then on 14
December Anne went to Halifax with Isabella, having been away for
a year and a half. *I fear our house is not the most regular,*[37] she may have
warned Isabella.

The timing was carefully planned – Eliza Raine had left Halifax a good two weeks previously. Without Anne and Samuel, there had been nothing to keep her there. Samuel had not stated his intentions to her and she still would have preferred his sister. She had sent Anne a glum reminder of their anniversary and of her twenty-first birthday, once a date they had dreamed of. But Anne had grown tired of Eliza. She no longer needed her and her £4,000 to liberate her from her parents. Thanks to her charm, wit and intelligence, she had achieved what Eliza had not: she had been taken in by the Duffins in York, and also by the Norcliffes. Compared to the vivacious Isabella and her wealthy family with a house in the city and a country home, the illegitimate half-Indian orphan Eliza seemed a poor prospect. Anne deliberately overlooked Eliza's reminder of their dreams of a future together. Eliza never had any parting words from her. *It has never yet occurred to me to like any one person less, because of liking any other person more,* Anne wrote of herself; *all my other friends would most exactly keep their places, and still be dear to me as ever.*[38] When Eliza realised there was no point waiting, she moved to Hotwells in Bristol to spend the winter in a milder climate and kept herself occupied with *deep philosophical works.*[39] *Upon the whole, her leaving our neighbourhood is rather a good thing for me,* Anne wrote to her brother; *home is, by this means, made considerably more agreeable.*[40]

Even without Eliza, though, the family home was not all that cosy. Anne regretted her father *being so unlike a gentleman.*[41] Her relationship with her mother was worse. Rebecca felt estranged from her oldest daughter. She was hurt that Anne had not wanted to live with her even as a child, and she showered her with reproaches. Jeremy also caused a lot of problems for Rebecca – *she is oftener right in some things than my father chooses to allow*[42] – and with money always tight and grieving the loss of three children, Rebecca had taken to drink. *My mother tipsy 25 nights.*[43] Anne had little pity for her. *At all events, it is not so precarious as my father used to imagine; nor do I think hers a worse life than any other in the family.*[44] After five weeks with the Listers, Isabella returned home ahead of time. Anne forced herself to stay another three weeks with the family, returning to Isabella in York on 1 February 1813.

The generous Norcliffes also felt Anne was a good influence on Isabella, and invited her along on a trip to Bath. Their four-day journey took in Sheffield, Derby, Birmingham and Worcester with all the attendant sights, and in particular all the porcelain factories, along the way to the spa town, *one of the most beautiful* [...] *in England.*[45] As Anne wrote, it was the first time she had left Yorkshire. Under the wings of the well-travelled Norcliffes, in Bath Anne learned the rules and manners of privileged society, cultivating her conversational skills and internalising the differences between an upper-class accent and her native Yorkshire dialect. *I am, and have every reason to be, as happy here as my dear Sam's most sanguine wishes can desire.*[46]

Before their return to Yorkshire, Anne and Isabella were allowed to spend a week travelling alone in May 1813. They viewed Salisbury Cathedral, the Earl of Pembroke's painting and sculpture collection at Wilton House, and Stonehenge. This first trip with a lover gave Anne a taste for such excursions, which she was often to repeat when the opportunity arose. She loved exploring new places and enjoyed the freedom afforded in unfamiliar settings – two women travelling together naturally took a shared room in guesthouses and had more privacy than in their family homes.

The Norcliffes headed north at the end of May. On the way back they visited Warwick Castle – *the finest thing of the kind in England* – and the ruins at Kenilworth. *In fact I shall return home quite a traveller.*[47] It was not hard for Anne to return to York, however. For there awaited her *no small pleasure in seeing again Miss M. Belcombe.*[48]

Mariana

1813–1817

In retrospect, Isabella Norcliffe may have cursed herself for introducing Anne to her *darling & almost adored Mariana* [...]. *Most sincerely do I wish you knew more of her; in my opinion it would be impossible for you not to like her. Added to a very strong understanding, she has the most Heavenly disposition I ever saw, a most affectionate and feeling heart, & an attachment to her Friends, which I am sure nothing but death can terminate.*[1] Isabella was to be wrong about that. She was right, however, when she compared Mariana and herself. *Never were two beings so perfectly unlike; she is milder than any thing I ever saw, & you know what I am.*

Mariana Percy Belcombe was a year older than Anne and lived with her family on Petergate, one of York's main roads that passes the minster, as did the Norcliffes when they were in town. Mariana's father, Dr William Belcombe, practised as a doctor. He and his wife Marianne had one son, Stephen, who was also to become a doctor, and five grown daughters: Anne, called 'Nantz', Henriette or 'Harriet', Mariana, Louisa – 'Lou' – and Eliza, 'Eli'. *Her sisters are very nice Girls, but in my opinion not one of them is in the slightest degree to compare to her.*[2] Anne shared Isabella's high opinion of Mariana. *She is indeed a charming girl, and, from the real worth of her character,*

29

7 *Bootham Bar, York,* showing Petergate, where Mariana Belcombe and Isabella Norcliffe lived. York Minster is in the background, copperplate by W. H. Bartlett.

has gained no mean portion of my esteem and regard.[3] Yet *all mental good qualities aside, your friend is a sweet looking girl.*[4]

The two of them, one twenty-one and the other twenty-two years old, probably entered into a sexual relationship in December 1812 when they spent two weeks together in York without Isabella. Over the course of 1813 they wrote each other sixty letters and Anne received eighty-seven letters from Mariana in 1814, one every fourth day on average. Like the diaries that Anne wrote from 1813 to 1815, they were later burned.[5]

Anne continued her relationship with the unsuspecting Isabella, especially as the Norcliffes had significantly more to offer than the doctor's daughter, Mariana, who lived in similarly modest circumstances to Anne herself. After returning from the south, Anne first visited the Duffins at Red House in Nunmonkton and hoped to be able to spend some time in York to see Mariana again. At this point, Anne received the unexpected news that her brother Samuel had died in an accident. *Poor fellow! He was drowned abt 3 o'clock in the afternoon [...] while bathing in the river Blackwater,*[6] Anne wrote at the bottom of his last letter to her. The last of the Listers' four sons was no more, and Anne had lost the only person she liked in her family. Against her original plans, she immediately returned to Halifax, accompanied by Isabella.

The death of her favourite brother was to turn into a blessing for Anne. Over the subsequent months, the wider Lister family discussed inheritance issues. The law gave Uncle James free choice of what to bestow on whom. Customarily, after his death the family estate would fall first to his oldest living brother, the childless Uncle Joseph of Northgate House, and after Joseph's death to Anne's father Jeremy. However, James had no intention of leaving anything to Jeremy, who was foolish with money and had already ruined his own small Skelfler House. So Uncle James was inclined to leave Shibden Hall to the Welsh branch of the family, the Listers of Swansea. Young and without financial support, Anne was opposed to this idea; she wanted to be the beneficiary of the family assets. However, marriage law at the time was a marvellous opportunity for fortune hunters, meaning families were reluctant to pass on property to daughters: poor Jane Boulton (née Raine) had meanwhile been put into a London mental asylum. So Anne tried to persuade Uncle James that she was *the last remaining hope and stay of an old, but lately drooping family.*[7] It was inconceivable for her to fall for a man only interested in her money, or indeed ever to be tied to a man, and pass Shibden Hall on to anyone else. *I love, & only love, the fairer sex & thus, beloved by them in turn, my heart revolts from any other love but theirs.*[8]

The inheritance issues were not yet resolved but the family decided to risk an experiment. Anne moved to Shibden Hall as her uncle's possible heir to learn about running the estate, which had interested her even as a child. For her, the land – *ancient acres* – epitomised her venerable descent. Anne herself never doubted for a second that she would be a capable successor to her uncle. At first, however, the greatest advantage to the arrangement for Anne was that Jeremy, Rebecca and Marian moved back to Skelfler House in Market Weighton in May 1815.

These changes did not make her any better off financially; Anne still had no income and relied on irregular sums of money given by her father, her godmother and her two uncles. She made sure to keep each sum to herself. *I take good care to let nobody know I have so much.*[9] Yet still her funds were barely sufficient to maintain a respectable façade. She found being dependent far more difficult than living frugally. As an unmarried woman from the landed gentry, she could take on no work other than as a teacher or governess without ruining her own and her family's reputation, but she dreamed of stealing away for a few months and *rambling, begging, and eventually gambling*[10] 200 or 300 pounds.

Uncle James and Aunt Anne – the other aunts had all passed away

– were not rich either. James kept only one horse for riding and no coach, so the ladies of the house had to walk to town. Shibden Hall was uncomfortable, a damp and draughty stately home. The three reception rooms on the ground floor had low ceilings, dark oak panelling and old-fashioned furniture: benches, carved chests and heavy chairs. The leaded windows, painted with crests, plants and mythical creatures, let in scant light to what was called the housebody, the main room of the building. Uncle James had set up his study next to the kitchen, where food was still prepared over an open fire. As the head of the household, he had the master bedroom, located on the left-hand side of the top floor and referred to as the Red Room, while Aunt Anne slept in the next room along. On the right-hand side of the floor, Anne made herself a kind of apartment; her privacy was the greatest luxury she enjoyed at Shibden Hall. Anne's realm consisted of a wide corridor, which she gradually furnished as a library and study, from which three uneven steps led up to her bedroom, now called the Edwardian Room. On entering and leaving, she had to be careful not to hit her head on the low lintel. Anne combatted the draughts by hanging colourful drapes on the ceiling and walls. When Isabella Norcliffe or Mariana Belcombe came to visit, this Oriental-like tent insulated the sounds of their whispers, giggles and, as Goethe put it, the *rock-a-bye bed's rhythmic, melodious creak.*[11]

Anne spent carefree hours there with Mariana. *Two good kisses at once last night & three this morning, after eight.*[12] In the eighteenth and nineteenth centuries, 'kiss' was a common euphemism for sex in English-, French- and German-speaking areas. It was the only term that could hint at physical love in poetry. The 'X's with which Anne recorded her masturbation in her diaries clearly echo the abbreviation for 'kiss'. She also used the word to mean an orgasm with a partner. *We drew close together, made love & had one of the most delightfully long, tender kisses we have ever had.*[13] Mariana had a good share in their lust together. *Two last*

33

night. M— spoke in the very act. 'Ah,' said she, 'Can you ever love anyone else?' She knows how to heighten the pleasure of our intercourse. She often murmurs, 'Oh, how delicious,' just at the very moment. All her kisses are good ones.[14] Later, Anne was to note: No one had ever given me kisses like hers. Mariana satisfied Anne far beyond sexual desire, because she did not see her Fred or Freddy[15] too much as a woman.[16] She ignored Anne's menstruation, which Anne described as an undesirable visit from my 'cousin',[17] and avoided anything that reminded me of my petticoats.[18] Mariana let Anne be the gentleman she felt herself to be.

After the first heady rush of love, Anne and Mariana ended up arguing. I cannot forget Mariana's conduct in the autumn of 1814,[19] Anne wrote in retrospect. She certainly behaved very ill and very inconsistently. It seems a strange mixture of selfishness and weakness.[20] Mariana shocked Anne with the news that a rich widower was wooing her – and she was not disinclined to accept his proposal. Charles Lawton owned Lawton Hall in Cheshire and a large amount of land from which he earned a considerable income. The Belcombes were delighted by his interest, seeing he was the most favourable prospect for any of their four unmarried daughters. No one minded that his conversation was shockingly gross and he was quite silly when at school.[21] Mariana's imaginings hit Anne hard. To sink January, 1815, in oblivion![22] she sighed even years later; never was so wretched in my life.[23] Beginning of 1815: whatever might be her regard for me it is very plain it bore but a very subservient portion to her regard for the good things of this world. I was in love or surely I could not have been so blinded and acted with such doting folly. Oh that I then could have given her up without a struggle.[24]

In fact, Anne provoked a major row with Mariana. She insisted her lover would never marry, and that the thing was going on decidedly to all I wished [...]. All was settled to my satisfaction. She came and staid with me a long while and I staid with her.[25] Mariana spent the spring and summer of 1815 at Shibden Hall, where Uncle James and Aunt

Anne also succumbed to her charm. She played cards with them in the evenings and brought life into the house, otherwise such a quiet place. Perhaps Anne was never happier than in these months of a threat thought overcome. *Surely no one ever doted on another as I did then on her. I fondly thought my love & happiness would last for ever.*[26]

In the autumn of 1815, Anne and Mariana left Shibden Hall to stay with the Belcombes in York. There, Mariana persuaded Anne to visit her parents and sister in Market Weighton. *I cannot forget the trick she once played.*[27] When she returned to York ten days later, it came upon her *like a thunderbolt:* Mariana was to marry. She *had heard from, and written to, Charles. He was coming over at Christmas and it was then November and the match would be soon.[...] I had scarce uttered on first hearing this but on reflection had determined to make no objection.*[28] Charles Lawton offered Mariana a respectable, comfortable life in his own country home, complete with servants, horses and coaches. Anne Lister, in contrast, had barely a penny, lived on the hope of perhaps inheriting a modest house one day, and could only dream of offering a woman a home – and it was uncertain whether that would be viewed as respectable in the eyes of society. Deeply hurt, she had to recognise that Mariana had weighed up her love and passion against Charles' material offer and found it wanting. *I could never understand [it]. If she married for love, she could not love me, & why engage me? If not for love, it was too worldly – not romantic enough for me.*[29] In fact, Mariana wanted both: the material security of marriage to Charles and the romantic affair with Anne. She flattered her lover with all kinds of promises: as a wealthy married woman she would be able to meet Anne much more often and also travel with her. *How, spite of love, it burst the spell that bound my very reason. Suppliant at her feet, I loathed consent but loathed the asking more. I would have given the 'Yes' she sought tho' it had rent my heart into a hundred thousand shivers. It was enough to ask.*[30]

Anne knew as well as Mariana that the marriage proposal could not be turned down. Mariana was almost twenty-six; if she rejected Charles Lawton her parents would have to go on supporting her. Mrs Belcombe begged Anne not to persuade Mariana against this advantageous marriage, as she had before. Mariana was to marry Charles *without caring a straw for him.*[31] Anne consoled herself with Mariana's promise for the future. Charles Lawton was forty-four. Considering their nineteen-year age difference, Mariana hoped to be widowed not too far along the line. Then she would move in with Anne at Shibden Hall with a pretty inheritance. The remaining time, of perhaps ten years, Mariana and Anne intended to regard as a trial of their great love. Anne accepted Mariana's suggestion. As a sign of their union, she put on the ring Charles had given Mariana; on her lover's finger she put a copy of the original.

Anne attended the wedding on 9 March 1816 and accompanied the newlyweds to Cheshire. Mariana's older sister Nantz went along as well, as was common at the time, to help the bride settle into her new life. They set off for Lawton Hall the same day, spending the wedding night at the Bridgewater Arms Hotel in Manchester. Anne tried to arrange *the time of getting off to bed the first night,* intervening as long as she could. Then she had nothing more to say.

Once at Lawton Hall, Anne presumably realised Mariana had made a wise financial move – and so would one day come to Shibden Hall a wealthy woman. Mariana's impressive new home was a magnificently refurbished mansion offering space for a large family, guests and plentiful servants (now converted into separate residential units). The stables and coaches were all anyone could have wished for. Previously a middle-class doctor's daughter, Mariana suddenly presided over a rich aristocratic estate dating back to the thirteenth century, which made Shibden Hall look like a rustic barn. We have no record of how Mariana's life at Lawton Hall began. Years later, Anne read to Mariana from her diary of the time, *of her conduct to me, her marriage, etc., and, not looking for a moment or two, found she had dropt at my feet, half-fainting. She had asked me to burn these papers, saying she should never feel secure till I did.*[32] Anne did as she wished.

The next surviving journal dates from August 1816, after a gap of six years. Instead of loose sheets, Anne now used thin exercise books with blue covers. The first surviving book is labelled Volume 2 and begins with the last days the two 'marriage helpers' spent with the Lawtons. Six months after the wedding, all of them travelled together to Buxton at the foot of the Peak District, then trying to establish itself as the 'Bath of the North'. Anne, who had already seen the original Bath, thanks to Isabella and the Norcliffes, could *conceive no place more stupid.* The baths were *dark low places,* the paths led through still sparse gardens, and their semi-circular hotel – a copy of the Royal Crescent in Bath – had no view, *a hill rising directly in front of it.* Anne and Nantz had small rooms far away from the Lawtons, *up I know not how many stairs.*

This seclusion gave Anne ideas. Mariana was sleeping with her husband and Anne felt entitled to compensation. Mariana's sister Nantz, with whom she had been living for half a year now, was thirty-one years old, unmarried and curious. On the first night at the Crescent, she came to Anne's room and lay on her bed until three in the morning. *I teasing & behaving rather amorously to her.*[33] The next day, the group began a regimented sightseeing programme; they viewed first Castleton, then a cave and a mine, and finally drove to the spectacular pass at Mam Tor. It rained cats and dogs from noon on. Soon after returning to the Crescent, they each retired to their rooms. That second night, Nantz lay on Anne's bed again until two, while Anne told her about the *feeling to which she gave rise. Lamented my fate. Said I should never marry. Could not like men. Ought not to like women. At the same time apologizing for my inclination that way. By diverse arguments made out a pitiful story altogether & roused poor Anne's* [Nantz's] *sympathy to tears.* The following night, the last before their departure, Anne took back

37

everything she had said about herself and asked Nantz *how she could be such a gull as to believe it*.[34] Nantz did not know what to think of Anne now – but she wanted to find out. On their way back to York the two of them came closer, and Nantz arrived for a visit to Shibden Hall two months later.

As was common practice among female friends, she stayed in Anne's room and shared her bed. There, Anne explained until four in the morning *my penchant for the ladies. Expatiated on the nature of my feelings towards her & hers towards me. Told her that she ought not deceive herself as to the nature of my sentiments & the strictness of my intentions towards her.* Anne told her openly that she felt attracted in the same way, purely sexually, by at least two other women, including another of the Belcombe sisters, Eli. Anne then asked Nantz *if she liked me the less for my candour etc., etc. She said no, kissed me & proved by her manner she did not.*[35] *We went to great lengths as we had often done before such as feeling her all over pushing my finger up her etc. but still did not get to the last extremity.*[36] Two days later, Anne lost patience. She spent a whole morning telling Nantz *she was acting very unfairly* and that she *ought either to make up her mind to let me have a kiss at once or change her manners altogether.* Another two days later, Anne finally noted down her mission accomplished. *Had a very good kiss last night. Anne gave it me with pleasure, not thinking it necessary to refuse me any longer.*[37]

Yet Nantz still could not relax. Having overcome her physical inhibitions, she was now feeling moral scruples. *She asked if I thought the thing was wrong – if it was forbidden in the bible.* Anne was prepared for such objections and *dexterously parried all these points.* She told her it was *infamous to be connected with both sexes – but that there were beings who were so unfortunate as to be not quite so perfect &, supposing they kept to one side [of] the question, was there no excuse for them. It would be hard to deny them a gratification of this kind. I urged in my own defence the strength of natural feeling & instinct, for so I might call it.*[38]

8 *Anne Lister*, miniature portrait painted in her youth by an unknown artist, Calderdale Leisure Services, Shibden Hall, Halifax.

Throughout her life, Anne emphasised how natural and thus necessary her desire was. *When we leave nature we leave our only steady guide, and, from that moment, become inconsistent with ourselves.*[39] Nantz seems to have been satisfied with this explanation, and to have enjoyed her visit from then on; after three weeks, Anne had to tell her that her aunt wanted a little more peace and quiet in the house. Or had Anne herself had enough? *I do not admire her but rather feel a sort of disgust for her she is not nice & her breath is disagreeable however her manners made me feel desire.*[40] As a parting gesture, Anne lent or gave Nantz one or two pounds of her own scarce funds. *I ought not to complain. Superior charms might not be so easily come-at-able on such easy terms.*[41]

GENTLEMAN JACK

Alone again, Anne turned to her books. During that autumn of 1816, she did a lot of reading on recent history, including biographies of Napoleon and Blücher and descriptions of the Battle of Leipzig in 1813 and the Congress of Vienna a year later. Three years after the Battle of Waterloo, where the Britons and Prussians had united to defeat France, Anne Lister felt sympathies for the former ally, bought a German grammar and began to teach herself the language of Kant, whose works had been described to her as the most significant contribution to recent philosophy. The only novel she read in 1816 was *The Balance of Comfort, or: The Old Maid and Married Woman*, in which the author, a Mrs Ross, recommended that women remain unmarried. When Anne was not reading she was helping Uncle James. She accompanied him in all weathers to supervise repair work, to negotiate with tenants and to schedule the sowing and harvest season. When the cook heard noises in the henhouse one night, she did not rouse elderly James but woke Anne instead, who fearlessly chased off the thief with a pistol.

These days of quiet reading and hard work were interrupted, to everyone's delight, on 29 January 1817, shortly before five, by the arrival of Mariana, whom Anne had not seen for five months. She was on the way to visit her parents in York, had left her luggage at the White Lion in Halifax and come up to Shibden Hall deliberately unannounced, so as not to have to inform her husband of her plans. She stayed for dinner and *we spent the evening most happily. A hack came a little after ten, and I went back to sleep with M— at the inn.* Not wanting to part the next morning, they travelled a little way together. Nestled close, they sat in Anne's favourite spot next to the coachman, although that draughty seat on top of the coach was not befitting for ladies. In Bradford, Mariana promised to spend a few days at Shibden Hall on her return journey, Anne took the stagecoach back and *got back to dinner, at Northgate. Got home to Shibden to tea.*[42] Such romantic interruptions to her everyday routine were very much to Anne's taste. She had not mentioned her affair with Mariana's sister.

Two weeks later, Anne waited for the stagecoach down in the town every day, only to return home disappointed four times in a row. Then Mariana knocked at the door unexpectedly just as dinner was being served, which the Listers took at around half past four. In the meantime, Anne's love life had become even more complicated. Charles Lawton had intercepted a letter from Anne to Mariana, which was *not in his favour certainly*;[43] in fact it was a catastrophe, as Charles read in it that Anne was hoping for his death so as to live on his money with Mariana. It was now inconceivable for Anne to stay at Lawton Hall again as in the previous year. Mariana hoped at least that *she could come once a year to Shibden, on her way to York*.[44] There was no imagining any more time together than that in the medium term. To continue sharing passionate, incriminating and daring thoughts in writing at least, Mariana learned Anne's *secret alphabet*.[45] After all, other letters might fall into Charles' hands. Having spent six days at Shibden Hall, Mariana had to return to her husband.

These days spent with Mariana rekindled Anne's love and likewise her torments. She wanted to share her life with this woman and no other, and yet she could hope to do so less than ever. When her uncle one day raised the subject of marrying, Anne *took care however to say that I never intended to marry at all. I cannot make up whether he suspects my situation towards Mariana. In the course of conversation I said, 'Well I think I could get on with Perce as well as anybody.'* 'Perce' came from Mariana's middle name of Percy. Yet James *did not apparently notice* Anne's insinuation that she could share her life with a woman. Either that or he did not wish to comment on the subject, as Anne complained in the same lines that *it is his general custom when you tell him anything never to speak*.[46]

To prevent herself losing her mind over the hopeless situation with Mariana, Anne plunged into an even stricter study regime. *If I was once to give way to idleness I should be wretched. Nothing but keeping my mind so intent upon study can divert the melancholy reflections which would constantly prey upon me on account of M–. Alas! They are even now a source of bitterness & disquiet that words can ill describe.*[47] Determined, she prescribed herself a rigorous timetable. *For the present, I mean to devote my mornings, before breakfast to Greek, & afterwards, till dinner, to divide the time equally between Euclid and arithmetic till I have waded thro' Walkingham, when I shall recommence my long neglected algebra. I must read a page or 2 French now & then and when I can. The afternoons & evenings are set apart for general reading, for walking, 1/2 an hour, or 3/4, practice on the flute,*[48] for which Aunt Anne accompanied her on the harpsichord. The flute was regarded at the time as just as 'masculine' as all the other subjects she was studying. Were Anne to come across a subject in her studies that had not yet been worked on, she intended to attempt the work herself. Writing was, after all, one of the few possible ways for women like her to earn money.

To keep herself under scrutiny, Anne started a new diary, leaving the loose leaves of her youth and the recent exercise books behind her. In March of 1817 she bought a bound book with around 300 blank pages from the bookbinder Mr Whitley. It was almost square, 20 by 24 cm, and about 3 cm thick. She wrapped the marbled covers in thin calfskin. On the flyleaf, she wrote a programmatic quote by the historian Edward Gibbon: *I propose from this day, August 24th, 1761, to keep an exact Journal of my actions and studies, both to assist my memory, and to accustom me to set a due value on my time.*[49] The habit was maintained up to Anne Lister's death; this diary was followed by another twenty-three volumes of the same type, all of which have been preserved. Shortly before her twenty-sixth birthday, she had found her form as a diarist. Going against her earlier advice to her brother Samuel, however, she did not write down the day's events every evening. She constantly made notes using pencil and paper and sometimes even chalk on slates, which she then edited as she entered them in the book. *In the morning, writing out a rough draft of my journal of last Saturday, Friday, Thursday, Wednesday & Tuesday*, she wrote on the following Tuesday, for instance. *After tea, wrote the rough draft of my journal of Monday 15 December.*[50] She kept to this time-consuming two-stage process for the rest of her life. As Anne always had high demands but scant funds, the time and money she invested in her diaries shows how important they were to her. She paid far less attention to the language she used than in her letters, though; she often wrote carelessly, in complex constructions, using redundant formulations, a limited vocabulary and at times rough terms.

Literally everything in the world interested her; her diary knew no bounds in terms of subject matter: from Prussia's political standing in Europe to the care of her toenails, she considered everything worth writing down – conversations, books read, smallpox immunisations, the conditions on a slave ship, her own feelings, departure times of stagecoaches or the clear span of bridges. Her daily notes on the weather, including exact temperatures, could be used to draw up climate graphs for Yorkshire. Thanks to her marked need to measure the time, many of her days can be reconstructed down to fifteen-minute intervals. *Alas! My watch stood again at 11. Je ne sais quoi faire! To be without a well-going watch is terrible to me, who measure all by time.*[51] Over the years, the extent of her diaries increased to the brink of unusability, as Anne realised. Details she might want to look up later were under threat of being lost in a tangled haystack of information. Anne therefore drew up several indices, for letters 'from' and 'to', for books and essays read and for their subjects. Although she found this task *very tedious*,[52] she continued to make these indices while writing. Every volume of her diary ends with a register in which she indexed her life. She also used her diary to help her understand herself better. *What a comfort* [are] *my journals, how I can write in crypt all as it really is, & throw it off my mind & console myself – thank God for it.*[53] About a sixth of the content of her diaries is encrypted. Anne spoke, very

parting, adding *false ringlets*, as was the fashion, at her temples or *pinned on each side of my hat.*[61] Still not a fan of bonnets as an adult, she experimented with small round hats, which were not the fashion for women or men, but entirely singular. Her generally conventional but black women's clothing was a style that suited Anne's personality. Along with her *deep-toned voice,*[62] it made her look androgynous in a way that was both provocative and attractive. *My manners are certainly peculiar, not all masculine but rather softly gentleman-like. I know how to please girls.*[63]

Though she often sighed over her skirts in her diaries, she never tried trousers. Dressed as a 'man' she would have been ridiculed in Halifax. She felt no desire to wear trousers while travelling where nobody knew her; she did not want to be an anonymous 'boy,' but to be regarded and respected as a member of a longstanding family. The only liberties she allowed herself were in the ultimate privacy of her room. *Began this morning to sit, before breakfast, in my drawers put on with gentlemen's braces.*[64]

With her diary and her clothing, Anne Lister had found key forms of personal expression. All she lacked now – as the potential inheritor of Shibden Hall, taking more and more pressure off her uncle – was a woman by her side. It was becoming increasingly unlikely that that woman would be Mariana. Charles Lawton was giving his wife restorative tonics and cold back rubs every morning, taking her to the sea every two months, *all this in hopes of a son & heir.*[65] He was still *terribly jealous of me. M– thinks we had better be cautious lest he should forbid her writing to me.*[66] At the end of May 1817, fourteen months after Mariana's marriage, Anne first began to *despair that Mariana and I will ever get together, besides I sometimes think she will be worn out in the don's service and perhaps I may do better.*[67] By early June, even her favourite study subject could no longer distract her. *Finding I could not attend to arithmetic, my mind being so entirely engrossed with Mariana, I began my epistle to her [...]. We have no chance of seeing much of each other so long as the don lives and may probably not meet for some years to come. [...] The thought made me so low that I cried and wrote alternately the whole morning. I do not doubt Mariana's affection but tis sad to live upon love so hard as this and many are the hours when I am wretched.*[68] The thought of Mariana's marital sex life was no less depressing: *I begin to fancy I shall not like another man's leavings.*[69]

Little by little, Anne withdrew. She complained about Mariana – *I am generally disappointed with her letters*[70] – and wrote to her without any encrypted additions, not including anything Charles could not have read. Having ended a letter with the words *my heart is yours and well as ever,* she hesitated. *This is the first time in my life I ever felt any remorse in saying anything affectionate to Mariana. I do not feel to have written truth, I do not think of her much.*[71] A year and a half after the wedding, she noted: *Alas, how changed. She has married a blackguard for the sake of his money. We are debarred all intercourse. I am not always satisfied with her. I am often miserable & often wish to try to wean my heart from her & fix more propitiously.*[72]

Anne's relationship with Isabella Norcliffe had been of much greater social benefit, but the Norcliffe family were currently on a long tour around Europe. Like Eliza, Isabella had never received a farewell letter from Anne and had to put two and two together. Since Mariana had married Charles Lawton, Isabella had got her hopes up again; *Miss Norcliffe had joked me and said she thought I should have been caught but I was now set at liberty again.*[73] And she did indeed come into Anne's sights once more. *As I was getting into bed I began thinking how little confidence I had in M– and how little likely it was that we should ever get together. I was very low. I felt that my happiness depended on having some female companion whom I could love & depend upon & my thoughts naturally turned to Isabella. I got out her picture & looked at it for ten minutes with considerable emotion. I almost wished to persuade myself I could manage her temper as to be happy with her.*[74]

Isabella had never doubted in that, and kept reminding Anne of her existence with letters and presents. She sent her an alabaster cupid on a bed of roses from Florence. *Poor Isabel, she never forgets me. Her thoughts & affections are constant and my heart keeps a faithful register. In spite of all, I think we shall get together at last.*[75]

Anne had not really managed to keep to her resolutions of that spring, too often distracted by the dissatisfying situation in which she found herself due to her love for Mariana. *This idleness makes me unhappy, and yet my mind is so unhinged I do not feel as if I could do much this morning,*[76] she lamented regularly in her diary. She was often annoyed with herself *for not having lately got up in a morning as early as I ought. It grieves me that I am ever in bed after 5.*[77] To keep up her discipline, she returned to her tutorials in mathematics and Classics, the subjects which she had let slide the least, with Mr Knight at the end of October 1817. *I can now read the Iliad pretty easily and have gone through it with great pleasure.*[78] After several preliminary examinations, she agreed a syllabus with Mr Knight and felt *happy at the idea of getting into a proper train again.*[79]

This regular activity helped her to get things tidied up in her private life as well. She went through her papers: *as I have never had my things fairly set to rights as they ought to be, 'tis high time to begin if I mean to get it done in my lifetime.*[80] She began by sorting all the letters she had ever received from Isabella, then *looking over poor Eliza Raine's letters. My heart bled at the remembrance of the past, poor girl! She did indeed love me truly.* Finally, she asked Mariana to *make a parcel of all the letters she has had of mine up to the present time and send them;*[81] in the wrong hands, these letters might be explosive. And she wanted to cut herself loose from Mariana. She hoped to be able to file her love away as she had done with her feelings for Eliza.

Once again, though, her hard-won mental equilibrium was tipped off-balance by death. Anne's Uncle Joseph and her mother Rebecca both died within the space of a week. The uncle at Northgate House down in Halifax had been ill for some time. Anne had paid frequent visits to him and her distraught Aunt Mary, describing his decline in minute detail in her diary. On 7 November Anne received the news from her sister Marian in Market Weighton that their mother had *a very bad cold, had the cramp in her stomach and a bad pain in her right side.*[82] Uncle Joseph died the next day. As the head of the family, Uncle James and Joseph's widow proved incapable of mastering the ensuing tasks, so Anne had to muster *all the fortitude & presence of mind I can command.*[83] She informed friends and relatives, ordered the coffin and mourning fabric for the family and staff, and wrote a death notice for the newspapers. She told her father in Market Weighton to come as fast as possible if he could leave her mother, as the burial should not be delayed too long. Jeremy made haste and arrived in Halifax on Monday, 10 November. By that point, Rebecca's cold had worsened to pneumonia. On the Tuesday, Marian alarmed Jeremy with the news that '*My mother in great danger yesterday, she is still however very ill.*' The letter *shocked and surprised* Anne enormously. She did not understand why her father had come when her mother was in such a bad condition, and felt for Rebecca, who *might indeed have felt herself neglected being left at such a time and having a child here who never went over to see her. To all this he answered not a word but as soon as he had drank his wine went to Northgate.*[84]

Anne had not seen her mother for two years. She had her reasons to avoid her, above all Rebecca's drinking, but now she was plagued by guilt. Uncle Joseph being dead, the burial could take place without them, and Anne urged her father to set out for Market Weighton with her at once – but they came too late. *Reached here about 4 this morning.* Rebecca had died two hours previously. *Not [...] seeing my mother ere she closed her eyes for ever, has indeed been a shock to me which no language can describe,* Anne wrote to her Uncle James later that morning. *She was insensible, Marian says, for a couple of hours before her death which was so easy, that the spirit seemed to flit away imperceptibly. This is indeed a great comfort, and we are thankful for it.* Anne felt *a calmness, a support, a strength within that is the mercy of heaven. My father seems composed and Marian more than I should have dared to anticipate.* As on Uncle Joseph's death, Anne took care of all that was necessary for her mother. She wanted to have Rebecca taken to Halifax to *put her where she is most likely to rest with her children*[85] in the family crypt, but her mother was buried in Market Weighton on 20 November 1817.

Anne did not write in her diary between the date of her hurried departure from Halifax on 13 November and 21 November 1817. There were other times, too, when she had no time for writing; she would reserve empty pages and almost always add the entries at a later date. For the death of her mother, however, she found no words.

Anne stayed with her father and sister until 7 December and then went to York, where she wanted to mend her relationship with Mr Duffin. He had fallen out with her because of Eliza Raine, whose life had taken a dramatic turn over the past three years. Having already lost Anne, Eliza was hit hard by Samuel Lister's tragic accident in 1813. With no prospect of ever being tied to the Lister family, she wanted to get her sister Jane out of the London asylum and live with her, but her foster father had prevented her from doing so. Eliza must have accused Mr Duffin and his mistress Miss Marsh of hypocrisy in an angry argument; while they were cheating on Mrs Duffin and lying to the world, they denied innocent Jane, the victim of a cheat, a life of dignity in the bosom of her family. That truth was a step too far. William Duffin now declared Eliza insane as well and handed her over to his colleague Dr Belcombe, Mariana's father, who also treated ailments of the mind and ran a private asylum in Clifton on the edge of York.

Anne sided with the powerful on the matter. She condemned Eliza's *senseless unpardonable attack upon Mr. Duffin* and criticised her *conduct stained with ingratitude.* So as not to upset Miss Marsh's feelings, she wrote that she would *never name her to you more.*[86] Following this betrayal, Eliza broke off all contact with Anne. Furious, she demanded her letters back, as well as a diamond ring and other objects that had once been meaningful to the two of them.

As the daughter of Eliza's doctor, Mariana Belcombe heard a great deal about all this and sensed that Eliza was being done an injustice. Anne had admitted to her that she and Eliza *had once agreed to go off together when of age but my conduct first delayed it & then circumstances luckily put an end to it altogether.*[87] Mariana had an idea of the part her lover might have played in Eliza's breakdown, so she asked her to respond to Eliza's letters and *as a favour done to herself, and as the best means of doing Miss Raine a service, to go and spend some time with her.*[88] Anne, however, was afraid of Eliza's courage for speaking openly to third parties, and preferred to stay at a safe distance in Halifax.

In the year after that, 1815, Anne suggested making Eliza a ward of the Court of Chancery, effectively removing her adult rights. Mariana's father, Dr Belcombe, opposed the idea though, as Eliza had *intervals of perfect Sanity, and has a correct recollection of what has occurred since her derangement began.* He hoped her state would improve after a year in his treatment, although she was *very wayward and obstinate, perfectly aware of what she is saying and doing, so much so that it may be difficult to prove her insanity to persons appointed by Chancery to examine her.*[89] Eliza stood by the truths for which she had been locked away, and Anne had a personal interest in having her declared insane. Coming from a madwoman, any confession about their former relationship would have borne less weight.

Another year later, Eliza, still living at Dr Belcombe's asylum, wanted to make her will and considered leaving her money to Anne, with whom she had once wanted to live. When the outraged Mr Duffin found this out he suspected Anne of planting the idea in

Eliza's mind and questioned her role in his foster daughter's life. This conflict was still smouldering when Anne came to York from her mother's funeral in December 1817. It was extremely important for Anne to restore things with Mr Duffin, as she was dependent on his hospitality in York. With Miss Marsh's support, they agreed it had been a *misunderstanding*.[90]

Three days after Anne's arrival, Mr Duffin accompanied her to Dr Belcombe's mental asylum in Clifton. Eliza *seemed pleased at my visit*, Anne wrote in her diary. *The first thing she said to me was 'Well! So you are in mourning for your mother!'* [...] *She afterwards asked me to take off my hat, felt my face, asked if I ever wore false faces and at last said she 'believed it really was my face'. She then bade me take off my right hand glove and observing the thick gold ring Mariana gave me, asked what I had done with the one I used to wear; then looking at my other hand asked significantly after 'all my friends'.* What Anne answered is not revealed in the journal. *She asked me what I had done with the gold chain she gave me and what with the pocket-handkerchiefs. I told her. When I said I never came to York without calling to see her she answered 'What! Never?' and seemed much pleased when answered 'No! Never.'*[91]

Anne's second visit to Eliza a few days later was not as harmonious to begin with. *At my request we were left a little by ourselves. At first she said she should take no insolence, no impertinence from me, that I had never done her any good and if I was impertinent we should come to blows. After a somewhat stern remonstrance on my part she said I had always thought nothing of her, that I might have genius, I might have talent but that I had made a bad use of them and indeed the world thought me a fool. She then grew more kind and asked to feel my face, to pinch my nose and feel my eyes* [...] *and desired me to sit by her on the sopha* [sic]. Mr Duffin entered the room at this moment, perhaps not coincidentally, and declared Anne's visit over. *Eliza had tears in her eyes – the only sensitive symptom I have observed since her malady.*[92] Anne knew better than anyone else who, what, and which circumstances had made Eliza allegedly lose her sanity. Her first lover would never leave Dr Belcombe's asylum. Anne wrote to her until around 1821 and did indeed visit her every time she was in York, until well into the 1830s.

Anne also wanted to improve her relations with Mrs Belcombe. Although – or because – Mariana was in York as well, her mother had refused to offer Anne a bed in her house. Mariana's mother took a similarly critical view of Anne's friendship with Mariana as Mr Duffin had of her relationship with Eliza. She resented her behaviour before and after Mariana's marriage. Charles Lawton had informed his in-laws about the lack of sexual harmony in the marriage and *complained to her father of M—'s coldness & he answered she required more dalliance.*[93] Meanwhile, there were rumours in York that *M— was parted from C— & returned to her father and mother; that she & C— were the most miserable couple in the world, & that, in fact, he had little or nothing; that he had killed his first wife; had not the very best character.* Anne tried to make *the matter look as well as I could but surely, in spite of anything I can say, people must think there would not be all these reports afloat without some reason or other.*[94] Mrs Belcombe recognised Anne as the reason why the Lawtons' marriage had not been a happy one and why it had become the subject of gossip.

Although Anne had distanced herself from Mariana over the past year, she still desired her. Two days after her arrival, she paid a visit to the Belcombes. Four of the five daughters were there, including Nantz and Mariana, whom she had last seen ten months ago. *Studiously avoided shewing any warmth to M— Had a few minutes tête-à-tête with Mrs Belcombe. We got upon the subject of romance. I said I changed my manners to M— as soon as I was properly told of the folly of them.*[95] According to this diary entry, Anne admitted there had been something less than sensible in her feelings for Mariana but claimed that she had now got over them.

Her daughter Mariana's relationship to Anne Lister had Mrs Belcombe as puzzled as the judges passing sentence on two Scottish teachers accused of 'indecent practices' at around the same time. Did such things even exist between women? A schoolgirl who had shared a bed with one of her female teachers – something no one found improper – had regularly woken up because the other teacher had lain down on top of her teacher and kissed her. *Then Miss Woods began to move, and she shook the bed, and she heard the same noise [like] putting one's finger in the neck of a wet bottle.* On another occasion, the schoolgirl was woken *by their kissing and whispering. She heard Miss Pirie say one night, 'You are in the wrong place,' and Miss Woods said, 'I know,' and Miss Pirie said, 'Why are you doing it then?' and Miss Woods said, 'For fun.'* Yet even such testimonies to lust shared by two women did not convince the judges. After eight years of extremely discreet procedure through various courts, the House of Lords acquitted Marianne Woods and Jane Pirie in 1819; *according to the known habits of women in this country, there is no indecency in one woman going to bed with another.* Despite all the signs that had also made Mrs Belcombe suspicious, the presiding judge had pronounced: *the crime here alleged has no existence.*[96] For Anne, this judgement meant a great deal of freedom; yet she still had to be careful, as the case itself implicitly shows. To Mrs Belcombe, she denied any physical relationship with Mariana, claiming, though, *that my regard for her was still the same as ever. I am not quite so certain of this.*[97]

Mrs Belcombe contented herself with this explanation and let Anne go out for a walk with Mariana, Nantz and Lou the next day. To prevent either of the two sisters with whom she was intimate from getting suspicious, Anne flirted over that evening's card game with Mrs Harriet Milne, the fifth Belcombe sister. A day later, Anne wanted to visit Mariana but *Mrs Belcombe prevented me* from entering her room; she was still distrustful although she could not put her suspicions into words. The next morning, though, Mariana got the better of her mother. *A little before 11, she herself suggested our having a kiss. I thought it dangerous & would have declined the risk but she persisted & by way of excuse to bolt the door sent me downstairs for some paper, that she was going to the close-stool. The expedient answered & she tried to laugh me out of my nervousness. I took off my pelisse & drawers, got into bed and had a very good kiss, she showing all due inclination & in less than seven minutes the door was un-bolted again & we were all right again.*

That same day, Mrs Belcombe invited Anne to stay with them after all. *M– and I talked it over. I did not like a bed to myself in the room next to the drawing room, on account of Nantz.* She was still there too and might come for a nocturnal visit like Mariana, which would give away Anne's affair with her. *I should petition for the little turn-up bed in M– and Lou's room*[98] – she rather liked Mariana's younger sister too. *Lou is certainly a quick, clever girl & seems remarkably* au fait *at Hebrew.*[99] While Mariana was in bed waiting for Anne, Lou was teaching her the Hebrew alphabet. Unlike Mrs Belcombe, Lou knew about her sister Mariana's relationship with Anne. *She, as well as Anne* [Nantz] *strongly suspects that neither M– nor I would much regret the loss of C–, but that we look forward to the thing and, in the event of it, certainly mean to live together.*[100] Anne was no longer so sure of that, though. *I have before told Lou I thought I had better take her on a running lease till Mariana was ready for me. Lou agrees and we are very good friends. What Anne* [Nantz] *thinks of it all I cannot say; she certainly is as fond of me as ever and would gladly do as much for me now as she did at Shibden.*

Mariana was not as glad. To Anne's surprise, she was *jealous of Lou. Tho' I laughed at the thing at first, I soon perceived it more real than I had imagined.* When they went to bed alone, *Lou being away we had a glorious opportunity for a kiss, but the annoyance occasioned by my attention to Lou had made Mariana cool, unwell and out of sorts and I let her be as quiet as possible.*[101] The next morning, as Anne was packing, Mariana looked at her with a changed perspective, now disconcerted on her own part. *Talked over my adventures in former days; M— said had she known them she would never have been introduced to me. Mariana wanted a kiss but I said it was too dangerous, that I really had no courage and that we had better practise a little self-denial.*[102] This was the first time these two passionate lovers had not come together when circumstances permitted.

Anne returned to Shibden Hall on 20 December 1817, having left hastily six weeks previously. A week later, Mariana paid her a visit on her journey back to Lawton Hall. Now they made up for what they had missed out on in York. *Mariana had a very good kiss last night; mine was not quite so good but I had a very nice one this morning.*[103] On only her third day at Shibden Hall, Mariana received a letter from Charles in the late afternoon. He ordered her to *set off immediately & travel as fast as she could to meet him in good time at Manchester this evening.*[104]

'Kallista'

1818–1819

I cannot live happily without female company.[1] Mariana remained out of reach and Isabella was travelling. Anne noticed the twenty-three-year-old Miss Elizabeth Browne at scientific lectures. *Having all the 4 preceding nights admired Miss Browne,* on the fifth evening she deliberately *sat just before her. Handed her several things to look at & contrived to get into conversation with her after the lecture was over. The lecture being longer than usual & I staying a good while afterwards to look at the apparatus, or rather at Miss Browne, did not get home till near 11.* During the next night Anne *did nothing but dream of Miss Browne &, tho' I woke at 6, yet had not resolution to get up but lay dosing* [sic] *& thinking of the fair charmer. She is certainly very pretty. She seemed evidently not displeased with my attention & I felt all possible inclination to be as foolish as I ever was in former days.*[2] The next evening, Anne sat directly behind Miss Browne and engaged her in another conversation after the lecture. *She evidently seems flattered,* Anne noted afterwards. *My attention to Miss Brown has been pointed these last two nights, I wonder if anyone has observed it?*[3]

Caroline Greenwood and her four sisters did indeed have an eye on Anne Lister's proclivities. Anne occasionally played music with them. The Greenwoods, a middle-class family in Halifax, were actually *very good and worthy and obliging,* but Anne considered them *a vulgar set.*[4] Earlier, *they fancied me quite taken up with Miss Norcliffe;*[5] now *they rallied me on the subject of my great admiration.* Caroline asked malicious questions about Anne's *choice in men, I said above all things, after good sense and good temper, good family and remarkably elegant manners*[6] – describing her ideal of herself. With ulterior motives, Caroline invited Anne and Elizabeth Browne to tea together. *Miss Brown is wonderful – handsome, or rather, interesting, gentle in her manners, entirely free from any sort of affectation & much more ladylike than any girl I have seen hereabouts,*[7] Anne wrote after the occasion. Elizabeth Browne was one of the *sweet, interesting creatures I should love;*[8] she was younger than her original ideal Mariana, yet *the most modest, unassuming, innocent girl (yet not wanting good sense) I ever met with.* She *has other things to do & reads by stealth,*[9] having to help her mother about the house. To Anne's delight, Elizabeth answered *when I asked her if she liked Lord Byron's poetry, 'Yes, perhaps too well.'* Byron was regarded at the time as the ultimate romantic hero and Anne had taken him as a role model. *I could soon be in love with the girl.*[10]

Over the subsequent weeks and months, Anne sought out every opportunity to meet Miss Browne. She ran into her at the library or at the lectures held by her former tutor Mr Knight at Halifax Parish Church, since he had been appointed vicar there. After one such lecture, Anne offered Miss Browne her arm and walked her home. *Having the two keys in my hand belonging to the seat* [in church] *I smiled and told Kallista if they were the keys of heaven I would let her in.* But Miss Browne gave Anne the run-around. *She made no reply. I observed she never does to anything at least bordering on a compliment.* Miss Browne did at least tell her she liked walking in the garden in moonlight, *for it made her melancholy. She owned to being a little romantic.* Anne *quite agreed* and rhapsodised that *a slight tincture of romance made a character more amiable.*

In person, Anne always called her new acquaintance Miss Browne.

Secretly, though, she called her *Kallista*,[11] Greek for 'most beautiful'. With her knowledge of Greek mythology, Anne was doubtlessly thinking of the nymph Kallisto, the favourite follower of the goddess Artemis, who roams the forests with her nymphs and uses her bow and arrows to kill anyone who tries to approach her or her women. When Artemis is hunting alone one day, Zeus takes on her form and seduces Kallisto – who enjoys the experience, believing she is in Artemis' embrace. Anne may have fancied herself in the roles of both Artemis and Zeus. She probably thought little of the consequences for poor Kallisto: as a punishment, Artemis changed her into a bear, which Zeus then elevated to the heavens as Ursa Major.

Anne's position in society forbade her from introducing the daughter of a small businessman – Copley Browne was a co-owner of a wire-drawing mill – into the Listers' illustrious circle. In the strictly hierarchical society of the day, paying and receiving visits – calling – was not something governed by one's own taste. Anne had to restrict herself to families with whom her uncle maintained contacts. The Listers considered themselves above all other families in Halifax, apart from the longstanding Waterhouses and Saviles. They socialised reluctantly with nouveau riche factory owners such as the Priestleys, Walkers and Rawsons, because their lifestyles were more luxurious and their political influence greater than their own. The Brownes, however, had neither title nor capital. Anne resigned herself to the situation. *Lamented, prayed God to have mercy on me & to help me & resolved never more to mention Miss Browne & to avoid her entirely. For the last time I will allow myself to try to meet her tomorrow.*

The next day, she searched half of Halifax to cross Miss Browne's path. When she at last *spied a suspicious bonnet*, she spoke to her, *paid her beauty several compliments & told her she was the best-dressed girl in town or neighbourhood.* Miss Browne thanked her politely for the compliments but also *said she was afraid of me,* whereupon Anne *assured her she had often frightened me so as to make me quite nervous.*[12]

Following these insinuation-laden confessions, they arranged to meet the next day at the library. Anne's vow never to see Elizabeth again was instantly forgotten. *What a strange being I am.*[13]

That next day, she went on the offensive. *My whole strain of conversation was complimentary & calculated to impress her with the idea how much I was interested about her.*[14] On their next walk five days later, *she now begins to shew that she is as much pleased with me as I can wish.* Miss Browne had admitted to Anne that *she envied my courage. This,* Anne responded, *might be gained at last by practice*[15] – only to proceed to action a few days later. As they were walking around the town they were caught in a sudden squall of rain. Standing outside an inn at King Cross, Miss Browne *consented after a few 'hems' and 'hahs'* to go inside. The landlady let them have a room to themselves and Anne had twelve minutes to pursue her agenda. *I told her her gown sleeves were rather too wide & that her frill was not put on straight. I took it off & put it on again, taking three trials to it before I would be satisfied. She did not seem to dislike the thing, nor to be unhappy in my society. I think if I chose to persevere, I can bring the thing to what terms I please.* As she fumbled at Miss Browne's breast, *I thought of what I should not.*[16]

Two days later, Anne went to Langton Hall to see Isabella Norcliffe again. She and her family had spent almost three years touring Europe, ending the trip with over six months in Brussels. She had never abandoned contact with Anne, and had sent minerals from Switzerland and *sweetmeats* from the south of France. While Anne was toying with Miss Browne, she dreamed of Tib. *I wish I was with Isabella & was happy with her. I will try to be so, if possible.* Since the difficulties with Mariana had begun, Anne had been persuading herself into new feelings for Isabella. *I have always loved her in spite of all & now,* Anne hoped, *Isabella's fondness, fortune & connections, if her temper be grown rather more tractable, will make me happy. I almost begin to feel that we shall get together at last.*[17] *Lay in bed thinking & building castles about Isabella.*[18]

Their reunion did not go according to Anne's wishes, however. Isabella did look *remarkably well*, but she was *fatter than when I saw her last*. On the very first night, Anne attempted to relight the fire. *Tried for a kiss a considerable time last night but Isabella was as dry as a stick & I could not succeed. At least she had not one & I felt very little indeed. She was very feverish, quite dry heat & seemed quite annoyed & fidgeted herself exceedingly at our want of success, saying she had grown fit for nothing & asking what could be the matter with her. It was certainly odd as she by no means seemed to want passion. I carried the thing off as well as I could, that is to say very well, tho' I confess I felt surprised and disappointed. Went to sleep in about an hour. Tried again just before getting up & succeeded a little better, tho' far from well.*[19]

Things did not get any better, as Anne established on the third night. *Isabella dotes on me & her constancy is admirable & her wish to oblige & please me overcomes every other, yet her passions seem impotent without the strong excitement of grossness & her sentiments are very far from being those I most admire. [...] She has seen a great deal of vice abroad & heard a great deal of loose conversation. Her mind is not pure enough for me.*[20] However, Isabella had never been the kind of sweet little creature that delighted Anne. The fact that she could not simply pick things up where they had left off may have had a cause Anne had not reckoned with: Isabella was in love with another woman.

Mary Vallance, the daughter of a Kent brewery owner, had met the Norcliffes on their Grand Tour of Europe and become a close friend of Isabella's sister Emily. She was staying with the Norcliffes, as after Emily's tragic death during their travels, Mary had become a kind of replacement for their youngest daughter. Although Isabella admitted to Anne that she found twenty-three-year-old Mary Vallance *irresistible*,[21] Anne could not imagine that Tib's relationship to Mary might be closer than their own. She asked herself *whether Miss Vallance would find us out.*[22] In fact, though, it took Anne a while to work out the truth about Isabella and Mary. Not until the end of her six-week stay did she find out that Isabella had asked Mary *to play the man*. Mary Vallance was less surprised by the suggestion than by the allocation of roles, because she actually *thought of Tib as a man*, as she confided to Anne, of all people. Mary *asked if I should not have married Tib if she had been a man. Astonished to hear me say, 'No.'* [...] *It seemed she had thought Tib always played the man with me* – an impression Anne could not let go unchallenged – *in which I think she was undeceived.*[23]

A disenchanted Anne left Langton Hall on 2 November 1818. After a brief visit to her father and sister in Market Weighton, she spent the four weeks before Christmas in York. Mariana's sister Lou Belcombe, with whom she had last time learned Hebrew, this time practically forced herself on Anne and *would rather have my love than esteem. I told her she did not understand my love & that she was too cold for me. She owned she appeared so but said she could convince me to the contrary.*[24] But either no opportunity arose under the watchful eyes of Mrs Belcombe, or Anne did not take it, having no interest in low-hanging fruit.

It was resistance that stoked her desire. As soon as she was back in Halifax, shortly before Christmas of 1818, Anne Lister 'happened' to meet Miss Browne, who was herself *on the watch*, so it seemed to Anne. At the Christmas service in Halifax Parish Church, they faced one another for the sacrament. *I fear I never received it with less feeling of reverence. Was thinking more of Miss Browne than anything else* – whether she would ever *mould her to my purpose.*[25] While Anne was strolling along *Callista Lane* on 8 January 1819, her crush came dashing out of the house and the two went walking arm in arm. Anne was *more inclined to be a little on the jocose than usual. I asked if she was still afraid of me. She said she could not help feeling a little so sometimes*, because, she added, *she thought I had a very penetrating countenance.* [...] *'Oh, oh,'* thought *I to myself, then, 'I have sometimes looked rather unutterable things.'* With a deep stare into Elizabeth's eyes, Anne told her: *I was, at some times, more anxious to be penetrating than at others.*[26]

On one of their next walks, Elizabeth confessed to Anne that *she had thought of me last night but so much that it had prevented her sleeping & she must not think so much of me after going to bed in future.* [...] *She had strange thoughts but could not help thinking she wished I had been a gent; that perhaps she should not have known me.* '*Oh, oh,*' Anne thought again. *I replied perhaps she had not more strange thoughts than other people.* [...] *She had wondered what I saw in her & thought perhaps it was her vanity that made her believe I liked her.* '*No, no,*' *said I.* '*I have given you reason enough.*' [...] '*I only wish you happy &, tho' I would rather, if possible, be in some degree instrumental to your happiness myself, for we all value the work of our own hands, I shall be satisfied to know you are happy, by whatever means.*' *Miss Browne;* '*Perhaps you will be disappointed in me. I may turn out very wicked.*' *I;* '*That is more likely for me to do, but we have all of us our weak side.*' *Miss Browne;* '*I have many.*' *I;* '*I fear you have not such an one as I should choose you to have if I could choose.*'

When Anne noted this conversation in her diary, she believed it would take only *a few more walks & perhaps she will understand her feelings better.*[27] But then an earlier hint dropped by Miss Browne became clear in March of 1819: Kallista wanted to marry a certain Mr William Kelly of Glasgow. *She is in love, it seems, & this gives me little hope of making much impression on her in the amatory way. Besides, I have not enough opportunity & dare not make any serious tempting offer. This would never do for me.*[28] Anne had to concede defeat. *She seems innocent & unknowing as to the ways of the world.*[29]

Anne's constant walks around Halifax arm in arm with Elizabeth Browne were the *talk & admiration (wonder) of the town,*[30] as Aunt Mary Lister of Northgate House reported to Anne. Caroline Greenwood asked Anne prying questions about what she got up to on her walks with Miss Browne. *I am settling the affairs of the nation with my prime minister.* Whereupon Caroline pestered Anne to *give my sentiment a name. I answered it was perfect esteem, but desired her to give it a name. She replied, 'Enthusiasm. A passion that would only last a short while.'*[31] Caroline's comments were laced with jealousy. Whenever Anne had visited the Greenwoods in the past, Caroline had dragged her to her room and played only for her on her glass harmonica. *She was glad to have an excuse to write to me, for the sake of having an answer back.*[32] Although Caroline Greenwood, like Lou Belcombe, offered herself up on a silver platter, Anne did not take the bait. She suspected Caroline wanted to lure her into a trap. *In fact, she makes a dead set, to all which I return no encouragement, but am very civil.*[33] Anne found it all the easier to resist Caroline's attempts, as she had a *head like a porcupine.*[34]

The only person to whom Anne spoke openly was her Aunt Anne. *She really is very good & is surely fond & proud of me. Talked of my fancy for Miss Browne. Told her I had gone to the lectures for no other purpose than to see her. She said she knew very well & that I should like Miss Browne better than Tib or M—, if I durst.*[35] An unruffled Aunt Anne accepted her niece's feelings for women. Uncle James made no comment, and so Anne had great freedom at Shibden Hall. Even her father let her have her way, on an undated occasion. *I had once had a person with me with whom I had gone to bed at ten & lain till one, two, three & later, the next day & my father would not have us disturbed.*[36]

On the evening when Anne spoke to her aunt about Elizabeth Browne, she also told her about her wish to travel. Inspired by Isabella's tour of Europe, Anne wanted to go abroad at last. She counted up her funds, which came to £50 – enough for a trip to Paris. Aunt Anne had never been to France either, so she joined forces with her niece and on the spur of the moment, they left for the Continent on 10 May 1819. Anne was twenty-eight years old, her aunt fifty-four.

They travelled via Dover and Calais, the journey taking six days. The women saved on three nights' accommodation by juddering through the nights in mail coaches. Whenever possible, Anne sat on the coach box to have a better view, enjoy the fresh air – and to get some exercise whenever the road led uphill and she could keep up with the horses. In Paris, they took rooms at the Hôtel des Ambassadeurs on rue Sainte Anne, near the Louvre. The guide recommended by Isabella picked them up every morning and took them to museums, Notre-Dame Cathedral and the Jardin du Luxembourg. One morning they left the hotel at six and travelled two hours to Versailles, only to find to their great regret that it had been plundered during the revolution. They walked through the park to the Grand and Petit Trianon and viewed the porcelain manufacture at Sèvres on their way back to Paris. They also visited a tapestry factory and admired the kitchen at the Hôtel des Invalides, where meals were prepared for four thousand private officers. Anne observed everything and made notes even on the public baths along the Seine, the laundresses in their boats and the inexplicable lack of traffic jams: *nothing to Northgate in Halifax on a busy market-day*.

Between their excursions, they would relax at a round marble table in a café, a pleasure not found in Halifax or in York. They treated themselves to rhubarb lemonade, *café au lait – very good* – and patisseries, watching the passers-by. They ate at the same restaurant every evening, another of Isabella's recommendations, working their way through the menu with great appetite and trying all the wines and champagnes. Anne and her aunt *laughed exceedingly* at a Chinese shadow theatre and on a Sunday evening – *we are shocked to confess* – amused themselves at the Tivoli gardens. There, Anne was drawn magically to the *Montagne Russe*, a precursor to the roller coaster, in which pleasure-seekers sped down an artificial hill in a small car. *I was seized, rather to the alarm of my aunt, with an unconquerable desire of descending: once she lured me*

10 *Anne Lister senior*, oil painting by Thomas Binns; Calderdale Leisure Services, Shibden Hall, Halifax.

away; a look behind brought back my malady and down I went. The shock was instantaneous.

Aunt Anne, too, enjoyed the trip hugely. At Shibden Hall she lived according to her brother's standards, leading a life more withdrawn than suited her nature. She and her niece made an excellent travelling team. Anne junior organised, negotiated and spoke to people – in clumsy French, as she was sad to note – while Anne senior ensured they appeared respectable. *Neither of us ever felt better in our lives, than during the seventeen days and a half of our stay in Paris.*[37] Anne dreamed of returning to Paris to study there. She had received a positive reaction at the Jardin des Plantes and the university to her idea of attending lectures on an informal basis.

On their return journey, they sailed to Brighton from Dieppe. Shortly before disembarking, the two helped each other to wrap around their bodies the yards of fine silk bought in Paris and put their clothes over the top. At customs, they declared only the aunt's minor purchases, two pairs of shoes, a wig and earrings. They went from Brighton to London, where they worked their way through a similarly packed sightseeing schedule. They stayed at Mr and Mrs Webb's very central Black Bear Inn at 220 Piccadilly and engaged a guide, as in Paris. As their first day was a Sunday, they took a long tour of the London churches and had walked sixteen miles by the evening. Over the next few days they visited the Tower, the British Museum – *delighted with the Elgin marbles* – Westminster Abbey – *nothing to the fine cathedral of York*[38] – and took a boat trip along the Thames. Anne climbed up ladders to the dome at St Paul's and savoured the view of the city from the Golden Gallery – but not the sky or the air, which, unlike in Paris, was contaminated by acrid chimney smoke. The workers' poverty, the women's misery and the horror of gambling halls and brandy dives *meet you barefaced.*[39] Anne had found Paris more civilised.

The Misses Lister went to the theatre every evening, extending their stay by a day to see the final performance by Sarah Siddons, *the finest performer that ever ornamented her profession. I had no conception of such acting, she was inimitably great – her voice, her declamation, her countenance, her action, more perfect than I could have conceived.*[40] After two months away, the two Annes arrived home on 12 June 1819.

Isabella, Mariana and Miss Vallance

1819–1822

Only twelve days later, Isabella Norcliffe came to visit. Although their reunion the past autumn had not gone well, Isabella was still very attached to Anne and thought the two of them were together. *Poor soul! She little thinks how things are. She feels secure. I scarce can bear it. I wish she knew all & all was settled.* As Isabella also had a vague prospect of one day inheriting her family's estate, she suggested to Anne that they move in together – if necessary along with her younger sister Charlotte, should the latter remain unmarried. Anne rejected the idea of living with both Isabella and Charlotte out of hand, *whether Tib ever has Langton or not. Then I could have no authority in Tib's house nor therefore, she in mine.* Isabella insisted on her suggestion. *'We might always be together. You visit me six months & I visit you the same.' When I hesitated she said, 'Well, but I can visit you six months & the other six, you can get somebody else.'*[1] Isabella knew she would always have to share Anne. During her stay at Shibden Hall, Elizabeth Browne returned to Halifax. *We were talking of her just after we came up to bed & Tib wanted me to take the first opportunity of giving her a kiss to see how she liked it & how she behaved on the occasion. I laughed & said, 'If anything particular happens, Tib, you will be more to blame than I.'*[2] That opportunity did not arise until weeks later, when Aunt Anne held a small social event and Anne invited Elizabeth Browne to Shibden Hall for the first time. *Just before we came in from the garden, contrived to be a few minutes alone with only Tib & Miss Browne. The former gave me a kiss & I made it an excuse to kiss Miss Browne on her lips, a very little, moistly. She looked shamefacedly* and pulled her bonnet lower over her face. *Miss Browne said kissing was an odd thing & people made quere* [sic] *remarks about it. 'These,' said I, 'none of us understand.'*[3]

Three days later, they met again at church. *In passing Miss Browne, smiled very graciously. I fancied she looked rather sheepish. What has she thought of my kissing her when she was here on Thursday?* Anne was never to find out. Miss Browne married Mr Kelly and remained one of the few women ever to resist Anne Lister's seductions. To Isabella's satisfaction, Anne from then on found *her company dullish.*[4]

Yet there was no advantage in it for Isabella. Anne noticed that *her habits are very little suited to mine. I could not live happily with her. At all events the experiment shall not be tried.*[5] Isabella preferred riding while Anne loved to walk, she had no interest at all in books, and in the library *Tib's manner there fidgetty & a little impatient. Would try to kiss me. She shall not go with me often again.*[6] When Anne wanted to read in peace, *she interrupted me desperately & I shall not be sorry to have my room once more to myself. I am never good at study when she is with me & I am weary of this long stoppage I have had to all improvement.*[7] In company, too, she felt uncomfortable with her oldest friend. *Isabel, much to my annoyance, mentioned my keeping a journal, & setting down everyone's conversation in my peculiar hand-writing (what I call crypt hand).* Anne put on a brave face but swore to herself: *Never say before her what she may not tell for, as to what she ought to keep or what she ought to publish, she has the worst judgement in the world.*[8] Aside from that, Isabella drank too much and things weren't going all that well in bed either. [Tib] *was for going to sleep, but I would have a kiss. She says it gives her a pain in her back.*[9] *I feel towards her differently, more coolly than I did.* [...] *I cannot feel that she is, or ever can be, all to me I want & wish.*[10]

Politics was one of the few subjects on which the two agreed. During Isabella's stay at Shibden Hall, on 16 August 1819, some 50,000 people demonstrated at St Peter's Field in Manchester for the repeal of the Corn Laws and a reform of electoral law. Imported grain from the Continent was cheaper than British corn, so the government had been raising high customs on imported corn since 1815. The resulting price rises benefitted landowners like James Lister while the poor starved. Legislation such as the Corn Laws highlighted the shortcomings of Britain's parliamentary system, with elections being neither secret nor general and favouring constituencies in the south of England and the landowning aristocracy. The large area around Manchester, Blackpool and Stockport, with just under a million inhabitants, had only two representatives in parliament; tiny Old Sarum in Wiltshire, one of the rotten boroughs, had just as many MPs. Although the unarmed protesters in their Sunday best at St Peter's Field were not a threat, six hundred hussars, a hundred and twenty cavalry from the yeomanry and several hundred infantrymen surrounded the crowd with two cannons. As the main speaker Henry Hunt was about to speak, the yeomanry received orders to arrest him. To reach the stage, they rode into the tightly packed crowd, cutting their way through with swords. Between eleven and fifteen people died, including four women and a two-year-old child, with four to seven hundred people injured. The state-sanctioned slaughter was soon dubbed the Peterloo Massacre, after the Battle of Waterloo. It left a deep impression on British collective memory, radicalised the reform movement – and hardened the government's stance.

The news of the Peterloo Massacre reached Halifax the same evening and two days later, five hundred people assembled on Skircoat Moor, not far from Shibden Hall. While her aunt and uncle feared looters, Anne discussed the events with Isabella until late at night. *The reform infection seems to have reached us.*[11]

Oh, that I had a kindred spirit & by whom, be loved. I have none & feel desolate, Anne wrote during the three months Isabella spent with her. This lament became a refrain over the course of autumn 1819. *I felt a sinking at my heart this afternoon. [...] I left all alone, none to love, to turn to, or to speak to. All will be dreary & forlorn. Oh, that I had a fit companion to dote on, to beguile the tedious hours. But I must study & never think of love & all the sweet endearments of life.*[12] As in the year before when she wanted to forget Mariana, Anne hoped study would distract her. It was unfair to blame Isabella for her not learning much in recent months; she had been notching up diary entries complaining about her own negligence for more than two years. Anne had not picked up her tutorials with Mr Knight after her mother's death. She rarely got up as early as she intended. In an attempt to trick herself, she tried sleeping on the floor. *This did not do. Did not awake till 7 & was so vexed to find it so late, I lay dozing till 9.*[13] To become reaccustomed to intellectual work, she wrote a 96-page report on her stay in Paris for Mr Duffin. Anne did not enjoy the laborious collation of facts and references but regarded the work as useful practice for a publication of her own, such as a translation of Plinius' *Naturalis historia*. She had *hope of a possibility of making something by writing*[14] and felt *ambition in the literary way, of my wish for a name in the world.*[15] Would she have regarded her diaries as her actual *oeuvre*?

Books, though, were only ever a secondary pursuit. *Oh, how my heart longs after a companion & how I often wish for an establishment of my own, but I may then be too old to attach anyone & my life shall have passed in that dreary solitude I so ill endure.* In this mood, Anne received a letter from Mariana with the suggestion of meeting her in Manchester for a night at the Albion Hotel. Mariana was jealous of Isabella and her long stay with Anne. Her mother and sister Nantz's return journey from Lawton Hall to York offered her an opportunity to meet Anne without Charles finding out. Such a rendezvous for a night was *foolish* in every respect. Anne's uncle and aunt *would think of the money it would cost & they would not approve*.[16] Above all, though, Anne had not seen Mariana for almost two years and had used that time to detach herself. *I had certainly never less idea, hope, or rather wish, of our being ultimately together than I have at present*.[17] From Mariana's letters, which bored her, she believed Mariana had grown apart from her. *I suppose she is more comfortable now than formerly with C–. She has her carriage & the luxuries of life and thinks proportionately less of me.* All in all, Anne considered Mariana *an unfaithful friend to Isabella, a weak & wavering companion to me. On calm & mature reflection I neither much admire her nor much esteem her character*.[18]

Despite all this, she travelled three and three-quarter hours to Manchester on 18 November 1819 and took a room at the Moseley Arms for an hour to make herself look presentable before she went on to the Albion Hotel. Having expected Anne earlier, the Belcombes had just gone out. Precious hours of an already short meeting were wasted. Tired of waiting, Anne had a guide take her to the site of the Peterloo Massacre. By the time she finally met the Belcombes at the hotel, *M– sadly disappointed. She met me affectionately enough & seemed rather nervous.* After dinner, Anne and Mariana withdrew early. Alone at last, they did not launch themselves upon one another in fits of passion, but plagued each other with questions about their sex lives. Anne wanted to know *how often* Mariana and Charles *were connected &, guessing, found might be at the rate of about twenty times a year.* Mariana asked about Isabella. Anne did not mention the fact that she slept with her whenever they saw each other. Mariana was *pleased to hear me say that, tho' Tib seemed fully to expect living with me, yet, at all events that would not be, for I neither did, nor could, feel anything like love towards her.* However, Anne *mentioned Tib's being fond of me as ever & the deceitful game I was now obliged to play as, of course, I could say nothing of my engagement to her. 'Indeed,' I said, 'is there, or can there be, any engagement at present? Was not every obligation on my part cancelled by your marriage?' She acknowledged that it was,* but suggested, *'You might make another promise now.' 'Oh, no,' said I, 'I cannot now.'*

Got into bed. She seemed to want a kiss. It was more than I did. The tears rushed into my eyes. I felt I know not what & she perceived that I was much agitated. She bade me not or she should begin too & I knew not how she should suffer. She guessed not what passed within me. They were not tears of adoration. I felt that she was another man's wife. I shuddered at the thought & at the conviction that no soffistry [sic] *could gloss over the criminality of our connection.* Mariana had never felt such scruples, as Anne noted with repulsion. *What is M—'s match but legal prostitution? And, alas, what is her connection with me? Has she more passion than refinement? More plausibility than virtue? Give me a little romance. It is the greatest purifier of our affections & often an excellent guard against libertinism. From the kiss she gave me it seemed as if she loved me as fondly as ever. By & by, we seemed to drop asleep but, by & by, I perceived she would like another kiss & she whispered, 'Come again a bit, Freddy.' For a little while I pretended sleep. In fact, it was inconvenient. But soon, I got up a second time, again took off, went to her a second time &, in spite of all, she really gave me pleasure.*[19] The next day, Anne was back at Shibden Hall by 8:45 in the evening.

Such extravagances could not remain entirely secret in a town as small as Halifax. In so-called refined society, however, Anne was not really rejected. Her family and friends might not like the look of her black clothing and took some time to get used to it, but they overlooked it. Anne was simply *odd*,[20] a term she also applied to herself. She used the word *oddities*[21] to refer to her masculine conduct and her love for women, which she acknowledged in hints. When the Greenwood sisters teased her on one occasion that *they heard I was going to be married* to Mr George Priestley, she not only denied the gossip, but also added *how very much I preferred ladies to gentlemen.*[22] Caroline Greenwood kept track of Anne's female conquests with *a broad grin.*[23] Anne took secret revenge with *foolish fancying about Caroline Greenwood, meeting her on Skircoat Moor, taking her into a shed there is there & being connected with her. Supposing myself in men's clothes & having a penis, tho' nothing more.*[24] Yet it was highly important to Anne never to be observed in *fondling circumstances.*[25]

Lower down the social scale, people treated Anne Lister with far less discretion, nicknaming her *Gentleman Jack*, referring to Jack-the-lad. Some thought Anne a provocation. *The people generally remark, as I pass along, how much I am like a man.* She was a little proud of that, in secret. But she also heard more vulgar comments. *At the top of Cunnery Lane, as I went, three men said, as usual, 'That's a man' & one axed* [sic] *'Does your cock stand?'*[26] In York, prostitutes offered her their services. *There were several bad women standing about the mail. They would have it I was a man and one of them gave me a familiar knock on the left breast & would have persisted in following me.*[27] In Halifax, too, people became intrusive. A *little-ish, mechanic-like, young man* spoke to Anne on the way to church, asking *if I would like to change my situation.*[28] Anne left him standing but remembered him immediately when she received a threatening letter from one 'William Townsend' on 1 October 1819. A second letter arrived a few weeks later, *beginning, 'As I understand you advertised in the Leeds mercury for a husband...' Saw no more but reclosed, three drops of sealing-wax & sent it back to the post office. I begin to care not much about these impertinent insults. Their intended shafts of annoyance fall harmless & I shall never read them. What the eye will see not, the heart will grieve not.*[29]

Yet she did not react quite so calmly to such hostilities as she wanted to believe she did. Towards the end of 1819, these anonymous letters began to arrive more often and Anne braced herself for a physical attack, even an attempted rape on one of her long walks.

*However, I will never fear. Be firm. Learn to have nerve to protect myself & make the best of all things. He is but a little fellow & I think I could knock him down if he should touch me. I should try. If not, whatever he said I would make no answer. Never fear. Pray against this & for God's protection & blessing, & then face the days undaunted.*³⁰ Anne believed God was on her side, as she was His creature too.

In early January 1820, a man asked Anne on the way into town *if I wanted a sweetheart. […] I heard him say, 'I should like to kiss you.'* A week later, *a man, youngish & well enough dressed, suddenly attempted to put his hands up my things behind. In the scuffle, I let the umbrella fall but instantly picked it up & was aiming a blow when the fellow ran off as fast as he could & very fast it was. I did not feel in the least frightened, but indignant & enraged.* When she got home she *told them during tea. My uncle & aunt think it is the man who writes these letters.* Uncle James also received post from 'William Townsend', complaining that Anne never responded to his letters. James would have liked *to stop it into his mouth* and stood firm by his niece, never suggesting she change her behaviour or her clothing. Anne and her aunt grew even closer. *Stood talking to my aunt by the kitchen fire, after my uncle went to bed, 3/4 hour, about the people calling after me, being like a man & about people's being insulted.*³¹ Except for sex, she could talk about anything with Aunt Anne, about her nature, her identity and all her *oddities.*

To escape the hate, Anne left Halifax for a while on 1 February 1820, joining Mariana on a visit to her family in York. Nantz was there too, as was Louisa, and the two of them left Anne and Mariana little space or time for one another. Nantz was *a little jealous. Says she knows me well enough. I never talk to her when I can get anything prettier or better.*³²

Anne was very interested in the court case against Henry Hunt, the main speaker at the assembly that had ended with the Peterloo Massacre. Although she was convinced of the *absurdity and impracticability of 'liberty and equality' in this world*,[33] she was none-theless impressed by the *great ingenuity and eloquence*[34] with which Hunt defended himself for four hours and thirty-five minutes. The court sentenced him to thirty months' imprisonment; the yeomanry men were acquitted, their superiors never prosecuted.

Meanwhile, York was at the high point of the season. One social gathering, one musical soirée, one party came hot on the heels of the last. In Halifax, Anne kept herself to herself; *one can hardly carry one-self too high or keep people at too great a distance.*[35] In York, however, she accepted every invitation and was a welcome, witty guest and a good conversationalist. In the midst of this social hubbub came the long overdue trial of strength between the former friends Isabella and Mariana, both of whom hoped to be Anne's wife one day. *Tib would really willingly marry me in disguise at the altar.*[36] When Isabella had to look on as 'her husband' retired to the bedroom with Mariana on the first night at the Belcombes' house, Anne ended up in a *little tiff with Tib.* The next morning, Isabella saw no reason to get up, where-upon Anne informed her that *taking snuff & lying in bed did not suit me & she knew it. Answer; I never found fault with M–, & proceeded to it. It was a pity I let her marry.* Mariana saw her chance to clear things up at last, and advised Anne *to tell Tib every now & then she did not suit me & not to let her dwell so on the idea of our living together.* Attacked on two flanks, Anne sighed to Louisa, *I should not like to be long in the same house with M– and Tib.*[37] She affected not to understand why both women wanted her to themselves. Neither Mariana nor Isabella ever *did, or ever could, interfere with each other. Both kept their own places.*[38]

On 30 March, Mariana and Anne retired to Shibden Hall for two weeks together. After all the annoyances, the two of them revisited their past again. Mariana wanted *to look over some of our old letters. In getting them, happened to stumble on some memoranda I made in 1817 on her conduct, her selfishness in marrying, the waste & distraction of my love, etc. Began reading these & went on thoughtlessly till I heard a book fall from her hands &, turning round, saw her motionless & speechless, in tears. Tried very soothing & affectionate means. She had never before known how I loved her or half what her marriage had cost me. Had she known, she could not have done it & it was evident that repentance now pressed heavily. [...] She grieved over what I had suffered & would never doubt me again.*[39]

As a sign of her trust and goodwill, Anne confessed to Mariana that she had been in love with Elizabeth Browne for a while. *M– said, very sweetly and with tears at the bare thought, she could never bear me to do anything wrong with ... anyone in my own rank of life. She could bear it better with an inferior, where the danger of her being supplanted could not be so great. But to get into any scrape would make her pine away.* Anne rather liked this jealousy. *I never before believed she loved me so dearly & fondly. She has more romance than I could have thought.* And so Mariana asked Anne to stop *being too attentive* towards other women, *having too much of the civility of a well-bred gentleman. [...] Sat up lovemaking, she conjuring me to be faithful, to consider myself as married and always to act to other women as if I was M–'s husband.* Anne agreed to do so and undertook to *now begin to think & act as if she were indeed my wife.* When Mariana asked her for a binding promise on her last night, however, *I said I would do or promise anything, but that she needed no further promise than my heart, at that moment, gave her. (I made no promises.)*[40]

Mariana sensed that she could not be sure Anne really felt bound to her. When Isabella's beloved father died in early June, Mariana asked with suspicion: *'My Fred, will this melancholy event make any difference to you or me? I shall not lose you, my husband, shall I? Oh, no, no. You will not, cannot, forget I am your constant, faithful, your affectionate wife.'*[41] Being reminded of her commitments had always annoyed Anne. *She seems to consider my last letter as containing a promise on my part. Now this I certainly did not mean & she ought not to take it so far.* Anne wrote back, *disclaiming very gently having given her a promise & bidding her send me back my letters & be careful, for a discover* [sic] *would be ruin to us both.* She herself felt *as much at liberty as ever.*[42]

With this in mind, Anne went to stay with Isabella at Langton Hall on 5 October 1820. There, Mary Vallance was already attempting to console Isabella over the loss of her father. Anne had stayed in contact with Miss Vallance by letter since they had first met under that same roof two years previously. At that time, Anne had explained to Mary who the man was in her relationship with Isabella. Now she lost no time in adopting this role towards Mary herself. After six days of glances, jokes and double entendres, Miss Vallance asked Anne to pay a visit to her room late at night. *I found her alone, and though Burnett* [the servant] *came in, she whispered me to stay. Began rubbing her.* Then Isabella burst in in her nightclothes, looking for Anne, who was actually sharing her room and bed. *Got quit of Tib and Burnett a second time and staid with her till 12.00. Burnett says her complaint is quite on her nerves. I know it is and I am the best doctor. I soon found out what was the matter, kissed and put my tongue in while I had the three fingers of my right hand pushed as far as they would go up there. Distinctly felt the stones of ovaria. She was ready and wide as if there was not virginity to struggle with. I spoke softly and asked if she liked me. She said yes and began to whimper and said it was not worth having and would send me to Isabella. I would not come until Tib was asleep. I don't think this really annoyed Miss V though she made another faint whimper when she said her love was not worth having. I bade her try me I really think I shall be going to bed with her by & by. She is ready enough but perhaps she likes me a little independent of her nervousness.*[43]

Isabella was not blind. Having once lost Mariana to Anne, now she saw clearly that Anne was taking Mary Vallance away from her. Anne paid no heed to the fact that Isabella was mourning her father. One night in bed, Anne confronted a drunk Isabella. *She still swore by all that is sacred she never took more than five glasses a day; one at luncheon, one at supper, one at dinner & two at tea.* When Anne insisted

Isabella was drinking more, *she called God & all the angels of heaven to witness it was a lie & wished herself at the devil if it was not false.* Anne *told her a great many home truths,* but Isabella fell asleep. The next morning, Anne – the daughter of a drinker – started again. *I told Tib she did not know the injury she did herself. She was now twenty years older in constitution than she was ten years ago &, in fact, much more an old woman than she ought to be at her age. I saw that this made an impression.* [...] *She was afraid I must be tired of her & could never like to be with her. She had rather do anything than cease to be loved & desirable to me.*[44] It never occurred to Anne that she herself might be driving Isabella to drink.

Anne's behaviour angered Isabella's sister Charlotte, who thought she was *very unfair on poor Tib, who preferred me to all the rest of her friends.*[45] *Indeed, Charlotte joked & told me, a while before, she supposed the cronyism had now got to such a pitch I could not live without the sight of Miss Vallance.* Anne withdrew slightly from Miss Vallance in reaction, shifting her attentions to a new guest, her old flame Nantz Belcombe. *Went to Anne's room after dinner & Charlotte came and we staid an hour.* Anne retired at 11 o'clock. *Only a few minutes with Miss Vallance and then went to Anne, a little before twelve & staid two hours. At first, rather lover-like, reminding her of former days. I believe I could have her again in spite of all she says, if I chose to take the trouble. She will not, because it would be wrong, but she owns she loves me & perhaps she has feelings as well as I. She let me kiss her breasts but neither she nor her room seemed very sweet to my nose. I could not help contrasting her with Miss Vallance, & felt no real desire to succeed with her. At last, she said, 'Now you are doing all this & perhaps mean nothing at all.' Of course I fought off, bidding her only try me, but I felt a little remorse-struck.*[46]

Shortly before Christmas, the next guest arrived, Harriet Milne née Belcombe. Nantz and Mariana's sister was unhappily married to Lieutenant Colonel Milne and York's gossip had it she kept several lovers. Much to Mariana's despair, Anne had flirted with her openly the past March. Now *in the evening, Mrs Milne played. Hung over her at the instrument. Afterwards, sat next to her and paid her marked attention.* At bedtime, Anne stayed another *near ½ hour in Mrs Milne's room.* Next that night, Anne spent *near an hour with Anne Belcombe. She told me of my attention to Mrs Milne & that I had taken no notice of her or Miss Vallance & that she was sure Miss Vallance had observed it & felt as she* [Nantz] *did. Said I could not help it. Mrs Milne was fascinating.* While she was at it, Anne knocked on the next door. *Then went half an hour to Miss Vallance. Got out of her that she had observed me to Mrs Milne & was a little jealous. Anne* [Nantz] *then came to my room, having expected me again in hers, & staid almost till I got into bed. Her love for me gets quite as evident as I could wish.*[47] Despite all this closed-door diplomacy, Anne seems not to have had a *kiss* that evening, although or perhaps because she was negotiating with three women in parallel. The only one she did not have anything to do with that night was Isabella.

On 8 January, the party went its separate ways. Anne's farewell from Mary Vallance was *not very tender. Indeed, I get lukewarm about her.*[48] That was the end of the affair for Anne. *I care not about my connection with Miss V. She gave me licence enough.*[49] Mary married soon afterwards and disappeared from Anne's life. Harriet, Nantz and Anne went to York together, where Anne stayed with the Belcombes – in Nantz's room, *whom I easily persuaded to sleep with me.*[50] They resumed their affair for a week and then Anne returned home. *I shall not think much about her but get out of the scrape as well as I can, sorry & remorseful to have been in it at all. Heaven forgive me, & may M– never know it.*[51]

To keep Mariana from suspecting, Anne spent four hours writing a letter to her, *very affectionately, more so than I remember to have done for long.* Shortly after flirting with four women at the same time and sleeping with three of them, she assured Mariana she loved her *as warmly as ever. Yes, Mary, you cannot doubt the love of one who has waited for you so long & patiently. You can give me all of happiness I care for &, prest to the heart which I believe my own, caressed & treasured here, I will indeed be constant & never, from that moment, feel a wish or thought for any other than my wife.* Anne craftily dated her oath of loyalty to the future, restricting it to the moments in which she lay in Mariana's arms. *Every wish that love inspires & every kiss & every feeling of delight shall only make me more securely & entirely yours.*[52]

Mariana read Anne's letter as the promise she had not got out of her at their last assignation. *I have not exactly given her a promise in a set form of words but I have done nearly, in fact, the same thing, so that I cannot now retract with honour.*[53] Mariana sought a renewal of the vow between them because Charles was refusing to provide for her financially after his death if she did not give him a son. She had no legal claim to an inheritance from him and had relinquished her father's inheritance in favour of her unmarried sisters when she married. As Charles' first marriage had produced no children either, Mariana was *seriously desirous of executing the prostitution of herself in disguise to any man who could make up the deficiencies & get her with child for the sake of fixing her importance by being the mother of an heir to Lawton.* Nothing came of this idea, however. *I know the scheme was originally my own proposing but she persisted in it till I utterly disclaimed it, shocked, as I said, at the serious idea of such a thing. Wherewith her morality?*[54] In fact, Anne may have been more repelled by the thought of Mariana having sex with yet another man. With Charles just as unhappy with Mariana as she with him, he informed her *she could not expect him to be quite correct during so long an absence.*[55] That meant she had even fewer inhibitions about living out her desire for Anne, especially as her lover might inherit Shibden Hall. *Well, I am satisfied to have done. I love her & her heart is mine in return. Liberty & wavering made us both wretched & why throw away our happiness so foolishly? She is my wife in*

honour & in love & why not acknowledge her such openly & at once? [...]
The chain is golden & shared with M–. I love it better than any liberty.[56]

At the end of July 1821, Mariana and Anne met in Newcastle-under-Lyme in Staffordshire, to become godmothers to the first daughter of Stephen Belcombe and his wife Harriet. They were both nervous, having not seen each other for over a year. Anne needed *two glasses of wine* to prepare herself for the sight of her lover, who was *looking well, much improved in appearance since I saw her last*. As they did everywhere, the two women shared a room at Stephen and Harriet's house. They did not get a wink of sleep the first night; Mariana wanted Anne to repeat her promise before they made love. *Somehow did not manage a good kiss. Refused to promise till I had really felt that she was my wife. Went to her a second time. Succeeded better and then bound ourselves to each other by an irrevocable promise for ever, in pledge of which, turned on her finger the gold ring I gave her several years ago & also her wedding ring which had not been moved off her finger since her marriage –* this ring was not the one from Charles, but the ring Anne had given her. *She seems devoted to me & I can & shall trust her now.* They planned to *solemnize our promise of mutual faith by taking the sacrament together when next we meet at Shibden.*[57] The day after this 'wedding' their godchild, at Anne's request, was baptised in the name of her 'mother', Mariana Percy. *The child behaved remarkably well* and received from her godparents a set of silver cutlery and a silver cup, *altogether, five pounds.*[58] Anne and Mariana enjoyed their 'honeymoon' for a week and then the carriage came to collect Mariana from Lawton Hall. She and Anne agreed *every morning at 10 ¾, to read a chapter in the new testament,*[59] so as to be doing the same thing and thinking of one another once a day, despite the distance between them.

Anne stayed a few more days with Stephen, Harriet and her godchild. At night she felt *a queer, hottish, itching sensation* [...] *about the pudendum.*[60] She remembered Charles' admission of infidelity and the initial problems in bed with Mariana and wondered, *can*

C– have given her a venereal disease?[61] The next morning, she talked to Stephen, a doctor like his father. *Mention M– & my suspicion of venereal. He said he was treating her as for this & suspected it, tho' there were certainly some symptoms against it.* As Stephen admitted *he scarce knows what to think of M–*, Anne shifted his suspicion to Charles. Stephen thought *C– looked so innocent the other day, he hardly thinks him guilty. However, he has met with men in his practice, & who bear very good characters, who have played their wives this trick.* Anne could hardly admit she was suffering the same symptoms but she did want his medical advice, so she claimed to know *someone in the same situation. A young married woman, poor, who had tried much advice without relief & therefore asked Steph for the prescription he gave M–.*[62]

With Stephen's prescription, she hurried to the apothecary in Halifax to have *Piper cubeba* made up for her – a slightly antiseptic pepper solution. *Just after tea, poured a tablespoonful of this lotion into a cup & used it with a bit of sponge. It did not feel sharp & I think will do me good.*[63] She also found an old prescription from Mr Duffin, using ground calomel mixed with oil for vaginal injections. The active ingredient was a mercury-based mineral prescribed for hundreds of ailments. As her discharge was increasing, *trying to use my two ivory syringes that were Eliza Raine's. Let the common one fall & broke off the top of the piston but afterwards got to manage very well with the uterine syringe.*[64] Calomel is not soluble, so fortunately Anne Lister's body would not have absorbed the toxic mercury she inserted into her vagina. On the way to the apothecary, she bought the first volume of Rousseau's *Confessions* from Whiteley's Bookshop.

Uncle James and Aunt Anne were very surprised. Aunt Anne *asked so many questions she almost posed me. I said it was to soften my hands.* Anne could not possibly express her anxieties. Even her well-meaning aunt would have assumed Anne had had premarital sex with a man, losing her virginity and her reputation. Infection from one woman to another was beyond the realm of what could be said. *I believe she suspects something, for she said, 'Well, you're a queer one & I'll ask no more.'*[65]

Anne's fidelity to Mariana was soon to be put to the test. That autumn, Nantz Belcombe started making eyes at her again in York. *I did feel slightly, but am really much altered in these matters since my more thorough engagement to M–.* Three days later, though, Isabella arrived in town as well. She appeared at nine in the evening at the Duffins' house, where Anne was staying, although she could not *feel comfortable because far from independent.* Anne therefore walked Isabella back to her accommodation, the Black Swan, *& slept with her.* [...] *A kiss of Tib, both last night & this morning.* Anne noted soberly: *but she cannot give me much pleasure & I think we are both equally calm in our feelings on these occasions.* She felt she had not really cheated on Mariana. *For my own part, my heart is M–'s & I can only feel real pleasure with her. I hope Tib will not have caught any infection from me. At the moment of my offering to sleep with her, I forgot this, & afterwards there was no retracting.*[66]

In York, Anne bought a gig for Shibden Hall, a half-covered two-wheeled carriage pulled by one horse, which cost £65, including a harness and lamps. She drove it to Market Weighton, where she was to prepare the sale of Skelfler House because her father could find no way out of his debts. *The mare a little awkward at 1st, & I had not driven over a hundred yards before I ran against the wheel of a cart. However, we came along very well afterwards.*[67] She covered the nineteen miles in three and a quarter hours. The estate where she had spent part of her childhood was in a shocking state. *Such a wreck of property I never beheld.*[68] She arranged with a London agent for the entire property to be auctioned in March. Her excursion to Selby was more pleasant, with Jeremy teaching Anne to drive the gig. She made a proud note in her journal that the return trip had taken only a quarter of an hour longer than the first leg. Alone on the box again on the way to York, however, she was forced to whip the horse and bribe it with warm beer.

Meanwhile, Mariana had also arrived in York, but as her mother was there too, and mistrusted Anne as much as ever, the two of them retired to Shibden Hall for a week after Christmas, living almost the way they intended to in the future. They had previously *agreed we would have things nice sometime, our tastes suit.*[69] Now they were *very fond of each other & perfectly happy together.* Otherwise stubborn and sensitive when it came to clothing and style, Anne even let Mariana teach her *to do my front hair & we laughed heartily at my awkwardness.* On the eve of Mariana's departure they were *consoling each other & latterly in playful dalliance & gentle excitement. Our hearts are mutually & entirely attached. We never loved & trusted each other so well.*[70]

Two weeks after Mariana left, Isabella came to visit. She seems to have turned a blind eye to Anne's affair with Mary Vallance. She stayed a whole two months and was on her best behaviour. She imitated famous actors and Catholic priests at mass, making everyone laugh. *Tib is affectionate, seems happy here & is quieter than she used to be.* They entered into a not entirely playful competition as to who could drive Anne's gig better. Although Anne had had another collision with a cart and almost tipped over, she thought herself *as good, tho' not quite so stylish a driver as she.* The only problem was: *melancholy enough at the thought of going to bed with Tib. I cannot even affect any warmth towards her.*[71] But Anne knew where her duties lay.

Isabella, on the other hand, knew Anne, and she wanted to find out who she currently had an eye on and whether she didn't want to sleep with Eliza Belcombe. *Said I should not like it, & that I was much altered of late in all these matters. Tib laughed, looked incredulous, bade me not say so, & added, 'It would be unnatural in you not to like sleeping with a pretty girl.'* Anne did not tell Isabella about renewing her vows with Mariana. *She appears to have no suspicion of my living*

[with] *& loving seriously, any other than herself. Poor soul, I know how she will take it when the truth comes out.*[72] But Isabella knew precisely where the greatest threat lay. Three weeks after her arrival at Shibden Hall, they ended up in a heated argument over Mariana. *After dinner, long & rather sparring conversation with Tib about M—, of whom she is perpetually jealous. She says I am not to think she has ever been gulled. She thinks M— is almost tired of C— & wants to have me. I fought off, saying I should not like another man's leavings.* Though Anne still did not tell Isabella about her vows to Mariana, she talked as in the past *of the impossibility of Tib & I living together because she must be with Charlotte.* She did, however, give a vague hint for the first time that *I should get someone & hoped Tib would come and see me. She would if she might sleep but never otherwise, but I might go & see her if I did not take my companion with me.*[73]

During Isabella's stay at Shibden Hall, Anne's aunt by marriage, Mary Lister, passed away. Northgate House fell to Uncle James, who soon received enquiries as to whether he intended to rent out the elegant townhouse. James could have used the income, but Skelfler House was about to be sold and his brother Jeremy and niece Marian would have nowhere to live. Uncertain as to whether he had to let his brother have Northgate House cheaply, James asked the worldly-wise Isabella *if she did not think the whole town would be up if my father did not live at Northgate, to which she replied 'Yes!', she thought it would. I unluckily & thoughtlessly said, 'How different M— would have judged.' Tib took this in desperate dudgeon. Nothing I could say would appease her. She saw through me — she saw what I was — I had been guilty of the utmost grossness — she wished I had M— with me &, for her own part, it was well she was going so soon & she would never trouble me anymore — she had come for the last time. I did all I could to pacify & asked her to give me a kiss. She said she did not want one. I then said, 'Ask for one when you do,' & then went downstairs. She was out of sorts all the after-noon & evening, tho' downstairs almost all the time. She said nothing when we came to bed. I waited a minute or two to give her an opportunity & then went to undress.*[74]

The row was rekindled the next morning. *First she wished I had M—, then she was sorry for what she had done, would not do so any more, etc. Could not bear to think she did not suit me. Loved me better than anything in the world. It would be my fault if we did not live together. I quietly told her we never should & persisted that she did not suit & it was best to be candid at once. She cried a little & said she was unhappy. I bade her cheer up & said there was no reason why we should not always be very good friends. She could not bear me to talk so. However, I gave her a kiss or two & we got the time over till twelve.* Isabella left the next day. *She said she would come again next year. I hope not. I am much happier not to have her & am glad enough that she is gone.*[75]

The Ladies of Llangollen

1822

For James Lister, the death of his sister-in-law Mary was a good reason
to write his will. Anne had repeatedly reminded her uncle that she had
been considered as heir in 1815–16. *I said I should wish to have all the
estate here, ultimately. 'What, all?' said my uncle, smiling. 'Yes, all.'*[1]
Anne knew her uncle *had no high opinion of ladies – was not fond of leaving estates to females. Were I other than I am, would not leave his to me.*[2]
She therefore assured him she would never marry and Shibden Hall
would not end up in the wrong hands, even hinting at her hope that
Mariana *would one day be in the Blue Room, that is, live with me.* While
she was at it, she confided in her uncle and aunt that Mariana *would not
have married if she or I had had good independent fortunes. [...] My uncle,
as usual, said little or nothing but seemed well enough satisfied. My aunt
talked, appearing not at all surprised, saying she always thought it a match
of convenience.*[3]

By her uncle's side, Anne had not only learned the practical side
of running the estate but was also now dealing with the business
correspondence, sometimes even writing two versions of letters to
help her hesitant uncle make decisions. She had proved herself such
a good estate manager that her uncle made her his heir in his will
of June 1822. However, she was to share the income from the estate

with his remaining siblings, Anne senior and Jeremy, until the end of their lives. Uncle James also undertook to pay Anne £25 twice a year from then on – the first sum of money that Anne could ever count on, at the age of thirty-one. Aunt Anne would give her any sum she required on top of this. In the previous year she had spent some £70; her savings amounted to £113 at the beginning of the year. All in all, she could keep herself above water, but compared to the way she saw herself and the things she wanted in life, it was a modest standard.

Travel was one of the things that had been far too rare in Anne's life for her taste. The moment she had regulated her future finances, she and her aunt set out on a tour of Wales in July 1822. They were an experienced team since their trip to Paris, and the gig granted them new-found independence, especially as the Listers had also bought another horse to pull it, which Anne named Percy after Mariana's middle name. They reached Chester in pouring rain on the second day, having arranged to meet Mariana there, who intended to come over from nearby Lawton Hall. They missed one another, however, just as they had in Manchester. By the time they had finally both arrived that evening, Anne *had got into a sad agitation and fidgettiness.* Although they were *delighted to see each other, yet somehow I felt very low.* Anne's mood was not improved by their *two kisses last night, one almost immediately after the other, before we went to sleep.*[4] She asked Mariana *how long she thought it might be before we got together, & she seemed to fight off answering, on pressing further she said she felt some delicacy on this subject & did not like to talk openly of it even to ourselves, for, tho' she did not love him, yet kindness & obligation made her feel a wish to avoid calculating the time or thinking of it except in general terms.* Aside from that, Mariana told Anne about a Mr Powis, whom she liked a great deal. *All this has made a great impression on me &, I know not how it is, I cannot shake it off.* [...] *She seemed as fond of me as ever, yet all the night when I was almost convulsed with smothering my sobs, she took no notice, nor was affected at all apparently.* [...] *I know not how it is but she, as it were, deceived me once.* The fact that Anne always had one to three lovers alongside Mariana did not make her doubt her own constancy. *Somehow or other, seeing M— has been no comfort to me.*[5]

Anne and her aunt continued on the road, reaching their secret destination that same day: Llangollen, the home of Lady Eleanor Butler and Miss Sarah Ponsonby. The 'Ladies of Llangollen' were originally from Ireland but had lived in self-imposed exile in this Welsh village for forty-two years. One rainy March night in 1778, they had tried to run away together but had been caught. After two months of negotiations, their wealthy families let them go but gave them very little money. Once in Llangollen, they rented a simple cottage, which they transformed over the years – adding dark carved oak inside and outside, leaded stained-glass windows and historical bric-a-brac – into an ornate olde-worlde home that they called Plâs Newydd, meaning New Hall. They were to live in the house and tend its gardens for fifty years. The orchard was planted with nectarines and melons, the flower garden boasted forty-four kinds of roses alone, the shrub garden was full of lilac, laburnum and dogwood. Gravel paths led to a little temple and a well, with wooden bridges crossing the small Cyflymen Stream. Cows grazed outside the house – and today only they are missing; everything else has been preserved or restored.

The world had known all about the two women's escape attempt and their life together in their rural paradise from 24 July 1790, when the *General Evening Post* printed their story. *Miss Butler is tall and masculine, she wears always a riding habit, hangs her hat with the air of a sportsman in the hall and appears in all respects as a young man, if we except the petticoats which she still retains. Miss Ponsonby, on the contrary is polite and effeminate, fair and beautiful.*[6] The article was slightly free with the facts – Lady Eleanor was a pudgy fifty-one-year-old at the time – but it brought its readers fairly close to the overarching truth. The two did indeed dress in a significantly more

The Rt Honble Lady Eleanor Butler and Miss Ponsonby.
"The Ladies of Llangollen."

From an original Drawing.

S Ponsonby

Eleanor Butler

11 *The 'Ladies of Llangollen'*: Miss Sarah Ponsonby (left) and Lady
Eleanor Butler (right), lithograph by an unknown artist.

conspicuous manner than Anne Lister. Both Eleanor and Sarah wore dark gentlemen's jackets, starched gentlemen's collars with ties, and black top hats. They kept their hair short but strongly powdered, a style long since out of fashion.

Such eccentric manners in a remote setting awakened visitors' curiosity, and the women soon had a steady stream of them: Sir Walter Scott, Wordsworth, Mme de Genlis and the British aristocracy made a beeline for them. The German gardening enthusiast Prince Pückler called them *the two most famous spinsters (certainly the most famous in Europe).*[7] Unexpectedly, the ladies pulled off a trick that ensured their physical and social survival: what was 'out' was suddenly 'in'. They masked their actual poverty as a conscious retreat into a life at one with nature, inspired by Rousseau. And they styled their insubordinate love as an ideal romantic friendship, deeper, freer and thus nobler than any heterosexual marriage. What had begun as escape and exile developed into the epitome of a philosophically elevated, enviable ideal life, a magnet for visitors, and a business model. Their paradise was paid for by their guests; *none ventured a second visit without bringing a contribution of carved oak, which was the regular passport.*[8] The Ladies of Llangollen became a top sightseeing destination, merging with their house and garden to form a singular work of art.

Anne Lister had read about them in a newspaper article around 1810 *& had longed to see the place ever since.*[9] Mariana had already been there and dreamed of living with Anne the same way. So Anne was very disappointed to hear from her landlady at the King's Head Hotel, Mrs Davis, shortly after her arrival that the eighty-three-year-old Eleanor Butler had a bad cold and was not seeing visitors. Anne and her aunt nonetheless walked straight to Plâs Newydd, *which is really very pretty*, and then wrote the following note: *Mrs & Miss Lister take the liberty of presenting their compliments to Lady Eleanor Butler & Miss Ponsonby, & of asking permission to see their grounds at Plâs Newyd in the course of tomorrow morning. Miss Lister, at the* *suggestion of Mr Banks, had intended herself the honour of calling on her ladyship & Miss Ponsonby, & hopes she may be allowed to express her very great regret at hearing of her ladyship's indisposition.*[10] Having pulled out all the stops on the politeness scale, Anne was invited to view the grounds at 12 o'clock.

I quite agree with M— (vide her letter), the place 'is a beautiful little bijou', shewing excellent taste, Anne noted after a tour with the gardener the next day. *They kept no horses but milked 6 cows. Said I, 'Can they use the milk of 6 cows?' 'Oh, they never mind the milk. It is the cream.'* Anne's expectations were more than met. *It excited in me, for a variety of circumstances, a sort of peculiar interest tinged with melancholy. I could have mused for hours, dreampt dreams of happiness, conjured up many a vision of ... hope,*[11] because two women had managed to make a home together and be happy with one another for an entire lifetime. Plâs Newydd in Llangollen became a utopian place of consolation, not only for Anne Lister but for many women who love women up to the present day.

Strengthened and crestfallen at the same time, Anne continued on her tour of Wales with her aunt. On 15 July 1822, they climbed Mount Snowdon. *The ascent was much easier than I expected. There was no danger attending [...] and the exertion required was more on account of the length of the way than anything else.* Anne had not expected her aunt *to go to the top and therefore took a boy with us to conduct her to Llanbellis.* Along the way, though, two gentlemen joined them and Aunt Anne took one of their arms, *enabling her to get up to the top. Arrived there we looked about a few minutes, and then, foolishly, sat down in the little hut, on the stone benches. All the party felt chilled, and took a little bread and brandy except myself. Indeed the two gentlemen drank all of the two pint bottles of brandy our guide had taken.* As it was late, they took a shorter but extremely steep path back to the valley. *Had I had any idea what it was, I should not have thought of my aunt doing it. However, by dint of patient labour, and constant hold of the guide, she got down, frightened as she was, yet apparently less so than Mr Reid.* They did not reach the small inn at Llanberries until twenty to ten. *I know not that ever I was more heated. I had scarcely a dry thread about me.*[12]

After ten days of Anne steering Percy and the gig without accident through wild valleys, past ruined castles, along cliff tops and all the way to the sea, they returned to Llangollen. Anne immediately asked Mrs Davis about Lady Eleanor's health and was told they had feared for her life during the night. *The damp this bad account cast upon my spirits I cannot describe.* [...] *There is a something in their story & in all I have heard about them here that* [...] *makes a deep impression.* She was just entrusting her disappointment to her journal when she received the unexpected news that Miss Ponsonby *will be glad to see me this evening to thank me in person.* Anne spent two hours preparing for this meeting with the sixty-seven-year-old 'Mariana', *washing & cutting my toenails, putting clean things on.*

At ten past seven, Anne knocked at the door of Plâs Newydd and was asked into the breakfast room, waiting one or two minutes for Miss Ponsonby. *A large woman so as to waddle in walking but, tho', not taller than myself. In a blue, shortish-waisted cloth habit, the jacket unbuttoned shewing a plain plaited frilled habit shirt – a thick white cravat, rather loosely put on – hair powdered, parted, I think, down the middle in front, cut a moderate length all round & hanging straight, tolerably thick. The remains of a very fine face. Coarish white cotton stockings. Ladies slipper shoes cut low down, the foot hanging a little over. Altogether a very odd figure* – Anne used the adjective she often applied to herself. Sarah Ponsonby may well have gained the same impression of her guest, who looked equally unconventional. *Yet she had no sooner entered into conversation than I forgot all this & my attention was wholly taken.* [...] *Mild & gentle, certainly not masculine, & yet there was a* je-ne-sais-quoi *striking.*

Anne politely complimented her hostess on *the beauty of the place* and asked after Lady Eleanor. She had been through three operations and was at risk of going blind but her partner was still confident; Eleanor did in fact live another seven years. According to Miss Ponsonby, she was a great connoisseur of the sixteenth-century Italian poet Torquato Tasso and had written *elucidatory notes* on his *obsolete manners and phrases*. That gave Anne Lister the courage to ask apparently innocently, but with ulterior motives, *if they were classical*. *'No,'* said she. *'Thank God from Latin & Greek I am free.'* Following this disappointing response, *I observed that she might think all the classics objectionable — Yes! They wanted pruning.* Having not got far with classical authors, Anne tried her luck with contemporary writers. As she had once quizzed Miss Browne, she also asked Miss Ponsonby whether she had read Byron. *She was most afraid of reading* Cain, *tho' Lord Byron had been very good in sending them several of his works. I asked if she had read* Don Juan. *She was ashamed to say she had read the 1st canto.* Sarah Ponsonby did not let her guard down in front of Anne, maintaining the pose of a chaste spinster. Anne allowed herself one last insinuation when Miss Ponsonby asked her which Mr Bankes she had referred to in her note; *the great Grecian*, Anne responded, to give Miss Ponsonby an opportunity to react to her ribaldry. When that fell flat, Anne tried a more forthright approach in the garden, in an attempt to find out more about the relationship between Miss Ponsonby and Lady Butler. *I envied their place & the happiness they had had there. Asked if, dared say, they had never quarrelled. 'No!' They had never had a quarrel. Little differences of opinion sometimes. Life could not go on without it, but only about the planting of a tree, and, when they differed in opinion, they took care to let no one see it.* On their walk together, Anne talked a little about herself and Shibden Hall, but not about her dream of growing old with a woman too. Sarah Ponsonby understood her nonetheless. *At parting, shook hands with her and she gave me a rose. I said I should keep it for the sake of the place where it grew.*[13]

When the Listers took the same rooms in Chester as they had on their way out, Anne doubted more than ever that she and Mariana might turn Shibden Hall into their own Plâs Newydd. *I sat musing on M–, thinking I wasted my life in vain expectation, hoping for a time which she is too delicate to like to calculate. Somehow I cannot get over this.* It took her seven glasses of wine to fall asleep. *'I was unhappy,'* said I, *'the last time I was here. I cannot be worse now.'*[14]

Back in Halifax, her loneliness felt more painful than ever. As she had done in the past, Anne wrote letters to revive her feelings for Mariana. *Again seated quietly in my own room at Shibden, where the happiest hours of my life have been spent with you,* she wrote to her. *You have a shrine in every thought, & every feeling is an altar of remembrance. Interest in your welfare pervades the whole temple of my existence, & anxiety for your happiness is the high-priest that does the service of my soul. God grant that an affection so deeply rooted, so intensely strong, may be a comfort to us both, & form one bright spot in our lives on which the shadows of misfortune never rest.*[15]

Mariana was very grateful for Anne's description of her visit to the Ladies of Llangollen. *'Tell me if you think their regard has always been platonic & if you ever believed pure friendship could be so exalted. If you do, I shall think there are brighter amongst mortals than I ever believed there were.'* A child of her time, Mariana regarded all sexual desire – not only lesbian – as a sinful weakness that admirable individuals were able to resist. Anne, however, did not believe in abstention. *I cannot help thinking that surely it was not platonic. Heaven forgive me, but I look within myself & doubt. I feel the infirmity of our nature & hesitate to pronounce such attachments uncemented by something more tender still than friendship.*[16]

While Anne was in Wales, Mariana and Isabella had been in Buxton at the same time, though not together. They met on social occasions – and both tried to show the other in a poor light in their letters to Anne. Mariana wrote that Isabella *'looks fat & gross. She danced on Wednesday & looked almost vulgar. I could not keep my eyes off her or my mind from you.' They had a squabble on Friday evening, just before M– began to write.*[17] Isabella, meanwhile, emphasised maliciously that Charles Lawton *is certainly better looking than I expected, & is certainly very gentlemanly in his manners, but his figure is dreadful.* [...] *Just before he took his leave, he said that he never saw anything so extraordinary as my likeness to you; upon which M– exclaimed with a silly face, that it was paying me a very great compliment; on any other occasion I should have said the same thing, but I was so astonished at hearing him mention your name, that I was (as we say in Yorkshire) perfectly dumbfounded.*[18] Others, too, noticed the similarity Charles Lawton had commented on between Anne and Isabella; one Mr Lally from York thought that was the reason for their altercations. *Two jacks would not suit together.*[19]

On Anne and her aunt's return from Wales they found Jeremy and Marian Lister ensconced at Shibden Hall, although Skelfler House had not sold; in the generally poor economic climate, no one wanted to invest in a run-down estate. Jeremy had auctioned off the cows, sheep, horses and pigs, however, along with all the farm machinery and his own household goods. His brother James had offered to rent him Northgate House at a price Jeremy could not afford. Otherwise so tight-lipped, Anne's uncle told her how embarrassed he was by Jeremy's behaviour, and that Marian too *is like my mother & my uncle would not trust her.* James and Anne agreed that the two of them would be best off *going to France,*[20] where they could lead a better, cheaper and more comfortable life, all in all, than in England. They could not come up with any more elegant way to get rid of Marian and Jeremy, so Anne said she was willing to find a place for her father and sister to live in France. At least this meant she could return to Paris.

On the evening of 29 August 1822 they drove to Kingston-upon-Hull and boarded a steamship for the first time in Anne's life, arriving in London on the 31st and staying two days. Anne noticed a great

12 Anne Lister's diary, 15 September 1822. Anne Lister often switched from uncoded to encrypted writing mid-sentence; West Yorkshire Archive Service, Calderdale, SH: 7/ML/E/6

deal of construction work in comparison to 1819 but was distracted by her father: *I am shocked to death at his vulgarity of speech & manner.* Everything about him was too loud, too vulgar or too jovial. The fact that she looked conspicuous herself did not stop her from criticising her wildly gesticulating and occasionally spitting father. *I am perpetually in dread of meeting anyone I know.*

In Dover, the sailing ships on which Anne and her aunt had crossed the Channel three years previously had been decommissioned. They chugged across to Calais in only two hours and fifty-five minutes. Jeremy had barely set foot on French soil before he had digestion problems and *talks of being dead in two or 3 days.* Instead of continuing to Paris, they stayed in Calais for the time being. *I always say to myself, temper, temper, temper, i.e. keep your temper.*[21] Anne walked on the beach on her own and enjoyed the food at their hotel, washing it down with more wine than usual. Marian found the *women's caps 'frightful', and the potatos* [sic] *too long and sweet, and bespeaking that the people do not know how to cultivate them.*[22] Of her father, Anne wrote: *I do not think he likes France hitherto. He told me this morning he thought we should all go back together for he is sure Marian is tired already. I think my father is, whatever she may be. He is constantly saying Frenchmen are what they were 50 years ago i. e. what he knew them in Canada & he seems neither to admire them or anything about them.* Jeremy had barely left his room, however. *What can he mean to do? He cannot be long at Shibden nor afford to live at Northgate. The prospect seems darksome but he appears to take it very quietly. He must order for himself & I shall fidget myself not more than I can help.*[23]

After a week, they did travel on to Paris. While Anne wore her feet out in search of a home for Jeremy and Marian, her father's complaints returned and he declared he had never intended *to stay longer than the money lasted he had in his pocket, and said at Calais he had seen enough of France already.* He claimed he had only come to Paris for Marian's sake. What he really wanted was *to board and lodge in some clergyman's family in some retired pleasant part of England*, saying he had read such advertisements in the *Yorkshire Gazette* before their departure. *Oh! That I could have guessed or divined this before we set off!*, [24] Anne sighed in a letter to her aunt. She was not entirely innocent in the whole fiasco, however, having intended to persuade her father to try out a life that would not suit him. With Jeremy and Marian not appreciating the sights of Paris and Anne unable to enjoy them in their company, they broke off their stay on 28 September. Back in Halifax, Jeremy did not in fact look for lodgings with a clergyman's family; he was neither willing nor able to bring order into his failed existence. Out of brotherly concern and fear of gossip, James had no other option but to let Jeremy and Marian live in the large Northgate House with its expensive upkeep.

Anne escaped to Isabella Norcliffe at Langton Hall, staying almost a month. Isabella was *much improved*, Anne thought, unlike Mariana's envious description. *She takes much less wine now*, she wrote, *only four glasses a day.* They continued their sexual relationship where they had left off. *Better kiss last night than Tib has given me for long.* In the morning, Isabella found Anne injecting medicine into her vagina for her persistent discharge. *I denied, but won't use the syringe again, however gently, when she is in the room.* [25] Nonetheless, she dared to do something she had not in Halifax or York, for reasons of discretion. In the neighbouring village of Malton, where nobody knew her, she went to a doctor and told him *I had caught it from a married friend whose husband was a dissipated character. I had gone to the cabinet water-closet just after her.* Without a physical examination, his diagnosis was as vague as Stephen Belcombe's. He prescribed mercury pills, which were not helpful. Anne's perpetual *horrors for fear of infecting Tib* did not stop her from having sex, though. *I had a very good kiss last night. Tib had not a very good one.* [26]

On this stay too, *We talked about M—*. Isabella had noticed that her attempt to put Mariana down had had no effect. Now she claimed *she likes her as much as ever. Nothing can ever make her dislike her again. If she lived with me, Tib would come & see us &, tho' M slept with me, Tib would not dislike her.*[27] Anne's diary does not reveal whether she saw through Isabella's tactical self-denial. She returned to Shibden Hall at Christmas.

'Frank'

1823

Over the next few months in Halifax, Anne made a new friend: *I never met with such a woman before.*[1] They met in February 1823 at a lecture series on scientific subjects. Miss Francis Pickford had read Jane Marcet's *Conversations on Chemistry and Natural Philosophy* to prepare for the course and ended up in stimulating conversation with Anne. The two had first encountered one another in Bath in 1813; whenever Francis Pickford visited her sister in Halifax, the town gossips – from whom Elizabeth 'Kallista' Browne had once *heard me compared with Miss Pickford*[2] – expressed surprise that Anne and Francis were not closer friends. The well-read Francis Pickford considered Anne *congenial with herself,* but her attempts to get to know her better had always been rebuffed by Anne's aristocratic pride. Now, Anne established that Miss Pickford *seems sensible & in my present dearth of people to speak with I should well enough like to know more of her. I talk a little to her just before & after the lecture &, if she were young & pretty, should certainly scrape acquaintance* – as she had with Elizabeth Browne at an earlier lecture series. *How I can still run after the ladies!*[3]

Two days later, Anne drove Miss Pickford to her sister's house in her gig after a lecture. The speaker had used the pronoun 'she' to refer to the air, which gave Anne an opportunity for all manner of double entendre. Miss Pickford picked up the thread and *spoke of the moon being made masculine by some nations, for instance, by the Germans. I smiled & said the moon had tried both sexes, like old Tiresias, but that one could not make such an observation to every one. Of course she remembered the story? She said yes,* but did not remark that Tiresias had felt nine times more lust as a woman than as a man. *We parted very good friends.*

Unlike with Miss Browne four or five years previously, Anne and Miss Pickford were soon calling on each other. *I talked very unreservedly & we seemed to suit & like each other very well.*[4] Among other things, they talked about whether and how educated women had to hide their knowledge. *Miss Pickford thought gentlemen, in general, pleasanter than ladies. I said my feelings with the one & the other were quite different. I felt it more incumbent to talk sense & felt more independent with gentlemen, but there was a peculiar tenderness in my intercourse with ladies & if I was going to take a walk, I should infinitely prefer a pleasant girl to any gentleman.* This was an important message about Anne to her new friend; *if she has much nous on the subject, might let her into my real character towards ladies.*[5] Miss Pickford admitted in return that she had a close female friend, a Miss Threlfall.

To Anne's disappointment, 'Frank' Pickford, as she was called, was more of a gentleman. *I wish she would care a little more about dress. At least not wear such an old-fashioned, short-waisted, fright of a brown habit* – like Sarah Ponsonby, meaning a men's jacket – *with yellow metal buttons.*[6] Miss Pickford thought *as to not noticing dress, etc., she supposes me like herself. How she is mistaken!*[7] When it came to others, Anne had a great sense of *fashions,* with a tendency for *noticing these matters so narrowly. A lady's dress always strikes me, if good or bad.*[8] The *sweet, interesting creatures* that made Anne weak at the knees all dressed well in a ladylike style; Frank Pickford was not one of them. *She is a regular oddity* and was too similar to Anne herself. *She is better informed than some ladies & a godsend of a companion in my present* scarcity, *but I am not an admirer of learned ladies,*[9] wrote the equally learned Anne. *I would rather have a pretty girl to flirt with. She is clever for a lady, but her style of manner & character do not naturally suit me. She is not lovable.*[10]

Francis Pickford seems to have felt differently. She contrived to meet Anne on walks on the lonely moors, finally admitting one evening at Shibden Hall *to growing a little romantic now & then. Surprised me by hinting that Miss Threlfall would, perhaps, be jealous of me &, altogether, it absolutely occurred to me that, if I chose it, I could even make a fool of Miss Pickford. My aunt observes she looks at me as if she was very fond of me. She certainly softens down a little with me & flatters me both in word & action in every way she can.*[11] But Anne did not like to be seduced. *She is too masculine & if she runs after me too much, I shall tire.*[12]

Miss Pickford did not interest Anne as a woman; but she did want to find out more from her, especially as Frank had once told her about *putting on regimentals & flirting with a lady under the assumed name of Captain Cowper. It did not seem that the lady ever found it out but thought the captain the most agreeable of men.*[13] *In my mind thought of her using a phallus to her friend.*[14] She spent two weeks working on her. *Went on & on. Talked of the classics, the scope of her reading, etc. & what I suspected, apologizing & wrapping up my surmise very neatly till at last she owned the fact, adding, 'You may change your mind if you please,' meaning give up her acquaintance or change my opinion of her if I felt inclined to do so after the acknowledgement she made. 'Ah,' said I, 'That is very unlike me. I am too philosophical. We were sent on this world to be happy. I do not see why we should not make ourselves as much so as we can in our own way.' Perhaps I am more liberal or lax than she expected & she merely replied, 'My way cannot be that of many other people's.' Soon after this we parted. I mused on the result of our walk, wondering she let me go so far, & still more that she should confide the secret to me so readily.* This was not all that surprising, considering the way Francis felt towards Anne. Like her, Anne had to reveal herself at some point to every woman she wanted to seduce. *I think she suspects me but I fought off, perhaps successfully, declaring I was, on some subjects, quite cold-blooded, quite a frog. She denied this but I persisted in that sort of way that perhaps she believed it. I shall always pursue this plan. I would not trust her as she does me for a great deal.*[15]

They continued their conversation the next day. Miss Pickford hoped Anne would make a similar confession. *I said I knew she could not have made the confession if she had not supposed I understood the thing thoroughly. She answered 'No, certainly.' I dilated on my knowing it from reading & speculating but nothing further. She was mistaken. 'No, no,' said she, 'It is not all theory.' I told her her inference was natural enough but not correct. Asked if she had heard any reports about me. I said I had only two very particular friends. Miss Norcliffe was out of the question from her manners, habit, etc., & the other, M—, was married which, of course, contradicted the thing altogether. Asked her which of them it could be of whom the report could be circulated. At last she said it was M—. I said I knew the report & should not have cared about it had it not annoyed M—. For my own part I denied it, tho' Miss Pickford might not believe me. Yet, in fact, I had no objection to her doubting me for, had I had the inclination for such a thing, I should have pleased myself by trying &, could I have succeeded, I should have thought myself very clever & ingenious & that I must be very agreeable, but I must say, really, Miss Pickford, it seemed, could make herself more agreeable than I could. I wished I had her secret. I dwelt a good deal on having had no opportunity, & the frogishness of my blood. She told me I said a great many things she did not at all believe. Whether she credits my denial to all practical knowledge, I cannot yet make out. However, I told her I admired the conduct of her confession & liked her ten thousand times more for having told me. She was the character I had long wished to meet with, to clear up my doubts whether such a one really existed nowadays.*[16]

Anne kept up her act until Miss Pickford's departure. *'Now,'* said

I, 'the difference between you & me is, mine is theory, yours practice. I am taught by books, you by nature. I am very warm in friendship, perhaps few or none more so. My manners might mislead you but I don't, in reality, go beyond the utmost verge of friendship. Here my feelings stop. If they did not, you see from my whole manner & sentiments, I should not care to own it. Now do you believe me?' 'Yes,' said she, 'I do.' Alas, *thought I to myself, you are at last deceived completely. My conscience almost smote me but I thought of M–. It is for her sake that I first thought of being, & that I am, so deceitful to poor Pic, who trusts me so implicitly.*[17]

Presumably, Francis Pickford did not believe Anne at all, understanding that she was lying. *'Is this,'* said she, *'your philosophy? Does your conscience never smite you?'*[18] She took a noble step back without exposing Anne. This clever woman could have become a genuine friend; they might have lent each other mutual support as two women who loved women. But Anne Lister did not seek friendship between equals. *I am now let into her secret & she forever barred from mine. Are there more Miss Pickfords in the world than I have ever before thought of?*[19] When Francis left Halifax at the beginning of September, *I stood watching her so long the people might stare at me.*[20] From then on, their letters concerned only chemical gases and Armenian grammar.

Mariana and Isabella

1823–1824

There is one thing that I wish for. There is one thing without which my happiness in this world seems impossible. I was not born to live alone. I must have the object with me & in loving & being loved, I could be happy.[1] A deep longing for a life partner was just as much part of Anne's existence as her steadfast dialogue with herself in her journals. Despite her renewed engagement to Mariana in July of 1821, however, she thought of her less and less. *Were I to meet with anyone who thoroughly suited me, I believe I should regret being at all tied.*[2] Mariana, she thought, *has not that fineness, that romantic elegance of feeling that I admire & that she scarcely understands me well enough to make me so happy as perhaps I once too fondly thought. Perhaps I require too much. It must be an elegant mind joint with a heart distilling tenderness at every pore that can alone make me happy.*[3]

Nonetheless, Anne was immediately willing to go along with Mariana's suggestion for a reunion. When Mariana passed through Halifax in the mail coach, Anne was to get on and go along with her. On the morning of 19 August 1823, the *suspense and anxiety of waiting* made her restless and she decided to walk towards the coach. She left Shibden Hall without breakfast at about half past seven, in drizzling rain, and marched ten and a half miles up into the moor to Blackstone

Edge, a dramatic escarpment, meeting the coach there three hours and ten minutes after setting out. *Unconscious of any sensation but the pleasure at the sight of M—,* a windswept and sweaty Anne held up her hand to halt the coachman, proudly and breathlessly announced that she had walked from Halifax, opened the door, stumbled up the three steps and collapsed onto the seat next to Mariana and her sister Lou. *M— horror-struck. Why did I say I had walked from Shibden? Never saw John's eyes* [Mariana's servant] *so round with astonishment; the post-boys, too; & how fast I talked! Thought to have met me at Halifax. Why did I come so far? Why walk? Why not come in the gig?* Anne gave hasty explanations and tried to laugh off Mariana's reaction, until she realised it was her boisterous joy at seeing Mariana that repelled her friend, who was appalled that she had taken the three steps into the coach in one go, most unladylike. *The poisoned arrow had struck my heart and M—'s word of meeting welcome had fallen like some huge iceberg on my breast.* Instead of embracing or holding hands in front of Lou, they ended up arguing. Anne's emotions *were in tumult.* She fell silent for five minutes to gather her wits. *'I meant to have gone with you'* to Scarborough, said Mariana, *'but now perhaps ...'* Anne was about to reply, but *'Now,'* said she, *'you are going to vex me. Hold your tongue.'*

They appeared to have made up by the time they arrived in Leeds, but Anne felt miserable. She brought up the late breakfast she had eaten on the way. *M— blamed the milk. It was not that. I laughed & said it was the shock of 'the three steps'.*[4] At the Belcombes' house in York, Anne and Mariana attempted to talk it over that night. *She had a feeling she could not describe.* Mariana was afraid of being caught out and *would make any sacrifice rather than have our connection be known.* Anne reassured her *she need not fear my conduct letting out our secret. I could deceive anyone. Then told her how completely I had deceived Miss Pickford.*[5] They had a sexual reconciliation, but at home in Halifax, the episode caught up on Anne again. *The '3 steps' business haunts me like a spectre. I cannot throw it off my mind; it is my 1st thought in a morning & last at night.* Mariana's concern over losing her reputation seemed to her like the *paltry selfishness of coward fear.*[6] She felt Mariana had never loved her as much as Anne loved her, due to Mariana's propensity for material matters – and so it was Mariana's fault that Anne had to cheat on her. *How I could have adored her had she been more of that angelic being my fancy formed her. No thought, no word, no look had wandered then.*[7] *But mine are not affections to be returned in this world.* In the light of Mariana's chronic venereal disease, Anne feared *knowing her had perhaps been the ruin of my health & happiness.*[8]

Mariana tried to explain herself in a letter. She assured *my Fred* of her unaltered love, *tho' the tongue may sometimes, at unawares, speak unpalatable truths.* Mariana regretted her behaviour at Blackstone Edge but insisted *absolutely I feel jealous for you of everyone's good opinion & I would not have you excite wonder, even in a post-boy.*[9] These words horrified Anne so much that she quoted them three times over in her diary. *M– has not the way, I see, to lull me into sweet forgetfulness.*[10]

Still, Anne went to Scarborough on 12 September 1823 to spend a week with Mariana and her sisters Louisa and Eli; *the 'three steps' business so in my mind, I seemed coolish, I daresay, & formal* to begin with. Her robust march to Blackstone Edge had already made the rounds. Anne's black woollen dress, worn on the beach and in the town every day, caused no less consternation; *all the people stared at me. M– owned afterwards she had observed it & felt uncomfortable.*[11] At the sophisticated resort, Mariana saw her lover through new eyes. *We touched on the subject of my figure. The people staring so on Sunday had made her then feel quite low. [...] She knew well enough that I had staid in the house to avoid her being seen with me. 'Yet,' said I, 'taking me altogether, would you have me changed?' 'Yes,' said she. 'To give you a feminine figure.'* Anne's masculine allures, which had fascinated and excited Mariana for nine years, now disturbed her. *She had just before observed that I was getting mustaches* [sic] *& that when she first saw this* *it made her sick. If I had a dark complexion it would be quite shocking. I took no further notice than to say I would do anything I could that she wished.*[12]

When Mariana said the next day that *it was lucky for us both her feelings were cooler. They tempered mine,* [...] *my feelings now began to overpower me. I thought of the devotion with which I had loved her, & of all I had suffered. I contrasted these with all the little deceits she has put upon me –* forgetting her own. *My heart was almost agonized to bursting. The tears ran down my cheeks.* Anne suggested to Mariana *never to be with her again till we could be together entirely, but I stopt* [sic] *short, tho' not before she guessed that I meant offering to be off altogether. This seemed to affect her.* After Anne had cried almost all night long, Mariana spent the next day crying. *She thought I should be happier without her. She was always giving me pain. I could do better without her than she without me.*[13] Anne vowed to herself: *I will not be much in M–s way. When I can give her éclat it will be very well. At present I cannot. She owns this sort of thing makes her feel uncomfortable. Is she ever conscious that she is at all ashamed of me?*[14]

The dismayed lovers returned from Scarborough to York to attend a concert festival at the minster. Anne was glad to be able to stay at the Norcliffes' townhouse, where she shared Isabella's room and bed. Mariana feared that closeness to her rival might be a threat to her and she visited for breakfast or dinner, not letting the two of them attend the theatre without her. *I sat between M– and Isabella.* On 24 September they were among the five-thousand-strong audience to hear Handel's *Messiah,* performed by four hundred musicians in the choir and orchestra. *The 'Hallelujah Chorus' transcendentally fine. Cramer, the leader, says there will never be such a thing again during the life of this generation.*[15] At the Belcombes' home, Anne even met one of the soloists, Angelica Catalani, whom she had heard many years before with Eliza. The world-famous singer had been invited to dinner at six but appeared an hour early; *nobody being ready, I staid & had a little tête-à-tête with her.* [...] *Madame Catalani is certainly a very handsome, elegantly mannered & fascinating woman. I stammered on in French very tolerably. Saw M— merely for a moment.* In comparison to the worldly artist, Mariana seemed *too commonplace. Her sensibility seems rather weakness of nerve than the strength of affection. She thinks a good deal of her appearance & dress.* Once again, Anne returned to the humiliations Mariana had visited upon her. *She is subject to a feeling of shame about me, such as at Scarbro'. I fancy she would sometimes rather be without me ... She is not exactly the woman of all hours for me. She suits me best at night. In bed she is excellent.*[16]

Anne had a direct comparison, as she had now gone back to Isabella. Despite having argued terribly not long before, they continued their sexual relationship without further ado in York. When Anne spent several weeks at Langton Hall, Mariana joined them. *I felt oddish when they came & did not go downstairs quite immediately. This Blackstone Edge & Scarbro' business so clings to my memory I can't shake it off.* Instead of enjoying her two lovers' company, *I felt low & unhappy & could have cried, with pleasure, all the evening.* She agreed with Mariana *when she said she would give anything to efface the last three months. Alas, they have altered me.*[17]

Back in Halifax, she was alarmed by a message from Isabella. *'I have been unwell since last Friday & it has turned to the fluor albus* [i.e. leucorrhea or 'the whites'] *& most violent.'* Anne was immediately certain she had infected her. *All this struck me like a thunderbolt. My heart sank within me as I thought of the injury I was so unsuspected of having done her.* Unsuspected? Anne had been sleeping with Isabella for two years, despite her concerns. *Remorse struck me deeply. Oh, M—, M—. What have you done?* Anne accused her other lover, who certainly was not the one who had infected Isabella. *Surely, said I, I am more sorry for poor Isabella than you were for me.*[18]

Isabella arrived for a long visit to Shibden Hall in mid-January of 1824. *She never expects to be well of this complaint & it inconveniences her very much. [...] Poor Tib. I will, at any time, make up for it all I can by double attention & kindness. If she knew the truth, what would she think?*[19] This redoubled attention towards Isabella showed itself in Anne getting up at 5:30 to see to the horses in the stable. From seven to nine, she studied Greek and French, from nine to ten overseeing work on the estate. Isabella joined her at ten for breakfast. Between eleven and two, Anne kept an eye on the workers again, and then went for a walk with Isabella. They sat down to dinner with Anne's aunt and uncle at half-past four. After that, Anne took care of her correspondence before they all met up again for coffee at eight. At ten o'clock, Anne was the first to retire, writing her journal before going to bed. *How heartily I wish she was gone. I already begin to count the days,* Anne wrote after five weeks. Isabella was drinking too much again and *poisons me with her snuff. I can hardly bear being in the room.*[20] They argued over banal matters – whether six horses had ever been driven by three postilions in England – and about Anne's arrogance. *Never knew anyone have so much pride. She could not bear it. She was not fit to be here. Would not soon get herself into the scrape again.*[21]

After Isabella had left on 24 March 1824, Anne reviewed the situation in her diary. *Her feelings were never finely acute. Now they are blunted a good deal. [...] Her memory is worse. She tells her stories much oftener over than she used to do, forgetting that she has told us the same again & again. She is growing gradually larger,* for which Anne blamed the alcohol and the ten hours a day spent in bed. *How I could have loved her. Yes, how adored her, had she had that temper & conduct which temperance & good sense might easily have secured. But, alas, it has not been so.* As in Mariana's case, Anne placed the blame for not being able to love her as she would have wanted squarely on Isabella's shoulders. *Had Isabel been half she might have been, my affections never could have strayed to M– or to any other. But no more. God bless thee*

Tib. Our interests are separated forever, but still, when I forget myself, I almost love thee. No, I do not love thee but love thy happiness.[22]

The summer after their tour of Wales in 1822, Anne and her aunt travelled around the Yorkshire Dales. At the end of July 1824, Anne drove her aunt in the gig to the Lake District, where they enjoyed the views and the food in good inns such as at Bowness on Lake Windermere: *Soup (with vegetables in it, very good), a most excellent & beautifully dressed (boiled, and then a little fried or crisped) pike. A roasted fore-quarter of lamb, potatoes and peas, 2 little sweet puddings, a tart & jellies. All most excellent. We never enjoyed a dinner more.*[23] The food at Shibden Hall was much more basic, on Uncle James' instructions – all the more reason for the two Annes to treat themselves once a year.

Aunt Anne was increasingly suffering from rheumatism, but Anne junior wanted to take her walks in the Lake District. Out in the gig and passing the start of a footpath across the hills Anne had heard of, she decided spontaneously – against the advice of their local guide – to go on a two-day excursion. In the next village, Rosthwaite, she hired a cobbler as a guide and arranged to meet her aunt the next day in Scale Hill in Loweswater, with their servant George Playforth taking her comfortably by road in the gig. They parted ways at twenty to four. Anne intended to walk across the northern half of what is now the national park in one late afternoon. The ascent proved steeper and harder than Snowdon in Wales; the path was barely secured, with loose stones costing her strength. After fourteen miles they reached a farm, where they could have asked for accommodation for the night. As the sun was still up, though low in the sky, Anne preferred to continue to Calder Bridge, another six miles away. But they lost their bearings on the way down. They did not reach Gosforth, further south than Calder Bridge, until late at night. They had walked over twenty miles without pause and Anne was absolutely exhausted. She had turned down bread, cheese and water along the way; as when climbing Mount Snowdon, she had not wanted to eat or drink because of the great physical effort. At the Lamb & Lion in Gosforth, Anne was *parched to death with thirst,* but was so suspicious she drank only a little boiled water with gin. Her feeble, dehydrated body could not keep down the simple fare available that late at night, and she had to lie down in her sweat-soaked clothes, having brought no change of clothing with her. This spontaneous excursion might easily have ended in disaster. Anne blamed her guide. *If left to myself I should not have so lost myself. I said repeatedly we must be wrong, but that my guide must know better than I did.*[24]

The next day, she walked along the valley to Calder Bridge, rented a horse there and rode sixteen miles along the country road to the meeting place with her aunt. For the remaining days of their trip, she concentrated on food.

By this point, Anne had been suffering from the venereal disease she had contracted from Mariana and passed on to Isabella for three years. Having consulted first Stephen Belcombe and then Dr Duffin, she had later gone to the doctor in Malton. She tried the painful and futile remedy of leeches on her back. In the end, Anne felt forced to tell her aunt and uncle. Aunt Anne had often asked concerned questions and had been shown Anne's discharge-soaked sheets by the maid. *My aunt took it all quite well. Luckily, thinks the complaint easily taken by going to the necessary, drinking out of the same glass, etc.* She and Uncle James gave Anne money for an examination in Manchester by Mr Simmons, *a plain-appearing, plain-mannered man.* Anne told him she was anxious *to know that the complaint did not go beyond the vagina. He hoped not. Asked if I had had many children. From the impulse of the moment I said, 'Lord bless you, no. I was never married.'* She could not allow herself to care what the doctor thought of her. *He then proposed an examination. I said I should not think it right to refuse to submit. The handling hurt me & I felt it quarter or half-hour afterwards but otherwise I did not mind it much. These things are chiefly in idea for, strictly speaking, there is no real indelicacy in submitting to a thing of this kind when so necessary.*[25]

Yet Mr Simmons was unable to cure Anne. Weakened by her complaints, she wrapped herself in blankets in the cold, damp, draughty Shibden Hall even at the height of summer, wearing leather knee-warmers made specially for her; she feared *I should be rheumatic, like my aunt.*[26] In the end, Anne had the courage to hint to Aunt Anne that *the grapes & pears of Paris did me more good than anything.* Her aunt sympathised. *She is really very good & anxious about me.*[27] Although Uncle James had pointed out *how poor we are & always have been; our ideas above our means,*[28] he gave her £125 for three months in Paris.

Maria

1824–1825

On 24 August 1824, Anne Lister left Shibden Hall with her maid, Elizabeth Wilkes Cordingley, in the finest weather. She took the mail coach again and reached London in a day and a half, with pauses only to change horses. To keep Cordingley amused, uncertain of how enthusiastic she was about the journey, Anne showed her the sights in *the metropolis of the world.* Anne wanted to see a house of correction on this visit, where the inmates had to keep a treadmill moving over ten hours of monotonous motion. She presented herself to the authorities to get permission to view Coldbath Fields Prison, prompting surprise at *the singularity of the application, and the no less unique manner of the applicant.* But she would not let them fob her off. *Surely in a metropolitan prison there is nothing indelicate or offensive – nothing, I presume, which a female might not, with the strictest regard to propriety or decorum, inspect.* When she was eventually let into the prison, where three hundred and fifty men, women and children performed penal labour, she tried out the treadmill for herself. *I got upon it for two or three minutes, and have nothing to say against it – cannot imagine how it can do any harm.*[1]

In Paris, Anne lodged in Mme de Boyve's pension at 24, place Vendôme on the corner of rue de la Paix. Anne's room was *comfortable,* but *123 steps from the ground – yet there is a story* [sic] *above*

*me – the situation excellent, but, like every part of Paris, noisy beyond
description. Ill-hung rattling carriages perpetually rolling over a rough
pavement, make a din more easily imagined than expressed – the whole
house vibrates like the needle of a mariner's compass.*[2] The mainly
English guests were curious about Anne, seeing as *The Times* –
and other newspapers as a result – had reported on her visit to the
treadmill. *It seems I have got the reputation of being 'a character'.*[3]
Anne let her *inquisitive, curious look*[4] wander over the other guests,
settling on the *nice little figure* of Mrs Maria Barlow, or more precisely *directed to her bosom.*[5] Mrs Barlow was almost thirty-eight,
four and a half years older than Anne, came from Guernsey and
had been not unhappily married to a Lieutenant Colonel Barlow,
who had fallen at the Battle of Salamanca in 1812. Her thirteen-
year-old daughter Jane was attending school in Paris, and so the
two had been living at the pension for the past year. *Mrs Barlow and
I are become very good friends. We always walk out together, and I find
her very pleasant.*[6]

Maria Barlow took Anne along to art exhibitions, showed her
the Louvre's Egyptian collection, and after Louis XVIII died on 16
September they watched his funeral procession together as well as
the coronation festivities for the new king, Charles X, from the windows of their pension. Mrs Barlow also found her a French teacher,
Countess Galvani, who had to give lessons since her husband had
vanished into thin air, along with a sum of public monies, and
Napoleon had confiscated her assets as a result. During the lessons,
Anne subjected this well-read lady to her usual examinations. The
cool and collected Mme de Galvani commented on every classical
or modern work Anne brought into conversation that it was *a little
free but so were all the poets* [...] and *all historians. Perhaps it was not fit
for quite young girls to read but women come to years of discretion might
read anything of the kind.*[7] While Anne soon liked her *exceedingly,*[8]
Mme de Galvani was not quite certain whom she was dealing with;

she thought I was a man, whereas *Mrs Barlow herself had thought at first I wished to imitate the manners of a gentleman.*[9]

So as to speak French outside of her lessons with Mme de Galvani, Anne conversed with her landlady, especially as Mme de Boyve *is very handsome – she has very good French manners; and I admire her.*[10] She began flirting with her and believed *I could make my way if I could speak better.*[11] At the same time, Maria Barlow was trying to become closer friends with Anne. *Her eyes sparkled when she saw me & she was evidently afraid lest anyone else was coming. She surely wished to have me tête-à-tête. She rather flatters me on my talents & agreeableness & I gently flatter her on being ladylike & pretty. She asked me if I had any male correspondents. I said one, between seventy and eighty, mentioning Mr Duffin, & said I was no believer in platonic attachments. Preferred ladies' company to gentlemen's. Did many things ladies in general could not do, but did them quietly,* and emphasised *I should not marry.* Routinely and not knowing quite why herself, *I begin to rather flirt with her but I think she has no consciousness of it, or why she begins to like me.*[12]

Ten days later, however, Anne considered Mrs Barlow *sillily vain*[13] and was glad to welcome a newly arrived guest: the twenty-five-year-old Mademoiselle de Sans, *French but born in England, who speaks both languages equally well. Out of health. Pale and rather interesting in appearance.*[14] Anne was soon engaged in *arrant flirting.* Mrs Barlow was offended, as she considered herself Anne's best friend in Paris and *would better like to have all my attentions herself. She rallies me about being inconstant, yet pays me great compliments every now & then.*[15] In the presence of two attractive women, Anne was in fine fettle. *In the evening rattled away so & flirted with Mrs Barlow.* That did not go uncommented by Mlle de Sans. *'I see you talk to her as you do to me.' 'No,' said I, 'I am not the same to any two persons.' She seemed satisfied. Fancies me serious with herself and flirting, perhaps, with Mrs Barlow. They are all jealous of my attentions.*[16] Anne enjoyed stoking the two women's competition and went a step further the next evening. *Felt pulses, mistaking Mlle de Sans' several times – deliberately. 'Indeed,' said she, 'if you were a man I know not what would be the end of all this. I think Mme de Boyve would be right. I should be married before the year's end.' She certainly likes me. Mrs Barlow, too, has made up to me, particularly today. Has said several times she was jealous. Sat with hold of my hand tonight & looked as if she could like me. [...] Joked and called me her beau.* To say goodbye, Mlle de Sans first shook hands with Anne, *then saluted me in the French manner,* with air kisses next to Anne's cheeks, *& then in the English manner,* in other words a real kiss. Anne did not let such an opportunity go to waste. *I immediately kissed her again, with a little more pressure of the lips, saying, 'That is Yorkshire.'*[17]

Following this small victory by Mlle de Sans, Mrs Barlow went on the offensive the next day and *somehow she began talking of that one of the things of which Marie Antoinette was accused of was being too fond of women. I, with perfect mastery of countenance, said I had never heard of it before & could not understand or believe it. Did not see how such a thing could be – what good could it do.* As with Francis Pickford, Anne put on a show of naivety. *I said I would not believe such a thing existed* – something Mrs Barlow, like Miss Pickford before her, found hard to believe. *She knew she was not telling me anything I did not know before. [...] I told her she had more sense than I had & could turn me round her finger & thumb if she liked. 'No,' she said, 'it is Mlle de Sans.' 'No, no,' said I, 'you understand this sort of thing better than she does.' [...] We agreed it was a scandal invented by the men, who were bad enough for anything. She is a deepish hand &, I think, would not be sorry to gain me over, but I shall be on my guard.* Mrs Barlow did not forget to mention *that she was not so calm and cold as I supposed.* That same day, Anne drove out with Mrs Barlow's rival and *made love to Mlle de Sans in the fiacre. Said I began to think I neither knew her nor myself. Knew not what was the matter with me, etc. She owned she had had many offers.*

Said she was just the sort of girl for it, she could attach anyone, etc. She was poorly & low but still coquetted very well. I cannot help fancying she, too, is a knowing one.[18]

The next day, Anne and Maria Barlow – who claimed 'it' was mentioned in the Bible – read the Apostle Paul's Epistle to the Romans together. *'Yes,' said I, 'the first chapter,' & pointed to that verse about women forgetting the natural use, etc. 'But,' said I, 'I do not believe it.' 'Oh,' said she, 'it might be taken in another way, with men,'* adding for safety's sake, *'as men do with men'. Thought I to myself, she is a deep one. She knows, at all rates, that men can use women in two ways. I said I had often wondered what was the crime of Ham. Said she, 'Was it sodomy?' 'I don't know,' said I, then made her believe how innocent I was.* As she had done with Francis Pickford, Anne claimed *we were a cold-blooded family in this particular. Warm as I was in other things, this one passion was wanting. I went to the utmost extent of friendship but this was enough.* Yet unlike with Frank, she whispered in Maria Barlow's ear *I should like to be instructed in the other (between two women) & would learn when I could.* To fire Anne's imagination, Maria Barlow lent her a book, *Voyage à Plombières*, pointing her in the direction of page 126 *where is the story of one woman intriguing with another.* That evening, Mrs Barlow sat down next to Anne in the pension's drawing room & *every now & then I felt her near me, touching me. My knees, my toes or something.* Anne *payed* [sic] *what attention I could to Mlle de Sans but Mrs Barlow evidently wished to engross me. We came up to bed together. Asked her to come into my room & she would but for fear of increasing her cold. She certainly makes absolute love to me. Tells me I don't know her – she can love deeply, etc. [...] I really must be on my guard. What can she mean? Is she really amoureuse? This from a widow & mother like her is more than I could have thought of. I am safer with Mlle de Sans.*[19]

The younger woman, however, fell seriously ill and had to take to her bed. Anne and Mrs Barlow visited her together. *While with Mlle de Sans, she let me have my hand up her petticoats almost to her knee. At last, she whispered, 'Do not yet.'* Chatting in Anne's room that same day, *she afterwards let me do it nearly as high.* In the end, Anne *held her hand and would not let her go. 'If,'* said she, *'you do in this way, you will prevent my coming again.' Of course, I desisted.*[20] Anne defended herself: *it would be Mrs Barlow's fault if I behaved foolishly again,* and *dwelt on the folly of encouraging what could not be returned.*[21]

Barely had Maria Barlow encouraged Anne Lister to take action, when she withdrew. Anne suspected she was afraid of gossip at the pension, and suggested they go on a short trip *that we must be five or six nights on the road & must share our room & bed. 'Then,' said I, 'would you not relax?'* She had then said she hoped not.[22] Anne began to think Mrs Barlow was hesitant because she was dealing with a woman. '*You have been married – you must make comparisons,*' she said to her, and thought, *if I had a penis, tho' of but small length, I should surely break the ice some of these times.* To confirm her suspicion, *I pointed out two phalli*[23] as they were viewing a collection of classical art together, but Maria Barlow would not be drawn out by them, either. Eventually, Anne dropped the mask that Maria had always recognized as such and told her about Eliza Raine. *Said how it was all nature.* [...] *I had thought much, studied anatomy, etc. Could not find it out. Could not understand myself. It was all the effect of the mind. No exterior formation accounted for it.* Her 'natural', i.e. 'toyless' kind of love, Anne said, was not to be confused with *Saffic* [sic] *regard. I said there was artifice in it. It was very different from mine & would be no pleasure to me. I liked to have those I loved near me as possible, etc. Asked if she understood. She said no. I told her I knew by her ways she did & she did not deny it, therefore I know she understands all about the use of a –.* Even in this encrypted passage, Anne Lister left the key word out of her journal. To prevent Mrs Barlow from possibly becoming interested in 'Saffic regard', *I mentioned the girl at a school in Dublin that had been obliged to have surgical aid to extract the thing.*[24]

Maria Barlow remained ambivalent. For weeks, she claimed she *only wishes to be friends*, at the same time admitting *she, too, was a little crazy*.[25] When Anne visited Maria late at night and was *stooping over her, the waist of my new gown hung off a little. She put her hand down on the left side, almost touching the nipple of the breast, evidently wishing to feel it. She felt the stuffing but made no remark. I let her do it, observing I should hope to do the same. She did not much notice this but with a half no.*[26] A half no only encouraged Anne. *In wishing her good night she quietly let me put my arms around her waist & gently press her & very gently kiss her. She stood too, with her right thigh a little within my leg, in contact – which she has never permitted before,* as Anne noted for 3 November 1824, recording a week later: *She now stands nearer to me when I kiss her, yet she always withdraws the moment it becomes obvious that I am excited.*[27] The next day, Maria visited Anne in her room. *I had kissed & pressed Mrs Barlow on my knee till I had had a complete fit of passion. My knees & thighs shook, my breathing & everything told her what was the matter.* [...] *I then leaned on her bosom &, pretending to sleep, kept pottering about & rubbing the surface of her queer. Then made several gentle efforts to put my hand up her petticoats which, however, she prevented. But she so crossed her legs & leaned against me that I put my hand over & grubbled* [groped] *her on the outside of her petticoats till she was evidently a little excited, & it was from this that Mlle de Sans' maid roused us,* by knocking on Anne's door and inviting her to visit her mistress. Anne called out through the locked door: *I was sorry, I could not, I had got so bad a headache. The fact was I was heated & in a state not fit so see anyone.* She turned her attention back to Maria, but *while I was grubbling pretty strongly,* she said, *'You know you pinch me.'* Anne grew tired of her one-sided efforts and asked Maria, *'Can you not love me one little bit for all the great deal I love you? If you do not love me, I cannot forgive you. You are too cruel thus to sport with the feelings of another.'* There were some feelings Anne kept to herself, though, entrusting to her diary that Maria *looked eight & thirty. Her skin &*

complexion were bad. I thought of all this when kissing her & thought it would not do for always.[28]

Up until then, Anne Lister had always written in her diary when and under what circumstances she had sex with her lovers, and how many orgasms they each had, without detailing exactly what happened in bed. Faced by Maria Barlow's prolonged resistance, Anne now extended her diary's function: the act of writing came to stand in for the act of love. In complex detail, Anne described inch by inch how far she had got with her hands, lips and tongue, savouring in writing what was still refused to her in real life. When Anne retired to bed with a headache on one occasion, she spooned with Maria. *I had my arms around her, she lying with her back to me, my right leg under and left leg over her. I got a hand towards her queer by degrees. She so turned round that my left hand got to her very comfortably and by degrees I got to feel and handle her. I got her gown up and tried to raise her petticoats also but, finding that this would not do (one of her hands prevented it), I was contented that my naked left thigh should rest upon her naked left thigh and thus she let me grubble her over her petticoats. […] Now and then I held my hand still and felt her pulsation, let her rise towards my hand two or three times and gradually open her thighs, and felt her as well and distinctly as it was possible to do over her petticoats, and felt that she was excited.*[29]

On another occasion, she pulled Maria onto her lap and went *from little to more. I became rather excited. Felt her breasts & queer a little. Tried to put my hand up her petticoat but she prevented. Touched her flesh just above the knee twice. I kissed her warmly & held her strongly. She said what a state I was putting myself into. She got up to go away & went to the door. I followed. Finding she lingered a moment, pressed her closely & again tried to put my hand up her petticoats. Finding that she would not let me do this but still that she was a little excited, I became regularly so myself. I felt her grow warm & she let me grubble & press her tightly with my left hand whilst I held her against the door with the other, all the*

*while putting my tongue into her mouth & kissing her so passionately as
to excite her not a little, I am sure. When it was over she put her handkerchief to her eyes &, shedding a few tears, said, 'You are used to these
things. I am not.' I remonstrated against this, declaring I was not so bad
as one thought me & injustice like this would make me miserable, etc.* [...]
*I loved her with all my heart & would do anything for her. Asked her if she
loved me a little bit. 'You know I do,' said she. I still therefore pressed her
to let me in tomorrow before she was up, when Mrs Page* [Maria's maid]
*was gone with Miss Barlow to school. She would not promise. Asked me
what I would do. I said teach her to love me better. Insinuated we had now
gone too far to retract & she might as well admit me.* [...] *On leaving me,
her face looked hot, her hair out of curl & herself languid, exactly as if
after a connection had taken place.*[30]

Anne Lister was wrong; Maria Barlow was not looking for casual
relaxation. She was the mother of a girl who would soon be of marriageable age, and she had to act responsibly. When Anne asked her
by the fire for the umpteenth time *if I had no hope of making her dearer
to me,* Maria answered, *'No, never, till we are married.' 'Oh,' said I,
'can nothing persuade you to anticipate?' 'No,' said she, 'I hope not.
You would then leave me very unhappy.' 'Why?' said I. She answered,
'Because it would be wrong. I should fret myself to death.'*[31] Maria did
not want sex before marriage, but she sensed that Anne was unwilling or unable to make a commitment. *She observed my wedding ring.
I said this ought to bind me but this was pure friendship.*[32] On further
questioning, she did reveal Mariana's name, but she claimed, *I have so
long loved her in a different way.* Aside from that, *Mariana always said
if I met with anyone I liked better, she would be no tie upon me.* Maria did
not believe her: *Tonight she insinuated what might have passed, saying,
'But of course you would never tell me.' I turned this off dexterously as
usual & I think, considering Mariana's marriage, she feels unwillingly
constrained to believe me.*[33]

Anne had to respect that Maria *after all* [...] *has behaved well & at present I see I have no chance of succeeding further. She says I never shall till I have the right to do so & she would not let me gain the right now even if I were at liberty for she would make me leave her & wait till I had tried whether I really know my own mind & could really be happy with her or not.* Nothing was further from Anne's mind, having been wedded to Mariana Lawton and Isabella Norcliffe in parallel for some twelve years. *How she is deceived. Why have I done this? [...] Poor soul! I begin to feel that I have really attached her & that I cannot find it in my heart to deceive her more.*[34]

At the end of November, Anne's stay in Paris was approaching its end without her having sought medical advice. Pears and grapes had not cured her discharge. A letter from her concerned aunt, which Anne read aloud to Maria, made her admit, *'I came to Paris for my health' & afterwards said something of 'suffering for one's folly.' [...] She was a married woman. Her husband was the origin of the thing. I had not got it quite fairly, meaning that she knew of it & ought not to have admitted me.* Maria's reaction to the confession was friendly and understanding. *She joked me that I wished to know everything,*[35] and recommended Guillaume Dupuytren, head physician at the Hôtel de Dieu hospital and personal doctor to Louis XVIII and Charles X. Anne told him the history of her ailment as though she was Mariana and was married to Charles Lawton. *Was he gay with others?* Monsieur Dupuytren asked. *Yes, at first with servants in the house,* was Anne's answer, going by what she knew from Mariana. *'Aviez-vous des rapports frequents? Once a week? Once a fortnight?' 'Yes,' said I, 'about so often at first. Then once a fortnight & afterwards once a month, till I was, all at once, ill & since then, not at all.' 'How old are you?' 'Thirty-two'* (a slight understatement). *'How old is he?' 'Fifty-two.' 'How long married?' 'Eight or nine years.' He said I was young. It was odd he had been so — without any connection with me. Had he no inclination? He did not shew any. Did we sleep together? Yes. Had he no erections? No. Had I much pleasure with him? Pas beaucoup. He said he must examine me. I said it was very disagreeable. Could it be done without? He seemed a little impatient & said would I say yes or no. I very quietly asked if it was absolutely necessary. He said yes. 'Well then,' said I, 'it must be done.'*[36] After the examination, the doctor told her to stop rinsing with zinc sulphate and to collect a new prescription from him in a week's time.

Guillaume Dupuytren was a respected surgeon and scientist, but his treatment drove Anne to the brink of collapse. Although she was thin, he prescribed a *meagre diet* without meat and made her take a one-hour bath every other day at 35°C, which felt rather cold to her. Above all, however, he prescribed her *rubbing with mercury*.[37] Up until the early twentieth century, mercury ointment was considered an effective remedy for gynaecological problems and syphilis, which Anne was less likely to have contracted, as syphilis and gonorrhoea are not so commonly passed on through lesbian sex. Admittedly, research has made little progress on the matter since Dupuytren's times: of all sexual varieties, sex between women is still the least studied by medical science. Anne's symptoms of itching and prolonged discharge indicate trichomoniasis. Unlike other sexually transmitted infections, this parasite is easily transmitted from woman to woman; most men do not even notice they are infected. Nowadays, Anne Lister would be cured by antibiotics within a week. Her French doctor, however, weakened her with a diet and baths and poisoned her with mercury rubbed into her legs and vagina. *I begin to look pale and ill and always feel worse in an evening. I feel rather more inclined to spit,*[38] she noted after only a week of this treatment. After a month, she was *certainly much reduced in strength*.[39] The mercury ointment had brought on profuse bleedings. *I used to sit on the pot & bleed like a stuck pig.*[40]

Anne only hinted at her worsened health in her letters to her aunt and uncle. Instead, she used the treatment by the famous doctor as an excuse to extend her stay in Paris; her ever-helpful aunt and uncle sent her the £100 she asked for. That gave Anne time to turn another matter to her advantage. The pension at place Vendôme had proved rather cramped. Anne persuaded Maria to rent a flat of her own for herself and her daughter, where Anne and Cordingley would move in for the rest of their stay. *In spite of all, I have no serious thoughts of her at present, tho' I am so far seducing her. Oh, this is terrible.*[41] Furnishing and maintaining an apartment was more expensive than living at the pension, but Maria complied with Anne's wishes despite her limited means. She hoped a shared household might be the start of a binding relationship. They found a charming apartment in *a beautiful and excellent situation* on the third floor at no. 15, quai Voltaire, commanding *one of the finest views imaginable of the Seine, the Tuileries gardens, the Louvre, &c.*[42] Maria Barlow had the salon, the dining room and two bedrooms wallpapered (the kitchen and servants' rooms were in the attic), bought furniture, curtains, carpets, bedding and linen, and built a nest for Anne and herself. Anne pretended to her aunt, who expressed surprise at the change of accommodation on 15 January 1825, that Mrs Barlow was the driving force behind it. *She has very kindly given me an invitation to pass the remainder of whatever time I may be still in Paris, with her, and I feel so entirely as if I should not know what to do without her, that I have very gladly accepted her invitation.*[43] *If one is at all unwell, there is no nursing like English. The French do not appear to understand this sort of thing and I have found Mrs B— the greatest comfort in the world. She has always taken care I had everything I wanted, has ordered about my baths, &c., &c., and has, in fact, done all I could not do well myself. I certainly feel myself in good hands altogether, and am now decidedly better.*[44] Did Aunt Anne understand the hints in Anne's letter?

During the time in which the two women were choosing curtain fabrics and wallpaper, Maria abandoned her resistance. *I soon took up her petticoats so as to feel her naked thighs next to mine. Then, after kissing with my tongue in her mouth, got the middle finger of my right hand up her & grubbled her longer & better than ever, she seeming rather more at ease than before & taking it with more emotion & apparent pleasure, which made me keep dawdling there a long time. She seemed more moist than before.*[45] On moving into their shared home, Maria then grew as free as Anne had hoped. *She nothing loth last night,* Anne wrote in her diary the next morning, and after the first week she noted: *She is quite at ease with me now. Jokes me about having done too much & my being exhausted, & declares she will not let me, saying she is exhausted too. 'No, no,' said I, 'I am not, but certainly you are not. I am the most of the two.' She smiled. I blamed the mercury for weakening me. She can certainly bear all I can do well enough & she shall have it.*[46]

To Anne's surprise, her *nice little bedfellow* was more active than her previous lovers. Whereas Mariana and Anne only cast furtive glances at each other while dressing, for instance, Maria sat *by the fire watching me wash the mercury from my thighs & then wash and dress. She admired my figure, its masculine beauty, saying I was very well made.*[47] Anne's greatest surprise came after a *strong excitement last night just after getting into bed. She said again this morning, it was the best she had ever had. Had a very good one an hour before we got up, slumbering all the while afterwards. In getting out of bed, she suddenly touching my queer, I started back. 'Ah,' said she, 'that is because you are pucelle* [virgin]. *I must undo that. I can give you relief. I must do to you as you do to me.' I liked not this & said she astonished me. She asked if I was angry. No, merely astonished. However, I found I could not easily make her understand my feeling on the subject & I dropped the matter altogether.*[48]

Anne Lister's private word for female genitalia, 'queer', is a surprise in itself. *It appears to be a distortion of the word 'quim' or 'queme', a slang word used to describe the same area of the female body,*[49] Helena Whitbread argues. In Anne's lifetime, 'queer' was an adjective meaning 'strange', 'odd' or 'wrong'. She used the word frequently in that sense too. Aunt Anne applied it to her niece on one occasion (*you're a queer one*).[50] Indeed, Anne Lister's secret expression for the centre of female lust would one day become an umbrella term for lesbians and gays, bisexuals and trans people.

While Anne always wanted to get to her partner's *queer*, she resisted Maria Barlow's foray. Maria's desire to penetrate her repelled Anne. *This is womanizing me too much.* [51] In twenty years of intense sexual activity, Anne had never been penetrated by any of her lovers. That role was reserved for her. She even considered her hymen intact. During her gynaecological examination by Dupuytren, *I was only afraid he should find out I was not married but he certainly did not make this discovery.*[52]

So what did Anne have done to her in bed? Despite the mass of detail she gives us of her sexual activities in her journals, she focuses only on her partners. We can reach some conclusions, however. Before a reunion with Isabella Norcliffe, Anne once imagined *what sort of kisses she would give.*[53] Anne would not let her lovers penetrate her, then, but they could touch her and bring her to orgasm, and she knew more than one sexual position. Of all things, Mariana, Anne and Isabella's infection gives us some clues as to specific activities. The trichomoniasis parasite is carried in mucous membranes. Women can infect women by stimulating themselves and their partner, passing infected vaginal secretions via their fingers. The *kisses* in Anne Lister's journals probably not only refer to sex in general and orgasms in particular, but can also be taken literally in some cases, as oral sex. When Mariana later found out about Anne's affair with her sister Nantz, *She asked anxiously if I had really gone the utmost length & asked for my honour that I had not. I gave it. Could I do otherwise? But owned I had done all but absolutely 'kiss'.*[54]

Both Anne and Maria hoped for a honeymoon in their apartment at quai Voltaire, but they each understood that to mean something very different. Anne, now almost thirty-four, was sharing a home with a

woman for the first time in her life, and hoped for undisturbed sex with
my little one. To her surprise, she found that Maria was willing to play
along with her gentlemanly act but ignored it in everyday life. Maria
*lets me see too much that she considers me too much as a woman. She talks
to me about being unwell* [i.e. menstruation]. *I have aired napkins before
her. She feels me, etc. All which I like not. Mariana never seems to know or
notice these things.*[55] The latter had always desired her 'Freddy', whom
she never wanted to deflower, and *is contented with having myself next
to her.*[56]

During her version of the honeymoon, Maria dreamed of a lasting
marriage. On the very first night she *hinted at what she sacrificed. She
meant virtue, I suppose, but I merely said I could sacrifice everything for
her; Shibden, my friends, every prospect I had. I scarcely said it ere the
feeling of insincerity on this point struck me.*[57] Maria too realized this
was a lie. Anne had told her *that I should love her always. 'Yes,' said
she, 'as long as you can.' Has she a presentiment? For she often speaks in
this way, that I shall, by & by, get the better of my fancy for her.*[58] Maria
grew more and more sad as a result; *she was not a crier in general, yet
how many tears she shed for me.*[59] She feared *that she loved me too soon.
In plain English, she was too much like a mistress. She was not my wife.*[60]
*I consoled her. Said I would marry her if I could. Spoke of the purity of my
affections.*[61] Yet to herself, she admitted it was *an imprudent connection.
[...] Mrs Barlow has no friends whose acquaintance can serve me as an
introduction. She has no money & there is Jane. [...] I have never seriously
thought of having her. [...] But I have suspected Mrs Barlow of being deep
& thus have acted like a rascal in so gaining her affections.*[62]

One morning in bed, Maria said to Anne, *'There is something you
have not told me.' I denied it in such a manner that she more & more
suspected it & said she knew Mariana had been more to me than I had
allowed. She asked if it was before or after her marriage. Said I, 'Oh,
do not ask me. Never name the subject again.'* Anne got up and went
to wash, but after half an hour she thought better of it, went back

to Maria and *told the whole story of Mariana's marriage – everything correctly, only would not allow, that is disguised, that I had had any connection with her since her marriage.*[63] Shortly before that, Mariana had sent greetings to Maria Barlow in a letter. Always concerned for her lovers to get on well with each other, Anne wished for Maria to send greetings back. Maria, however, thought *it would not be true, nor her sending. She could not be half so civil. She 'could throw her into a ditch'.* Anne felt some consternation. *I see she is fond of me but she would be desperately jealous, worse than Mariana, whom I could more easily cheat.*[64]

Maria had had a life before Anne too. Two admirers were seeking her attentions, a Mr William Bell from her native Guernsey and Mr Hancock, a wholesaler in London. Before Maria had let down her resistance, Anne had been whispering in her ear, *'Don't marry and forget me.'*[65] After only nine rather up-and-down days of living together, Anne entreated Maria to *marry & consult her own welfare, hinting as gently as I could the uncertainty of my circumstances & that I would not for worlds be any tie upon her to prevent her marrying. In fact, I had been musing over Mariana's letter & had even before thought it would be best to prepare a little hole to creep out at. Perhaps she thought of this, but I denied it all when she asked me why I was so suddenly changed as to advise her so much to marry. Poor soul! The tears trickled quietly down her cheeks the whole time.*[66]

Anne stayed in Paris until 31 March 1825. She and Maria visited the prison cell at the Conciergerie where Marie Antoinette had awaited her execution, and viewed documents from the case against Joan of Arc next door in the Sainte Chapelle, where the archives of the Palais de Justice were housed at the time. All in all, however, despite costing her aunt and uncle another £70, Anne's stay had not been a success. Neither was she cured of her affliction, nor had she significantly improved her French, seeing as she spoke only English with Maria Barlow. Anne had frittered away seven costly months in

Paris, distracted by a sexual affair that had absolutely no significance to her. *I was sorry to leave her but yet, somehow my sorrow was not so deep as I expected. I felt no inclination to shed another tear about her.* [...] *Somehow my heart is not so deep in the business as it ought to be & I scarce know why I have gone on, & led & been led on. Very strangely, it seems like a dream to me.* [...] *How will it all end? I cannot help thinking she has played her cards better than I have.* [...] *I fear this is the worst scrape I have ever been in.*[67]

Anne arrived back in Halifax on 11 April 1825. Her uncle and aunt were *very good to me. They say nothing is wrong I do & are delighted to see me back again.* In fact, it had been very hard for them to do without their niece. Aunt Anne was *very rheumatic. Could scarcely move from her chair. Screaming with pain every now & then. I have never seen her so bad.*[68] Uncle James also seemed more sickly and immobile than before; he *must always have someone at his elbow to assist in the management of his affairs.*[69] She visited tenant farmers in his name, signed a contract on his behalf for the first time and supervised the re-routing of a public footpath, moving it from the courtyard of Shibden Hall to an appropriate distance from the house. She abandoned the meagre diet, cool baths and mercury, and returned to better health.

Maria, however, took to bed with a high fever after Anne's departure. *I thought I was near my end,*[70] she wrote to Anne, making it clear in letter after letter that she did not want to let her go. *You have taught me much untaught before,*[71] which she could not forget and which was why she did not want to take up either of her admirers. Anne picked up the erotic energy with which Maria wrote her letters and *slightly alluded to our connection. No-one could possibly understand it but herself. I said I still sighed after happiness gone by with a sigh more deep & long than she might think.*[72] To herself, she noted *I must be serious in recommending her to marry Mr Bell or make up my mind to have her myself.* [...] *If she had a little more money I should not hesitate a moment, but, alas, it would be a bad connection for me. But my heart is somewhat won upon.*[73]

Plagued by indecision, she asked her aunt and uncle for advice. *My aunt had talked my uncle over while I left them. They would like to see how & with whom they are likely to leave me.*[74] Aunt Anne and Uncle James encouraged Anne to bring the woman of her choice to Shibden Hall during their lifetime. Anne told them about her increasing frustration with Mariana. As *Charles would not die to please anyone,* [...] *all chance whether Mariana & I are together. Should I find anyone who would suit me better, & should Charles live, Mariana will lose me.*[75] She also spoke to them about *Mrs Barlow & mentioned the real state of the case between us very honestly. They both seemed very well inclined towards her. Were I really wishful to have her I am sure they would throw no obstacle in the way. On the contrary, they appear much in her favour. I told them she had four hundred a year & my aunt and I agreed this evening she might be better for me with this than Mariana with five hundred* – especially as Maria had cared for Anne very well in Paris and her uncle and aunt were becoming more and more frail. *But tho' I speak most highly of Mrs Barlow & that it would be my own fault if I was not happy with her, yet I owned I was very odd & perhaps I should, after all, like a person with more éclat about her.* [...] *My aunt is for Mrs Barlow.* [...] *But, alas, I feel it would not do.* [...] *From the very first I have fancied her hurrying me into the thing.* [...] *And even now the idea occurs to me of Mr Bell's being made a means of making me engage myself to her.* [...] *I am determined to be cautious. I may hereafter choose better.*[76]

And so Anne wrote Maria a pathos-laden letter persuading her to marry Mr Bell. *Maria! the more you are firmly rooted in my remembrance and esteem, the more I feel myself incapable of enduring the thought, that it could be possible to promote my happiness by any means less conducive to your interest, than to mine. I have considered the matter deeply, I have weighed it on the balance with the most impartial justice in my power, and, taking it for granted that Mr B—'s circumstances are in every respect, as favourable as I have been given to understand, I am quite sure I should not be happy under the self-reproach of having prevented you giving him the answer he must deserve, and, must expect.*[77] In overblown sentences, Anne prophesied to Maria that she would learn to love Mr Bell, emphasising her own great sacrifice. *The letter will do very well. I have shed many tears over it. I know not how it is, my own style affects me. Well may she feel it. Such beautiful sentimentality will probably not be addressed to her by anybody.*[78]

Mariana

1825–1826

In early August of 1825, Anne accompanied her rheumatism-plagued aunt to take the waters at Buxton, where she had consoled herself with Nantz after her sister Mariana's wedding nine years previously. Anne also sought out the resort physician, whose prescription proved as ineffective as all the others, however. Maria had responded to Anne's advice to marry Mr Bell with the words *I may love you to the latest breath of my existence. That privilege cannot be taken from me.* Now, a military band in Buxton reminded Anne of Paris, where she had heard similar music with Maria. *My heart turned towards her. I felt as if I could write instantly, 'Maria, live for me. Do not marry. Come what may, I will be yours.'*[1]

Mariana Lawton sensed that this woman in Paris might become a threat to her. She had last seen Anne over a year ago, for only three days. They had last spent any decent length of time together almost two years before. So she suggested to Anne that she might come over to Buxton for a day and, to test the waters, Mariana added that she would take a room at a hotel if she didn't make it back that same evening. Anne answered by return of post: *your thought of getting a bed at Clayton's lodgings rather surprised me. Should you come alone, you will find my room very comfortable.*[2] Upon which Mariana announced she was staying not one day but ten. Mariana's coming put Anne in a very restless mood. *For the moment I thought more of Mariana and less seriously of Mrs Barlow.* That same evening, though, she *relapsed into my carelessness towards Mariana and tenderness towards Mrs Barlow.*[3] In her indecision, she and her aunt *talked all the evening about Mrs Barlow or Mariana. Very candidly about both.* Of Mariana, she felt *if I knew I should never see her again, assured of her being well and happy, I should get over it without much trouble.*[4]

When Mariana arrived in Buxton, Anne *received her as well as I could but felt restrained. It was the second night of her 'cousin'. Pretended it would do her harm to have a kiss yet, at last, as if unable to resist, she not discouraging it, had one.*[5] What was inhibiting Anne was less Mariana's menstruation or the thought of Maria than her concern for her own health. In Paris, Anne had decided *I must have no further connection with her. She will certainly infect me again.*[6] On the second night, Anne still *felt restrained. Glad to make the excuse of her having her 'cousin' & pretended to sleep, then to awake excited, she nothing loth, & we had a short kiss.* Not until the third night was she back in her stride. *Had Mariana twice & about two kisses each time. Lay awake talking till six this morning. Told her honestly of the doubts I had lately had about her.* [...] *I reassured her, saying that my telling her all this was a proof I had changed my mind.* [...] *I said I now found if I could not be happy with her, I could not without her & that, if happy at all, I must be made so by her.* Anne also told her about Maria Barlow. *I owned I had done all I could to gain her affections.* [...] *I might try her as fair game.* [...] *Owned we had slept together & the state of my health was the only thing that had prevented nearer intercourse. Made her regard for me appear pure & beautiful.* Unlike Maria, who made no attempt to hide her jealousy, Mariana either felt or pretended affection for Maria and *said how interesting she must be.*

When Anne read her last letters to Maria out loud to Mariana, however, her lover almost fainted. *She bade me take off her wedding ring, which had never been off since I myself put it on, & put it on again in token of my return to her. I could not, but in agony of sobbing said it could only mark that there had been a time when my heart had left her, which I now felt had never been the case. She therefore bade me leave the thing undisturbed & I kissed it in proof of my re-promised faith. Asked if she forgave me. Oh, yes, yes, it was the thought of the fearful danger of losing me that she had escaped, which so agonized her. We mutually professed our love, agreed we both wanted to sleep & therefore got into bed, lay quiet & went to sleep without attempting to have a kiss.*[7]

They made the next night a new wedding night. Mariana told Anne that her womb had prolapsed, according to her doctor. *I said I should like to feel it. Just put up the right middle finger, brought it back bloodied, surprised to find no entrance into the womb. Said I really could not be quite sure but I thought Charles had never broken the membrane. It was very odd but I would feel again another time. 'Then,' said Mariana, half in wonder, half in joke, 'I am the virgin Mary still.' She said Charles had never gone higher, she thought, than an inch, if so much, & from her account I do not think he has ever been able to do the business.*[8] Presumably Mariana was denying her marital sex exactly the way Anne made a secret of her sexual escapades. Anne, however, was intoxicated by the idea of having deflowered Mariana, forgetting her period had started on 30 August. Yet just as they had received their godchild after the last renewal of their vows, this time they felt they had enjoyed their real wedding night, after at least eleven years of 'marriage'.

Over the next few days, they slept together at every opportunity – late in the evening, at night, in the early morning and during the day while Aunt Anne went out for a drive. *At 12 1/4 Mariana and I went upstairs. Began to be on the amoroso. Pushed up my right middle finger. Cordingley interrupted us. At it again. Gave her a good kiss &, not pushing hard, merely pushing up & down – no blood followed. [...] I had done the business better than I had thought & she was now no longer a virgin, at which we were both well satisfied. My having had to do this for her seems to have delighted us both. It proves that Charles has had not much power & that she has never belonged but to me.* Having more power in her loins than Charles was too sweet a thought for Anne to doubt, especially as Mariana encouraged the idea. *My having found her still a virgin, in fact, was a great comfort to her. She would die as she had lived, mine & mine only. She really does seem devoted to me & will make me happy. I love her. We will understand each other better in future & I am satisfied.*[9]

To extend their joy, Anne wrote to her Uncle James that Aunt Anne was doing better but the doctor advised they stayed another two weeks. The instant Uncle James sent the required £70, Anne and Mariana set off without Aunt Anne on a three-day tour of the area in the Lawtons' light open carriage. They viewed Haddon Hall, Alton Abbey and the house and gardens at Chatsworth, enjoying the famous tart at the village of Bakewell. *Three or four all at once last night & one more, a good one, at four this morning.*[10] They had barely returned from their mini-honeymoon to Buxton when Charles turned up unannounced. At the Crescent, Anne almost ran into him, but she pretended not to have seen him as she came down the stairs, turned around and sought shelter in the women's section of the baths. He left after only three hours.

Mariana, Anne and her aunt left Buxton on 21 September. In Manchester, where they stayed overnight, the lovers gave each other intimate parting gifts. During the preceding nights of love, Anne had *owned that, tho' I had never given any of the hair of my own queer to anyone, yet I had asked for & received it from others. I had some among my curiosities now. She would know whose. Guessed everybody she could. At last guessed Mrs Milne & my blushing or looking conscious made her suspect. I saw she felt hurt & hastened to contradict. I had blushed at the thought of her guessing so nearly, for it was her sister Anne* [Nantz] *to whom I had alluded & I had last night said that Anne had made up to me*

& that we had gone far in flirting, tho' Mariana thinks not how far. I said I had completely persuaded Anne there was nothing more than friendship between Mariana and me.[11] Whether Nantz or Mariana believed that is another matter. In any case, Mariana wanted to be part of her curiosities collection. She *cut the hair from her own queer & I that from mine, which she put each into each of the little lockets we got at Bright's this morning, twelve shillings each, for us always to wear under our clothes in mutual remembrance. We both kissed each bit of hair before it was put into the locket.*[12]

Mariana also bought Anne a wedding ring to bear witness to their new marriage. As they strolled around Manchester, however, it seemed to Anne as though Mariana was ashamed of her again. Mariana admitted *she could not bear to have our connection known or suspected & conscience made her cowardly. She shrank from having the thing surmised now, but declared that if we were once fairly together, she should not care about it. I might tell our connection to all the world if I pleased.* And so discord crept into their harmony at the end of the trip. *On getting into bed last night, tried Mariana for a kiss but she was quite dry. Told her of it. She said I had set her wrong by being so queer while we were out. I said no more. Made no further attempt & we soon fell asleep. Awoke at two o'clock. A little play & two good kisses at once.* [...] *Awoke again at seven & then had three good ones all at once & she put the ring on & I promised not to take it off till Christmas. I may change my mind when I please. She will let me off whenever I like & when I wish it, I am merely to send her back the ring & she will understand me & give me no further trouble.*[13]

Mariana took this third set of vows made with Anne seriously. They were barely parted before she wrote her a long love letter. *So long as life shall last, I will be your lover, friend, & your faithful wife. If I can be anything more, teach me what it is & that I will also be, with all the truth & power of one who lives for thee & thee only.* [...] *Yours and only yours let me always be. That is, so long as it makes you happy to have me so. But one minute beyond this, one moment beyond the time that you can give me yourself in exchange & you shall hear of me no more. Yet I will never be another's.*[14] Without Mariana physically by her side, however, Anne's memories of her new old bride faded fast. Two tender letters from Maria Barlow in Paris made Anne doubt Mariana again. *She is another man's wife. I am solitary.*[15] To keep herself distracted, Anne took care of Shibden Hall, had trees felled and 2,500 oaks and 1,300 beeches planted. The future lady of the manor knew she had no time to lose with the trees if she wanted to benefit from them herself. Without informing her thrifty uncle, she bought three hundred more beeches at her own expense. She also had the old privy in the courtyard of Shibden Hall filled in and a new *cabinet d'aisance* built.

Anne spent Christmas of 1825 at Langton Hall with Isabella and Charlotte Norcliffe, along with Mariana's sister Harriet Milne. In the same place five years previously, Anne had flirted hard but without consequence with Mrs Milne, what with having her hands full at the time with Miss Vallance, Nantz Belcombe and Isabella Norcliffe. The last time they had seen each other, a year and a half previously, Anne once again enjoyed *very flirting style of manner & conversation & some double entendre. Bad enough. She likes it. I feel no esteem for her & flirt & make a fool of her, & perhaps myself, too, for doing it.*[16] Now, Anne told Harriet on the day after her arrival *she might succeed better* than Mariana. *She might manage me. Ladies always ruled, etc. Said how dangerous she was. She said she could excite the feelings of others & keep her own calm.*[17] After a walk in the Wolds together, *I made absolute love. Said Mariana was not warm & nobody knew her better than I did. Mrs Milne was warmer. [...] Perhaps she, Mrs Milne would suit me better.* At dinner *she began pinching my feet upon which I became gradually empassioned. She saw this & went on, evidently pleased with the effect she produced, perfectly evident to, and understood by, her tho' not by the rest. Tho' Mrs Norcliffe kept talking to me, at last I got up & left the room.* With

Anne sleeping in Isabella's room and Harriet in Charlotte's, they got no further this time, either. As Anne was packing her things, *Mrs Milne came for a moment. I kissed her. She said, 'Don't forget me. Say "I love you, Harriet."' 'It is not love, it is adoration. But do you love me?' 'Yes. I do love you.' 'Well, don't look cross at me the next time I see you.' 'How can you say so. You have me quite.' She kissed me with open lips. I might have taken any liberty I pleased. 'You have me.' Yes, thought I. She would see us off & stood at the door in the cold.*[18]

Anne went on to York, where she stayed with Mr Duffin, whose wife had died three months previously; now fifty-five, Miss Marsh hoped she would at last be able to marry her lover, twenty-three years her senior. Anne spent half a day with her thoughts fixated on Harriet Milne. *We have both gone too far to retract. I thought & think of this. Poor Mariana!!! How can I trust myself? I know not yet how keen remorse will be or if I have too little virtue left to feel it deeply. I cannot, do not respect Mrs Milne. I told her seriously she must not now be nonsensical with anyone else. I could not stand it. I could be desperately jealous. She has no conduct. She would intrigue with anyone. How can I trust such a woman?* Her mind still on Harriet, Anne chatted with Mr Duffin's niece that evening; *turned to obscure lovemaking. She said I was very odd. [...] She was evidently interested, she scarce knew why. [...] Thought I to myself, 'Here I am flirting again, not contented with my folly with Mrs Milne. How can I trust myself?'*[19] Two days later, she continued her flirt with Mariana's other sister Lou Belcombe. Lou had offered herself to Anne on several occasions. The most recent had come in a letter, proposing they live together. *My whole conversation odd & foolish & if Lou had a grain of nous, she must understand it. At last I said nothing was impossible. Perhaps I should fall in love with Lou. I never felt anything more like it. 'Why should you not?' asked Lou. I said, 'What! Engaged to one sister and in love with another?' 'Yes,' said Lou, 'with two of her sisters'* – alluding to Mrs Milne. That same evening, Anne chatted with Miss Duffin again. *Surely she might almost smoke* [suspect] *me. I went a little too far.* [...] *Were I at liberty to try, I might succeed. But 'tis indeed foolish to flirt in this way & shew myself for nothing. But somehow I seem as if I could never resist the opportunity. A woman tête-à-tête is a dangerous animal to me. What with Mrs Milne and my folly to Lou and Miss Duffin, what would Mariana say? 'Tis well she is in ignorance.*[20]

At the turn of the year, back in Halifax, Anne received post from various women. *A regular love letter* came from Harriet Milne. *Is it possible that I can have feelings which have never yet been roused into action? Affections that were dormant till you called them forth?* Anne found Harriet's direct style exciting. *She wishes to lead me on,* but she told herself *I must not get into a scrape with her.*[21] A few days later, an unsuspecting Mariana sent a *very kind letter. It gave me a pang of remorse to think of my folly with Mrs Milne, but Mariana's affection consoles & fortifies me again.*[22] And finally, Maria Barlow wrote from Paris, having been told by Anne that she and Mariana had *sworn fealty anew* in Buxton, *& this, after having known me, makes the case absolutely decisive. There is no other form left to adopt but that of friendship.* [...] *I have received my divorce! I am resigned & may you be happy with her destined for you.*[23]

In the midst of this tumult of competing females, James Lister died. On 26 January 1826, Anne was just brushing her teeth *when (at 9 1/2 by the kitchen clock) Cordingley rapt* [sic] *at my door and bade me go down directly – my uncle was laid on the floor. Ran to his room (my aunt almost in an hysteric of grief, supported by Cordingley, in the hall). Saw him fallen at the foot of his bed.* He had presumably had a heart attack while getting up. *Alas! It was too late. All was over. Ran down to my aunt. Did all I could to compose her.* Anne had her father and sister fetched from Northgate House and took care of a worthy funeral for the head of the family.

On the very day of his death, James' relatives gathered at Shibden Hall and listened to Anne reading out his will. As agreed while he

13 *James Lister*, oil painting by Joshua Horner (assumed);
Calderdale Leisure Services, Shibden Hall, Halifax.

was alive, James left his entire estate to his niece. As long as his siblings were alive, however, she had to share the annual income equally with them. Anne senior, Jeremy and Marian also had a lifelong right to live in Shibden Hall. As Anne had been favoured by Uncle James, Marian was to become Jeremy's sole heir. While Aunt Anne grieved a great deal for her fraternal companion and Jeremy and Marian were also in tears, Anne remained cool. *'Lord, I am a sinner. There is not that sorrow there ought to be.' Felt frightened to think I could think, at such a moment, of temporal gains – that I was now sure of the estate. 'Are others,' said I, 'thus wicked?' & knelt down & said my prayers. [...] He was the best of uncles to me. Oh that my heart were more right within me.*[24] James Lister was laid to rest in the family crypt at Halifax Parish Church on 3 February 1826.

Anne became the fifteenth Lister of Shibden Hall; the first had been her great-great-great-great-grandfather Samuel; Anne was of the seventh generation after him. The fact that fourteen Listers had owned Shibden Hall before her was due to many sons and daughters in the family not marrying and the inheritance frequently being passed on to younger brothers. Jill Liddington[25] calculated that the Listers had only owned Shibden Hall for two hundred years, not the three hundred Anne claimed. Her aristocratic pedigree was not as old as she would have others believe, or as she liked to believe herself.

As soon as Anne had become lady of Shibden Hall, the two women who believed or hoped themselves to be married to her came to pay visits. The first to put in an appearance was Isabella Norcliffe. Despite her recent unhappy stays at Shibden Hall, she sounded out the possibility of living together, asking Anne unceremoniously how much money she now had at her disposal. As always, they slept together – *A kiss last night of Tib. Perhaps I may never have another*[26] – and as always, they argued over petty matters. Isabella *called me a fool & an ass before George* and claimed *my aunt & I were laughed at for our pride.*[27] After seventeen days, Anne was once again *glad to have got rid of poor Tib.* [...] *I would not live with her for all the world.* But even as lady of Shibden Hall, she laid stake by their friendship. *Her family importance, etc., used to please me. Now I am ashamed of her. In fact, it has been of use to me to know the Norcliffes & being intimate at Langton does very well,*[28] so she did not want to break off all contact with Isabella.

Mariana Lawton arrived at Shibden Hall two weeks later, *pale & thin & ill.* For Mariana, the moment they had both been waiting ten years for had come. Not through Charles' death but through the death of Uncle James, the opportunity had arisen to live out their dream of a life together. Her departure had been preceded by ugly scenes with her husband. *Charles worse tempered than ever. He had not spoken to her of four days before she set off,* so she had merely left him a short note to say goodbye; *she did not, at that moment, know if she should ever return. Half a word would make her leave him but I urged her going back, at least for a time. My uncle's death was so recent it would look as if she took this opportunity of parting from him to come to me. She was for going back to her own family. I objected to this. Charles might not live long & then all would be right.*[29] For many years, Anne had accused Mariana of not standing by her. Now it was Anne evading the issue. While Mariana had previously been concerned for their reputation, now Anne thought they should not show themselves to be a couple. It is likely that such concerns were only part of the truth – once again, Anne was not even sure if she still wanted Mariana. *'Oh,' I last night said to myself in bed, 'I would rather go abroad without her.' Wished to be a while at liberty & have my fling in Italy.*[30] 'Going to Italy together' was a phrase for sex in Anne's secret language. As long as they could still only dream of such trips, she would go with Mariana 'to Italy': *Slept very little last night. Talked almost the whole time till about 4 in the morning. Went to Mariana four times, the last time just before getting up. She had eight kisses and I counted ten.* As in Buxton, when Anne confessed all about Maria Barlow to Mariana, she now admitted *the subject of Harriet Milne & how I committed myself on the Sunday, but declaring I had gone no farther. Mariana had suspected it & the assurance things were no worse was a great comfort to her.*[31] She *forgave me but was horrified at Harriet Milne's depravity.*[32] Being keen to live with Anne, Mariana was not in a position to put pressure on her.

Mariana had only been at Shibden Hall for three days when Anne received a letter from Charles Lawton, *to say I had some time ago done him the honour to make an overture of reconciliation, which he regretted he did not directly accept as then he might not have had to apply to me on this present occasion.*[33] He had in fact rejected an attempt at reconciliation from Anne after her uncle's death. Mariana had written to her how tactfully Charles dealt with her grief for the loss of James Lister. In response, Anne sent him a letter containing *what I consider a very handsome offer of reconciliation between Charles & myself, tho' without any 'constrained or uncomfortable compromise of my feelings'.*[34] Charles, however, said only to Mariana, *'I never felt ill-will towards Miss Lister. I was hot & angry at the time but I have never thought of it since.' 'Then why did you not speak to her in Buxton?' 'I never saw her at Buxton.' 'Yes, you met in the passage.' 'I don't know that I did, & was not likely to put myself in her way. I should have no objection to shake hands with Miss Lister – but don't talk anymore. I want to go to sleep.'* That had not been enough for Anne; she planned to *let it rest forever. I care not about it. Charles' manner is not enough conciliatory for me.*[35]

Shortly after this failed approach, Charles' surprising letter arrived, *insinuating that his not accepting my offered reconciliation, & that circumstances respecting her own family, had been the cause of her* [Mariana] *leaving home.* That was a questionable interpretation, but it allowed Charles to take a step in Anne's direction. *If I was still inclined to hold out the hand of friendship he would meet me in all sincerity of heart. What he wrote was in perfect confidence – I knew not how much he wanted a friend. If all was known, he might not seem so much to blame.* That, however, was the plain truth, and no one knew it better than Anne Lister. Charles asked

Anne not to show his letter to Mariana, whereupon she told her about it immediately. *We lay about quarter-hour, talking & chuckling over the thing. Whatever happened, his writing to me & the way in which I would behave, would acquit me to the world.*[36] Once reconciled with Charles, Anne would be able to meet Mariana far more easily and frequently. Things could not have gone better from Anne's point of view; she was all the more determined about sending Mariana away again before her two-week visit was over.

Mariana Lawton was serious about leaving her husband. Her first step was to go to her family in York and from there to Langton Hall, where she encountered her sister Harriet Milne, with whom she had a bone to pick; yet she had to keep quiet so as not to give herself away. Mariana *suffered much.* Harriet and Charlotte relished telling Mariana how Anne had stayed up with them the previous Christmas *three hours one night, telling them <u>indecent stories</u>. Fred, this should not be.*[37] Anne, meanwhile, received a second letter from Charles. *He seems to hope she will return thro' the influence of Steph when she 'has given herself time for cool reflection. I cannot, my dear Miss Lister, believe you would consider me so faulty as I may appear & wish you, knowing all circumstances fairly, were left to judge between us.' Declares he has always felt the sincerest regard for her & wish to make her happy.* Anne was certain on the matter. *She must go back. It will be best on all accounts.*[38] And so Mariana was pushed and pulled on three sides to return to her husband: by Charles, by her brother Stephen and even by Anne. But Mariana was not prepared to give in without conditions. *'I told him, Fred, that my affection was gone, my esteem shaken. That I had no feeling left that could support us under a repetition of annoyances I had had to contend with. Consequently it was not likely that I could meet them again with calmness. That, thro' Steph's and your <u>interference</u>, the present disagreement might be made up,'*[39] – but only until the next. She did not disguise her deep disappointment towards Anne. *'I was sorry to say I could find it in my heart not to go back but <u>you say I must</u>. Well, Fred, your will must be done.'*[40]

Even before Mariana went back to Charles, Anne's calculation paid off. Grateful for her support, Charles made no objection to Mariana spending all of May at Shibden Hall on her way back to Lawton Hall. Outsiders thought them *man & wife*.[41] Earlier on Anne had confided in her older friend Eliza Priestley – *almost the only gentlewoman in this town*[42] – that she would not really settle at Shibden Hall *till I had some friend ready to settle with me. Wished I had one now. It would be a great comfort to my aunt as well as myself.*[43] In conversation with Mariana, Mrs Priestley now said that Anne would not change much at Shibden Hall. *'Ah, I don't think so,' said Mariana, inadvertently, 'I think we might.' The we was tell-tale. Mrs Priestley had noticed it & looked as if it was not lost upon her. Mariana coloured deeply – talked of 'we' & 'we' as much as she could afterwards in such a manner as to turn it off, but probably only made bad worse. On Mariana's telling me this as we returned, we both laughed heartily. I told her Mrs Priestley would instantly guess all about it.*[44] Anne was not concerned, however. At some point she would live with a woman at Shibden Hall, so it was a good thing to get people used to the idea early on. And although she did not want to have Mariana by her side forever at the moment, she did get on well with her. *She will know & manage me better in future. I do not, cannot, doubt her affection. I think we shall get on well together in time to come.*[45]

To stand her ground as the lady of Shibden Hall with absolute control over the estate's income, Anne Lister had to ward off attacks from her father. Despite being overlooked in his brother James' will because of his inability to do business, he was now acting the lord in front of tenants and suppliers and bribing Anne's business partners to make side arrangements in his favour. Anne got to grips with business matters, prices for wood, broken stones, labour. On the first semi-annual payment day, when Anne accepted the rents in person, she refused her tenants the reductions previously granted by Uncle James. *They will think me 'very hard'.* Hoping not to get off to a bad start with their new landlady, *all the tenants have paid every farthing. This, too, is more than I counted upon.*[46]

Another reason for Anne refusing Mariana's wish to move in with her was that Aunt Anne wanted to spend some time in the south for her rheumatism. That suited her niece very well. They had hoped to return to Paris together since their pleasant weeks there in 1819. That had not been possible while Uncle James was alive. Now, though, Anne bought a large travelling carriage for £220, with plenty of space for the two of them, plus their servants and luggage. They would hire horses from one posting to the next, travelling comfortably in their own home. Anne felt she had ordered her business matters at Shibden Hall and hoped to see Rome and to spend two years travelling. Mariana was to go along with them as far as Paris.

On 16 June 1826, the staff at Shibden Hall lifted fragile Aunt Anne into the fully packed carriage. Her longstanding servant George Playforth accompanied them, in charge of the coach and the luggage. The new maid, MacDonald, took the place of Cordingley, who had had enough of travelling. Jeremy and Marian Lister moved into Shibden Hall during the two Annes' absence. Northgate House had to stand vacant, as the tenant Anne had found died suddenly before moving in, and Jeremy proved incapable of finding another.

To begin with, Anne Lister senior and junior spent some days with Mr and Mrs Lawton in Liverpool and Dublin, not least so as to demonstrate to all their acquaintances in Yorkshire and Cheshire that Mariana had not left her husband and that her husband had made up with Anne. At the Royal Hotel in Chester, Anne met Charles for the first time in ten years. *Charles soon came in. Went up & shook hands with him & said I was glad to see him, as if nothing had passed disagreeably between us. All passed off remarkably well. [...] Mariana says he was very nervous all the morning. We both behaved uncommonly well. My manners soon set him at his ease. I had two glasses of Madeira at dinner & three of port afterwards.* [...] *Charles retired at 10. My room next to theirs & Mariana & I came in in 5 or ten minutes. She undressed in my room. So did I, quite, & in half an hour we had been in bed, had two or three kisses & Mariana was gone to Charles.* After this successful start, the next few days were very relaxed. They travelled together to Parkgate on the coast, where the marital bedroom at the hotel was so stuffy that Charles was *glad to have it to himself & Mariana slept in mine.*[47] *Two very good kisses, last night, at once. We got into the other bed this morning that it might seem as if we had not slept together.* Even Anne had to pay due respect to Charles, whom she heard snoring on the other side of the wall at night. *He is very attentive to my aunt & all goes on beautifully.*[48]

In Liverpool, Mr Duffin joined the Lawtons and the Listers, and was later to report in York how well Charles, Mariana and Anne got on. They spent three days viewing what was at that time the largest port in the world. Having grown fat on slave trading, it was the point of exit for all the goods produced in the industrial heartlands of Manchester, Sheffield, Leeds, Bradford and even little Halifax. From Liverpool, the group went on via Wales to Dublin, where *all of us much struck with the magnificent appearance of the public buildings & the width of the streets.* The food was delicious, the accommodation excellent, and in the evening they enjoyed Shakespeare's *Comedy of Errors*, of all things. But things did not continue in this merry vein. Anne drank *a glass of warm lemonade. Charles never heard of such a thing. Nobody would, or ever did, take it but myself. Then he began about Mariana's shawl & mine being for winter, not summer. Nobody wore such here, etc. Tiresome. I am sick of travelling with him.*[49]

Anne had to grit her teeth for a while longer, though, because after the trip to Ireland they visited Lawton Hall, Mariana's home, where Anne had not been for ten years. Anne took the opportunity to quiz the servants. *Charles as bad as ever out of doors.* [...] *Calling after women & talking to them. Uses very gross language. Said to have been, the other day, in the plantation with a low, bad woman. Will walk with any sort of trull. The Irishman who assaulted the dairymaid the other day declared all the servants were bad & he was not worse than his master.* […] *Mariana will never end her days there. Her leaving Charles would not surprise any of them.* As if to confirm the gossip, Charles secretly took Anne aside, led her to the gatehouse and showed her a little boy he said he had fathered with the gatekeeper's wife, Mrs Grantham. Anne thought the boy sufficiently *stupid-looking* to be his son. Having not had any children with either of his wives, Charles did not want to officially acknowledge the child but he did not want to deny him either, and he asked Anne to tell Mariana so in confidence. Mariana was more horrified by talking about it than by the fact itself, something she had been expecting for years. She demanded absolute discretion from Charles – *no wife would bear these things*[50] – and gave him such a talking to that he let her leave for Paris with Anne and her aunt without contradiction the next day.

Maria

1826–1827

During the preparations for her long stay abroad, Anne had bombarded the pragmatic Maria Barlow with hundreds of questions. How much did it cost to hire horses from Calais to Paris? Was there an English doctor in Orléans? Could she get hold of a wheelchair for Aunt Anne? Maria took care of everything but kept her answers neutral. *How can she be so cold so soon?* Anne wondered, only to interpret Maria's reserve as a tactical pretence: *she is deep, she wants to catch me.*[1] Still, Anne thought, *I must see her again. Let me try my regard for her – see how she looks & how she could please me now when Mariana is mistress of my thoughts & hopes.*[2] Anne neglected to tell Maria that she was bringing not only her aunt with her, but also Mariana Lawton.

The group arrived in Paris on 2 September 1826; Maria had reserved hotel rooms for them. *We had got into the Rue de Rivoli when Mariana saw a little figure in white dart out of the Hôtel de Terrasse and call out to the postboys to stop. Said Mariana, 'Mrs Barlow.' There was Jane, too. Mrs Barlow as pale as death. I felt a little less so. Jumped out of the carriage. Met her* and introduced her to Aunt Anne. *Her attention to my aunt unbounded. Evidently rather constrained to me & I to her. Mariana had come upstairs to our room & did not come down till Mrs Barlow was gone, who staid surely about 1/2 hour. I walked home with her & went upstairs into her salon for a few minutes. In crossing Tuileries gardens, mentioned Mariana's being with us. Mrs Barlow agitated. Said I had behaved dishonestly not to tell her before. Should have written on purpose from London & she would have got out of the way – gone into the country. 'And I have seen her,' said she. 'I took her for your lady's maid & wondered to see another ugly woman stuck up behind'!!! I took no apparent notice of this splenetic, ill-judged speech.* Instead, Anne told her *it was not my fault Mariana was with us, etc. She would stay perhaps a few days* – in fact, Mariana was to spend six weeks in Paris at Anne's request. Eventually, Anne asked Maria for her help finding an apartment. *'Why,' said she peevishly, 'should I settle Mrs Lawton?' This struck me much.*[3]

Over the weeks that followed, Anne tried to make up with Maria and at the same time keep Mariana amused. Mariana had come to Paris to shop and Anne took her to all kinds of stores, which Mariana left kitted out with new hats, handbags, writing paper, tailored dresses and stays. At dinner on the third day, Anne said, *'Perhaps I might go to Mrs Barlow,' & this had spoiled poor Mariana's appetite – but she would have me do whatever seemed best.* Anne did not visit Maria until the next day, when she and Mariana were out apartment-hunting and passed the quai Voltaire, where Maria and Jane were still living. Anne claimed she just wanted to say hello and left Mariana with the concierge. *Mariana waited for us patiently 55 minutes tho' I had promised to stay only 1/4 hour. She had been overwhelmed with miserable reflections* – Mariana knew only too well what was possible with Anne in half an hour, or even in seven minutes if need be – *but behaved beautifully.*[4]

Maria's behaviour, however, was less to Anne's taste. Anne tried to explain to her that Mariana was to remain her first wife, but Maria was welcome to be her wife number two again. *I said I had done Mariana injustice – been mistaken about her – en revient toujours a ses premier amours* [sic]. *'Then,' said Mrs Barlow, 'you love her. You love another & you tell me so yourself. I did not think you could have so soon forgotten me & met me thus,' etc., and we had a scene. At last I said I durst not presume to talk of love without her express permission under my present circumstances, which could not be changed, etc. She said she could permit it – it was different now after the manner in which we had lived together. 'Well then,' said I, 'I love you as well as ever,' & prest her hand. (Alas! I felt something like disgust.) She smiled as if she had gained a victory & I hurried off.* At the hotel, *I felt shocked as I returned, musing on what had passed. She will take me on any terms. Poor Mariana! I looked, she & my aunt said to each other,* <u>very</u> *ill. I daresay I was as white as a sheet.*[5]

Six days after their arrival, Anne, her aunt, Mariana and their servants moved into an airy and spacious apartment at 6, rue de Mondovi, close to the Tuileries. They were now paying less for accommodation than at the hotel, but eating out every day was expensive and Aunt Anne was still not stable on her feet. Anne soon had to dismiss a cook for financial reasons. *Mariana and I went shopping, buying bread, butter, groceries – tiresome but necessary. What folly to have English servants. They can do nothing of this sort for you & ten times worse to provide for them yourselves!* Anne could neither cook nor run a household – but Maria Barlow could. That gave Anne an idea: once Mariana had left, Maria could move in with them. But Mariana was *against our having her here to keep house for us. Says she will never consent to it. My aunt thinks Mrs Barlow is trying to make up to her.*[6]

Anne had to admit that her efforts to coerce her various lovers into good relations with each other had been in vain on this occasion. Maria thought *she is mine by right. Nobody – no married woman – can have so good a right to me as hers.* Having run into Mariana by chance at church, she later caused *quite a scene. Said I behaved ill to her – did not care for her – treated her with no respect – was a slave to 'that creature'. I found fault with this manner of expression. Said my circumstances were fixed. […] All this seemed to upset her. She cried. Sent me away then called me back. I was weary of her & really cared very little, except to be pothered & annoyed. Poor Mariana waiting* – for an hour and a quarter in a nearby shop – *very good-humouredly.*[7]

Mariana knew better than Maria that Anne would not be won over with accusations; that called for lenience and good temper. Anne showed her around Paris, they went to the theatre often, Mariana took embroidery classes and Anne went back to Mme de Galvani for French lessons. In the evenings they *sat up, eating grapes and talking, as we generally do.* They *talked earnestly about Mariana's leaving Charles. She has a sad dislike or misgiving about going back to Lawton. Thinks she cannot get over this business about Mrs Grantham – cannot stay.*[8] Anne felt sorry for Mariana but continued to persuade her to stay with Charles and wait for his death. *If possible, she had best get the upper hand & stay it out. I would make myself happy & comfortable. It might make a difference of five hundred a year to us besides the additional respectability.*[9]

On 7 October Anne accompanied Mariana to Boulogne-sur-mer and handed her over to Charles. Anne stood on the pier and watched the ship sail. *The sea was very rough & as I watched the vessel heave among the breakers my heart heaved with it & I hoped Mariana & I would never meet to part again.*[10]

Back in Paris, Anne immediately resumed her affair with Maria Barlow. Mariana had *agreed that I should try whether she would really take me on any terms or not. If she would, I would be shocked & be off. If she would not, of course I should stand excused from lovemaking scenes.*[11] Maria did not say no, and Anne was not shocked and did not make off. Mariana need never know.

Originally, Anne and her aunt had planned to spend the winter on the Mediterranean, but Aunt Anne was too unwell to travel. In January of 1827 they took a smaller, cheaper apartment on Place neuve de la Madelaine. Having forged a close friendship with the building's live-in owners, the lively Séné family, Aunt Anne did not want to move on in the spring either, especially because she felt well looked after by her English physician, Dr Scudamore, and their household problems had calmed down, thanks to Maria Barlow's laundrywoman and her butter and vegetable suppliers. She therefore encouraged her niece to go on a long trip without her. Anne asked Maria Barlow along, who was happy to accompany her to Switzerland and northern Italy, with Jane. As Aunt Anne needed the servants George Playforth and MacDonald more urgently, her own carriage had to stay in Paris.

In beautiful summer weather, Anne, Maria and Jane set out by post coach on 15 June 1827. Via Nancy, they reached Strasbourg where visitors were still allowed to climb the cathedral tower to the top: at that point *the view is magnificent – worth all the trouble – the Rhine, the mountains of France and Germany.* [...] *We crossed the famous quarter-of-a-mile-long bridge of boats over the Rhine, and sat an hour in a German cottage at the picturesque extremity of the town of Kehl, where we had sourish cream and German bread. The Rhine at Kehl is a magnificent river – its waters were turbid from the great quantity of rain that had fallen in the mountains; its current rapid as in Caesar's time.* They continued via Colmar to Basle, where Anne initially felt she *never was more comfortable at any Inn in my life. My room is on two sides surrounded by the Rhine. We are a little way from the wooden bridge that connects the great and little Basle.*[12] Then, however, the vicinity to the polluted water caused the worst diarrhoea in her life.

In Basle, Anne met a coachman from Berne who was waiting for travellers to his hometown. Anne, Maria and Jane went on a day's excursion to test out his carriage, including two horses, and then rented it for a good price for an undetermined period – the only thing important for him was that they ended up in Berne. And so Anne did get her trip in her own 'caravan' in the end. From Basle, they went on to Baden, where Anne was reluctant to leave the warm spa water in her private bathing cabinet. In Schaffhausen, they admired the *falls of the Rhine. It was worth to travel all the way from Paris.* She adored Lake

Constance and the surrounding area too; *literally, our eyes are always more tired than our legs. The scene changed almost at every step, that our visionary powers have, absolutely, no rest.* In Constance *the people seem to meet together, all hereabouts, to sing, in an evening, and really sing, all in concert, very well.* They could not understand a thing, with Maria speaking as little German as Anne, who had never got further than flicking through her grammar book.

The three women gained their first impressions of the Alps on their way through the Swiss canton of Graubünden to Italy. From Coire, *the celebrated Via Mala having even surpassed our expectations,* they spent a night in Splügen *among the snow-mountains* and *between walls of snow twelve or fifteen feet high, crossed the Splügen mountain* [...] *and descended by one of the most frightfully magnificent roads in Europe into the fine valley of Chiavenna.*[13] Via Lake Como, Bormio, Merano and Bolzano, they arrived in Verona, the Roman arena of which thrilled Anne, a fan of all things Latin. After a day trip to Lake Garda, they continued via Vicenza and Padua to Venice.

In Italy, tensions among the party became palpable. Like Mariana Lawton, Maria Barlow had grown embarrassed by the clothes Anne wore on their travels, which she considered unkempt and shabby. Anne spent hours of every evening writing her impressions of the day in her diary instead of discussing them with her travelling companion, who felt rejected. Besides which, Maria was not in good physical condition. She had been suffering from cystitis since the crossing to Tyrol, where they had almost got stuck in the snow on the pass and had to spend an ice-cold night in a mountain cabin. In Italy, the heat was too much for her. With her enthusiasm for adventure, Anne felt held back by Maria. Whenever Maria wanted to stay in a beautiful spot for a while, Anne shooed her onwards. They continued to Milan via Este, Mantua and Cremona. Lugano and Lago Maggiore were ticked off the list before they headed back to Switzerland via the Simplon Pass. At Lake Geneva, they strolled in Lord Byron's footsteps and then went on to Chamonix, to climb the Mer de Glace, the largest glacier on Mont Blanc. They stayed a night at the travellers' hospice on the Great Saint Bernard Pass, where Anne went walking alone, got lost in the descending darkness and would not have found her way out of the snow if the Saint Bernard dogs hadn't barked at the sound of her calls, guiding her way back.

Impressed by the Alps, Anne persuaded Maria and Jane to conclude the trip with an extended mountain tour. In Berne – *surely the prettiest town in Europe*[14] – they took leave of their coachman and took a new guide, who arranged a two-week hiking tour of the Bernese Highlands around the Jungfrau Massif. They sent their heavy luggage ahead from Kandersteg to Interlaken. Three mountain guides brought Anne (on foot) and Maria and Jane (on mules) via Andermatt, Grindelwald and Wengen to Lake Thun and Lake Brienz. For Anne, this hike through the Alps, with its physical exertion during the day and simple mountain cabins by night, became the highlight of the trip. Jane, on the other hand, was *tired of mountains*.[15] They returned to Paris via Lucerne and Zurich, Geneva and Lyon, arriving back on 24 October.

There, they found Aunt Anne hale and hearty in the company of Isabella Norcliffe, who had used Anne's room, taken her aunt on plenty of outings, and told her all the latest Yorkshire gossip. She left again on 12 November, along with her cat, which she had brought with her all the way from Langton Hall. However, Aunt Anne did not yet want to return home, so Anne could look forward to another winter in Paris.

She did not wish to spend it with Maria, however. The long tour had driven a wedge between them. Anne also found her lacking in *éclat*, social standing and wealth. Anne had reached *the wrong side of 30*[16] and would have to pick up the pace if she wanted to catch herself a suitably rich aristocratic woman who would satisfy her needs in romantic, sexual, pecuniary and social terms. The young widow

Mme de Rosny had much of what Anne desired: youth, beauty and connections to the French court. At the beginning of 1828, Anne left her aunt alone in the apartment on Place neuve de la Madelaine and moved in with her new lover – allegedly to perfect her French. In all other areas, however, Mme de Rosny turned out to be as much of a disappointment as her predecessors. As Anne had not had her own coming-out at the English court, she could not be received by the French royal family, despite all Mme de Rosny's connections. And she too was short on money; she probably lived on the commissions she charged for arranging smuggling deals to England. Rather than losing more precious time with Mme de Rosny, Anne decided to visit an old friend in Scotland, Sibella Maclean. Having to see to things at Shibden Hall as well, she entrusted Aunt Anne to the care of Maria Barlow and left Paris on 17 March 1828.

Her first stop on the way north was Lawton Hall. On her last farewell from Mariana, a year and a half previously, Anne had wished she would never have to part from Mariana again. Now, matters looked different; *her manner was warmer than mine. I said I was harassed tho' in fact I felt more as if I had been so long absent from Mariana I did not know what to do with her. She looked tall and big. She seemed to have grown taller. I felt awkward & said to myself, 'Why, what have I to do with having such a woman?'*[17] As always, they slept together.

Sibella

1828–1829

Back at Shibden Hall, Anne found the house and grounds badly kept. Paths were overgrown, walls had collapsed, hedges were untrimmed – even though Jeremy and Marian had moved in partly to prevent the house from falling into neglect. Yet even inside the house, a rotten staircase had not been repaired, and Anne could tell the carpets had not been beaten since her departure almost two years earlier. She took care of everything immediately, with her characteristic energy. She also found a tenant for Northgate House, the lawyer Mr Scratcherd and his family, and negotiated the sale of part of the large Northgate grounds for the construction of a new church, as growing Halifax now had some 18,000 inhabitants. The sale brought her £711, most welcome in a financially difficult year in which Aunt Anne still had to pay the rent for the Parisian apartment.

Anne had barely seen to the necessary chores in and around Shibden Hall before she set off for Scotland to see Sibella Maclean, the daughter of the fifteenth Laird of Coll, an island in the Inner Hebrides. Anne had met Sibella eight years previously, in 1820, at a gathering in York. *On catching the first glimpse of you, Bless me! Who's that? She's an elegant looking creature!*[1] What attracted Anne was Sibella's ancient aristocratic provenance, which she felt was reflected in her outward appearance. *With all your shyness, (not too much), there is a look that looks 'the chieftain's daughter'.*[2] Anne thought Miss Maclean *one of the most ladylike, pleasing women I ever met with in my life. I have seldom seen manners that I prefer; and, when seated at the head of her own table, she is perfect.*[3] Anne could well imagine such a woman at the head of *her* table. *I would rather spend my life with Miss Maclean than any one.*[4]

In the years since 1820, Anne had renewed her vows with Mariana three times, seduced Miss Vallance and Nantz Belcombe, slept countless times with Isabella Norcliffe, flirted with Harriet Milne, Lou Belcombe and Francis Pickford, spent a long time living in Paris with Maria Barlow and then a few weeks with Mme de Rosny. During all these entanglements, Sibella Maclean had been an iron in the fire that Anne Lister sought to heat up from a distance, to forge and shape to her will. In numerous wordy letters, she never told Sibella what she was doing – or with whom – instead trying to initiate a flirt by means of complex rhetorical figures.

On her remote island, Sibella was rather surprised to receive so much post from Anne. Six years her senior, she complained that Anne's letters had no content, and forbade her from sending mere fine words. *Surely you must fancy I flatter you more than I have the smallest intention of doing,* Anne responded. *I never say what I do not think. A sense of duty, and, perhaps, of something like your highland pride, makes me fear and scorn to be untrue, and bind me to sincerity as the brightest gem in honour's crown.*[5] Confused by such answers, Sibella kept up her reserve towards Anne, insisting on being called 'Miss Maclean' when Anne would have liked to use her forename, and considered Anne *a character*, whose *mind is not formed in the ordinary mould.* For years, Sibella did not understand what Anne wanted of her, and asked her to write only *what might be read aloud verbatim.*[6]

In 1824 the two saw each other again for two days at the home of mutual friends. Anne told Sibella of her wish to share her life with a woman and gave her a brooch in which she had once kept a lock of Eliza Raine's hair. *I care not for wealth, nor honours, nor all the pomp of circumstance this world of shadows can bestow. Give me but one kindred spirit with my own, and a dinner of herbs would seem to me a meal at which the gods might dine. With such a one I could be happy in a palace or a prison.*[7] After this second meeting, Sibella found Anne all the more *incomprehensible – an enigma you cannot solve.* And so Anne went as far as she dared in writing. *Perhaps I am 'odd, very, very odd'.* [...] *You promised to indulge all my whims. Well might I exclaim to you or to myself – she knows not what she promises!* 'But I shall not visit you in Shibden till you tell me why I do not understand the promises I have made.' *I can tell you at once. If you do not understand my style of writing, how can you understand me, how the <u>whims</u> you have promised to indulge.* [...] *I cannot tell you on paper: it would require more explanation than you are aware.* [...] *There is something (but it breathes not of dishonour) that parts me from the world I meet with.* Sibella required only *that little key that would open all my letters, and all I have said to you. One little key would be enough; for few people are more simply natural than myself, or more generally consistent with themselves.*[8]

An aggravating factor in Anne's long-distance seduction attempt was the fact that Sibella found romance ridiculous. *You do not, you cannot admire what is usually meant by romance, in any shape. Your good opinion of the person possessing such romance, must necessarily suffer more or less on this account.*[9] Anne tried to shake off Sibella's sober principles. *But inasmuch as romance may, in this day, mean affectation, I am unconscious of having any of it. That my feelings run on in a current peculiarly their own, increasing knowledge of the world makes me more and more aware; but that I never turn them from their natural course you will more and more believe as your acquaintance with me becomes more intimate and correct.*[10]

That was precisely what Sibella did not want, at first. In 1825 she seems to have found the 'key': an acquaintance from York told her the gossip that was already making the rounds about Anne and her Scottish friend. She cancelled her invitation to Anne. Anne accompanied her aunt to Buxton instead and spent several lustful weeks with Mariana. Nevertheless, she went on sending Sibella letter after letter. By 1828 Anne had finally ground down Sibella's defences. She could find no more excuses to turn down Anne's wish for a joint tour of Scotland – or perhaps she wanted to find out once and for all what Anne wanted of her.

On 19 May 1828, Sibella welcomed Anne to Edinburgh, showed her around the city and introduced her to friends and relatives. The two of them spent two months of that summer exploring Scotland by steamer, coach, rowing boat and farmer's cart. *We have seen all the ruins, cascades, glens, castles, lakes, forts, &c., &c. We have visited twenty-one of the principal lakes, traversed the fertile Carse of Gowrie, and looked down from the top of Ben Nevis. We have been comfortable everywhere; and I have learnt to think Finnin haddock, Loch Fine herrings, barley scones, and mutton hams among the best of good things.*[11] There were some hikes Anne had to take alone, however; at forty-three, Sibella did not have the strength. *She looks, and is, thin and delicate.*[12] And she had a cough that had not gone away for years.

What else happened in Scotland is still unknown; Anne Lister's diaries from 1827 to 1831 have yet to be decrypted and published. There are typed summaries of the coded passages held at the West Yorkshire Archive Service, Calderdale, in Halifax, which were made by Vivien Ingham and Phyllis Ramsden when they read through all the diaries between 1958 and 1969. According to these, Anne told Sibella about her earlier relationship with Mariana on 2 June. On 4 and 5 June, Anne wrote a long passage about Sibella which remains encrypted, and then on 7 June another five lines. From 16 to 29 June Anne wrote extensive passages which Phyllis Ramsden also neglected to paraphrase but instead described as *personal* or *of no interest.*[13] Ramsden gave an involuntary explanation of what she meant by that in 1970, in an essay about Anne Lister: everything Anne had written in code was *of no historical interest whatever* and *excruciatingly tedious to the modern mind*.[14] Thanks to the many coded passages from other years, which Phyllis Ramsden also paraphrased, and which have since been transcribed more fully and published by Helena Whitbread and Jill Liddington, we can translate Ramsden's judgements very precisely. *Personal* refers to expressions of Anne Lister's lesbian desire and *of no historical interest whatever* means descriptions of sex. In other words, Phyllis Ramsden turned Anne Lister's secret alphabet into her own code, communicating what was unspeakable without speaking it. Ramsden's summaries of the long encrypted passages written in the second half of June 1828 suggest that Anne made her progress with Sibella step by step. As with Maria Barlow, the approach had taken up more time than Anne's enjoyment of her success.

The moment Anne had achieved the primary goal of her journey, she suggested Sibella should spend a while living with her and her aunt in Paris. Seeing as her father had no objections, Sibella agreed; a winter in a warmer climate could only do her good. They intended to set off as soon as Anne had dealt with her tasks at Shibden Hall. A new road to Bradford and Leeds was being built nearby. Anne admired Godley Lane, cut deep into the hillside and laid out on high embankments: *a stupendous piece of work, it will be the greatest possible improvement in the roadway to the whole neighbourhood*.[15] However, it was not to run too close to Shibden Hall, so Anne demanded that the authorities change its route. She also began work on the old house itself. To minimise damp and draughts, she had drainage laid down to the foundations and part of the exterior wall rebuilt. The windows in the downstairs rooms were also re-fitted, which had to be done with the utmost care due to the valuable old panes. The sloping surface in front of the main entrance was levelled to form a spacious terrace. These changes led to arguments with the building's other inhabitants. *My father and Marian and I have certainly few sentiments and opinions in common,* Anne sighed in a letter to her aunt in Paris. *My patience is nearly exhausted, tho' I know not of how much I may have need even yet. [...] Our return either to Shibden, or to England, is very little advisable under the existence of present circumstances.*[16]

To put some distance between herself and Jeremy and Marian, Anne went to visit Mariana at Lawton Hall at the end of October, even though Sibella Maclean had been waiting for her in London since 29 September. But Anne did not want to go to Paris until she had received the money for the sale of the land at Northgate House. Anne confessed her affair with Mme de Rosny to Mariana and was granted her forgiveness, as ever. She failed to mention there was a woman waiting for her in London whom she imagined at the other end of her table at Shibden Hall. Yet even after the formalities for the land sale were finally notarized on 20 January 1829, Anne did not go to Paris. Instead, she spent three weeks taking the air at Scarborough with Mariana, through whom she had infected herself again, having been free of symptoms in the meantime. When Anne returned to Shibden Hall for three weeks in March, she hoped to tie everything up so she could stay away for another two years.

On 21 March 1829, Anne travelled with Charles and Mariana Lawton and Lou Belcombe down to London, where Sibella Maclean had been waiting for her for six months. Sibella had taken the opportunity to seek the treatment of a Mr John Long, who correctly diagnosed her constant cough as tuberculosis but deployed disconcerting methods to try to cure it. He told Anne about his *grand discovery*: three piglets squashed to death by their mother had been thrown onto the dung heap; one crawled down again, brought back to life by the warmth of the fermenting dung. This observation convinced Mr Long not only of the curative powers of warmth in general, but also of this particular variety: he *wished he could bury his patients in a dunghill.* For Anne, it was clear on their very first meeting *the man must be mad.*[17] Sibella, however, placed great hope in him. He predicted she would die if she were to go to Paris and forgo his expensive treatment.

The charlatan Mr Long was not the only point of contention between Sibella and Anne. Sibella presumably made accusations; instead of living with her in the mild temperatures of Paris, Anne had preferred to spend the cold winter months in Yorkshire with Mariana, who played a role in Anne's life that Sibella could not divine. According to Phyllis Ramsden's excerpts from Anne's coded journals, they argued every day. In the end, Sibella decided in favour of Mr Long and against Anne. For the first time ever, a woman left Anne.

Vere

1829–1832

While Anne was arguing with Sibella Maclean she did, however, make friends with Sibella's aristocratic relatives in London, particularly with the widowed Lady Louisa Anne Stuart. Anne had always got on well with older ladies. Lady Stuart's rather impressive Pembroke Lodge in Richmond Park was also home to Sibella's niece Vere Hobart, the sister of the fifth Earl of Buckinghamshire. The orphaned Vere was supposed to spend the summer with Lady Stuart's son, the British ambassador to Paris, Charles Stuart, first Baron de Rothesay. As an unmarried young woman, however, she needed a suitable travelling companion. Now thirty-eight, Anne Lister was only too happy to take Vere along to Paris. Anne left a note at the British Embassy the day after their arrival, whereupon the ambassador's wife, Lady Elizabeth Stuart de Rothesay, a daughter of the third Earl of Hardwicke, paid a personal visit to Anne and invited her to a soirée at the embassy on 30 April. There was no greater honour for an English traveller in Paris.

The evening became a social pinnacle of Anne's life to that date. Wearing a newly tailored black ball gown, enrobed by a dresser hired especially for the occasion, and equipped by a hairdresser with a *chapeau de bal with bird of paradise plumes*, Anne savoured the glamour of the two thousand guests; *never was I so entourée de noblesse*. [...]

Titles English and foreign, stars, garters, &c., &c., a brilliant assemblage. Anne admired Lady Stuart de Rothesay, *a blaze of diamonds,*[1] with the *sovreign nack* [sic] *she has of always having something apt and agreeable to say to everyone.*[2] Her ward Vere Hobart danced with Ferdinand-Philippe, Duc de Chartres, the son of the later citizen king Louis Philippe, *but it was impossible to get near her; and I literally had never an opportunity of speaking to her.*[3]

Over the subsequent months, Anne was invited not only to official functions at the embassy, but also to private circles, particularly once the dowager Lady Stuart had arrived from Richmond in June. She suggested they spend the summer together in Belgium and Germany. Anne was all the more glad to take her up on the offer, seeing as Vere Hobart was to join them. From June on, Anne was *trying to flirt w. Miss H.*, although Vere was rather *flippant*, in fact *rather a goose*, as Anne pronounced after they visited a museum together. Not that that made the young single woman with aristocratic relatives and the prospect of an impressive dowry any less attractive in Anne Lister's eyes.

They set out in two carriages on 14 August. This time Aunt Anne let her niece have the use of their travelling carriage along with their servant George and maid Cameron; Lady Stuart travelled in a second coach with Vere. Over the next few days and weeks, Anne noted down moments in code, which Phyllis Ramsden paraphrases as follows: *flirting with V. H. – walking with V. H., – talking to V. H. – discussing V. H. – flirting with Miss V. H. – slight disagreement with V. H. – on better terms with V. H. – criticising V. H.* There were five lines on 21 August considered by Ramsden of *no interest.*[4]

The group arrived in Brussels to cool and rainy weather on 22 August. A disappointed Anne recorded: *Never in my life did I see such a parcel of narrow, winding, crooked streets – there is nothing to form a fine capital.*[5] They viewed the battlefield at Waterloo and went on to Namur, through the Maas Valley to Liège for a few days in Spa.

In comparison to Anne's travels in Scotland with Sibella Maclean or Switzerland with Maria Barlow, Lady Stuart went to far greater expense, visiting acquaintances at every turn and acting more formally, which appealed to Anne Lister but not to her budget.

The group eventually arrived at Aix la Chapelle, at that time a sophisticated spa town that Anne liked *much better than I expected*.[6] But when the dowager Lady Stuart decided to take the waters there, Anne grew bored. The nearby Rhineland was of more interest to her, much praised by English tourists at that time. To Anne's regret, Vere refused to go along, despite speaking good German. An acquaintance of Lady Stuart's, Lady Caroline Duff Gordon, *a very agreeable person*,[7] proved more adventurous. It was only with her that Anne came to the extensive viewings and long hikes she had hoped for on the journey. Lady Gordon thought her contemporary Anne *sensible, agreeable, and to the purpose*.[8] Anne in turn valued her *constant good humour in travelling. Had we gone from pole to pole, I really do not think we should have sparred one single instant*.[9] She did not note anything 'of no interest' on their travels together. They got as far as Darmstadt, where they experienced the opera's *admirable orchestra, beautiful scenery and dresses, but bad singing. Francfort is a capital town; and we all regretted not being able to stay longer than two days.* They liked the spas of Wiesbaden and Ems but had problems with the language. *It is absurd to say that French is spoken everywhere on the Rhine. Merely a few Innkeepers speak it, and one has all the difficulty in this world to get on with German.*[10] The famed landscapes of the Middle Rhine elicited little enthusiasm from Anne. *From Coblentz to Cologne, in returning, we went in the steam boat, and liked it well enough. We did not go more than 6 or 7 miles an hour, and had therefore time enough to see the views. What a pity to hear a very great deal of praise of anything before one sees it! We were all but disappointed with the Rhine scenery taken collectively – taking it by piecemeal, there are, it must be allowed, some very fine things.*[11]

Returning to Aix la Chapelle, Anne then accompanied Lady Stuart and Vere Hobart through constant rain across the Netherlands and northern France to their ship's pier at Calais. During these last three weeks, Anne attempted to move her relationship with Vere along – *(v. dull) talking etc to V. H.*, as Phyllis Ramsden notes at several points in her summaries.[12] Once Vere was back in London and Anne back in Paris, they exchanged only pleasantly polite letters, however. With no reason to hope Vere was the woman who would give her access to the upper echelons of society, Anne toyed with the idea – for the first and last time in her life – of *whether she should marry some old nobleman on her own terms, to get 'rank'*.[13] No suitable candidates announced themselves.

As always when Anne could find no one to fall in love with and seduce, she devoted herself to her scientific interests. She attended lectures by Georges Cuvier, the founder of palaeontology, at the Collège de France in the winter of 1829–1830; she was fascinated by his *Recherches sur les ossemens fossiles des quadrupèdes* (1812). Thanks to a letter of recommendation from one of her new aristocratic acquaintances, he received her at the Jardin des Plantes. *Stayed a few minutes with this first naturalist of his age – very civil and gentlemanlike, & gave me a student's ticket to the cabinet d'histoire naturelle*.[14] She attended Professor Audoin's lectures on comparative anatomy. He put Anne in contact with a medical student by the name of Julliart, with whom she undertook dissections. On the first occasion, Julliart brought a dead rabbit to the Listers' apartment, then a live one; *felt a bit queerish to see the poor animal killed & then begin cutting it up directly – but as M Julliart said one must get accustomed to these things.* They soon moved on to dissecting a human hand. *No smell, but somehow the cutting at a hand so like one's own had an odd effect on me.*[15] Anne's next dissections were of a human ear and then a woman's head. It is not known where the head came from. Anne, who had kissed so many women, took on the dissection of the face. She preserved the *bits* in rectified spirits and kept them in a cabinet she obtained especially, which also contained a skeleton and several skulls.

Did Aunt Anne find these exhibits unpleasant? Did her niece want to lead a student life at the age of thirty-nine? Anyway, Anne rented a room in another house in the Quartier Latin at 7, rue St Victor. *Aprl. 16. For the first time I am at my desk here writing my journal. How light & airy my little apartment – I shall do very well here, much better for study than rue Godot. I look into a court & a little garden at the bottom – the sparrows are chirping – I hear the clock of the Panthéon church of St. Geneviéve. I am quite comfortable & have brought my letters to answer.*[16] A hundred years before Virginia Woolf's 1929 essay, Anne Lister had a room of her own in which to work and think.

In May of 1830, Lady Stuart de Rothesay enquired as to Anne's plans for the summer. *Said I thought of going to the Pyrenees – she hoped she could see me there, said I should be delighted. And I know not which first proposed going together, which she said she should like very much.* Anne thought so too. However, such a high-class travelling companion caused considerable costs even before they set off. Anne had her travelling coach refitted, renewed her wardrobe, bought six pairs of shoes, had a new livery made for George Playforth, and paid her maid Cameron to take lessons in hairdressing so that Anne would look good on the road. Before their departure, King George IV died, which meant Cameron also needed a black silk dress and George a black suit. But Anne regarded all this as an investment in her future: *Me voilà en train (I am coming on).*[17]

The group left Paris in three carriages on 21 July 1830: Anne in her own with servants and luggage, Lady Stuart de Rothesay with her two young daughters in a landau, and a third carriage for her servants and luggage – twelve people in all. They arrived in Bordeaux on 26 July; *so hot, hardly resolution to dress at all.*[18] On 28 July, unsettling news arrived from Paris, where the July Revolution had broken out. The last Bourbon king, Charles X, a reactionary, had ordered the dissolution of the Chamber of Deputies, limited the vote and restricted freedom of the press. In response, tradesmen, workers and students built barricades on the streets against the authorities – including beneath Aunt Anne's windows, while she was all alone in Paris. After three days of violent clashes, the king abdicated and fled to England. In southern France, the revolution was felt only indirectly: newspapers were not printed, the Tricolore was flown instead of the white and gold flag of the monarchy, and Anne was surprised to find she could not cash a bill of credit from the Rothschild bank. Rather anxious, the group sought shelter with the British consul in Pau. After days of great uncertainty, Lady Stuart received news from her husband, instructing her to continue with her vacation as planned. Aunt Anne reported to her niece that all was calm again and the 'citizen king' Louis Philippe was being proclaimed monarch that day, 9 August; she selflessly wished Anne pleasant travels. Anne did not recognise that her aunt had been desperate with fear during the days of the revolution, just as she did not see through the British ambassador's tactical reasons for having his wife put on a pretence of normality.

As on the trip around Belgium and Germany the previous year with Lady Stuart's mother-in-law, Anne soon grew bored of the high society to which she aspired. *I am heartily sick of this life of trammel,* she complained. *I get no real walking, am getting fatter and all day tortured by dress too tight. Oh, that I was unknown and walking and riding about at my ease.*[19] Usually, she would have tried to liven up the trip with a flirt. But the wife of the British ambassador was taboo, even for Anne Lister. Expeditions to Eaux Bonnes and Eaux Chaudes only made her all the more keen, having already crossed the Bernese Highlands, to see the higher mountains of the Pyrenees. Starting from Luz-Saint-Sauveur, where they stayed for three weeks, she finally had the longed-for opportunity. Without informing Lady Stuart, Anne hired a guide, Pierre Jean Charles, packed a rucksack with crampons and a change of clothes, and announced to her surprised travelling companion, at the end of a picnic at the famous Cirque de Gavarnie, that she'd see them in four days' time. Anne later reminded Lady Stuart *how grave you looked*, but her friend did give her a *piece of chocolate and the five-franc-piece*[20] to take along.

Anne and her guide spent the night in Gavarnie, where they hired a local smuggler who knew the mountains well. In the early morning of 24 August, Anne started by *arranging my dress, etc. Loops & strings put to my old black merino that I have all along rode in here, so as to tie it up round me*,[21] and then climbed in the finest weather with her two guides to the top of the Brèche de Roland (2807 m), a spectacular natural breach in the main crest of the Pyrenees. Today's visitors pass only the remains of a glacier, but in Anne's time the ice was still *so steep that, in spite of iron cramps strapped round our feet, and long iron pointed sticks in our hands to hold by, it was with some difficulty we got up it. In the next glacier, still worse than the other, one of the guides with an axe cut little steps for himself and the rest of us, that we could just stick our toes into, and, one after another, we all got safe over.* At 12:30 they were standing in the legendary gap, enjoying the view for ten minutes. *Getting to the bottom did not give us much trouble – my foot slipped, I found myself sitting instead of standing, and, in this way, glided down so nicely they all thought I had done it on purpose.*[22] In the Spanish part of the Pyrenees, they headed south and spent the night in a modest shepherd's hut near Góriz. They got up at 3:15 the next morning and spent four hours climbing Monte Perdido (3,355 m), the third highest mountain in the Pyrenees. It is now the heart of the Spanish Parque Nacional de Ordesa y Monte Perdido, and can be reached by practised mountain hikers without mountaineering equipment. Anne Lister also found the ascent *more fatiguing than difficult. The view was magnificent, particularly towards Spain. It was not, however, entirely for the view I had gone up – I was curious to try the effect of the air at so great an elevation, but none of the inconveniences so often complained of, affected me at all. I felt only that the breeze was light and exhilarating.* Up there, *it was the perfect solitude, the profound stillness that gave me a sensation I had never had before.* The descent took them three hours; along the *magnificent gorge d'Ortessa* – the 'European Grand Canyon' – at the end of a long day they reached Torla, at that time still a *picturesque little town.*[23] Anne collapsed that evening, as she had after her extremely long hike across the elevations of the Lake District. *They brought me goat's milk – it was no sooner down than up again. Then called for wine* and got *an enormous bottle of vin de Carignan, like a rich cordial. A little of this with water and a large plate, 3 bunches, of grapes was all I could take.*[24] She later recalled, *no moment of my life has made a deeper impression on me, than the moment of my return from Mt Perdu.*[25]

The next morning, she had barely *greased my shoes with the oil of the lamp, or poor things they seemed as if they would hardly last me home,*[26] when along came the village priest to pay his respects. *We contrived to understand each other in Latin. He immediately asked if I was <u>christiana</u>. I guessed there was but one step in Spain from christian or Roman Catholic to heretic or infidel, and said yes. This opened to me every drawer of the sacristy, and even the very pipes of the organ.* A policeman also asked sceptical questions, *having been informed that I had been <u>drawing military plans!</u> You would have laughed to see the careful examination of my little note book,*[27] Anne later played down the incident in a letter to her aunt. As the notebook contained neither sketches of the landscape nor passages in suspicious secret code, she was allowed to mount the mules she had ordered with her guides and ride back to France via Ordesa, San Nicolás de Bujaruelo and Port de Gavarnie. They reached Gavarnie at nine in the evening, spent another night there and walked back to Saint-Sauveur the next day. The only person she told of her experience was Lady Stuart de Rothesay, who welcomed her with some relief, *for it was not quite a lady's expedition.*[28]

Four days later, Anne hiked via the Col du Tourmalet mountain pass – which the Tour de France cyclists ascend every year –
to Bagnères de Bigorre, and booked accommodation for the whole
group in the spa resort. During the three weeks Lady Stuart spent
taking the waters, Anne again got bored. She took her servants
Charles and Cameron back deeper into the Pyrenees to Bagnères
de Luchon on the border with Spain. Despite a dire warning from
Lady Stuart, Anne wanted to give in to the temptation to cross the
border a second time. *The scenery on the Spanish side of the Pyrenees
seems so much bolder and finer than on the French.*[29] She had also taken
a fancy to the constantly knitting shepherds there *and the fine black
eyes, and long black braided hair of the women.*[30] Not taking her leave of
Lady Stuart, she crossed the border at Bosost, spent one night in Las
Bordas and the next in Vielha. The next morning, she was stopped
by two soldiers. The Spanish authorities feared the July Revolution
might cross over from France and were arresting every suspicious
foreigner in the border region. Many years later, an insinuation of
Anne's suggests she was arrested and was to be put into prison in
the provincial capital, Jaca. We do not know whether she talked the
soldiers there round or bribed them, but Anne was then escorted to
Benasque, where she took part in a festival without letting her guards
bother her. *We had music and dancing and singing. The fandango and
bolero delighted me, and the fine wild notes of a young whiskered Don,
who accompanied himself on the guitar, seemed to inspirit us all. I never
in my life ate such fine, large, delicious grapes or drank such rich, strong
wines.* She returned to Bagnères de Bigorre via Port de Venasque and
the Hospice de France.

Lady Stuart greeted her with accusations. She had heard rumours
of Anne's arrest. She excoriated Anne's adventures, which put her
on the spot as the wife of the British ambassador. *I think she does
not much like my character of enterprise.*[31] For the remaining six weeks,
Anne stayed obediently by her side. They travelled via Toulouse,

Narbonne, Montpellier, Nîmes, Arles, Marseille and Toulon to Hyères, where they stayed for ten days. All in all, Anne did not think much of the French Mediterranean coast. *The clear blue sky – the scented air was delightful; but, save the dark green orange-gardens of Hières, there was a glare that blinded me. All is too white.*[32] On 1 November they began their return journey along the Rhône Valley, staying in Lyon and arriving back in Paris on 14 November 1830.

There, it was not only the stumps of felled street trees used for the barricades that reminded them the July Revolution had taken place. The legal and political fallout of the *Trois Glorieuses* almost led France into another war, something which was also feared in other parts of Europe. Belgium had seceded from the United Kingdom of the Netherlands. Anne Lister's friends at the embassy were facing the aftermath of the intrigues the ambassador himself had contrived during the July Revolution. Ignoring the neutral stance imposed on him by the British government, Lord Stuart de Rothesay had tried to manoeuvre another man onto the throne rather than the citizen king Louis Philippe, causing diplomatic difficulties for Britain. When a new government came to power in London under Earl Grey, Lord Stuart was not only recalled from Paris but dismissed from the diplomatic corps entirely. The Stuarts had to leave the embassy by Christmas.

This was a heavy blow to Anne Lister. And another piece of news also scotched her hopes for better social standing: Sibella Maclean had died. *She is the first friend I ever lost. I know not quite what is my feeling; but it is one of great heaviness and heart-sinking, though I know that her release was a mercy, and what all must have desired.*[33] As part of her grieving process, she copied their entire correspondence into her diary.

Instead of savouring her breakthrough to high society, Anne had to take stock of her financial position in the politically turbulent winter of 1830–1831. She and her aunt were spending too much money in Paris. Shibden Hall had brought in an income of £1,062 over the past year. The trip to the south of France had cost Anne £300 instead of the £200 she had expected. There being no sign of a rich match on the horizon, Anne had to try to make more money out of her assets by means of investments and business ideas. Returning to England was all the more expedient because a war would have cut Anne and her aunt off from their funds. For Aunt Anne as well, there was *no alternative but her going back to Shibden; there is so much excitement here; who knows how it will end!*[34]

However, neither of them were keen to return to Shibden Hall, where Jeremy and Marian Lister were now setting the tone. *The servants dine at one o'clock,* Anne learned from a letter from her sister. *My aunt we cannot imagine will object to dine with my father at two o'clock, and you, of course, have a tray, as usual;* Anne had always eaten later than the rest of the family, not valuing their company. *I must say I think your having so many servants, considering the accommodations, a serious inconvenience.* Anne might be able to keep her servant George but she was told to let her maid go, *as they cannot interfere with the house servants, or in the kitchen in any way.* There were no capacities for Anne's and her aunt's laundry so it would have to be dealt with elsewhere, Anne's finer items might possibly be washed early on Thursday mornings. Marian also wanted to put a stop to any plans of her sister's for Anne's own estate. *I think it is absolutely necessary that not a word is said relative to alterations either in the house, or out of the house, my father will not agree to them, he cannot endure them, and I assure you it can but create in both unpleasant feeling.* Marian set rules for the future use of sugar, then asked her sister to give good notice of her arrival. *And now my dear Anne I fancy I have mentioned everything that can signify, for it surely is not needful to say that we shall do all in our power to make my aunt and yourself comfortable, though of course my father must of necessity live in his usual quiet regular way.*[35] Aunt Anne and her niece must have exchanged dark looks after reading this letter. Hoping for a bolthole to escape the inevitable conflict, Anne kept her room on rue St Victor for £17 a year. The two left the city on 23 May 1831. Aunt Anne had spent almost five uninterrupted years in Paris.

Six days later they arrived at Pembroke Lodge in Richmond Park, where they stayed two nights with the dowager Lady Stuart and Vere Hobart. Since their parting in Calais, Anne had attempted to flirt by letter with *meiner lieben lieben Vere*[36] – my dear, dear Vere, writing in German. Vere was open to Anne's suggestion to spend the next winter together in Italy. As a taste of things to come, Anne sent a surprise package to Pembroke Lodge after her departure. *My dear Miss Lister, I have nothing in the world to tell you (which you will say is a promising commencement to my letter)*, but, Vere continued her letter, *I must say how delicious we found your Marseille figs, [...] safe and dry and unsticky, and as sweet to my nose as the figs to my palate. [...] I marvel much at your parting with them so easily, you see how I would have acted in similar circumstances – gobbled them up, to be sure.*[37]

At Shibden Hall, life with Jeremy and Marian was as uncomfortable as anticipated. Against Marian's instructions, Anne immediately had a ground-floor room divided, erecting an interior wall, adding two windows in the exterior wall and installing a fireplace so that Aunt Anne could lead a warm life without having to climb stairs. Having given the necessary orders around the house, Anne fled to York only two and a half weeks later. There, however, her old friends the Duffins and Belcombes bored her, and things were no better at Langton Hall, where she spent three weeks in July with Isabella Norcliffe.

So off Anne went on a spontaneous trip to the Netherlands in early August, taking Mariana Lawton along for lack of alternatives. They spent three weeks visiting Rotterdam, Utrecht, The Hague, Leiden, Haarlem and Amsterdam and admiring localities so *beautifully clean and neat, you might eat off the streets.*[38] Yet it was an *ill-fated journey to Holland.*[39] We do not know what exactly happened, as the ten pages left blank in Anne's diary were never filled. On the return journey they stopped in London, where at the King's Theatre they heard Nicolò Paganini, *whose wondrous fiddling on one string surprised and kept us awake in spite of a rather restless night the night before on board the steamer.* On the way north they visited the cathedrals of Norwich, Ely, Peterborough and Lincoln – but *no ecclesiastical building I have ever seen equals York cathedral.*[40] Anne was back at Shibden Hall on 24 August 1831.

She could stand it only for a few days. On 10 September she left for Manchester to try out a brand new invention: a train ride. The line to Liverpool, regarded as the 'mother of all railways', had been opened a year previously. For the 35-mile stretch, bridges and viaducts had been built, foundations were sunk in a bog, cuttings were made through rock, and a tunnel was dug beneath the centre of Liverpool to extend the tracks all the way to the port. Anne wanted to take a look at this feat of engineering, boarding a train at 7:15 in the morning. *We went twenty miles an hour, but so comfortably and steadily, one might have been writing, if one chose it, all the way.*[41] She reached Liverpool by 9:10. Anne began her return journey an hour later. *Better understanding the thing, got into the very last carriage, a sort of open German waggon (merely the top covered) with glass windows all along the back so that we had a back view all along the line of rail-road – far the best place for seeing.*[42] She was back in Manchester by 12:06. *It was impossible not to be surprised, and gratified at the steam expedition.* As a shareholder in canals, Anne was nonetheless pleased to hear that the plan to extend the railway via Halifax to Leeds had been abandoned for the time being. *Great doubts whether it would pay,* she informed her aunt. *You may therefore set your mind at ease about the Calder & Hebble Navigation.*[43]

From Manchester, a restless Anne travelled on to London, where she once again stayed with the dowager Lady Stuart and Vere Hobart. Anne asked Vere to say for certain whether they would spend the winter together in the south, if possible in Rome and Naples. Vere, however, asked to think it over until 20 October; *Vere is being court-ed*,[44] Lady Stuart told Anne. Anne tried to make the best of the situation and passed the four weeks of waiting with a trip along the south coast of England. On her return to London, Vere was *not making a point of crossing* the water;[45] cholera had reached Europe for the first time, and had already claimed several thousand lives in Vienna and Berlin. As Vere had been told to seek out a milder climate for health reasons, the Stuarts suggested that she and Anne should spend a few months on the Channel at Hastings. Not wanting to return to Shibden Hall and unable to go abroad alone, Anne pretended to welcome the suggestion.

The two women arrived in Hastings on 25 October 1831; they found a house at 15 Pelham Square, which they rented until the following spring. It had two ground-floor reception rooms and two bedrooms above. The rent included cleaning, lighting the stove and preparing meals, otherwise *I have thrown all the cares of housekeeping on Miss Hobart who really manages very nicely, far better than I should do.*[46] They took excursions and Anne walked on the beach a great deal, with or without Vere. Vere helped Anne to learn German, and Anne accompanied the *charmingly singing*[47] Vere on the pianoforte.

Anne was soon coming up with *plans for living together – if Vere can be persuaded to it*, as Phyllis Ramsden paraphrases Anne's coded diary passages. Yet as early as 10 November there was a first *tiff with Vere* over *her callers*. The vicinity to London meant Vere's social life was not interrupted, in fact it seems she had more visitors than ever, with eligible bachelors in particular paying calls, hoping – as did Anne Lister – to use the opportunity to chat with the rich heiress away from the eagle eyes of the dowager Lady Stuart. After *another tiff* things came to a head over Christmas. *AL stays in bed all day, to avoid one of Vere's beaux!* Anne had agreed to spend the winter in damp, rainy, windswept Hastings so as to extract Vere from her family's influence and win her over. Now, though, things could not be further from intimate togetherness in their house by the sea. *Vere thinks AL very 'odd'*, without seeing the sexual character of Anne's 'oddness'. Anne concluded the year with a page and a half of coded notes about *Vere*.

She began the new year *flirting with Vere Hobart* and had a *dalliance with VH* on 8 January, but the very next day *Capt. Cameron calls on VH*. This captain proved to be the most serious of Vere's admirers. *AL rather cross with VH* (16 January), *AL regrets her stay at Hastings with VH, AL takes umbrage at VH* (17 January). *Refuses to come downstairs for VH's caller* (19 January), *re VH – AL in pathetic state of psych. confusion abt. her. AL offended, VH tries to cajole her. Still sulking a bit*. For February too, Ramsden notes a great deal of *scene and reconciliation – peacemaking, another scene etc. (boring & repet.)*. Anne felt *both repelled and attracted* by Vere, but was still *talking to VH. abt possible travelling arrangements*. March sees long encrypted passages day after day, *comments on VH*, which Phyllis Ramsden summarises with the words: *AL unhappy – cannot accept that she has failed to captivate VH*. In mid-March, Anne allowed herself *more histrionics with VH – VH quite unmoved*.

Still, Anne did persuade Vere to think about the material aspect of a lasting relationship with her: *asking questions abt AL's income, etc.* and *joking talk abt their money*.[48] Vere Hobart believed Anne Lister had an income of £5,000 a year, an assumption the mistress of Shibden Hall chose neither to confirm nor deny. *Then jokes with Miss H. that our match would be off on account of pecuniary matters and we both laughed and called each other mercenary*. On the morning of 15 April, Anne summed up their 'marriage negotiations' before they went to church together: *Well if it was not for the petticoats the thing would be clear enough. Yes that it would be said she. Perhaps said I laughingly it is pretty much the same thing in spite of them.* It was not; *how little dream what so few hours would bring forth.*[49]

For Captain Cameron came calling again that day and Vere *asked him to dinner – the murder is out – we talked it over – she will not say 'no' – so it is done.* Donald Cameron hinted to Vere even before the meal that he wanted to propose. *Twenty minutes with Miss H–, laughing and joking, but found the tears starting as I kissed her forehead and ran away. 'What, are you going?' said she – but I was off, saying, 'Oh, I dare not look behind me.'* In the privacy of her room, Anne cried her eyes out. For five months she had done nothing but court Vere, all in vain. She pulled herself together for dinner. *On going down, saw them on the sofa together & both looking so satisfied, I suspected how it was. The moment we left the dining room about eight, he staying behind quarter-hour, she told me it was all over - he made his offer in a very flattering manner to her, done it very well & she had accepted him.* Anne brought herself to say *I was very glad of it. She gave me her two cheeks to kiss. I kissed both, first one then the other, but said nothing – she moralized a little – said how a moment changed our whole lives, but she thought she should not repent.* Anne drank a polite cup of tea with them both *& soon came upstairs – a little before nine – & left them to their happiness. What a sudden change for us all – for me too. She will go to Italy, but not with me.*[50] *Cried & sobbed bitterly for an hour last night, then began to be more composed, but could not sleep till three – awoke about six – up at seven – to the pot – long very thick piece with some difficulty.*

Her pride returned that morning. *I neither want her pity nor her ridicule, both of which I might count upon, did she know my folly. Well, one word has made greater separation between us than thousands of miles could have done. She is no longer anything to me. My eyes are swelled up – I am not fit to be seen. Perhaps washing will do good. But I shall get over it.*[51] It was not easy. Phyllis Ramsden notes on the next few days: *AL v. upset – scenes, reconciliations – do – more sparring – still arguing – ditto.*[52] Vere remarked that *we now clashed more than ever. However,*

it came out when I said Donald was a lucky man, that she thought [...] I
thought she was making a <u>mésalliance</u> & I might give that impression to
others. [...] She is more in love with the novelty & nice-ness of being mar-
ried than with Donald himself & she is shockingly touchy. [...] She has a
damned bad temper – suspicious, jealous, incredulous – I am far better
without her.[53]

Vere's engagement meant all Anne's plans for the future were obsolete. They gave up the house only a week later. Although cholera had
spread to France and England, Anne still wanted to travel. *I am taught*
to think cholera an <u>epidemic respecter</u> of fearless, temperate, flannelbelted
persons, and shall not therefore let it disturb my plans at all.[54] She ordered
three 380-page diaries from her bookseller Whitley in Halifax, plus a
dozen 50-page notebooks; she wanted to stay away a long time and see,
experience and write down a great deal.

One thing Anne still needed, though, was a travelling companion
– for company, respectability and not least to cut costs. Only one
day after Vere Hobart accepted Donald Cameron's proposal, Anne
wrote to the *always good humoured*[55] Lady Caroline Duff Gordon,
with whom she had undertaken her successful trip along the Rhine
in 1829. Lady Gordon had made several travel suggestions since.
Besides tho' <u>married</u> to each other, we could be a <u>fashionable</u> pair and
be as <u>independent</u> as we chose and each go her own way. What do you
think? Anne had not taken up the idea, although she *should have has-*
tened to accept the most amiable offer of <u>Marriage</u> that surely ever was
made.[56] The reason at the time – Vere Hobart – was no longer a hin-
drance. Anne accompanied Vere back to London on 25 April 1832
and went straight to Lady Gordon in Cheltenham. The lady's ironic
understanding of marriage, however, was so modern that it included
separate accounts, even when travelling. That was exactly what Anne
did not want. *I have difficulty enough as to the usages of high society.*
[...] But I have ten times more on account of money. Anne had wasted a

small fortune over the past few months on the south coast, first on a trip to kill time and then with Vere in Hastings. *My high society plans fail – unknown & without connections, money should abound. I have had my whim – tried the thing – & pretty much it has cost me. I shall in future perhaps do more wisely & within my compass.*[57] That same night, she wrote to Aunt Anne to announce her imminent arrival at Shibden Hall; *all things considered, it seems for the best to look after business concerns without further loss of time.*[58]

Ann

1832–1840

Anne Lister returned to Shibden Hall on 7 May 1832, not having spent more than a few weeks there since 1826. Marian, Anne complained, crowed over the household like the *cock of the dung-hill.*[1] She had had enough of her sister, even on the day of her arrival; *we shall never agree – the less we see of each other the better – I like her less & less.*[2] Jeremy Lister did not speak a word to his prodigal daughter. Marian informed Anne of his opinion of her. *My father does not like my walk etc.*[3] Anne avoided joint mealtimes and only spent an hour or so with her family in the evenings for her aunt's sake; *my aunt the best, but with all her goodness to me, sadly tiresome as a companion – the rest insufferable in point of vulgarity.*[4] *I must get away somewhere – the money is the thing – I must invent something or other very shortly – but off I must go.*[5]

Two weeks after her return, Anne escaped to her usual exile at Langton Hall with Isabella Norcliffe, where Mariana Lawton also put in an appearance. Anne explained to her oldest friends and lovers that she dreamed of a *dame de compagnie […] who is sensible, & comfortably well-mannered,* who would be prepared to *go where I like.* She should *do no work but help me to dress, to take care of my things, & make others do the rest. […] I don't mean to sit at a table with the woman who does my dirty work*. Isabella and Mariana could no doubt imagine what else Anne expected of such a woman, *laughing and quizzing me.*[6] Her grinning friend informed Anne on that occasion of *the appellation Isabella says people give me – of tuft-hunter.* Did people know about Anne Lister's pubic hair collection? Anne would have had to pay her *dame de compagnie*, which gave the whole matter something *too anomalous, rather sleazy, & I should [...] give it up,*[7] just as the idea of *a peasant 'wife',*[8] which she had nurtured over the past years of involuntary celibacy. In her mind she went through possible candidates of her acquaintance, *the MacKenzies, Lady Elizabeth Thackray & Miss Hall – to try first for Miss MacK–. Thought of Miss Freeman & Miss Walker of Lidgate as people here. Louisa Belcombe & Miss Price in York, besides Miss Salmon. Surely I shall get some companion by-and-by.*[9]

The top billing went to twenty-nine-year-old Ann Walker from the neighbouring village of Lightcliffe, twelve years Anne's junior. The Walkers were 'new money' to Anne, owners of steam-powered weaving mills, and thus below the classes she chose to mix with. Ann Walker's grandfather had built an empire as a cloth-maker, trader and landowner. The family had three properties in Lightcliffe. Ann was born in 1803, and grew up with her older sister Elizabeth, and younger brother John at the family's main home, Crow Nest, a large Georgian manor house surrounded by spacious grounds. It was at an evening occasion at the Walkers' home that Anne Lister had first worn black, fifteen years previously. Anne had made an impression on young Ann; four years later, *Miss Ann Walker of Crownest* [sic] *overtook me, having run herself almost out of breath. Walked with her as far as the Lidget* [sic] *entrance to their own grounds & got home at 6:40. Made myself, as I fancied, very agreeable & was particularly civil & attentive in my manner. I really think the girl is flattered by it & likes me. She wished me to drink tea with them. I hoped for another walk to Giles House & the readiness she expressed shewed that my proposition was by no means unwelcome. She has certainly no aversion to my conversation*

& company. After parting I could not help smiling to myself & saying flirting with this girl has done me good. It is heavy work to live without women's society & I would far rather while away an hour with this girl, who has nothing in the world to boast but good humour, than not flirt at all.[10] When they took that second walk a year later, Anne did admire Ann's *pretty flaxen hair*[11] and also found her *very civil, etc, but she is a stupid vulgar girl. [...] I have no intention of taking more walks, or letting the acquaintance go one jot further.*[12]

That had been ten years earlier. Since then, a series of deaths and blows of fate had put an end to Ann Walker's sheltered life. Her parents both died within six months of each other in 1823. Her father left a complicated forty-eight-page will designed to prevent his assets from being divided for generations to come. The main heir to the family fortune was nineteen-year-old John; each of the sisters received a smaller share, from which they gained an income of about £600 a year, as Anne Lister knew. With these handsome sums in mind, John Walker had ruled that his daughters' inheritance was for their *sole and separate use*, not to be transferred to *any person or persons with who she may intermarry.*[13] John Walker might have anticipated dowry hunters but he had not reckoned with his daughters' naivety, longing for love or susceptibility to emotional blackmail. Against the express will of her trustees, in 1828 Elizabeth married George Mackay Sutherland, *a subaltern infantry officer without a sixpence*[14] stationed in Halifax, with whom she moved to Scotland. On his demand, Elizabeth transferred all her personal assets to him, even though her father had stipulated they were for her alone. Captain Sutherland's lucky ticket turned into the first prize when his young brother-in-law John died out of the blue on his honeymoon in 1830. As he had not left a will, the entire inheritance was divided between Elizabeth and Ann: business shares, stocks, properties and land to the value of some £45,000. George Sutherland harassed his wife, heavily pregnant with her second child, until she signed to place *the property coming to you, as one of the Coheiresses of your Brother, at the complete Disposal of Captain Sutherland.*[15] He even tried to get his hands on his sister-in-law's share – if not for himself, then at least for his first-born son Sackville. The unmarried Ann Walker found it hard to resist and therefore made her young nephew her heir in 1831. From then on, *the Sutherlands and Miss Walker and the Priestleys are all queer together,*[16] by which Anne Lister meant they were estranged.

The arguments over the inheritance depressed Ann Walker, and during that very summer of 1832 when she ended up on Anne Lister's list, she suffered another major loss: her secret fiancé Mr Fraser died unexpectedly. The young woman seemed thrown off track, with rumours of *insanity* and *mental derangement* circulating about her. *Her mind warped on religion – she thinks she cannot live – has led a wicked life etc.*[17] Rich, without protection, confused and alone, Ann had never seemed more attractive to Anne Lister. She paid her a neighbourly visit lasting an hour and three-quarters on 10 August 1832. *We got on very well together. Thought I, as I have several times done before of late, shall I try & make up to her?* A week later, Anne *called en passant on Miss Walker of Lidgate – & sat with her tête-à-tête from 10 to 1! Talked of household economy – got on very well.* [...] *Thought I, 'she little dreams what is in my mind – to make up to her – she has money and this might make up for rank.'*[18] She calculated *the object of my choice has perhaps three thousand a year or near it, probably two-thirds at her own disposal. No bad pis aller – even if I liked her less – a better take than Lady Gordon or perhaps Vere either.*[19]

Whereas the Listers had previously called on the Walkers only rarely and out of neighbourly duty (their properties being adjacent), Anne now began visiting Ann Walker every few days. *Miss W– & I do certainly get on marvellously – she seems quite confidential & glad to see me.*[20] Ann Walker, who had literally chased after Anne Lister eleven years previously, enjoyed the undivided attention she now received from her neighbour; *she always thought I had a tincture of romance about me.*[21] She came in her carriage for a visit to Shibden Hall, conversed with Aunt Anne for a quarter of an hour for politeness' sake and then took Anne along to town with her to go calling and running errands. At Throp the gardener's, *I am to choose shrubs for her & she for me.* Then Ann dropped Anne off again at Shibden Hall. The two had never spent a day like that together before; according to Anne Lister it lasted from 11:50 until 5:30.

Two days later, Anne *incurred a cross thinking of Miss Walker – first time.*[22] To her chagrin, Ann went on holiday to the Lake District with her best friend Catherine Rawson soon afterwards. Anne used her absence to work on her new landscape garden. While there was little she could change about Shibden Hall, she wanted to make the grounds more impressive. Inspired by her travels and especially by the Llangollen Ladies' Plâs Newydd, she transformed the gently sloping fields between the house and the Red Beck stream about five hundred yards away into a single open space. She had the hedges torn out, the fields changed to lawns, unattractive trees felled, and planted oaks, horse chestnuts and yews, roses, juniper, and, along the stream, willows, in groups or as eye-catching solitaires. Anne spent every morning commanding a small army of workers, who put into practice what she'd read the evening before in John Claudius Loudon's *Encyclopaedia of Gardening,* a parting gift from Ann Walker. She was fond of helping out with the work herself. Jeremy and Marian eyed the changes with suspicion, convinced *I shall not have income to keep these things up. 'I shall find it out,' she* [Marian] *said, 'by & by.' She expects to be the richest, & that I shall be obliged to sell.*[23]

Anne's highly strung sister, eccentric father and rheumatic aunt might well have been off-putting for Ann Walker. To seduce her, Anne needed a place where they could be undisturbed – and so she had a little cabin built with a view of the lily bank of the Red Beck, in the lower part of her landscape garden. Upon stone foundations, walls of young oaks were built and covered with moss. The little house had

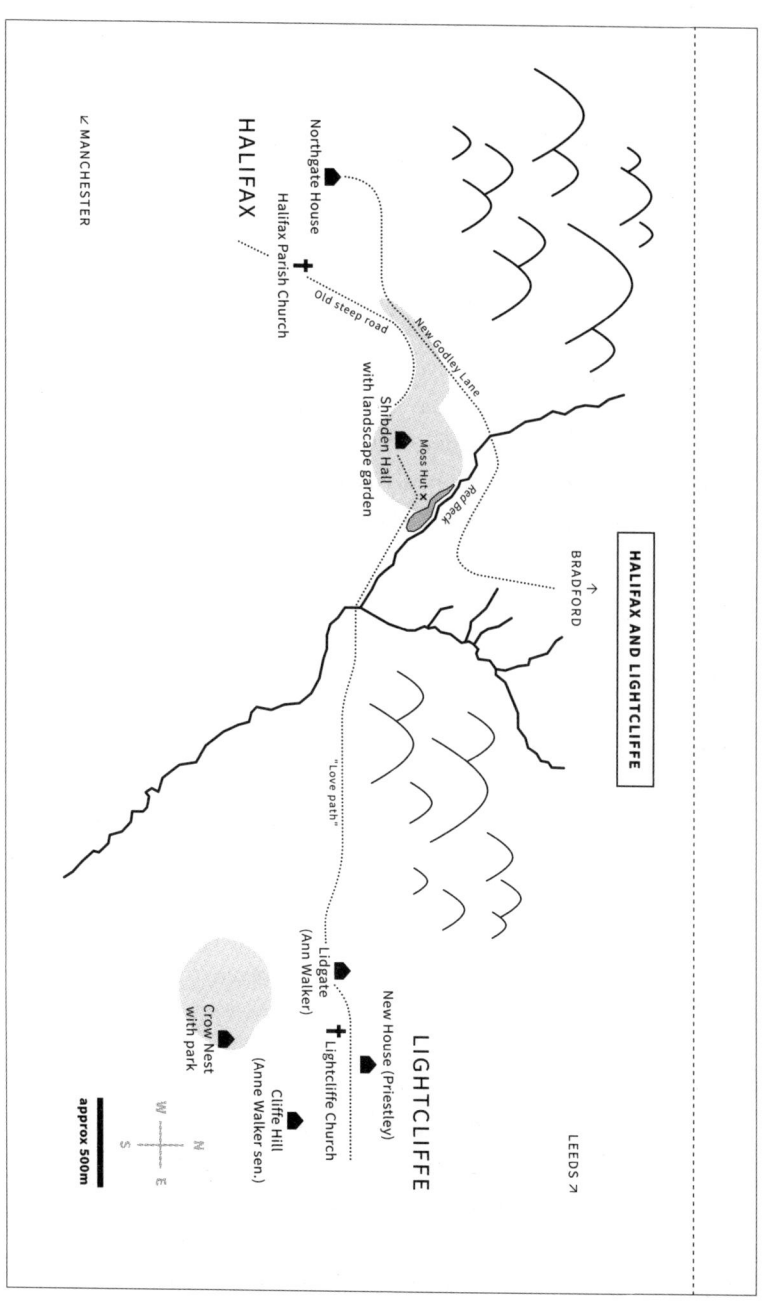

14 Map of Halifax and Lightcliffe, Laura Fronterré.

a roof of rushes, and Anne planted evergreen yews and cherry laurels to keep it out of sight of Shibden Hall. Always fond of innuendo, she also planted plenty of sycamores, known since Shakespeare's days as 'sick of amour' trees. Everything was ready to receive Ann Walker.

The latter *had always an idea that her thirtieth year would be a very important one.*[24] Thinking of Anne Lister every day during her stay in the Lake District, she began to connect that idea with her. She had hardly returned home on 25 September before Anne Lister paid her a call. She had been fantasising lustfully about Ann again before getting up in the morning, and took the 'love path' that would soon be much used in both directions. She walked through her landscape garden, past the moss hut to the stream, along the Red Beck to the end of the garden, climbed a steep hill to the road, walked down to the next valley and back up to Lightcliffe. After almost two miles, which she covered in just over half an hour, Anne Lister reached the smallest of the Walkers' buildings to the left of the road, Lidgate, where Ann Walker lived alone. On the right of the road was the entrance gate to Crow Nest, the vacant family seat. A little way further along the road was the Priestleys' New House, where Anne had once been a regular caller. Eliza Priestley was Anne's oldest friend, and knew Anne wished for *a lady for my future companion.*[25] Her husband was Ann Walker's cousin and estate manager. Not far from them lived Ann Walker's godmother of the same name, at the spacious Cliffe Hill.

Ann Walker was so glad of the visit that Anne turned up again the next morning at the same time. She came for breakfast at eight, stayed for lunch at two and then showed Ann her new moss hut, which had a solid floor and light garden furniture; *said I had built the hut on purpose for her.*[26] Ann Walker was delighted and *sat & sat in the moss house, hardly liking to move. Of course I made myself agreeable.* Anne steered the conversation round to travel and Ann *seems to take all I say for gospel* [...] – *she consults me about her affairs* and *falls into my views of things admirably.* At dusk, she walked Ann back to

Lidgate; *on parting she said she knew not when she had spent so pleasant a day – I believe her.* On her walk home, a satisfied Anne thought: *she is more in for it than she thinks,* and envisaged the future. *We shall have money enough. She will look up to me & soon feel attached & I, after all my turmoils, shall be steady.* To her surprise, she noted: *I really did feel rather in love with her in the hut, & as we returned. I shall pay due court for the next few months – & after all, I really think I can make her happy & myself too.* [...] *How strange the fate of things! If after all, my companion for life should be Miss Walker.*[27]

The next day, Anne retired to her new moss hut and began work on her future with Ann Walker. *Incurred a cross thinking of Miss Walker – I shall think myself into being in love with her – I am already persuaded I like her quite well enough for comfort.*[28] *I begin to think her at times pretty.*[29] Ann Walker, for her part, had no need to persuade herself of anything. Beguiled by Anne, she walked the love path on a surprise visit to Shibden Hall the next day, allegedly to get Anne's advice on a tenant. Anne took her straight to her hut and whispered so many sweet nothings that they were *bordering on love-making.* [...] *Our liaison is now established,* she believed, and vowed to *make the poor girl as happy as I can, so that she shall have no reason to repent.* [...] *I myself am surprised at my so rapid success & at the novelty of my situation. Perhaps after all, she will make me really happier than any of my former flames – at all rates we shall have money enough & I don't fancy she will be close or stingy or <u>cold</u> to me.*[30]

Unlike Sibella Maclean and Vere Hobart, from the outset Ann Walker understood and welcomed Anne Lister's advances. She told Anne the next day *she had often looked at all her things & said what was the use of having them with nobody to enjoy them with her? She said it all seemed now like a dream to her.* During the night, she had been thinking *whether she could make me happy & be a companion for me. She said how happy she now felt & looked so, as we sat on the sofa.* Anne lied, saying she *had made up my mind in May – the moment I was at*

15 Halifax 1836. This was the view Anne Lister had on her way from Shibden Hall into town. Halifax Parish Church is in the foreground; the bridge on the right is next to Northgate. Copperplate by N. Whittock. Calderdale Leisure Services, Shibden Hall, Halifax.

liberty to do so — so that it had been well enough digested by me, however sudden it might seem to her — & that I gave my happiness into her keeping in perfect security.[31]

During their next five-hour rendezvous in the moss hut two days later, Anne told Ann that *if she felt a quarter the regard for me I did for her, I should be satisfied — but if she ever should feel half, I should be more than happy.* Then she made a marriage proposal of sorts to her. *Proposed her living with me at Shibden,* the advantages of which *I advocated skilfully &, I think successfully.* [...] *Said that less money needed be paid out than she perhaps imagined. Explained that there would be more éclat & independence even for her at Shibden.* She also revealed her financial situation, claiming she *expected to have ultimately two thousand a year* — a significant exaggeration. *I then asked if she thought*

ANN: NEIGHBOURS

she could be happy enough with me, to give up all thought of leaving me.

This proposal put Ann Walker in something of a dilemma. She was accustomed to very different comforts to Anne and hoped to live at Cliffe Hill after her aunt's death; *she spoke of her great attachment to the latter.* Moving into the down-at-heel Shibden Hall must have seemed an absurd idea. She ignored Anne's attempt to open financial negotiations and *never let slip her own income.* Instead, she explained *she had said that she would never marry – but that, as she had once felt an inclination not to keep to this, she could not yet positively say she should never feel the same inclination again. She should not like to deceive me & begged not to answer just now. I said she was quite right – praised her judiciousness – that my esteem and admiration were only heightened by it – that no feelings of selfishness should make me even wish for my happiness rather than hers – that I would give her six months [...] to make up her mind.*[32]

There was nothing that would make Ann Walker come round more easily, Anne was convinced, than good sex. She fell back on her old trick in the moss hut: *On the plea of feeling her pulse, I took her hand & held it some time – to which she shewed no objection.*[33] In fact, Ann was just waiting for her neighbour to put her words into deeds. When Anne came to Lidgate at 10 in the morning on 4 October, *I had my arm on the back of the sofa – she leaned on it – looked as if I might be affectionate, and it ended in her lying on my arm all the morning & my kissing her & she returning it with such a long continued passionate or nervous mumbling kiss – that we got on as far as we, by daylight, mere kissing, could – I thinking to myself, 'Well, this is rather more than I expected – of course she means to take me.' Yet on pressing the hardness of my case in having to wait six months, & begging for a less length of probation – she held out, saying her mind was quite unmade up – & I must not hope too much for fear of disappointment. Yet she asked me to dine with her at five & stay all night.* Having reacted with such reserve to Anne's proposal, Ann Walker was very open to her sexual advances, suggesting her own bed for the last step rather than Anne's romantic but uncomfortable moss hut. Unlike Anne, she did live alone in her house, after all. But Anne could only accept the invitation to dinner: *Very sorry could not do the latter while my father was unwell & my sister absent. Thought I, 'I see I shall get all I want of her person, if I stay all night.'*

So as not to arouse suspicion, Anne hurried home and returned to Ann's house later that afternoon. Her neighbour had dolled herself up and *put on an evening gown*. After dinner, her servant left the two of them alone and *she sat on my knee, & I did not spare kissing & pressing, she returning it as in the morning. Yet still I was not to hope too much – she said I was infatuated – when the novelty was over I should not feel the same – & I might not find her a companion for me.* Ann Walker seems to have been observing her neighbour's habits for many years. *We were so affectionate – we let the lamp go out – long continued (mumbling moist) kissing, I prest her bosom – then finding no resistance & the lamp being out – let my hand wander lower down, gently getting to her queer – still no resistance – so I whispered surely she could care for me some little? 'Yes.' Then gently whispered she would break my heart if she left me – she then said I should think her very cold (how the devil could I?) & it came out: how that her affections had been engaged to one of the best men – that they could not be transferred so soon – for he had only been dead just three months – & she got to crying.* At the moment of surrendering herself to Anne Lister, Ann Walker thought of her deceased secret fiancé, Mr Fraser, and was overcome by the contradiction of lust and grief. *I begged a thousand pardons etc etc – declared it was only thro' ignorance that I had ever been so sanguine etc etc – & thinking a scene would then come beautifully from me, seemed in a paroxysm of stupid tho' deeply sighing grief and stifled tears & declared myself hopeless – said my conduct (or, rather, my hoping) was madness. All this was very prettily done. I however promised to see her tomorrow & we parted in all the pathos due to the occasion.*[34]

Anne was equally surprised by Ann's advance and retreat. *I scarce know what to make of her. Is she maddish? I must mind what I say to her. Be cautious. Hang it! The queer girl puzzles me.* She was particularly disturbed by Ann's open desire. *'Cold,' thought I! 'No sign of that – more likely, she will try what I can do for her before giving the answer, & I don't think I can do enough.'* She had said that *if she once made up her mind she thought herself as much as married to me for life. Well, I may try her, or rather let her try me – & go what lengths the first night I sleep there. She certainly gulled me in that I never dreampt of her being the passionate little person I find her, spite of her calling herself 'cold.' Certainly I should have never ventured such lengths just yet without all the encouragement she gave me. I shall now turn sentimentally melancholy & put on all the air of romantic hopelessness. If I do this well, I may turn her to pity.*[35] Anne was appalled that Ann had accepted her declarations of love and *thinks me over head-&-ears with her – she is mistaken – her mumbling kisses have cured me of that.*[36]

Anne set off for Lidgate the very next morning. *I explained how sorry I was – would have been the last to have intruded on her feelings etc etc – under circumstances of such recent grief,* and renewed her promise to wait six months for Ann's answer to her marriage proposal. Ann had composed herself overnight. *She took me up to her room – I kissed her & she pushed herself so to me, I rather felt & might have done it as much as I pleased. She is man-keen enough.*[37] Over the next few days they ventured ever further, but with differing intentions. Anne was interested in Ann's money; Ann wanted sex. *It seems I can have her as my mistress & may amuse myself – she kissed me & lay on my arm as before, evidently excited.* Anne kissed her back *& pressed very tenderly & got my right hand up her petticoats to her queer, but not to the skin – could not get thro' her thick knitted drawers, for tho' she never once attempted to put my hand away, she held her thighs too tight together for me.* [...] *I wonder what she will say when I have once fairly <u>done my best for her</u>.* Ann Walker clearly wondered the same thing, and *asked me to* *spend the whole day & stay the night on Tuesday.*[38]

Yet this visit did not lead to what Ann Walker wanted either. *Kissing & pressing her as usual. – She put the blind down – lucky – James had come in on trivial errands twice. And Mrs Priestley came at four – I had jumped in time & was standing by the fire – but Ann looked red & I pale, & Mrs P– must see we were not particularly expecting or desiring company. She looked vexed, jealous & annoyed.*[39] Anne's best friend, Mrs Priestley, knew precisely what was going on. In days gone by, she had not only tolerated Anne's preference for women but even defended it. *Speaking of my oddity, Mrs Priestley said she always told people I was natural, but she thought nature was in an odd freak when she made me. I looked significantly & replied the remark was fair & just & true.*[40] Now, however, that it was her husband's cousin at stake – and her assets – Mrs Priestley's tolerance came to an end. *She only staid a few minutes & went off in supressed rage.* Ann Walker did not care. She was not on good terms with her cousin Mr Priestley, a trustee of her father's will. *Miss W– laughed & said* we *were well-matched – we soon got to kissing again on the sofa. At last I got my right hand up her petticoats & after much fumbling got thro' the opening of her drawers & touched (first time) the hair & skin of her queer – she never offered the least resistance.* In the midst of the action, Ann asked: *'If you never had any attachment, who taught you to kiss?' I laughed & said how nicely that was said – then answered that nature taught me. I could have replied, 'And who taught* you*?'*[41]

Anne Lister was vexed from the very beginning by the way Ann did not hide her desire. She always found it unpleasant not to be the first lover in a woman's life and thus have to face comparison. She much preferred virgins. *Damn her, she is an old hand & has nor shame nor anything – she certainly takes all very much like one of the initiated.*[42] Her suspicions alighted on Catherine Rawson, with whom Ann had just been in the Lake District, and whom Anne had tutored years ago in Latin and Greek. At the time, Anne had pronounced *I do not think*

SH: 7/ML/644/1

I have considered & re considered
all you so kindly said to me on
Saturday, or however painful what to
me to tell you, yet I must tell you
that as my convictions with respect to
its being wrong & against my duty remain,
I think we had better not meet again
till I have read my sisters letter; for
my wretchedness only brings misery
upon you, & mine seems to increase
every day — I know not what to do for
the best —

Monday Dec. 24th 1832.

16 Letter from Ann Walker to Anne Lister, 24 December 1832; West
Yorkshire Archive Service, Calderdale, SH: 7/ML/644/1.

Catherine will make much out as a scholar. She seems better suited to be made a beauty of.[43] Now that Ann Walker mentioned having previously talked to Catherine Rawson about moving in together, Anne suspected *Catherine's classics might have taught her the trick of debauching Miss W—. Yes, Miss W— has been taught by someone. [...] Have she and Catherine been playing tricks?*[44]

Anne preferred to go home than stay overnight, having been caught almost in flagrante by Mrs Priestley. *How changed my mind,* she noted; *I am cured,* especially as Ann, like Vere before her, simply did not respond to her proposal. *I care not for her – tho' her money would suit.*[45] And so Anne went to breakfast at Lidgate again three days later, *love-making & kissing* Ann all day long on the sofa. *As it became dusk we crept closer & I, without any resistance, got (for the first time) right middle finger up her queer. [...] She whispered that she loved me – then afterwards said her mind was quite unmade up & bade me not be sanguine.*[46] Anne, who had taken many women only *on my own terms,* as lovers in other words, was appalled at the role reversal that Ann Walker undertook; *she would like to keep me on, so as to have the benefit of my intimacy without any real joint concern.*[47]

On Ann's third invitation for Anne to stay the night, she finally relented. After a day spent paying calls and shopping together in Halifax, they spent a *very cozy evening* at Lidgate and went upstairs at 10:15. Anne undressed *& then went to her room – had her on my knee a few minutes & then got into bed, she making no objection – & staid with her till twelve & three-quarters – rubbing gently. [...] She seemed so tender & able to bear so little (I think she was more <u>intact</u> & innocent & virgin than I had latterly surmised) that I contented myself with handling her gently & love-making. She feared she should never be able to satisfy me. [...] She whispered to me in bed how gentle & kind I was to her, & faintly said she loved me, 'or else how can you think,' said she, 'that I should let you do as you do?' In fact, tho' I never allow that I have 'hope', surely I ought not to despair – she surely cannot go on as she does, meaning to say 'no'.*

Ann Walker had had to ask three times before Anne finally went to bed with her. In the morning, though, she woke up far from happy. *Miss W– not well – lay on the sofa all the day & I sat by her very affectionately – gave her her gruel.* Ann thought *she was suffering from having had me last night*, and struggled (or appeared to struggle) to recover from the loss of her virginity. She *never thought I should have made her suffer so much – would never let me do so again. I took all this very well,*[48] just as she took in her stride the information Ann had given her that night about her income: Ann received £2,500 a year but could only spend £1,000 of it freely; that was far less than Anne had assumed. They had both got what they had been waiting for – Ann sex, and Anne hard figures – but they both woke disappointed.

And yet they both wanted more. In the nights that followed, Anne caressed Ann and *gave her, as she owned, pleasure,*[49] until she managed to shorten the proposed waiting period: Ann Walker now wanted to decide by the end of the year whether to live with Anne, and was toying with the idea of travelling with her in January. She had set this time aside for her friends the Ainsworths, but Mrs Ainsworth died suddenly in a carriage accident. Ann's shock was doubled by the advances made to her by the freshly widowed Mr Ainsworth, asking her for a secret correspondence. A tearful Ann gave Anne his letter to read. *'Oh ho,' thought I, 'all this is very clear' – and I candidly told her what I thought,* namely that Mr Ainsworth aimed to win Ann's heart before her relatives could send him packing. To Anne's surprise, however, Ann did not feel capable of rejecting his advances outright. *This led to my saying that she must now decide between Mr A– and me,* and gave her until Monday to do so. Anne made this ultimatum on a Thursday.

Ann panicked. *Fearing she should not be so happy with him as she might have been – never knew till now how much she was attached to me – should make comparisons, too, in poor Mr Fraser's favour – and torturing herself with all the miseries of not knowing what to do.* After a good two weeks of sex with Anne, she also *felt repugnance to forming any connection with the other sex*. She not only asked Anne to stay with her that night but also *promises me a lock of queer's hair in the morning – and I am to cut it myself if I like!*[50] *We fretted ourselves to sleep last night – she lay on me as usual to warm her stomach & then lay in my arms – but I was perfectly quiet & never touched her queer.* [...] *Just before getting up, I got scissars* [sic] *– took up her night-chemise & attempted to cut the lock, but kissed her queer – gave her the scissars – said she must cut it for me herself – & threw myself into the great chair. She soon gave me the* golden *lock – threw herself on the chair by me. We wept (& kissed).* Ann was overwhelmed by her feelings for Anne. She had been certain of Anne's love and it was only her move of using Mr Ainsworth to put her under pressure that made it clear to her what she had to lose. *She hung upon me & cried & sobbed aloud at parting;* according to Anne's conditions, they were not to see each other again until the day of her decision. *'Well,' said I to myself as I walked off, 'a pretty scene we have had, but surely I care not much & shall take my time of suspense very quietly – & be easily reconciled either way.'*[51]

Ann Walker, however, spent a tormented weekend. On the Monday she sent Anne a small purse containing two pieces of paper, one saying 'yes' and the other 'no', along with a letter. *I have endeavoured to express myself in the most gentle & delicate manner possible & rather to imply than say what I really mean. It is a most difficult note to write – and, had it been possible, I would rather have been silent for the present – until grief has become more subdued.* [...] *I find it impossible to make up my own mind. For the last twelve months I have lived under circumstances of no common moment, and with my health impaired & with vivid regrets of the past, I feel that I have not the power fairly to exercise my own judgment. My heart would not allow me to listen to any proposal of marriage, and this is in effect the same. I would simply go on & leave the event to God.*

And on these grounds, I once thought of asking if you would act upon *your original intention, and consent for us to travel together for a few months. Again I feel this unfair to <u>you</u>. I promised an answer — and I am at your mercy. I have written the words on a slip of paper & put them in the purse. I have implicit confidence in your judgment, & if you still think it better to decide today, the paper you draw first must be the word — or, if you prefer, let your good aunt draw. And then we neither of us decide — you may <u>think this an evasive termination of my promise</u>. Forgive me, for it is really all I can say. Having heard you once say that in one case* [i.e. no] *I must give you up as a friend, I find myself as incapable of consenting to this, as I am for deciding under my present feelings what is to be my future course of life. Whatever may be the event, I shall always remain your faithful & affectionate A. W.*

Anne realised she had asked too much of Ann. Ignoring the pouring rain, she took the letter and purse straight back to Lidgate. *She was nervous when we met — but I looked calm & we soon got on tolerably — we kissed and she was affectionate as usual, as far as I would let her.* Anne explained that she *could not leave to the decision of chance what ought only to be decided by her* [Ann's] *own heart.*[52] Having been unable to force the decision, Anne was prepared to wait until 2 January, as agreed. Two days later, Ann surprised Anne with a confession of an earlier relationship with Mr Ainsworth: *if she married him, it would be from duty — I pressed for explanation & discovered that she felt bound to him by some indiscretion — he had taught her to kiss, but they had never gone so far as she & I had done.* Anne thought such loyalty ridiculous. *I reasoned her out of all feeling of duty or obligation towards a man who had taken such base advantage. She said there was no other obstacle between us — & she should be happier with me.* [...] *I asked her if she was sure of this. 'Yes, quite.' 'Well, then,' said I, 'consider half-an-hour & decide.' In half the time she asked if I would take her & gave me her word & 'Yes' & hoped I should find her faithful & constant to me. Thus, in a moment that I thought not of, was I accepted & the matter settled. I kissed her.*[53]

But Anne had got her hopes up too soon. When she wanted to seal their engagement with a ring ordered discreetly in York, Ann sent it back. *I cannot take it, my love, till I have fewer torments of conscience than I endure at present.*[54] Anne had managed to set aside Ann's scruples over Mr Fraser and Mr Ainsworth, but the new problem was more serious. *She had doubted whether it was right to engage herself to me, if this sort of thing was so bad between two men, it must be so. I answered this in my usual way: it was my natural & undeviating feeling etc etc.*[55] Ann was also *much troubled with anonymous letters,*[56] warning her of Anne Lister — who had been attacked again that autumn. *An impertinent fellow with a great stick in his hand [...] made a catch at my queer. 'God damn you,' said I & pushed him off.*[57] Unsettled by such attacks and by reading homophobic Bible passages, Ann Walker could not fully enjoy the sex she so desired with Anne. *Talking last night till two — said she should not suffer for me — so declared I would not grubble her — she excited as she lay on me & I pretended great difficulty in keeping my word — I felt her over her chemise & this all but did the job for her. She owned she could not help it & that now she had got into the way of it. [...] Thought she should be getting wrong with somebody when I went away. 'Oh,' thought I, 'this is plain enough.' Yet still she talked of her sufferings because she thought it wrong to have this connection with me. We argued this point.* Anne suspected the problem lay elsewhere: *But she is quite man-keen, & the wrong with me is that I am not enough for her.*[58]

Anne thought, *in spite of all her declarations to the contrary, I begin to suspect he* [Mr Ainsworth] *really has deflowered & enjoyed her.* When they made love, Anne always had the feeling *she must have some man or other — I can never satisfy her.*[59] Against her usual way, Anne had not so far used her euphemism *kiss* when writing about Ann, instead speaking only of *gently grubbling.* They had not yet been truly uninhibited and passionate with one another. *Said to myself as I left her, 'What a goose she is.'*[60] *How can such a girl make me happy?*[61]

The cooler Anne became, the more honest she was towards Ann.

This proved more successful than all her false declarations of love and attempts at emotional blackmail. Ann was *evidently courting me more as I court her less.* Initially, that took effect in bed too. *Without any persuasion she came to me at once last night – and, forgetting all the wrong, she lay in my arms all the night – and had three good long grubblings, nothing loth.* [...] *We awoke at seven and talked till eight – now that she sees me inclined to be off, she wants to be on again, said no more about the wrong, but began to think she was throwing away her happiness & said she could not bear to part with me.*[62] Anne raised the pressure on Ann by insinuating for the *first time, that our present intercourse, without any tie between us, must be as wrong as any other transient connection.*[63] It was not that lesbian sex itself was a sin, in other words, but that all sex before marriage was. This argument did stir something in Ann Walker, but she still could not bring herself to say 'I do.' *She wants my services & time & friendship & to keep her money to herself.*[64] A desperate Ann cried a great deal, promising this and that, but Anne Lister *attached in reality no importance to all this, well knowing that tomorrow she might be all on the other side of the question.* By Christmas of 1832 Anne knew she would not get an answer from Ann. *I never saw such a hopeless person in my life – how miserable – said I to myself, 'thank God my own mind's not like hers – what could I do with her?'*[65]

Instead of an intimate betrothal to Ann Walker on 31 December, *parted in tears, both of us, I saying I never did or could understand her.* Anne spent New Year's Eve alone. *Well! Here is the end of another year! How different this new year's eve from the last! tho' in each case, unsuccessful love-making.* [...] *Vere married & off at Rome,* [...] *Miss W—, as it were, come & gone, known & forgotten – & myself, what I have never been before since fifteen – absolutely untied to anyone. I never stood so alone – & yet I am far happier than I have been of long – I am used & reconciled to my loneliness.* In the same breath, Anne looked forward: *some way or other, what adventure will come next? Who will be the next tenant of my heart?*[66]

In the new year, Ann Walker sent a letter expressing her fear that she would burn in hell for having sex with Anne. *'Why,' said I to myself, 'this explains all. The poor girl is beside herself.'*[67] Elizabeth Sutherland, up in Scotland, had meanwhile gained the same impression and invited her sister to Inverness. Ann Walker did not know whether she wanted to go or not, but let Anne help her pack. On 16 February 1833, Captain Sutherland and his mother arrived to pick her up. On an earlier occasion, Anne had found *Captain Sutherland better in appearance and manners than I expected, very well.*[68] Now she could not refuse him her respect, he having managed – unlike her – to marry one of the rich Walker heiresses. *Some talk with Captain S–; said I thought the complaint chiefly on Miss W–'s mind; but she was perfectly herself on all subjects but that of religious despondency.* Worldly-wise Mrs Sutherland asked Anne *if any love affair was on her mind.* *'No,'* Anne answered without batting an eyelid. To say goodbye, Anne *grubbled a little last night & touched & handled her this morning.* Then she accompanied Ann to the carriage and waved adieu. *'Heaven be praised,' said I to myself as I walked homewards, 'that they are off & that I have got rid of her & am once more free.'*[69]

SEPARATION

Alone again, Anne Lister focused on business matters. A check of her finances revealed that she and her aunt had a joint annual income of only £825 – divided between them, not even half of what Ann Walker had at her disposal. Anne had to borrow several hundred pounds to invest in new business ventures. Like all Northern industrial towns, Halifax was booming. *Never in my life did I see a more smoky place than Bradford.* The number of high chimneys there had doubled over only a few years; *the same may be said of Leeds.*[1] Anne knew that one day *we shall do all by steam, from carrying ourselves to boiling our potatoes. But they must have coal to have steam,*[2] which was why she wanted to exploit the coal seams underneath her land. She read books on geology and thought about how and where to start a mine and how to transport coal away from it.

The past year – 1832 – had gone badly for her, not only on the marriage front. Frightened into action by France's July Revolution in 1830, Earl Grey's government was attempting to correct the worst excesses of the old peerage system before the population started demanding rights by violent means. Grey and his Whigs represented the industrial middle class; Anne was a Tory, interested in defending the privileges of the land-owning aristocracy. While she outwardly rejected Grey's electoral reform, she admitted its necessity in her diary. Grey was forced to resign when the House of Lords rejected his Reform Act, prompting rioting. In Halifax, protesters were seen *parading a straw figure of the king with a petticoat over his head (& then burning him)*.[3] The possibility of a revolution became a national threat, so Earl Grey was re-accepted into government and his act was passed after all on 7 June 1832, abolishing several dozen infamously rotten boroughs and re-drawing constituencies to correspond better with the size of the electorate. In former days, the whole of Yorkshire had had only two members of parliament; since the 1820s the number had grown to four. Now Halifax alone, with its population of around 20,000, would be sending two MPs to Westminster. Of course, women didn't have the vote, and only those men who had rented land for at least £10 a year for at least sixty years (or whose fathers had), or had held land of their own, worth £50 or the corresponding assets for at least twenty years had the privilege. In Halifax, that amounted to about 7.5 per cent of the population; the overwhelming majority still had no voice whatsoever. To exclude land-owning women like Anne Lister from the vote, the ballot was explicitly restricted to *male persons*; the threat of female emancipation meant a male-only electorate was written into law.

That did not stop Anne from casting more than one vote, however, when the first post-reform ballot was held in Halifax in December of 1832. The election was neither general nor secret: votes were cast publicly at polling stations. This gave Anne Lister the opportunity to persuade all her tenants now granted a vote to cast it for her favoured Tory candidate, twenty-eight-year-old James Stuart Wortley – a nephew of the dowager Lady Stuart. *Had John Bottomley, having sent for him to tell him to vote for Wortley tomorrow – had 1/4 hour's talk – he promised to vote for him.* The tenant told her the Whigs had paid them all visits and some of them *had all been at him, & some said they would not employ him again if he would not vote their way, but he told them how I wanted him to vote – and seeming to care nothing about it but that he thought he ought to oblige me. It is quite useless to leave such men as he uninfluenced – he knows nothing & cares nothing about it, & is likely best satisfied with the idea of pleasing somebody he knows.*[4] Yet despite Anne's untiring political campaigning and inventive methods, at times bordering on blackmail, her candidate came in last. The two seats in the House of Commons went to the Whigs.

Politically frustrated and without the prospect of a new love affair, Anne Lister could no longer stand to live with her family at Shibden Hall. A good year after her return, she left again for pastures new in her own travelling carriage, accompanied by her new maid Eugénie and her manservant Thomas – George Playforth had been shot dead in a hunting accident. She was heading for Paris and would see where she might go from there. In London, she met Lady Stuart, her daughter-in-law Lady Stuart de Rothesay and Lady Vere Cameron née Hobart, who had just given birth to her first child. After leaving Vere, Anne had kept a stiff upper lip towards her and managed to write letters of *affectionate chit-chat to Miss H–.*[5] For the sake of good relations with the Stuart family, Anne pretended there was nothing she'd rather hear than Vere's stories about her wonderful months honeymooning in Rome, Naples and Florence.

After a few summer weeks in Paris, during which she saw Maria Barlow and decided on *no nonsense*[6] with her, Anne accepted an invitation from another friend from her Paris days, Lady Harriet de Hageman, who was now living in Copenhagen with her husband. From there, Anne hoped to continue to Russia, her dream destination ever since Isabella's well-travelled brother had announced: *whoever had not seen St Petersburg, had seen nothing.*[7] She left Paris in scorching heat on 18 August. To see a little of the German lands on her way, she travelled slowly and never by night. *I like Germany exceedingly*, Anne wrote to her aunt. In Trier, she was impressed by the Porta Nigra city gate and the Roman baths, recently excavated *at the expense of the Prussian King*. Via the Mosel valley – *magnificent* – they reached Coblenz, *a fine-looking town*. She viewed Limburg and Marburg on the River Lahn. She took great interest in the modernisation of these medieval towns, where *the ramparts and fosses are turned into good gravel-walks and handsome pleasure grounds*. Eventually she reached Cassel, *a very handsome but stupid town*. She preferred Göttingen, as a letter of recommendation from the Paris Jardin des Plantes opened the doors to the university collections for her, and also to the anatomist and anthropologist Johann Friedrich Blumenbach, then at the height of his Europe-wide fame. He showed Anne a mummified corpse, probably one of the 'Nedlitz mummies'. Anne *was sorry to leave the nice little town, and good, reasonable inn*. Had she not caught a cold on her journey, she would have liked to travel through the Harz region; as it was, however, she went on via Einbeck to Hanover, the original residency of Britain's ruling Hanoverians and capital of a kingdom in its own right; *a very good town, and they say one of the gayest and pleasantest on the continent in winter*. She enjoyed Bremen and its town hall, but liked Hamburg even better. *I know nothing finer than the Jungfernstieg (pronounced Youngferstee), and the fine place (square), round the basin of the Alster.* Everywhere in the region, she found *the inns, however odd-looking, comfortable enough*, except for *the evil of scanty bed-clothes, scarcely large enough to cover a person.* She was shocked by the state of the roads, however. *All Hanover seems a bed of sand. All the paved roads they have, have been made since the peace* [1814]. *What did they do without them? – their wheels must have been perpetually up to the naves in dry sand, or mud.* The last stretch of the route presented a particular challenge. *The road from Hamburg to Lubeck is the worst I ever saw in my life, a rough granite boulder pavement full of holes. I never thought of getting safe to Lubeck; but we really did arrive without any accident or breakage at all.*[8] Lübeck was another town Anne was reluctant to leave. On the evening of 17 September, she took a steamer from the neighbouring port of Travemünde, which dropped her off in Copenhagen by one o'clock the next afternoon thanks to its eighty-horsepower engine.

There, Anne stayed at the Royal Hotel but ate at the Hagemans' home every evening. Lady Harriet soon took her on a two-day excursion to Roskilde, the former capital, in whose cathedral the Danish kings were buried. She also introduced her to the *charming person* Countess Blücher, who took Anne along to the theatre – *the dancing was fair; but the women had such bad legs*[9] – and to evening receptions held by the ambassadors of the Netherlands and Sweden. Anne exulted: *I have every prospect of getting into all the best society here, and of passing a very pleasant winter.*[10] She boasted to Mariana Lawton, *I am always au courant des affaires. I see the Corps Diplomatique and leading people, and the business of nations has always interested me more than village scandal. Excuse the expressions but my mind seems as if it had room to stir in.*[11] Anne believed she had made her breakthrough into society when she was received at the Danish court, for which she had a new dress made. *One cannot appear in black on a royal birthnight, so, for the first time these 17 years, I was in white satin.*[12] Yet her arrival in high society was not a complete success: she mistook a maid of honour for the queen. Nonetheless, Anne wrote to her aunt, *as I am so well off here, stay the winter.* And as she was *so pleased with Germany,*

I think of travelling about there next spring – but not knowing German is terrible; so I have made up my mind to have a master.[13] From Germany, she intended to travel on to Russia, *if you are well enough to allow of my going in comfort.*[14]

However, the reverse was the case. Anne received a first unsettling letter from her sister in mid-November. Another letter from Marian arrived on 28 November, prompting Anne to pack her bags and set off for Halifax two days later in the hope of caring for her aunt or at least seeing her one last time. But there were no ships leaving Copenhagen at that time of year. Anne had to take the arduous land route to Hamburg and a ship from there to London. She was lucky that the British embassy found her a travelling companion, Lord Hillborough, a diplomat in his mid-forties on his way from Norway to Paris as a courier. He presented Anne as his wife, with his diplomatic passport granting them easier access to post horses for Anne's carriage on the islands of Zealand, Funen and Jutland. They travelled day and night to catch a ship from Hamburg to London on 3 December. Yet heavy rain and muddy roads meant they did not reach the city's Altona Gate until 5:30 in the morning of 4 December. The next steamer to London did not leave for three days. Anne wrote anguished letters home, knowing they were unlikely to arrive before she did.

Anne and her two servants set sail on 7 December. The passage to London usually took two days but the weather had got even worse. The *Colombine* had to moor again in nearby Cuxhaven because the two sixty-horsepower engines were making no progress against the wind and waves. During the night the storm became a hurricane, loosening the moorings; the bowsprit smashed against the pier. They stayed in Cuxhaven for five days until the damage was repaired and the weather had improved somewhat. Anne had been seasick in her bunk at night, even in the protected harbour at Cuxhaven. On the open sea, she could not keep down a sip of tea or a morsel of dry bread; even looking at her watch made her vomit. Thomas and Eugénie were no better off.

The *Colombine* docked in London at 2:10 in the morning, three days later. Anne fled to the nearby Ship Tavern, which was *a dirty-looking place, no help for it, anything better than on board*. It was a Sunday, so the coach could not be unloaded that day, costing Anne even more time on the way to her aunt, with no idea whether she was alive or dead. She did not arrive at Shibden Hall until 19 December, almost three weeks after leaving Copenhagen. *Found my aunt a great deal better than it was possible to expect from the alarming accounts I had received. She was delighted to see me & had counted upon my coming, that I shall never repent not having hesitated about it.*[15]

That was only half the truth, however. She told her aunt's doctor *it was <u>unfair</u> and absurd to send for me in such circumstances – I had come at the risk of my own life & that of my servants – he said it was not his doing – he wished Marian not to send for me, but she did it in her fright.*[16] Four days after her arrival Anne left again, preferring to spend Christmas at Langton Hall with Isabella Norcliffe and her old friends.

MARRIAGE

At Langton Hall on the day after Boxing Day of 1833, Anne received a letter from Ann Walker, who had just returned from Scotland and had gone to Shibden Hall to ask after her. She had spent ten unhappy months with the Sutherlands, fending off the advances of a debt-ridden relative of her brother-in-law who had been the reason for her invitation in the first place. The Sutherlands charged her a thousand pounds for her stay. Ann Walker had learned the hard way that she would never have a relationship in which her fortune did not matter. Of all her dubious suitors, however, the woman among them was her favourite; she had pined over Anne Lister during her time in Scotland. As in the previous autumn, Ann Walker again took the initiative. Knowing

ANN: MARRIAGE

Shibden Hall was ruined for Anne Lister, she offered her a home with her. *Whilst you are in England I hope you will consider my little cottage as your own. I have plenty of accommodation for your servants, and 2 rooms entirely at your disposal.* Aside from that, she asked Anne to accompany her again to Stephen Belcombe, Mariana's brother, who had taken over his father's practice in York and also treated depressions.

Anne answered immediately, announcing her arrival at Lidgate for 4 January 1834. While Ann Walker *will count each day and hour to my arrival,*[1] Anne Lister spoke to Stephen Belcombe about her. The previous year, she had seemed to him to have *nothing the matter with her but nervousness – if all her fortune could fly away & she had to work for her living, she would be well.*[2] Arriving at Shibden Hall, Anne spent exactly an hour and ten minutes with her family and then walked through the rain and darkness to Lidgate at ten past nine. *Miss W– delighted to see me – looking certainly better in spirits than when I saw her last; but probably this improvement is merely the result of the present pleasure and excitement on seeing me. Dinner (a mutton steak) then tea and coffee – and went upstairs at 11:40.* In bed, they talked until four in the morning. *She repented having left me. [...] Miss W– talks as if she would be glad to take me – then if I say anything decisive she hesitates. I tell her it is all her money which is in the way. The fact is, she is as she was before, but was determined to get away from the Sutherlands and feels the want of me. [...] I touched her a little but she soon said it exhausted her. I had my drawers on and never tried to get near, knowing that I could not do it well enough. I am weak about her. Oh, that I may get well rid of her.*[3]

For the next eight days, Anne moved into Lidgate. It took them four nights to come together physically again. *Goodish touching and pressing last night – she much and long on the amoroso and I had as much kiss as possible with drawers on.*[4] There was not much more to be had. *No touching and grubbling last night and she snored so loud I could not sleep. 'Why should I be so annoyed?' said I to myself and resolved to get rid of her as soon as I could.* But Ann now wanted to keep Anne and this time seemed *quite decided to take me and leave me all for my life and I said then I would do ditto.*[5]

With this proposal of a will, Ann Walker took a large step in Anne Lister's direction. The latter loved and desired Ann less than ever but needed her money more urgently than before. And so she hoped to take their relationship into the future after all. Ann wanted Stephen Belcombe to treat her, so they left for York on 13 January 1834. The doctor probably understood the way things stood between the two women; he had been friends with Anne for years and she had told him *all about the business between Mariana and me – very good friends, but our living together at an end. He seemed surprised & sorry but behaved remarkably well.*[6] Now he was to cure Ann's ailments. Her menstruation had stopped for almost a year and she complained of back pain.

Ann rented three rooms on the edge of York, so as to spend several months under the doctor's care. Before that, for a good week Anne showed her the East Yorkshire countryside of her childhood. Under Dr Belcombe's regime, Ann walked every day, sketched, learned French, read and wrote Anne such discreet love letters that they *might be cried at the market-cross.*[7] In return, *Miss W– had begged me not to write anything particular – not to get ourselves laughed at.*[8] In reality, though, she *longs to see me again – thinks it longer than all the time in Scotland – talks of coming over for 2 or 3 days on the 8th or 10th – if I will let her.*[9] They were reunited at Ann's house. *During a long grubbling said often we had never done it so well before. I was hot to washing-tub wetness & tired before it was half over. We talked & never slept till five.* From then on, they regarded that 10 February 1834 as their wedding day. *She agreed it was understood that she was to consider herself as having nobody to please, & being under no authority, but mine.*[10] *She is to give me a ring & I her one in token of our union as confirmed on Monday.* Anne got a gold wedding ring, Ann a ring with an onyx, black to symbolize Anne. They planned a later honeymoon in Paris. *She will pay and I will make all answer as well as I can.*[11]

Over the next few months, Anne and Ann visited each other in York and Halifax and attempted to improve their marital sex life. *No drawers on last night – first time and attempt to get really near her – did not succeed very well, but she seemed tolerably satisfied.* Referring to the following night, Ann said it was *not quite as well as last night, but I think we shall do in time. She seems very fond of me – is very proper during the day but very sufficiently on the amoroso at night that I (am) really sure I soon shall be satisfied with her and I really hope we shall get on very well together.*[12] Soon after the beginning of Ann's treatment in York, her periods returned, which she and Anne regarded as a fortuitous start to their marriage. *One good one last night and both asleep directly. Twenty minutes dalliance in the midst of dressing.*[13] Both of them were relaxing more and more. *Looked at her queer and played gently.*[14]

Seven weeks after their wedding, Anne began to let close friends in on their relationship. She and Ann visited the Norcliffes at Langton Hall together. *Went to Charlotte for a moment. 'What did I bring Miss W– for?' They said she was crazy and she, Charlotte, believed it.* Similar talk was heard in Halifax, as Catherine Rawson had told Ann Walker. *I merely said 'No' – if I had thought her so, should not have taken her there.* Having gained an impression of Ann for a day, Charlotte crept into Anne's room late at night and *seemed ashamed* of thinking her mad. Anne *explained and said I thought of settling with Miss W–. C. N– thought I had better not determine too soon, but take time to let it amalgamate gradually. I said it had already been amalgamating the last eighteen months, and I thought that long enough and I thought I had made up my mind – but begged Charlotte not to name it. Nobody was so much in confidence as she – she thanked me, said she had no idea I knew Miss W– so intimately or would not have said what she did.* Anne assumed Charlotte would go straight to Isabella and the Belcombe sisters and tell all. That very night, she woke Ann to tell her they were now established as a

17 Shibden Hall before Anne Lister's alterations, *c*.1835,
lithograph by John Horner, from: *Buildings in the Town and Parish
of Halifax. Drawn from Nature and on Stone by John Horner*, 1835;
Calderdale Leisure Services, Libraries Division.

couple among her York friends. *One last night and ditto this morning.*[15]

Ann wanted to be open with her doctor but Anne was uncomfortable with the idea because of her special relationship with his sister. *I will not tell M— that Miss W— and I are positively engaged – and advised Miss W— not to name it, as she asks my leave to do it, to Steph – say he had better hear it from M— than from Miss W— or me.*[16] Stephen would not hear anything from Mariana, however, because Anne was deliberately feeding her half-truths in her letters. *Do not fancy from all this, I am at all more likely than I allow 'to fetter myself too soon or too tightly'.*[17] But Mariana saw through Anne. *'Dearest Fred, I have received your letter*

— the die is cast and Mary [i. e. Mariana] *must abide by the throw. You at least will be happy.'* [...] *Miss W— being at my elbow, put the letter into her hands. But she has no idea of the real state of our former connection — wondered — but I talked all off as well as I could, and she thinks it is merely about as Catherine Rawson will feel about her, Miss W—.*[18]

Although Anne hated living with her father and sister, she could still not imagine living anywhere other than Shibden Hall — especially as she hoped to change the dynamic in her favour with Ann by her side. Aunt Anne gave her blessing to the announcement that Ann Walker would be moving in. To her surprise, her father also made *no objection — on the contrary, I could bring no one my father would like better.*[19] Marian's reaction too was open and friendly; Anne *laughed and asked which would suit me best, M— or Miss W—? She thought the latter — would be more convenient and then agreed with me that she would suit me in every respect the best.*[20] Starting with Uncle James, who had set the tone quietly but decisively, Anne's entire family accepted her love for women.

Anne had barely prepared her family for Ann Walker moving into Shibden Hall when the latter questioned the arrangement. *'Will it be wise to irritate or brave public opinion further just now? For the same reason, ought or can I accept your kind proposition about Shibden?'* Her usual indecision — *does she mean to make a fool of me after all?* Anne was hurt by Ann's refusal to take *the straight course of shewing our <u>union</u>, or at least <u>compact</u>, to the world,* and regarded it as an *affront! Does this seem as if she really thought us united in heart and purse?*[21]

Yet she knew it was not only fear of gossip in Halifax but also the state of Shibden Hall that gave Ann pause; *true, the house is not worth much altering — should do little or pull it down at once.*[22] Building a new house was too expensive, however, so Anne called in the architect Thomas Bradley to modernise Shibden Hall and make it look palatial. She wanted Ann Walker to see with her own eyes that Anne was raising her to her level, as she understood it. A road through the Lister wood was to link the house with the new Godley Lane. A lodge was to mark the entrance to the property, for which Anne wanted one of York's city gates to serve as model. She intended to finance all this using Ann's money. To gain an overview of Ann's property and income, Anne employed Ann's steward Samuel Washington after her own steward had died, so both estates could be managed jointly. That spring Anne bought land on Godley Lane so that one day a pathway would make transport of coal easier to and from the coalmine. Unable to pay even the deposit in full, she assured her contractual partner that *Miss W– was at Shibden and would, I was sure, advance what was wanted.*[23]

Ann Walker was too much in love to object. Under significant pressure from Anne, she eventually was *quite satisfied to let Lidgate house and land next spring.*[24] The months with Stephen Belcombe and his family had done her good. He *seems now aware of the business between Miss W– and myself.*[25] On 20 May, Ann's thirty-first birthday, Anne Lister collected her in York and took her to Richmond in North Yorkshire, where they holidayed for a few days. *Two last night & one this morning but not very good ones – we had spoilt them a little by grubbling as we came along in the carriage.* In Richmond, they were joined by Ann's drawing master Mr Brown. They sought out the picturesque Yorkshire Dales for nature studies, and the remarkable sandstone formations at Brimham Rocks. While Ann sketched, Anne went walking. Mr Brown kept himself to himself. *Real playing and squeezing and pressing for an hour and a half last night and almost as long this morning. She says she gets fonder & fonder of me and certainly seems to care enough for me now. I think we shall get on very well. Nobody would care for me more or do more for me.*[26]

HONEYMOON

Back in Halifax, they found Aunt Anne in tolerably good health – and set off on their honeymoon. They left in Anne Lister's travelling

carriage on 5 June 1834, accompanied by her new servants George
Wood and Eugénie. They drove through the north of France, making
many stops along the way, visiting the royal burial sites at St Denis and
finally arriving in Paris, where they stayed at the Hôtel de la Terrasse.
Anne probably told Ann that she had stayed there with her aunt in
1826, perhaps also mentioning that Mariana Lawton was with them,
but she certainly kept Maria Barlow's fit of jealousy to herself – and the
fact that she had tried to convince first Mariana and then Maria in bed
that she had only ever loved one of them.

I like Paris so much, I shall really regret leaving it so soon, Ann Walker
wrote to Anne Lister senior, addressing her with an affectionate *my
dear aunt*.[1] Anne in turn wrote to her aunt about *Miss Walker, whom I
shall in future call Adny*.[2] She did not mention how she arrived at that
pet name. In her journal, she switched from *Miss W–* to *A–*. Anne
had seen plenty of Paris over the years, so the two of them went on
to Switzerland after only a week. In Geneva, they took a hotel room
with a view of the mountains, the lake and the Rhône. 'Adny' asked
Anne to inform her aunt *she is very well, and very happy. I really think
she is both. She requires to eat oftener than I do; but we manage very well
about this*. While Anne skipped lunch, Ann ordered fresh fish from
Lake Geneva. *Adny has had no tea since leaving Paris, and likes the café
au lait very much. Even I myself had no idea she would enjoy travelling
so much. She is sure she can ride 30 miles a day over any roads; and, if
there was any chance of riding to the top of Mt Blanc, there she would go.*[3]

Ann Walker was a passionate horsewoman, fond of riding a pony
along the love path between Shibden Hall and Lightcliffe, for example. Anne Lister preferred to walk but, as with Maria and Jane Barlow,
she was happy to put up with riding if it took her into the mountains.
From Geneva, they went on to Sallanches, where Eugénie stayed with
the carriage and most of the luggage while Anne, Ann and George
took mules to Chamonix. From there, they set out on a *most agreeable
and healthy excursion.* [...] *These seventeen days upon muleback, making*

what is called the grand tour of Mont Blanc, have quite cured us both. We have really done great things – people would hardly believe us if we told them. Adny's strength improved daily; and you can't think what a nice little traveller she is – always pleased – always <u>right</u>. Via Martigny, they reached the Great St Bernard Pass and spent the night at the hospice. Did Anne tell her wife she had almost been lost in the snow there in 1827? Along the Aosta Valley, they descended to Courmayeur and returned via the Little St Bernard Pass, *over snow, and ice, and rocks, and precipices. Such scrambling as nobody ever saw for four-footed animals in England,*[4] a proud Anne wrote to her aunt. The latter felt *very anxious about you, and often think if you do not take more care of yourself than you do in general, it will be as Mr Duffin used to say that your mind would wear your body out.*[5]

Happily back in Geneva, Ann Walker described the downsides of their Alpine excursion to the anxious aunt. *Anne has told you our route over the mountains, but she has not given you any description of the magnificent hotels we met with. At Mottets we slept between the cows and the hay loft, and at the village des Ferret there were two rooms, for us, guides, George, and the poor widow with eight children. We thought at first George must sleep at the foot of our bed, but a bed was at last contrived for him in the room with the family and the guides. In our little apartment, which was so low that we could touch the ceiling with our hands when we were in bed, we had two sickly children that cried a great part of the night. The people were very civil and attentive, and we were really very tolerably comfortable, and I assure you these little adventures not only served us to laugh at, at the time, but they made us feel the comfort and value afterwards of a good hotel. I am sure you would have been very much amused if you could have seen us in our mountain scrambles, trudging sometimes almost up to our knees in snow.*[6]

After this adventure, Anne and Ann spent another four weeks travelling through the Dauphiné and Grenoble, the Rhône Valley, Lyon and the Auvergne. In St Etienne – *as black and dirty as Low*

Moor – Anne was interested in the industrialised coalmines. Ann Walker wrote in a letter to Anne Lister senior: *We went down one or rather I should say Anne, for I descended only part of the way.* That was enough to come back up *so besmeared with black dust, that it was impossible to know the real colour of our skin.*[7] From then on, Ann did not accompany the untiring Anne on her every excursion; the latter had to climb the Puy de Dôme (1,465 m) at Clermont-Ferrand alone. Finally, they returned to London via Vichy and Paris, and Anne introduced Ann Walker to the dowager Lady Stuart. *I was delighted to find my London friends thinking me very wise, and to find Ann's shyness wearing off amazingly.*[8] On 28 August they were back in Halifax, having spent almost three months in France and Switzerland.

AT SHIBDEN HALL

In their absence, Samuel Washington had found a tenant for Lidgate for an annual rent of £100 for the length of ten years. Ann had part of her furniture brought over to Shibden Hall, along with her porcelain and all the bottles in her wine cellar. The two moved into a new shared bedroom in Anne's wing on the top floor; Anne used her old room for writing from then on. The other Listers welcomed Ann Walker very warmly. As in many families, the presence of an outsider had a calming effect on their quarrelling. For Marian, Ann was *now one of the family.*[1] So as not to get on each other's nerves in the comparatively cramped space, they ran three separate households: Anne and Ann, Jeremy and Marian and the immobile Aunt Anne, each with different mealtimes. In the evenings Anne and Ann would play backgammon in one of the reception rooms; when Anne had enough of losing, she *read aloud to her (she making charity baby clothes) from page 17–133 volume I, Niebuhr's Rome.*[2] Ann would have liked to have children, a wish Anne regarded as a latent threat to their relationship. Seeing herself as the husband, Anne concealed her menstruation from her wife. *No kiss.*

Had slept in cousin-linen with paper as usual underneath her nightwear. *A– never found out that I had cousin.*³ To show the outside world they were a respectable couple, Anne rented a pew in the front row at Lightcliffe Church for the two of them.

Ann Walker's relatives, however, were appalled by her moving in. Mrs Priestley, who was in the best position to assess the situation, refused to shake hands with Anne. Ann's aunt at Cliffe Hill was *crosser than ever. How tiresome! Gets upon poor A–'s nerves and undoes all good. Surely she will cease to care for such senseless scolding by and by – all sorts of bitterness against me.*⁴ From old Mrs Rawson, with whom Anne had always got on well, she found out that *all the town talking of A–'s coming here – so cruel to leave her aunt – & how did my father like so many families in the house – with her fortune so strange to give up her home and come and live so out of the world.* Anne retorted, *'What could A– and I do better? Both left alone – all of us better – & very comfortable – my aunt, father, sister – everybody pleased – people should know all sides before they judged.' 'Yes!' agreed Mrs R– and seemed satisfied. Miss Cliff-hill* [Ann Walker senior] *has asked Miss Mary Rawson of Mill-house to go to her – & and she is going next week, it seemed as if to live with her.* This was startling news for Ann Walker. *She burst into tears.* [...] *Had seen her – her aunt had spoken as if the girl had merely arrived by accident.*⁵

Ann Walker felt the need to justify her choice to the world, and to her sister Elizabeth in particular. *You may probably have heard already that Mary Rawson went to Cliff-hill on the 2nd October, Miss Lister was told (and from good authority), to reside – and at my Aunt's own proposal. I may only tell you that I have never heard one word of this myself* [...] *my aunt told me of her stay as if it was by mere accident she had come for the day & been left. I am really very glad & thankful that my Aunt had at least got someone… I have often felt uneasy about her – as it was not in my power to do more than I had done. I was the only unmarried Niece who could be with her, and I really did make her the proposal to live with her.* [...]

She took a fortnight to consider of the proposal and then said she thought 'old and young people did not suit'. I then fitted up Lidgate (you know, at not a little expense). When I was in Scotland, unknown to me, Miss Lister twice asked her to ask me to live with her, when she repeated the objection she made before; but no word was ever passed upon the subject, nor should I have named it to you or to anyone else, had it not been reported in Halifax that my 'cruelty in leaving Lidgate' had obliged her to ask Mary Rawson. No one had a better right or more ample means to please themselves than my Aunt and I think she is quite right having done so; but I think it scarcely fair that people should judge so harshly of me without at least hearing both sides; however necessary I thought it for my Aunt to have someone, I would not force myself upon her.[6]

To put a stop to the gossip and smooth the waves within the family, Jeremy and Marian Lister paid an official call on Aunt Ann at Cliffe Hill. Ann Walker senior presumably felt honoured by a visit from the aristocratic Listers, intended to bear witness to the warm relations between the Walker and Lister families. *A— & I walked afterwards* and were *very well received & sat there an hour.* The very next day, Anne sent Ann's aunt *the pheasant & brace of partridges received from I. Norcliffe (Langton) yesterday.*[7] But Ann Walker senior would not be bribed that easily. Relations remained tense and Ann could never be sure how she would be received when visiting Cliffe Hill.

Marian, too, was thinking of marrying. For years, her relationship with Aunt Anne's doctor, Dr Kenny, had unsettled her sister. Now there was a Mr Abbott in her life, a businessman who seemed to be well off, although there were few details to be had about the extent of his fortune. Her sister getting married and having children was a nightmare for Anne Lister. If Marian, now thirty-six, were to have a son, Anne's absolute rule over the family would be at risk. Would she not then be managing Shibden Hall on behalf of her nephew, the future lord, who would put the estate into the hands of the Abbott family? While Marian warmly welcomed Ann Walker into the family, Anne was trying to thwart Marian's marriage plans by any means necessary: she flattered her sister, issued open threats to cut her off if she married, talked her father into rejecting the marriage and even took Mr Abbott to task, informing him that Marian had nothing whatsoever to expect from her. She told her sister candidly: *No one can deny that I go straight forward in the path nature seems to have set out for us – it is you who step aside.*[8] The marriage plans came to nothing. Marian went on taking care of their father, who needed help after suffering a minor stroke.

Now that Ann Walker had moved into Shibden Hall, Mariana Lawton wanted to know how things stood and invited Anne to stay over Christmas of 1834. Anne, too, felt the need to clear things up and went to Lawton Hall alone. *I led the conversation to A–; said I really liked her, was more than comfortable and that whatever might be said, money had nothing to do with it. M– asked if it was true that she has three thousand a year – I said no, but our fortunes would be about equal and that we should have five thousand a year [...] I was thankful things were as they were, for I was determined to have someone and certainly could not have done better. Charlotte said A– was not ladylike and Mrs Milne thought she* [Mariana] *would not be flattered if she saw her successor – but that I could not do without money. [...] Said I had read her last letter to A–, but she did not understand it – I had told her all that was necessary, but not quite* all, *that is, not of our* connection *– nor did anyone know of this or ever would. This seemed to satisfy her.*[9] They slept in separate beds that night. The next morning, Mariana put Anne to the test. *M– came a little before eight and stayed till nine in bed with me – rather in pathetics – she cannot get over her love for me – but I behaved with perfect propriety.*[10] That said more than words ever could. On top of which, Anne did not want to be infected again; no doctor had been able to cure her but the symptoms had died down since she had stopped sleeping with Mariana.

Anne returned to Shibden Hall a loyal 'husband', late at night.

*A— jumped up & came to me in her dressing gown & cloak, delighted to
see me back again – had given me up in despair. Had tea – the 1st thing
we did was to laugh aloud at her droll figure & the bustle I had made –
explained, sat talking – told her I myself was astonished how little I had
thought of M–, either of going or returning – very glad to be back again.*
They were perhaps never closer than that night. *One very good kiss
soon after getting into bed and not long after this another not quite so good
but very fair.*[11]

By-elections were held in Halifax at the very beginning of the new
year, 1835. Anne supported James Stuart Wortley again, donating £50
for his campaign and hoping to *have the command of 20 votes.*[12] Since
their landslide defeat across the nation in 1832, the Tories had pushed
through addenda to the electoral law that put them at an advantage.
Any man was entitled to vote, for example, provided he paid £50 a year
in rent. In many places, Tory landowners parcelled their land into £50
rental units to create more voters who they could influence to vote in
their favour, as there was no secret ballot. Anne Lister, whose lease-
hold properties were not large enough for that method, used a different
trick: she raised Charles Howarth's annual rent on paper to £50, only
to lower it by £4 after the election. She let her tenants know she *did not
want anybody to change his opinion against his conscience for me, but I had
made up my mind to take none but <u>blue</u> tenants.*

The first seat went once again to the Whig candidate, Charles
Wood. The second went to Anne Lister's candidate, Wortley, with
only one ballot's majority over Edward Protheroe, a Radical. The
locals immediately suspected the election had been manipulated; *the
town was in a sad turmoil – the windows, glass & frames of many of the
principal houses, inns, & shops (blues) smashed to atoms – the 2 front
doors of the vicarage broken down – Mr Rawson's carriage (the banker
with* [whom] *Mr Wortley had been staying) completely broken up.* The
next day, Anne came across *a yellow mob of women & boys – asked if I*

was yellow – they looked capable of pelting me. 'Nay!' said I, 'I'm black – I'm in mourning for all the damage they have done.' This seemed to amuse them, & I walked quietly & quickly past.[13]

Two days later, a mysterious marriage announcement appeared in the newspaper. *Anne and Ann's steward Washington took coffee with us, and with some humming and ah-ing, pulled out of his pocket today's* Leeds Mercury *containing among the marriages of Wednesday last: 'Same day, at the Parish Church H-x, Captain Tom Lister of Shibden Hall to Miss Ann Walker, late of Lidget, near the same place.' I smiled and said it was very good – read it aloud to A– who also smiled and then took up the paper and read the skit to my aunt, and on returning the paper to W– begged him to give it to us when he had done with it – he said he would and seemed* <u>agreeably surprised</u> *to find what was probably meant to annoy, taken so quietly and with such mere amusement – said not a word of it to my father and Marian.* Anne was not quite as relaxed as she claimed. Having chosen the forename 'Tom' for tomboy and given Anne the rank of captain, the anonymous advertiser clearly intended to expose the two women as a couple. *A– did not like the joke – suspects the Briggs – so does my aunt.*

Rawson Briggs was the head of the Whigs in Halifax. The victims of this public ridicule thus thought the prank was politically motivated, in conjunction with the still controversial election outcome. Whenever the people of Halifax talked about the corrupt influencing of voters, Anne Lister's name was mentioned. She thus understood the ad in the *Leeds Mercury* as an attempt to frighten her. Only two days later, *Marian came into A– and me at breakfast this morning with an anonymous letter,* posted in Halifax, *directed to 'Captain Lister, Shibden Hall, Halifax', containing extract from the* Leeds Mercury *… and concluding, 'we beg to congratulate the parties on their happy connection.'* Someone wanted to make quite sure Anne and Ann saw the insult. Anne was determined to stay calm, including inwardly. *Probably meant to annoy, but, if so, a failure.*[14]

The announcement was also placed in the *York Chronicle* – a Whig newspaper – whereupon the *Halifax Guardian* re-ran it on 17 January 1835. Anne and Ann then demanded an apology from the editor, who claimed he did not come from the area and had not recognised the hurtful intent behind the announcement. The three announcements made a public mockery of Anne Lister and Ann Walker in all of West Riding. When Mariana Lawton asked about the matter, Anne played it down with some effort. *On discovery of the hoax, a handsome volunteer apology was sent by the Editor of one of the papers; & here the matter ended, for nobody was annoyed, & nobody cared about it.*[15]

That was not even remotely true. *Reports circulated here gainst A– and myself – my tricking or getting out of her all she had.*[16] While the town had previously tolerated Anne Lister's *oddities* with a mix of irritation and amusement, Ann Walker moving into Shibden Hall went too far for them. A female couple not hiding themselves away but living together and sitting side by side at church provoked Halifax society. Mrs Waterhouse did not mince words when Anne and Ann called on her; she *hoped A– would not learn to walk and be like me – one Miss Lister quite enough – could not do with 2 – one quite enough to move in such an eccentric orbit.*[17] A month later, Anne received *an anonymous letter (3 pages) with promise of another to A–; extreme abuse of me – pity for A–; sure she is unhappy &* [the writer] *will do all to aid her getting away from me & Shibden.*[18]

Aunt Ann Walker senior at Cliffe Hill also got wind of the rumours; *she thought A– had left all she had to me; and so she had, the next thing, to cut A– out* [of her own will] *for it.* That fear was premature, however, as Ann had not yet changed her will in Anne's favour, despite her promise. *A– pleased* [her aunt] *by saying she had left all to Sackville – nothing yet settled about me, but if A– did not marry, should probably stay with me and we should mutually give each other a life estate in all we could.*[19]

Before Ann Walker could alter her will and freely dispose of her fortune, she had to dissolve her joint assets with her sister Elizabeth. Ann had been keen to do so since her brother-in-law Captain Sutherland had secured the legal rights to his wife's share. She felt *ill-used altogether*[20] by the Sutherlands, especially as their ideas on how best to manage their joint assets were very different. The Sutherlands, far off in Scotland, demanded harsh measures against tenants whose rent was allegedly overdue, which Ann thought *silly and tiresome,*[21] as she knew the tenants in person. She and her steward Samuel Washington therefore worked on a detailed inventory of the joint assets, which were to be divided into two halves for herself and Captain Sutherland. She discussed the legal issues with her solicitor Jonathan Gray in York, who wrote to Captain Sutherland as Ann's representative.

Four weeks later, the Sutherlands did agree to the proposal, but Captain Sutherland *had taken amiss her having instructed Mr Jonathan Gray to write to him.* Angry that he could not dupe Ann as easily as his wife, he charged her *with involving him in ruinous law expense – a long rigmarole silly letter.*[22] Sutherland, who had previously employed a host of lawyers to get Elizabeth's share transferred to his name, had an idea of who was behind this professional approach. *I don't blame Miss Walker but those who from Interested selfish and wicked motives endeavour to bias her Mind.* Anne Lister, so Sutherland thought, had lured his sister-in-law into her home only to get her hands on the Walkers' account books and property titles. *As our Properties and Miss Lister's join, I cannot help expressing my extreme upset that the Titles should have been for Weeks at Shibden Hall, and which I of course should have decidedly objected to.*[23] The captain was accusing Anne Lister of nothing less than theft – first of the documents, then of the land.

He therefore reserved the right to inspect the Walkers' properties, land and business in Halifax before any possible agreement. To lend weight to his demands and dynastic claims, he took along

Elizabeth, heavily pregnant with their fifth child, and their eldest son, four-year-old Sackville. They stayed with Ann Walker senior at Cliffe Hill, where Ann also welcomed them. Anne Lister joined them the next day, where a tense silence prevailed. *5 or 6 minutes with A— before anybody else came to me — but she dared scarce speak*, as Ann had already argued with Sutherland over the property titles and account books. Anne took care of the atmosphere. *I agreeableized & talked much to the S—s, particularly to Captain S—. Mrs A. Walker & A— scarcely uttered.* Separately, first Captain Sutherland and then Anne and Ann went to York over the next few days and discussed matters with the solicitor Gray, who managed to settle the division of the estate amicably, despite the parties' mutual mistrust. The agreement did not bring goodwill and trust back into the estranged family, however. Ann, *looking thin and pale & tired*, told Anne *it is her sister not Captain Sutherland who is awkward.* Ann was more upset by the split from her sister than by her brother-in-law's avarice. *She cried all yesterday and was quite poorly but held up as well as she could. Mrs S— on the high horse, and A— stood up against it very well.*[24] Ironically enough, the conflict led to an improvement in Ann's relationship with her aunt. *Mrs A. Walker in very good sorts with A—, but fatiguée de ces Sutherlands.* Anne Lister provided constant support and encouragement; *talking all over did her good.*[25]

Captain Sutherland was suspicious of Anne Lister for good reason. Her own business investments were swallowing up more and more money but not paying off. Since the autumn of 1834, workers had been driving a mine, *to be called Walker pit in compliment to A—*,[26] into the earth at the highest point on Anne's land, close to the natural escarpment to the valley towards Halifax. When coal was extracted from 300-foot-deep horizontal tunnels it was to be transported to Godley Lane via the newly purchased property. The purchase price for the land was due in January 1835 and, although she took out another loan and borrowed money from her father, aunt and sister,

Anne could not put together the £3,500 she needed. Ann Walker gave her £1,500 towards it, £1,000 of it nominally as a loan at 4 per cent annual interest.

The conversion of Northgate House into a hotel called for even greater investment. After the last tenant died, Anne had hoped to sell the house, but did not get a high enough offer. She rejected a bid from a man wanting to convert the building to a hotel, simply because he was a Whig supporter. Instead, she began the necessary conversion work herself. *I spare no expense in making it as convenient as I can. There will be on the ground floor five sitting rooms, besides the bar and casino; on the first floor two sitting rooms connected with bedrooms, twelve bedrooms, bathroom, and three water-closets; on the second floor 30 bedrooms and three water-closets. There will be also two bedrooms over the coachhouse and taproom, and there will besides be rooms over some of the stabling near the house, that will dine and lodge a hundred soldiers (should so many billets ever fall upon the hotel) without the least crowding or inconvenience. There will be stabling for fifty horses and everything else in the two stable courts in proportion. I shall not grow rich upon this pile of building but if I do not lose much by it, and if I get a good tenant, one who will make everybody comfortable, I shall be satisfied.*[27] In fact, Anne expected a long-term return of ten per cent on her investment, which she estimated at £6,000. She toyed with various names for the new road to her hotel: *Gasthaus St, Gasthoss St, Alberg St, Inn St — the street not good enough to be called Adney St.*[28]

The foundation stone for the large guestroom, to be built as an extension to Northgate House, was laid in a ceremony on 26 September 1835. *There must have been a hundred people collected round the spot — 2 neatly dressed young ladies, some respectable-looking men and the rest rabble.* First of all, Anne and Ann and the builder, Mr Nelson, assembled a time capsule for future generations. Five coins with the king's head on them *were put into a large-mouthed green glass bottle;* also an inscription engraved on sheet-lead, rolled up tight. The message read: *The first stone of a spacious Casino, which will be annexed to a handsome hotel, to be erected at Halifax, was laid on the 26th day of September AD 1835, in the sixth year of the reign of King William IV, by Miss Ann Walker the younger, of Cliffe Hill, Yorkshire, in the name and at the request of her particular friend, Miss Anne Lister of Shibden Hall, Yorkshire, owner of the property.* Ann Walker, who *did her part very well*, made a speech expressing the hope that the hotel would be well received by the town and the local and further area, and continued, '*it will do credit to all the individuals concerned in its erection'. Ann deposited the bottle, and eight or ten men lowered down and properly placed over it the foundation stone, to which Ann then gave three right earnest strokes with her mallet.* After that came Anne: '*Mr Nelson, my friend Miss Walker has done me a great honour; and I trust her good wishes will not be in vain,'* adding, '*may the voice of Discord be never heard within its walls, and may persons of every shade of varying opinion meet together here in amity and in charity; and may none ever go away dissatisfied but such, if there be, whom good cheer and humour can't please!' I heard someone of the Crowd say, 'Very well'; A— and I hurried back into the carriage — 3 cheers were given.* After the ceremony, the workers went to Anne's own Stump Cross Inn for *a very good dinner & got so drunk none could look up yesterday [...] All very much pleased — said the Blues were the best — if it had been a yellow, they would have got nothing.*[29]

Shortly afterwards, Anne found out that the railway was now to be extended to Halifax; the route raised the value of previously insignificant plots of land belonging to Ann Walker in the valley and the station was to be built at Northgate, in the direct vicinity of Anne's hotel. Things could not have gone better. *The influence of the railroad is already felt. What will it be by and by, when even such old fashioned going people as I begin to follow in the train?*[30] It began to dawn on Anne Lister that she had been wrong about the future of the transport sector. In public, she advocated further expansion of the canal system, while making discreet but not very successful attempts to sell her and Ann's canal shares while they were still worth something.

Ann Walker took little interest in daily business matters and would have liked to hand control of her financial matters to a trustworthy person. But the trustee of her father's will, William Priestley, the husband of Anne Lister's former friend Mrs Priestley, was *not really a man of business – things went on better without him.*[31] Since visiting Germany, *his soul seemed wrapped up in German chorales and the great works, vocal and instrumental, of German masters.*[32] He played the oboe and clarinet, founded the Halifax Choral Society and organised concerts that drew respect around the country. But Anne Lister, too, proved to be neither a loyal administrator nor a good businesswoman. She was constantly asking Ann for money for the Walker Pit, for the Northgate Hotel, for buying properties and for another, even larger coalmine, Listerwick Colliery. *A– low at my having so many concerns – oh dear!*[33] For Ann, all these investments were untransparent, doubtful and unnecessary, as she had lived well on her diversely invested assets until her marriage. *She is afraid she shall not have enough for herself.*[34] The alterations Anne was planning to Shibden Hall also caused her consternation. Why spend so much money? *She will always long to be doing Cliff-hill – tho' she herself doubts whether that or Crow Nest will be the place eventually.*[35]

Their joint budget at home also caused tension. Anne Lister asked for £500 a year from Ann Walker for running the household, because she had spent that amount at Lidgate. There, though, Ann had lived more comfortably and independently on that sum and so now felt cheated. They argued on numerous occasions over the use of the carriages. *She said she should have gone over to Leeds today if she had had carriage & servant of her own – I quietly said she had two of each – I was very sorry I had prevented her... I said no more but came upstairs – keeping my temper beautifully, as I must say for myself, I have always done to her... I see there will be a struggle for the upper hand – I shall not give way, come what may.*[36]

In August of 1835, Anne and Ann went down to London for a shopping trip. On the evening before they left, Anne *explained affectionately and calmly* that she'd be visiting Lady Stuart alone, even though the dowager had given Ann a warm welcome on their return journey from France. *She cried* and recalled similar occasions when Anne had denied her to her aristocratic friends. *She thought the sooner we parted the better. I said my greatest and first wish was her happiness – if I could not make her happy, I only hoped someone else might succeed better etc.'* Anne judged her own behaviour *very kind and affectionate*. Ann's response was: *'Oh no,'* but she had expected very different. [...] *But if left to do my own way, I did not despair. She by-and-by came round, kissed me etc. I took all well, but thinking to myself, 'There is danger in the first mention, the first thought, that it is possible for us to part – time will shew – I shall try to be prepared for whatever may happen.'*[37]

Anne visited her high-society friends in London without Ann. At the home of the dowager Lady Stuart she met Lady Vere Cameron, who *said I must have a hoard somewhere, or coal or something must yield a great deal – how could I build Inns & talk of a house in London etc – hoped I should not ruin myself. 'I hope not,' said I, 'but if I do, my little friend Miss W– must help me out.' 'Come to me,' said Vere, 'I will keep you.' I said A– had a very good fortune – but I should take care – had no thought of a house in London perhaps for these 10 years to come.*[38]

Ann Walker's stay in London did not go well. She had opened a Sunday school in Lightcliffe, where she *after church, had 30 small school boys, whom Miss W– exercised in catechism*[39] – presumably a tough task for a woman with allegedly bad nerves; or perhaps evidence that she was more resilient than Anne Lister claimed. Hoping to put the school on a professional standing, she went to the British and Foreign Central School in London to look for two teachers, a man and a woman. This attempt was in vain, as *we fancied the system was a sort of gradual undermining of the Church and Tory politics.*[40] With her back complaints still persisting, Ann consulted the orthopaedist Sir Benjamin Collins Brodie, an eminent authority in his field who also treated the king. After the examination, though, the doctor merely made the terse comment that *she was just the sort of person for nervous pains but there was nothing to fear.*[41] Ann Walker's only option was household remedies; *rubbed A–'s spine with brandy for 20 minutes.*[42]

The two stayed a good week and then set off on a roundabout return journey. They viewed Warwick Castle and Birmingham and spent three days taking the waters at Buxton, where Anne had cuck-olded the newlywed Charles Lawton in 1816, also cheating on the bride by sleeping with her sister on the same visit. In 1825, she and Mariana had not been able to get enough of each other there; with Ann, all she got was *a kiss last night rather better than that the night before – but she moaned after it till she fell asleep in about half hour or less – but I took no notice.*[43] The lack of trust between them made their love life complicated; they rarely managed more than *a tolerable kiss.* [...] *She a little exhausted and said 'It is killing work,' of which I took no notice but seemed to sleep.* Earlier on in their marriage, Ann had already asked Anne why *she did not feel moisture from me as before.*[44] That problem was resolved, but mutual disappointment set in; *pretty good one last night, but she said I had half killed her and she would have no more, and she awoke me two or three times in the night to tell me she could not sleep.*[45] Anne ended up writing more and more often: 'No kiss.' When they did make love, it tended to be on Ann's rare initia-tive. *A goodish kiss last night – all her own bringing on – I never spoke but took it.*[46]

In Buxton the next morning, Ann was *sickish and reading the Psalms while I washed. She is queer and little-minded and I fear for her intellect.*[47] As was previously the case with Eliza Raine and Isabella Norcliffe, it did not occur to Anne Lister that she might be one of the reasons for Ann's tension. Back at Shibden Hall, she resolved *I feel now at last resigned to my fate and take it very quietly – she has no mind for me – I shall not meet with one that has, in this world. Let me be thankful for all the mercies and the blessings I have, rather than sigh for more.*[48] *I have been strongly impressed within these few days, even from little things in her own manner, that we shall not stick together for ever – she will want to be off. Well, be it so – I will try to manage my affairs as well as I can & let her go.*[49] For the time being, her attempt to gain unrestricted access to Ann's assets had failed. *Her whole manner too about money matters nowadays speaks plain enough that things are not to be as I at first expected.* Anne felt Ann Walker *would be glad to be at liberty again.*[50] In fact, it was Anne Lister whose *mind turns to the thought of being at liberty again.*[51] Ann, however, *had been fearing I should leave her & be tired of her etc.*[52] She could not overlook the contradiction between Anne's words and deeds.

Anne Lister spent more time on her business and private correspondence than with her wife, and especially on her journals. Her minute detailing of her life grew into an obsession during the 1830s. She lost all sense of what was worth mentioning and what not. Nothing prevented her from writing down for the hundredth time how fast she had walked from Shibden Hall to church. She made detailed notes of what she ate and what food she enjoyed, her digestion processes and their results, shape, size and consistency. When she had to put up with an hour's stopover on a night journey: *Opened the coach door & sat down, or squatted, in the bottom & made water, so that it ran out.*[53] She described her allergies in as much detail as her dental care regime. *For about an hour, scaling my teeth with a penknife. I have really got them pretty clear of tartar.*[54] Most of the entries ended with the sum of the lines she had just written. About half of the entire volume of Anne Lister's journals was written in the 1830s; she wrote an average of 750 words a day,[55] the equivalent of about two pages of this book. Both Mariana and Aunt Anne had complained about Anne's obsession with herself, in earlier times. Ann Walker now took drastic action; Anne complained she had *taken away the key of my study*[56] or *has locked up my journal.* The implicit invitation was water off a duck's back for Anne Lister, who was *beside myself at the disappointment.*[57]

In the winter of 1835–36, Ann Walker gave up explaining herself to Anne. *A– queerish and poorly or* <u>*middling*</u>*, as she calls it – I think temper goes for much of it. She cried last night, on my gently saying I thought she ought to tell me things fairly – she would not* <u>*mew*</u> *as she used to do – had reasons but would not tell.*[58] When their relationship entered its third year on 10 February 1836 and Anne *wished her many happy returns of the day on the 1st thing on wakening this morning,* Ann was *out of sorts at the day, at its being the anniversary of our being together – she can hardly perhaps own to herself that she repents, but she has a queer temper and perhaps fancies herself under restraint. My maxim is: neither to confide in nor consult her.*[59] That maxim may well have made matters worse.

But Anne could simply not afford to lose Ann Walker. In February of 1836 she borrowed £300 from Ann, followed by £100 each in March and April, then £50 here and £20 there. She made another attempt to cure Ann's depression, walking with her and taking more care of her. *A– would not take luncheon till I got her persuaded – at last told me she had been unhappy the last two weeks – had not pleasure in anything, never felt as if doing right. Would not take wine – was getting too fond of it – afraid she should drink – was getting as she was before – afraid people would find it out – & began to look disconsolate.*[60] To stop Ann from feeling guilty again, Anne also took care of matters of the soul. *No kiss. Lay talking to A– more than an hour & did her good. Would not let her say prayers, but read to her. [...] She thanked me & seemed eased.* Still, though, Anne thought *she is getting all wrong again in her spirits. I really fear for her intellect.*[61] She said the opposite to Ann's face. *No kiss. A– very low, till I accidentally told her I had no fear, nor had Dr Belcombe, of her going really wrong (in her mind) – she then cheered up & seemed better.*[62]

It was not only Anne Lister who was testing Ann Walker's nerves; she was also troubled by a conflict with the residents of a poor area by the name of Caddy Fields. They had always taken their drinking water from a stream that had its source on Ann Walker's property. When the water supply was suddenly interrupted and an angry crowd demanded their water, Robert Parker, Anne Lister's Halifax lawyer, recommended placing a barrel of tar in the source to make it undrinkable for at least a year and show these upstarts who the water belonged to. The people of Caddy Fields were beside themselves with rage, and *burnt A– & me in effigy*.

The water poisoning went to court but neither Robert Parker nor Ann Walker were charged with the crime; instead, the four workers who had sunk the barrel on their instructions were sent up before the judge. The court established that the water did not belong to Ann Walker but was public property, as an established right. The case made waves and the *Halifax Guardian* placed the blame on Ann Walker. *A– very low all today.* She looked *wretchedly & will hardly take wine fearing to take too much.*[63] Three days later, there was a stink-bomb attack on Anne Lister's new coalmine, using asafoetida; Anne's workers had to evacuate the pit.

In the midst of these conflicts, Jeremy Lister died. By now eighty-four years old, he had been bedridden for several days. Anne had sat with him for long hours, as had Ann and Marian. *Death could not come more gently, more easily – though at the bedside, I scarce knew that the last breath had passed away. Marian was more composed than might perhaps have been expected – I took her downstairs into the Kitchen – got her a little brandy and water to rinse her mouth with and a little drink and a biscuit.* It was on the day of Anne's forty-fifth birthday, 3 April 1836, at 4:40 in the morning. *My aunt wished me my health and many happy returns of my birthday – a melancholy birthday today! A– so low and in tears and her breath so bad, for she would take no luncheon – fancies she takes too much – that sleeping with her is not very good for me. Really, I know not how it will end. At this rate I must give up.*[64]

As the mistress of Shibden Hall, Anne arranged the funeral, which took place a week later with all due pomp and circumstance and was widely attended by the local community. At Halifax Parish Church, the *neatly bricked* family crypt proved *deep enough for 2 coffins above my father's.* Anne was casting a glance at her own grave, where she was to be buried only five years later. *In leaving the church (between the doors and gates) a woman among the crowd said 'There is not many tears.' 'No!' thought I, 'I have not shed one – nor did I shed one when my father was with me over my mother's grave, or over my uncle's – there may be grief without tears.' Thankful when all was over. Came immediately to A– & sat quietly with her. [...] A– rather better on the whole, but her mind or spirits are subject to sad lowness – tho' she has rather more lengthened gleams of cheerfulness today.*[65]

Jeremy's death brought Anne into possession of her father's third of the income from Shibden Hall. Nonetheless, she went on trying to per-suade Ann *that she had better give me a power to manage everything & give me a life estate etc.* Ann Walker may have hoped to have Anne Lister to herself at last, and *had no objection* [66] any more. In the spring of 1836 they sought advice together from Jonathan Gray in York on sev-eral occasions. Anne assured the lawyer, who had heard rumours about Ann Walker, that *A– had simply been low and nervous but never insane.*[67] She could only legally wheedle her partner's fortune out of her if Ann was of sound mind. In the end, they made each other beneficiaries of their full assets for life. Should Anne Lister die first, Ann Walker was to receive the income from Shibden Hall; after her death the estate would go to John Lister from the Welsh branch of the family, as Anne had as-sured her Uncle James. A ship's doctor with the East India Company, John Lister had made a good impression on Anne when she met him in Paris in 1831. Ann Walker formulated her will correspondingly. Both

Anne Lister and Ann Walker also added a special clause: should one of them marry – marry a man, that is – the right to benefit from the other's assets would expire.

These new wills brought back Ann Walker's scruples. *No kiss. A— very low – had been crying for over an hour before nine, then lay talking – she thought she could not make me happy.* Anne talked her out of that idea, though she knew Ann was right, and Ann returned to it a few days later. *Lay slumbering on the sofa – tea at 9 1/2 – long talk – A— thought it her duty to leave me – explanation – said I could not stand this – she must make up her mind and stick to it. She should have no difficulty in leaving me, but I thought her very foolish. The fact is, as I told her, she did not like signing her will. I told her she had best do it now and alter it afterwards. We should both look so foolish if she did not – it would make the break between us immediate – she had better take time. At last she saw, or seemed to see, her folly and said with more than usual energy she really would try to do better.*[68] Under all this pressure, Ann Walker signed her will in York along with Anne Lister on 9 May 1836. That did not mean the wills were valid, as they still had to be certified by two witnesses, but Anne Lister now granted her wife a little more peace.

By the time they returned from York, Marian was no longer at Shibden Hall. She did not want to live there without her father, whom she had taken care of since Rebecca's death and nursed at the end. She moved to Skelfler House in Market Weighton, which she had inherited from her parents. The two sisters did not say goodbye to each other.

Liberated from her sister and father, Anne immediately began to make significant changes in and around Shibden Hall. The ceiling in the large sitting room was to be torn down, extending the main body of the house, or 'housebody' upwards, so the staircase also had to be moved; a 'Norman Tower' was to be built onto the house on the west side, to accommodate Anne's library on its second floor and below that, on the level of the bedrooms in the old house, a water-closet, to put an end to cold walks across the courtyard. For the eastern side of the building, Anne planned new rooms for the servants. On seeing her architect's plans, which included even more buildings, Anne was *very well satisfied – only afraid of making the house too large-looking and important.*[69]

The upheaval in the house became too much for Aunt Anne. Her rheumatism had rendered her immobile for some time now. The death of her last brother – she had once been one of eight siblings – may have robbed her of her will to live. Six months after Jeremy, she died at the age of seventy-one on 10 October 1836. We cannot say whether Anne cried at the loss of her favourite aunt or not, as at the time of writing her diaries from that period have been neither transcribed nor edited, and no letters have survived.

Her aunt's death did not ease Anne's financial problems, as she had always hoped; her expensive business ventures were not yet making any profit. She was constantly asking Ann Walker for money, including £285 to pay for her aunt's funeral. On 3 January 1837, Anne was forced to take out a £15,000 mortgage on Northgate House at 4 per cent interest per annum. The bank refused to extend her any further loans, so Ann Walker gave her several sums of money and even paid Anne's mortgage interest. Despite this, Anne felt, according to Phyllis Ramsden, *bitternesses with AW about money – AW again refuses to help finance AL's estate projects.*[70]

With her debts in mind, Anne pressured her partner to have her will witnessed. Judging by Ramsden's extracts from Anne's coded diary passages, she must have worked on Ann Walker throughout the first half of 1837. *AW cross when signing her will is mentioned – AW out of sorts and bad tempered – AL must keep AW in better order – AW's bad temper; AL's money worries – ditto – re AW's will – AW upset.*[71] By mid-May, Anne Lister had finally persuaded Ann Walker. *A— satisfied & the will republished.*[72]

18 Shibden Hall, draft for an extension by John Harper, 1836.
Only the terrace and the smaller tower in the background were actually
built; West Yorkshire Archive Service, Calderdale, SH: 2/M/2/7.
Shibden Hall is now open to the public.

That did not restore peace, however. *AL in despair abt AW's mood-iness, etc. – talking to AW abt their feelings, problems, etc – more upsets.*
On 29 June, Ann had had enough. All her financial concessions could
not buy Anne Lister's love; just like Captain Sutherland, Anne would
be satisfied only once Ann had signed over her entire fortune to
her. *AW leaves AL note saying she is going to leave Shibden.* Was she
informing Anne of her decision in writing so that her silver-tongued
partner could not talk her out of it? The next day, there was a *stern
scene with AW, who cries,* followed by *more scenes.* Anne estimated her
money, calculating her income, etc. and forced another *discussion with
AW abt her leaving.* Ann Walker meant it seriously. She was *asking
sister for use of Crownest,* having rented out her own house, Lidgate,
on a long-term lease. Ann was even thinking of visiting her sister in
Scotland, despite their troubled relationship, as long as it got her out

of Shibden Hall. But Anne did everything she could to foil her intentions; *more discussion, more amicable*. By 16 July, after nineteen days of arguing, Anne had talked Ann around: *AW now inclined to stay at Shibden – AL drafts her a tactful letter to her sister,*[73] to cancel her visit and retract the request to live at Crow Nest.

But Anne had only managed to stop Ann breaking free from her; her basic problems continued. Only a month later, *AL in tears and very worried abt the outcome*. Once again, it was *re AW's possible departure*, followed eleven days later by *more of same*.[74] Ann Walker found it impossible to leave Anne Lister in the end. She needed emotional support, found it hard to make decisions and had no real alternative. Her relationship to her sister was in tatters, that with her aunt was difficult, and she had meanwhile argued so severely with William and Eliza Priestley *that she was not likely to enter their doors again*.[75] And so Ann stayed with Anne at Shibden Hall, in all her misery. *AW not speaking, AL depressed – AL and AW fall out again*.[76]

Anne Lister could always forget her worries when she was travelling. It seemed to be a good time for a trip: Northgate House had been converted and Anne had found a tenant via an advertisement in the *Leeds Mercury*, paying £300 a year as of 1 January 1838. Her second coalmine, Listerwick Colliery, was finished in April 1838. The seam was only about three feet wide but the coal was good quality. Anne decided to seize the day and fulfil her dream of visiting Russia, especially as Shibden Hall was even less comfortable than usual due to the building work. However, *AW doesn't want long sojourn abroad, but doesn't want AL to be abroad without her*.[77] In the end, they agreed on another trip to France.

FRANCE

Anne and Ann set off on 2 May 1838, in their own travelling carriage and accompanied by their servant George Wood. After a dramatic crossing from London to Antwerp – *24 hours' sea and 17 of them sickness* – they went on via Brussels to Liège, where the first centre of heavy industry on mainland Europe was in the process of developing. Being an operator of two modest coalmines, Anne Lister *went to the bottom of one of the deepest coal-pits, said to be 400 yards deep, so it might be. The descent by ladders was no joke.* Ann, who had gone along, gave up when Anne's lamp fell into the depths. At the bottom, Anne took a half-mile ride along a tunnel on the horse-drawn pit railway and crawled into the nooks and crannies where a hundred and fifty men were breaking the coal out of the seam with elbow grease, picks and crowbars. *The ascent in the panier (great wooden box that will bring up 2 tons of coal at once) took six minutes, the steam-engine pulled us having forty-horse power. I came up dirty and delighted.*

They stayed in Spa for four days, at Ann's request, before Anne hurried them up the River Maas to Huy, Namur and Dinant. They viewed Reims Cathedral – *but, after all, and as a Gothic building, I prefer York Minster to all I have ever seen*[1] – and visited the Moët champagne cellars in Epernay; they drank a whole bottle with their meal. They arrived in Paris on 29 May, staying at the Hôtel de la Terrasse again. But the next three weeks were not as enjoyable as their first stay together. Ann came down with a terrible rash on her face, collapsing in the crowded palace at Versailles. Still, Anne suspected *much of AW's 'illness' is humbug.*[2] Ann consulted an English doctor, who recommended the baths at St Sauveur and Barèges in the Pyrenees. That was fine by Anne. They hired a French maid, Joséphine, and set off for the south on 20 June via Chartres and Orléans, Tours, Poitiers and Angoulême, along the same route Anne had taken with Lady Stuart de Rothesay in 1830. From Bordeaux, however, Anne was on new territory. They travelled via Dax and Bayonne to St Jean de Luz on the Atlantic coast, not far from the Spanish border.

Spain had tempted Anne back in 1830, but France's July Revolution had meant she could do no more than cross the border illegally in the mountains. This time, eight years later, France was at peace but a brutal civil war was raging in Spain over the succession in the House of Bourbon. Prussia and Russia had sent money and weapons to the absolutist 'Carlists', while Britain had sent 10,000 auxiliary troops to the aid of the more liberal widowed queen. Up to 1839, 120,000 soldiers and countless civilians lost their lives. Anne wanted to take a jaunt to this stricken country. As there was *no getting to St Sebastian by land*, she rented a *little cockle shell of a boat and four rowers*, who proved to be smugglers. Out at sea, the waves were so high that Ann Walker asked Anne to abandon the reckless outing. But Anne refused to be done out of an adventure. She ordered the rowers to land again at Socha and sent Ann back to St Jean de Luz, accompanied by a boy. She herself continued the trip with her servant George, reaching San Sebastian four hours later. *Miserable doings – meat as of Pharaoh's lean kine* [cattle] *– poulets half starved to death before they were killed – the people ruined; and all beyond the walls a heap of rubbish.* Anne spent the night in modest accommodation. The next day, *a corporal of our artillery marines walked with me over the slaughter-ground of Hernani*, five miles inland from San Sebastian, *a miserable town, then full of our miserable legion.* Their route took them close past the Carlists' enemy troops. *'Whatever the Carlists do,' said my Corporal, 'the Christinos and British legion rob just as much; and I have often been ashamed even for our own artillery.' (About 120 marines then at St Sebastian) ordered to go to the different villages, eight or ten miles off, and take even the beds where people slept on, and what was worse oblige them to carry their own things thus plundered, to St Sebastian!*[3]

Anne returned to St Jean de Luz in the smugglers' boat that same day. She received a *poor reception* from Ann Walker, who had been worried about Anne and at the same time angry *at being dumped ashore so ungallantly from S. Sebastian trip.* Anne wrote *bitter comments* in her diary. Two months after the start of their journey, which had been intended to bring them closer again, theirs was an *unsatis-factory relationship*[4] just as before.

From 9 July, they stayed six weeks in St Sauveur, *as it was in 1830, the prettiest, pleasantest spot in the Pyrenees.*[5] Ann Walker bathed in curative waters, but most of all, they went on excursions to the surrounding mountains, usually on horseback for Ann's sake. They were accompanied by the mountain guide Pierre Jean Charles, with whom Anne had climbed Monte Perdido in 1830, and his friend Jean Pierre Sanjou. Their first tour took them to Mount Pimené (2,801 m), which can be hiked up to on foot apart from the last part of the ascent. They rode to Gèdre (1,011 m) with their guides the day before, spending the night at a simple hostel. On the morning of 24 July 1838, Charles woke them early. *I had ordered breakfast, café au lait for A. only, therefore I only took a mouthful or two of bread and drank a little water, meaning to breakfast on the mountain. Thankful afterwards that A. had breakfasted. Off at 6:10. All clear, the views of the valleys & mountains charming.*

After three and a half hours of strenuous uphill riding, they came to a hut where a shepherd made them *a thick porridge* of sheep's milk, maize and salt cooked over juniper branches. *It tasted strong, but really very tolerable. A. liked it. I cautioned her not to eat too much, saying it was strong. Charles thought it could not hurt anybody.* Although Anne was very hungry by that point, *I did not take much, but more, as I found afterwards, than my stomach would bear.* They continued up the mountain with some effort, first on the horses and then on foot. *The two guides, one on each side of A., got her on very nicely, I following.* In the end they reached the Pimené's Petit Pic, granting them beautiful views on the snow-capped mountains around it. *I saw that A.'s head would not, even if her legs would, carry her much higher, for the crete* [the crest up to the Grand Pic] *was indeed a crete, a giddy narrow ridge along which I felt my own head in its then aching state would be trop forte. My breakfast had disagreed with me & I had more or less of a bilious headache for the last couple of hours.* Despite all that, Anne and her guides climbed to the peak in only seven minutes. *It was a glorious sight to look upon – Vignemal and its glacier, the largest in the Pyrenees.*

Anne's descent was extremely risky; hikers are now advised only to climb the steep, narrow ridge if they are not at all afraid of heights. *Not difficult climbing, but so precipitous my head would scarcely carry me. Charles walked down & bade me do the same, which I did, in fact he taking hold of my hand.* [...] *But on getting back to A. & looking down again I felt as if I could not tell how we had managed to get up, the crete is so narrow one can't go along it without seeing down the precipice at each side. Poor A. turned her head away & could not bear to see us coming down.*[6] On the way back to Gavarnie, Anne vomited again from sheer exhaustion. As usual on her major excursions, she ate and drank far too little. They reached the hostel at Gavarnie at seven in the evening, after thirteen hours of climbing and descending.

Anne would have liked to ride on to Spain the next day, but Ann *did not know how she should bear another hard day.* So they merely viewed the Cirque de Gavarnie, had a picnic *and drunk to the beautiful cascade, & A. began to sketch and I to examine stones & the guides lay down on a rock at a little distance.*[7] Anne only reluctantly took this rest day for Ann's sake. She considered herself much more resilient. In retrospect, Anne thought it *next to impossible*[8] that Ann had also come along with her not much later to the Pic du Midi d'Osseau (2,884 m) – a peak now more frequented by mountaineers than hikers, despite iron treads – and *scrambled to the top.* In fact, though, Ann Walker seems to have had a more realistic and wiser assessment of her own – considerable – physical strength than Anne Lister, who was convinced her body knew no limits.

For this reason, Ann Walker did not take part in Anne Lister's greatest feat of daring in the Pyrenees. In Vincent Chausenque's *Les Pyrenées* (1834), Anne read that the Vignemale (3,298 m), the highest peak in the French Pyrenees, was *inaccessible du cote de France*, but

Charles told her *a man from Gèdre has discovered the way to the top.* Henri Cazaux and his brother-in-law Bernard Guillembet had in fact climbed the mountain for the first time the year before, on 8 October 1837. Both being guides, they now wanted to sell the official first ascent to high-paying tourists rather than claiming it for themselves. Although Cazaux and Guillembet had fallen into several crevasses, they assured Anne the route to the top of Vignemale was no harder than that to Monte Perdido, with no need to cross a glacier. All she had to do, they said, was ride four hours from Gavarnie to the last shepherd's hut and on the next day climb for six hours. When Anne heard that, she planned to go further than the peak and continue to Panticosa (1,636 m) in Spain, on another twelve-hour hike.

Saturday 4 August was the big day, but the skies clouded over at nine and Charles called off the tour. At that point a competitor turned up, Napoléon Joseph Ney, Prince de la Moscowa, the son of Napoléon's Marshall Ney. He hired Henri Cazaux to take him up the Vignemale that coming Thursday, *be the weather fine nor not.* As the weather had improved by Monday, Anne Lister summoned Charles and Pierre. The two of them collected Anne on horseback at three in the afternoon and took her to the hut, from where they would attempt the ascent the next day. Ann Walker stayed behind, but *had persisted in my having my crampons (those I bought for Mount Perdu in 1830) with me.* Nonetheless, Anne was puzzled when *Charles borrowed crampons at 1fr. per day, the wife of Cazaux having unexpectedly told Charles in passing through Gedre to provide us with these articles. How is this? Cazaux declared that we had neither glacier nor snow to pass. Charles had luckily brought a baton ferré for me.*

Equipped with this iron-tipped walking stick, Anne and her guides rode via Gavarnie (1,360 m) and reached the Cabane de Saoussat Débat at five past eight, meeting up there with Henri Cazaux and Bernard Guillembet. The five shepherds who lived in the bare cabin in the summer made them a sheep's milk paste, which Anne again did not eat. She stuck to her bread, two hard-boiled eggs, *2 biscuits in the breast of my dress*[9] and a flask. She had brought along a bottle of the best eau-de-vie she could get in St Sauveur for her four guides. In Halifax, she would not even have shaken hands with the nine men with whom she spent the night; here on the mountainside, they reminded her of *the Idylliums of Theocritus, and the Eclogues of Virgil. The shepherd of the high mountains is still nearly what he was 2,000 years ago. The shepherds of Arcadia had even fewer comforts than the shepherds of the Pyrenees; and, trust me the <u>antres</u> [caves], of the former, were little worse than the <u>cabanes</u> [cabins] of the latter.*[10] When Anne lay down side by side with the others on the bare rock floor, she found it *not comfortable enough to cheat one into sleep.*[11]

Anne Lister would have liked to set out at ten to midnight, but when she woke Cazaux he put her off until five to two. For the first tourist ascent of the Vignemale, Anne *was dressed as I have been ever since my arrival here, for riding, and as I was when I ascended the Mont Perdu – flannel waistcoat, and drawers & light small merino loose sleeves (as for the last 20 years), chemise, stays, short cambric muslin,* several petticoats, a light lined top *with high collar & long sleeves – broad-hemmed 3 frilled muslin fichu and over this double muslin handkerchief & double dark silk do, & then my black merino dress,* lightly padded and lined with silk. The dress sleeves were cuffed with white muslin, *for cleanliness – as usual – and a double pelerine lined with persienne to the dress, & crossed over my chest a light black China crape shawl. I had had tape loops put round the bottom of my dress & strings at the top & just before setting off, had my dress tied up all round me just about or above the knee. I wore white cotton socks & black spun-silk legs with tape straps, & strong leather quarter-boot shoes with nails in (made here for the purpose) & black sateen gaiters. I had my white cotton night-cap in my pocket and my clasp-knife of London 1826. I had in my breast pocket a whole black twilled silk handkerchief & ½ a light coloured foulard (the one I went to the top of Ben Nevis in 1828) & Charpentier's map of the*

Pyrenees, & my little rough note-book containing my passport. Yet I was lightly equipped & my heart was light. She also had with her a sleeping bag, thick wool socks with twenty five-franc coins hidden in their toes, one pair of lighter shoes, a woollen cape lent by Charles and a Maclean tartan coat from her long-deceased lover Sibella, a change of shirt and a nightshirt, which she had not worn the previous night.

Off at 2 ¾ – am. Sent back horses at 4:55. After breakfast, they went on by foot at 5:20. Contrary to Cazaux's claims, they did cross snow and did need the crampons. Anne vomited from the exertion along the way, as on Mount Pimené; instead of the promised six hours, they reached the peak after ten hours, at one in the afternoon. Anne wrote on a sheet of paper her own name and those of her companions: Henri Cazaux and Bernard Guillembet, Pierre Jean Charles and Jean Pierre Sanjou. She put the paper into a bottle she had brought along, sealed it well, and the men carefully piled stones over it – the first cairn on Vignemale.

At the peak, Anne abandoned her plan to continue to Panticosa. They viewed the glacier and began their descent at ten past two. They were back at the cabin at five past eight, after over seventeen hours of walking. *Tired, but would have pushed on to Gavarnie, but Charles said it would be dangerous to attempt such a road in the dark. Drank a good deal of boiled milk but did not eat more than a mouthful or 2 of bread. My dress quite damp from the brouillard on the col. Wrapt myself up in my cape and lay down about nine, the rest sitting over their soup.* Anne, however, not wanting to spend another night with nine men in the cramped shepherds' hut, got her way after all. At half past eleven, she, Charles and Pierre walked back to Gavarnie, arriving at the hostel at 1:15 in the morning. There, Anne got her own room and bed, shook out her clothes, washed her feet *and slept well.*[12]

Less than eight hours later, Ann Walker arrived in Gavarnie on horseback and the two women repeated Anne's 1830 excursion to Spain. *I saw my old friends again at Torla, and the prison I was to have been sent to at Jaca – it was less gloomy-looking outside, than I expected; and the town seemed good and prosperous.* They rode back via Panticosa, the place Anne had originally wanted to reach on foot from Mount Vignemale. *The hotel was so full, we slept on the dinnertables in the salle à manger and the guides in the stable. The cooking was French and excellent, the wines Spanish and delicious.*[13] After five days they arrived back in St Sauveur. While Ann Walker's *journey seems to have agreed with her marvellously*, after her extra trip up Mount Vignemale Anne Lister felt *strangely out of sorts, perpetual vertigo and sickness very often, particularly on horseback, all but vomiting – my head heavy, myself dull, oppressed.* At night she slept badly, *dreaming myself among unclimbable mountains.*

Yet things were to get worse still. Henri Cazaux sold the first ascent of Mount Vignemale a second time. He *had deceived the Prince de la Moscowa – had told him that I had not gone to the top, was sick on the glacier.* This offended Anne and she vowed she *would not pay Cazaux till this was cleared.*[14] After a vain attempt by Charles to convince the prince of the truth, Anne consulted a lawyer in Lourdes, a Monsieur Latapis, *about 50, rather rotund au milieu, & of agreeable lawyer-like manners. Told him I should be glad of his assistance, that the grievance was not serious, but that I felt myself un peu blessee and I hoped he could tell me how to set all right.*[15] The lawyer wrote a declaration for Cazaux to sign, stating that Anne had climbed to the top of the mountain on 7 August 1838. If Cazaux refused, Latapis would represent Anne in court. They drove back in the midst of heavy rainstorms.

The next day, Anne invited Henri Cazaux to the hostel at Gèdre to talk. Anne ordered wine, bread and cheese and *Cazaux made not the least objection to sign it, declared fully and openly that all I and Charles had said was true, and that I had got to the very top, and got up very well too.* She then paid his fee and gave him a decent tip to ensure that *nobody either destroyed the bottle or raised a higher column than mine.* The following day a triumphant Anne sent Charles to the Prince de la

Moscowa with the declaration signed by Cazaux. The prince uttered a *word against Cazaux which he (Charles) could not repeat to me.*[16]

Despite all this, Anne read an article in *Galignani's Messenger* – an English newspaper published in France – on 21 August 1838, stating: *The Prince of Moscowa and his brother, M. Edgar Ney, accompanied by five guides, made a successful ascent on the 11th instant, to the summit of the Vignemale, the second loftiest mountain of the Pyrenees, being only a few feet lower than Mont Perdu, and which has hitherto been thought inaccessible.* The thirty-five-year-old Napoléon Ney, Prince de la Moscowa, was not willing to cede the first ascent to a forty-seven-year-old spinster. Yet his rival refused to back down in this round either, and asked the editors of *Galignani's Messenger to insert the following paragraph in the next edition: 'We noticed, some days ago, the ascent of the Prince de la Moscowa and his brother, M. Edgar Ney, with five guides, to the summit of the Vignemale, hitherto thought inaccessible. We find that an English lady had, 4 days before, ascended with 3 guides to the same summit, which though inaccessible from the French side, is not more difficult of ascent from the Spanish side, towards the east, than high mountains in general. St Sauveur. Mon. evening 26 August 1838.'*[17]

Anne Lister's note was indeed published, but as an honourable woman would not want to see her own name in print, her rival was considered the first climber until 1968, and even today the route Anne Lister took to the peak of the Vignemale on Tuesday, 7 August 1838 is called 'Prince de la Moscowa'. In the meantime, at least, an anticline on Mount Vignemale has been named 'Col Lady Lister'. In her diary, Anne pretended not to care. *I thought not of certificate, nor cared more for mounting Vignemale than Mount Perdu, the ascent of which last mountain nobody believes. What matters it to me? I have made each ascent for my pleasure, not for éclat. What is éclat to me?*[18]

From the mountains, Anne and Ann continued their travels in the autumn to Nîmes, Montpellier and along the Rhône Valley to Lyon. They were not getting along well. According to Phyllis Ramsden, one bad row was only reconciled two days later. Ann *complains that AL makes all arrangements without consulting her.* Anne suspected *that much of the trouble with AW has its roots in her attitude to money, her great fear of overspending, running short.* Had Anne read her own journals, she would have found the exact same concern there; at times she was *reduced to thinking of really cheap places to go & live 'insruectively'* [sic] *until her income increases.*[19]

THE BRONTËS

Almost seven months after their departure, Anne Lister and Ann Walker arrived at Shibden Hall on 27 November 1838, late at night, during a snowstorm. That whole winter was to be snowy and bitterly cold in Yorkshire. Despite twelve open fireplaces lit around the house, the temperature in Anne's study on 19 December was −0.8 °C. Another snowstorm raged on 7 January. *Appalling windy night. I rocked in my bed. At 5:40 got up. It blew a hurricane. Soon after I got up Ann came. She had had a note from S. Washington to say that many panes were blown out at Cliffe Hill.* At noon, Anne and Ann struggled over to Lightcliffe to check on Ann Walker's aunt and the damage to her house. Large trees had toppled to the ground. *It took us an hour of hard work to push back again against the wind.*[1]

A young Emily Brontë was also struggling through this unusually hard winter. Having grown up in Haworth, only twelve miles away from Halifax, she had been working as a teacher at Law Hill School since the September of 1838. The school was located in the village of Southowram, close to Shibden Hall. It was during that winter that Emily Brontë's ideas for *Wuthering Heights* (1847) matured. Jill Liddington (2001) puts forward a convincing theory that the snow-covered heights of the title have far more in common with the countryside around Halifax than they resemble the Yorkshire Dales. The novel's famous main conflict might even have been inspired by Anne Lister and Ann Walker.

Emily Brontë was certainly aware of them. The school's head-mistress, Elizabeth Patchett, knew Anne Lister personally and most likely hinted at the local gossip about the two neighbours. Through Law Hill School, Emily met numerous relatives of Ann Walker's. A walk she often took led her close to Shibden Hall. Perhaps she could have encountered the passionate pedestrian Anne Lister along the way. Ann Walker may have overtaken her on her daily ride to visit her aunt at Cliffe Hill. Emily Brontë no doubt came to her own con-clusions about the two women who lived together and sat together in their church pew: they were united by a forbidden love like that between Heathcliff and Cathy.

Aside from that, the writer must have got wind of the long-standing conflicts over inheritance in the Walker family, which are reflected in the second narrative strand of *Wuthering Heights*. During that winter, the large family was plagued by a particularly hostile atmosphere as the Priestleys openly distanced themselves from Anne Lister and Ann Walker. Like every great novel, *Wuthering Heights* does not indulge in interpretations and is not based on a single source of inspiration. Yet Emily Brontë's impressions of Anne and Ann are clearly written into it. *What sex is Heathcliff anyway?* Scholars have asked. *Even to raise the possibility of a homoerotic* Wuthering Heights *helps.*[2] While some interpret Heath*cliff* as reminiscent of Anne Lister, Emily Brontë may also have been thinking of Ann Walker and her house *Cliffe* Hill in Light*cliffe*.

Emily must have told her sister Charlotte Brontë about Halifax, because her work too includes motifs from Anne Lister's life. Charlotte also knew the Clifton Asylum well, the institution run by Stephen Belcombe, in which Eliza Raine was held.[3] After one of her visits, Anne noted that her first lover *spits perpetually* and *is so dirty and obstreperous*[4] that her *gowns are now made, as to the sleeves, like a strait waistcoat, so that she can do no mischief, otherwise she would have struck me.*[5] While Emily Brontë was working on *Wuthering Heights*,

Charlotte was portraying Eliza Raine in *Jane Eyre* (1847) as the locked-up, mentally disturbed Bertha Mason, a Creole woman from Jamaica, a 'half-caste' like Eliza Raine. In her second novel, *Shirley* (1849), Charlotte Brontë took Anne Lister as a model for her titular heroine. The rich landowning woman is not interested in marriage candidates but in good business, uses a male first name – which only changed gender as a result of the publication of the novel itself – and ends up in a pragmatic marriage. Shirley and her real love, her best friend Caroline, marry brothers.

It was not only the hard winter that made life at Shibden Hall uncomfortable. During Anne and Ann's absence, only *my little study was finished, the rest of the house seemed nearly as we had left it.* Workers and building materials had to be obtained to continue the interior, the Norman tower and the new servants' quarters. *It was high time to be at home again.*[6] Construction on the Listerwick Colliery had also come to a halt. To run the colliery, a three-storey building was needed to store ropes, tools and material, with an office and rooms for the supervisors. All that cost money which Anne did not have. *AL overcome with anxiety & remorse*, Phyllis Ramsden notes only a week after her return; and then, the next day: *AL upset & hysterical abt her debts.*[7] Since becoming mistress of Shibden Hall, she had invested more than £20,000 in her various undertakings but had not generated any significant income.[8]

Once again, Ann Walker came to her aid with a generous cash injection. *A— had sent to the bank for three hundred pounds – she had put up ½ in a little parcel & brought it me with a look of pleasure that affected me – I took the parcel with a mere 'thank you', adding, 'I shall not say much.'* That same evening, Anne suggested a new regime for the costs of running Shibden Hall to Ann. *To my surprise she said she could not do that <u>and</u> do for her estate, which was in worse order than mine. [...] She cried and said it was very hard – she had no comforts herself. This upset me. [...] I left her about eleven, declining her invitation to* *sleep with her. My mind was made up to leave her. I longed for a nutshell to live quietly in and yet the thought of her and the parting distressed me.*[9]

But Anne still could not afford to leave Ann; *paying bills. Depressed abt them.*[10] In February 1839, Ann Walker helped her out with £50, and in May with £100. As Anne did not want to be dependent on these voluntary gifts, she made several attempts to gain unrestricted access to Ann's assets. She thought Ann's *reason is very weak*[11] and asked Ann's lawyer to *arrange for AW to make over management of estate to AL.* However, Anne not only underestimated her own wife, but also Mr Gray. He informed Anne such a measure was *not legal*[12] and that the agreement between Mr and Mrs Sutherland was a very different case. *I fancy he doubts me a little in this matter. Very well, it was to be let alone.*[13]

Anne Lister did not blame her lack of business success on her inferior entrepreneurial skills but on political conflicts. *The whole of our social system has been strangely altered of late years. The operative classes* spent more time *at radical meetings and beer-shops*[14] than at work. Exploited by the new capitalism, workers were beginning to organise and demand rights. *A fearful number of people have turned out for increase of wages* and formed trade unions, about which Anne Lister spread implausible claims: a member must *bind himself by a solemn and dreadful oath to obey their 'officers' in everything, even in murdering a bad master.*[15] She made life difficult for a tenant of one of her inns after union members met there several times. *I had told him as plain as I could speak, I would not have them at the Mytholm* [Inn], *& if he did not understand now, I should take some other means of making him understand – he must make up his mind to give up these meetings or leave the house.*[16] Anne was happy to persuade her tenants of all sorts of things; indeed, she did not disapprove of child labour. There were three hundred children employed in her wire-drawing mill in Mytholm alone, and children also worked below ground in her mines.

On 7 May 1839, more than a million signatures were submitted to the House of Commons in support of the People's Charter, calling for a restriction of the working day to ten hours, the right to a secret ballot for all men over the age of twenty-one, and other demands. That same day, Halifax town council requested troops against its own Chartists. Anne Lister provided accommodation for the third Dragoon Guard at her Northgate Hotel. *I should be happy to do anything I could for the town.*[17] She wrote to Lady Vere Cameron: *Heaven defend from Mobocracy! Democracy is not the word – the demos of antiquity was respectable; and the Democrats of old Athens would have spurned their namesakes of this present day.*[18] Strictly speaking, she was not wrong: The democrats of Athens held slaves, oppressed women and shared their power among only a few free citizens. The Chartists wanted more equality than that. On Whit Monday of 1839, they passed Shibden Hall along Godley Lane on their way to a major demonstration. A brass band played loudly to make sure Anne heard them. *There is a deep-rooted feeling of hostility against the dignities of the olden time that is very difficult to deal with. [...] What used to be sacred is no longer so.*[19] By 'sacred' she meant her own privileges.

By 1839, Anne Lister had made considerable dents in her inheritance and rendered her own home inhospitable with all the building work. Neither politics nor business life, neither her studies nor love had brought her success, happiness or satisfaction. To evade the realisation that she had failed at everything she set her hand to, she took flight one last time: *My love of travel is as great as ever.*[20] Only six months after returning from the Pyrenees, Anne wanted to set out on her long-postponed trip to Russia. Unlike the previous year, Ann Walker made no objections. Anne's problems had become her problems, and the tensions in her family meant she too was unhappy in Halifax. She and Anne had argued a great deal on their last trip to France but things may well have been even worse at home. Anne advertised for servants prepared to travel through Scandinavia to

Russia with them and found Mr and Mrs Gross, a German and his English wife. From Moscow, Anne hoped to visit the Orient. We do not know how much of this plan she revealed to Ann Walker, who imagined Moscow to be their final destination.

FROM HALIFAX TO MOSCOW

For their long journey, they packed several trunks full of clothes, shoes and hats for hot and cold weather, for vigorous hikes and for society occasions; they packed wooden crates full of books, a small camping stove and saucepan, cutlery and crockery, a stable travel desk with a built-in inkwell, papers, a letter opener, a ruler and two thermometers. Being a seasoned traveller, Anne gave instructions on how to pack their carriage. It weighed about 17 hundredweight (800 kg), with another 15 hundredweight (700 kg) of luggage on top.

They set off on 20 June 1839, making a last few purchases in London. Anne bought a compass, a telescope and an extra watch. At her bank, Hammersley, Anne collected her passport, which was issued to her and *my niece, Mademoiselle Ann Walker*[1] and her servants. Bills of credit from Hammersley could be exchanged for local currency at banks in large towns. Anne had therefore instructed her bank in Halifax to keep her account at Hammersley regularly stocked up. An emergency fund of £2,000 was set up with Hammersley's agent in Hamburg, which would be much easier to access from Moscow. Finally, Anne Lister and Ann Walker had their wills legally witnessed and deposited them with Hammersley.

Anne and Ann planned to have their carriage lifted onto a steamship in the London docklands at midnight of 2 July 1839 and to go straight from there to Hamburg. But both of them were overcome by unassailable *hydrophobia*.[2] They promptly cancelled the longer ship's passage and decided on the shortest maritime route, from Dover to Calais, which meant a far longer journey by land. To save at least a little time, they travelled non-stop from Calais to Copenhagen. As in 1833, Anne was shocked by the poor streets of the Kingdom of Hanover; *a mere track over the sandy plain, we could not get out of foot's pace. Peaty, heathery, sandy, marshy moor or common – must be bleak and dreary in winter. Sand, sand, everywhere*, in which the coach's wheels sank. To cross rivers, the horses had to be unharnessed and the carriage had to be loaded onto ferries. They reached Kiel via Oldenburg, Bremen and Hamburg. The captain of their ship to Copenhagen *said he had never before seen such a heavy carriage*.[3]

They landed in Denmark on 14 July and retired to the Royal Hotel. To Anne's disappointment, the only 1833 acquaintance of hers in the city was Monsieur de Hagemann, her friend Harriet's husband. He showed them around the royal palace and the Academy of Fine Arts, where the sculptor Bertel Thorvaldsen had just taken up residence after forty years in Rome. Anne described him as *to Copenhagen what Praxitales was to Athens. Our great regret was that he happened to be from home. An old friend of mine took us to his atelier – to his apartment – into his very study. It was interesting to see the books and papers of such a man lying up and down just as he had left them.* After four days they continued their journey as far as Roskilde, where Anne showed Ann the cathedral and introduced her to Harriet de Hagemann.

Up to that point, Anne Lister had been familiar with all the places they passed through. On 19 July 1839, she, too, entered new territory. The couple visited the old castle in Helsingør, Frederiksborg with its coronation chapel for Danish kings, and spent a long Nordic summer evening clambering around the Kronborg stronghold, where *Hamlet* is set, though according to Anne *there is more fancy than reality*.[4] The next morning they rented a ship that had space for their travelling carriage and sailed to Helsingborg. They raced along the coast to Gothenburg in thirty hours. Anne found the white beaches of Halland – now a hive of Swedish tourism – dull, *but everything Swedish new to us and therefore interesting. How odd to me to find myself with and without tongue! Not one word could we understand or make understood save in broken German.*[5] Their German servant spoke the language fluently, of course, but Anne was disappointed in him. He served them well in their mobile home, but when it came to dealing with postmasters, customs officers or innkeepers he seemed uncertain and unassertive. His wife, Grotza, however, proved to be a capable maid and also made friends with the staff at all the inns they stayed at, garnering important information – particularly when Anne and Ann stayed at an English-speaking hotel, Mrs Todd's in Gothenburg.

From there, they wanted to take a detour to Norway. The Norwegian roads being sandy, too, they left their heavy carriage and most of their luggage in the care of Mr and Mrs Gross, who stayed behind in Gothenburg. Anne and Ann bought a small, much lighter coach and hired a Scottish–Swedish coachman to take them around Norway, along the roads recommended in the brand new *Handbook for Northern Europe* (1838). Over the coming months, this travel guide became Anne's bible, and was consulted and compared with reality at every stage.

They set out on 26 July 1839. We know what they experienced up to 13 October thanks only to the letters Anne Lister wrote to her friends, as the next twenty pages of her diary remained empty; all the new experiences and incessant travelling kept Anne from transcribing her pencil-written loose notes. *We were charmed with Christiania,* Anne wrote to Mariana Lawton about the city now known as Oslo. *Nothing can exceed the beauty of its situation at the head of one of the largest and loveliest of the Norwegian fjords. But, said everybody, see Bergen, see Drontheim. We set off – the scenery from Christiania to Gaousta-fell* [Gausta, the highest mountain in the south of Norway, at 1,883 m] *is indescribable – the winding fjord, and little lovely lakes, and rock, and dark pine-forest, and towering mountains, and Norwegian cottages. But the weather became bad.* In Bolkesjö in the Telemark region, they lost two days to heavy rain; *and seeing that we had no present hope of better, we very reluctantly turned back.*[6] In Oslo, they bought gifts for their loved ones in England – Anne sent Vere Cameron a small barrel of anchovies – sold their light coach and returned to Gothenburg by steamer; *thankful to be on terra firma again. Never passed a worse water night, I was too ill to bear speaking or moving.*[7]

Reunited with their carriage and servants, they crossed Sweden to the east via Örebro, Västerås and Enköping. They arrived in Stockholm on 22 August; *with a southern climate, it would rival Naples? I had no idea of the beauty of situation of so many northern towns.*[8] Prompted by the recommendations in the handbook, Anne and Ann hired a new guide and undertook *our fortnight's tour, via Upsala (the pink mead at Upsala as good as the best pink champagne) to all the mines, from top to bottom, which was very interesting.*[9] Anne went to the most important Swedish iron ore mines of the time at Dannemora, the famous copper mine at Falun and the silver mine in Sala. While she was learning about mining technology in the hope of solving the Listerwick Colliery's groundwater problems, Ann preferred to sit in the sunshine and sketch.

We had enjoyed everything, and had met with kindness everywhere,[10] Anne summed up their stay in Sweden. *We liked the good, honest Swedes, who were always very civil, and always ready to do our liking.*[11] They also grew accustomed to the *fresh-strewed juniper* in their rooms; only the food was not quite to their taste; *tho' it is not the land of gourmands, tho' we had rarely met with butcher's meat except in great towns, and had drunk milk, or coffee, or the limpid steam, yet still we had been well, and fared well on pancakes* and *a soft cake they call limpa of which I was exceedingly fond.*[12]

Back in Stockholm, Anne and Ann confronted their fear of water and boarded a two-day ferry to Åbo/Turku. That took them into Russian territory, as Finland had been annexed by the tsar in 1809 and converted into a Russian grand duchy. Particularly on the coast, the previous centuries of Swedish rule have left their mark to this day, and their Swedish courier could negotiate in his native language at the mail stations. They made fast progress on the well-maintained roads, especially when *our driver was seated on the boot-box, and I drove his four horses abreast,*[13] in the Russian or ancient Greek style, rather than harnessed behind one another. They spent two nights in Helsinki, *the new capital of Finland,* which they found *quite charming.*[14] To end the predominance of Swedish Åbo, the new Russian rulers had declared Helsinki, an insignificant town closer to the Russian Empire, the capital. They erected neoclassical buildings modelled on St Petersburg; the senate square still resembled a construction site, so that Helsinki came across as extremely modern to Anne and Ann. *Our journey through Finland has been really a very agreeable and a very economical one, and we have seen the country and the people – the latter always civil and ready to do their utmost to please, and the former well-farmed and interesting.*[15] Anne wrote about everyday details such as the fresh fir branches placed on the thresholds of houses and the *beautiful white moss and dried yellow marigolds put at the bottom between the glasses* of the windows.

Shortly before Vyborg (Viipuri) they heard their first Russian and thought *the male costume this morning very pretty and picturesque – a white frock coat and red belt or blue.* The women wore *a strong linen, dark with narrow red stripes, [...] and a white handkerchief on the head.* When they reached the border to Russia itself, however, they were not allowed to cross. *Our books, I believe, were all taken out of the carriage and looked at. But, as desired, I copied the list I have and signed it, and enclosed it in an envelope and sealed it with my own seal, to be forwarded to St. Petersburg. I engaging to go within six weeks to the Committee of Censorship to claim the list. We are thus allowed to take all our books and things and go in comfort –* but only after an involuntary night at the border. The next morning, *our Subdouanier lifted the barrier and bowed and through and off we went.*[16]

On the afternoon of 17 September 1839 *we drove over the magnificent*

Neva into the city of palaces,[17] built on a swamp only some hundred years previously by tens of thousands of serfs and forced labourers and declared the capital of Russia. They took rooms at Mrs Wilson's English hotel and explored St Petersburg with an English-speaking guide. Anne and Ann stayed twice as long as intended, three weeks in all, and still had not seen everything by the end; *we cannot imagine anyone a finished traveller who has not been there. The amateur of pictures who has closed his grand tour without a visit to the Hermitage palace, ought to die of the spleen forthwith.* They visited the art collections three days in a row. On what was at that time Russia's only railway they went out to the royal palaces and gardens at Tsarskoye Selo. In the Botanical Garden on Aptekarsky Island, they made a long list of trees, shrubs and flowers they wanted to plant back home.

Although the censors did not object to any of their books, Anne and Ann did have to submit to the authorities' regulations and register themselves and their servants with the police, and also apply for and pay for a pass to continue their journey to Moscow. In comparatively liberal Britain, restrictions like these – on travel and thinking – prompted harsh criticism of Nicolas I, who was considered the most reactionary of the nineteenth-century autocratic rulers in Europe. The Russians could not read any criticism of his policies, however, as there was no free press in the country. That did not trouble Anne. She regretted *we were unlucky in not seeing the Imperial family,* which she nonetheless claimed was *one of the handsomest families in Europe.*

From St Petersburg, Anne and Ann travelled non-stop to Moscow, covering 435 miles in five days. On 12 October 1839 they took *a large excellent apartment here in a sort of Hotel Garni kept by an English family,*[18] and known as Mrs Howard's. They immediately set out on *a quiet reconnoitering walk by ourselves,* strolling down their street, Bolshaya Dmitrovka, to the Bolshoi Theatre, ending up on Red Square and coming across St Basil's Cathedral – *gorgeously grotesque – we have seen nothing like this church* – then walking through the gate of the Saviour Tower (Spasskaya) in the Kremlin. *What can exceed the view of Moscow from here – its motley grouping of European and Asiatic style, its hundred churches and its pomp of domes! I had no idea of such a scene – all my expectations were exceeded!*[19] Not until Moscow had Anne Lister found the time and inclination to return to her diary.

Over the next two weeks, a guide not only showed them the usual sights but also gained them access to private palaces when the owners were away. He even took them to the Moscow reservoir and the Sparrow Hills, a wooded ridge along the Moskva River, these days the 'green lung' of the huge city and the site of the Lomonosov Moscow State University. There, Anne and Ann viewed a sad spectacle that took place every Sunday: the departure of the exiled on their long march to Siberia. The German physician Dr Haas explained the procedure, telling them that new arrivals, *if they are ill* [...] *are sent to the hospital till cured or, if incurable, remain to die comfortably.* Anne imagined the five-and-a-half-month march to Siberia to be similarly comfortable. *Walk never more than 22 versts* (14.5 miles) *a day, and rest every 2 days.* The state paid for their food and clothing, she noted, and *none are sent for forced labour but those condemned to great crimes – murder, and was the other crime brigandage? The lesser delinquents merely sent to colonise the country, and some parts in the south have a better climate than Moscow.* To the woman who considered the London treadmill harmless, exile to Siberia seemed like a stay at a sanatorium, especially as *all who are sent as colonists, whether serfs at home or not, are freed.*[20] At the time, Britain transported its own criminals to Australia, including many of the Chartists Anne Lister so disapproved of.

Unlike in European St Petersburg, Moscow's streets were full not only of Orthodox Russians but also of Sunni Tartars, Galician Jews and Shi'ite Persians, Lutheran Germans, Circassians and Finns. Anne and Ann found the Russian Orthodox church service both strange and attractive in equal measure. *The Greek catholic worship is a step above the Roman catholic in splendour and antiquity. I have got accustomed to the Byzantine style of church, and gilded domes, and silver, and sky-blue, and sea green, and every colour you can name.*[21] They also took part in Muslim Friday prayers. *All that the Mullah or clerk (in white muslin turban and yellowish flowery-pattern caftan) requested of us was that we would not speak nor tread upon the carpets, and he civilly set us some sort of old box to sit on. Not a word spoken – never saw people more orderly.*[22] Anne was very impressed by the city she had been longing to see for so many years. *Without exception Moscow is the most picturesquely beautiful town I have ever seen. There is no draw-back, no poor, ugly part. All is only <u>more</u> or <u>less</u> good, and many parts are singularly beautiful. The first impression is most striking, and first impressions go on improving.*[23]

The weather turned painfully cold in October. Ann Walker, who thought they had reached their destination, had had enough, according to Phyllis Ramsden, and *would like to go home.*[24] Anne Lister wanted to wait until December to see whether the snowy roads would be passable by sleigh and then set off again for the south. Their conflict was overwritten by new social contacts arising from England. Anne had sent the British ambassador a letter of recommendation from Lord Stuart de Rothesay, with the request to put her in contact with the governor general of Moscow, Prince Dmitry Vladimirovich Golitsyn. At four in the afternoon of 7 November, Anne and Ann were received for a formal dinner at the governor's palace. Prince Golitsyn's niece, Madame Apraxina, was the hostess, and this honour meant that Anne and Ann were invited by other families of Moscow's aristocracy, including the director of the Moscow Botanical Garden, Alexander Grigoryevich Fischer von Waldheim, and his father, the zoologist and palaeontologist Gotthelf Fischer von Waldheim, a friend of Alexander von Humboldt and – another student of Georges Cuvier in Paris, though this was before Anne's time. Count and Countess Panin took great care of the two travellers.

Countess Alexandra spoke English – which was unusual for members of the Russian aristocracy, who usually conversed in French – and was *very good and talkative and agreeable.*[25] The Panins took them to the theatre, the natural history museum, the university printing press, a school for technical drawing, an orphanage and the Cholera Institute. Aside from that, the Countess took them along to a Russian steam bath – *and what a scrubbing I did get.*[26] Anne and Ann were also invited to society occasions; *handsome houses, balls in the best Parisian style, and a great many pretty girls. One dame in particular, is one of the finest women I ever saw, and Venus de Moscova.*[27]

This Venus was also lodging with Mrs Howard, initially, and was called Sophia Alexandrovna Radzivill née Urusova. She was three years younger than Ann Walker and married to a royal aide-de-camp. The princess actually had obligations as a lady-in-waiting in Petersburg, but the court and her husband had allowed her to move to her parents' home for the winter, due to ill health. She stayed at the hotel while waiting for her rooms at her parents' palace to be prepared. *A very agreeable, clever, stylish person,*[28] Anne wrote after their first meeting over tea. A week later they felt *mutually attracted.* On 12, 14 and 16 November, Anne wrote her conversations with the princess in her journal, in her code, which Ann could not read, and *wonders if they are seeing too much of each other.* Three days later, Anne decided they were seeing too little of each other and *finds AW's constant presence v. irksome.* For the first time, Anne did not regret that Ann spoke so little French and so could not follow everything Anne Lister and Sophia Radzivill had to say to each other. The princess, for her part, was curious and *asks AW's history.*[29]

Yet Anne was enticed even more by Persia and Baghdad than by Sophia Radzivill's beauty. To get there, she intended to cover the next long stretch to the Volga by sleigh and then continue along the frozen river to Astrakhan and finally cross the Greater Caucasus to Tbilisi. The Russian Empire had been expanding since the mid-eighteenth century, through a complicated series of brutal wars, up to the Black Sea and the Caspian. A fragile peace treaty had been signed with Turkey in 1829, but devastating conflicts still lay ahead for the region. To this day, Russia has never succeeded in incorporating the entirety of the Caucasus. Ambushes and armed uprisings were every-day occurrences in 1839. In Moscow, Anne and Ann heard the story of a French couple who were abducted by Cherkessians and never seen again after no ransom was paid. Nobody crossed the Greater Caucasus if they did not have urgent military or professional rea-sons to do so. While the men among their acquaintances competed over the best suggestions for their journey, the women advised them against it; they also declared Anne absolutely insane for attempting it in winter. Daytime temperatures in Moscow went down to −26 °C in mid-December, too cold for snow.

The icy weather and their acquaintances' appeals convinced Ann Walker of her wish to go home; the return journey would be adven-turous enough. When she also proved *v. hesitant abt expense of further travelling,* Anne was *in a panic* and categorically declared she would not go back under any circumstances. Count Panin then suggested Ann Walker *should stay in Moscow & let AL do the winter journey with another companion,* at which Ann responded, aghast, that she *'would rather die on the road than be left here.'*[30] There could be no compro-mise between the two of them. Phyllis Ramsden describes the situa-tion as critical: *Discussion of plans to separate when they get back home.* Yet abroad, Ann felt even more dependent on Anne, who was impos-sible to talk out of her plans – as ever. Ann Walker caved in the next day; *all put right with AW for the time being.*[31]

Anne Lister's only concession to the warnings against the trip was to take great care over their travel equipment. Her own car-riage would be of no use beyond Moscow, so Anne bought two new vehicles. The servants got a Russian *kibitka,* a simple wooden wagon with a canvas roof open at the front, which could be set on runners in winter and wheels in summer. For herself and Ann, she found a vehicle *between kibitka and coach*, with a passengers' cabin, doors and windows. The wainwright made two luggage crates to fit the coach, which were used as seating for the coachman outside and the ladies inside. On Count Panin's advice, mattresses were also made for the cabin, *to be buttoned up against the back and also at the bottom of the seat so as not to slip off. Advises our never sleeping on the sofas we meet with – will be devoured. But always put our own mattress in the middle of the floor, the vermin will then be some time reaching us.* Aside from that, the count recommended putting *hay at the bottom of the kibitka and over that a common carpet – the great thing will be to keep our feet warm.* To help on that front, they had knee-high leather boots made, lined, like their new heavy coats, with fur. They also got hold of a *wolfskin to throw over us in the carriage*[32] thanks to the count's advice, and a food heater operated by means of hot water. They were to be grateful for all the count's advice.

The question of who was to accompany them as servants was also highly important. Their maid, Grotza, stated point-blank that she would only leave Moscow for home. Anne gave her a good reference so that she could find another post until Anne and Ann returned to take her back to England. Her husband was prepared to come along to the Caucasus, providing he could turn back at the ladies' expense at any time if the conditions appeared too unfamiliar and difficult for him. More important than Mr Gross, however, was finding local staff who would bring them back safely from such remote regions. Via their Moscow links, they came across a courier for the state postal service who was to arrange everything related to horses, coachmen, roads and accommodation up to Tbilisi. Their hairdresser put them in touch with a former serf, George Tchaikin, who had bought his freedom for 2,000 roubles. He had been to Paris with a former master, learned French and gained an idea of what Western Europeans held dear. George was in the process of buying the freedom of his fiancée, twenty-three-year-old Dominica, who was known as Domna. Seeing she was a *nice-looking little person*,[33] Anne took her on as her new maid. Domna and George were to marry before their departure.

Snow fell at last in the second week of January 1840. With their new coaches, equipment and servants, Anne and Ann went on a trial run to Sergiyev Posad, home of the most important Russian Orthodox monastery, forty-five miles north of Moscow. *At first I felt smothered in our little machine. Opened and shut my little window from time to time to peep out as well as for air. Very fine day and we were quite warm enough by dint of cloaks and being so covered in.* However, *we slid along the hardened snow with a tremulous motion and noise like that of being near the engine in a steam-boat.* They spent the night in the monastery's guesthouse and viewed the monastery the next day. *How picturesque! How well worth coming to see! This fortress-like convent, this Kremlin sanctuary with its 8 picturesque towers and high white walls is very striking.*[34] They attended two services and even gained a brief audience with the abbot. They returned in the dark – also part of the trial run – and reached Moscow at two in the morning.

After this jaunt, Anne Lister could barely wait for their departure. Ann Walker, however, was *in the dumps – AL tries not to notice.* Upon which Ann Walker *resorts to utter silence, which infuriates AL – 'this not speaking I cannot bear,'*[35] Phyllis Ramsden quotes Anne Lister in her excerpts of the coded passages. Ann did not want to go along but still had a fur hat and coat made. Undeterred, Anne obtained the necessary passes and purchased the final provisions: candles, tea and sugar, a samovar and a lantern. Ann succumbed to her fate. They stored everything they did not take along in their travelling carriage, in Mrs Howard's coach shed. Anne exchanged Hammersley bills of credit for roubles at a Moscow bank. She was warned she would not be able to access her money by this means south of Astrakhan. During the night before their departure, Anne and Ann wrote a number of personal and business letters, knowing it would be a long time before they could do so again. Princess Radzivill received a note. Following *confidential talks* with her, Anne had weighted up the *pro & contra*[36] of an affair. They parted with tears in their eyes; *travelling would be unsupportable if one had often the pain of partings like this.*[37]

FROM MOSCOW TO THE CAUCASUS

They left Moscow on 5 February 1840. To make fast progress, they stopped only to change horses during the first forty-eight hours. *Only just snow enough for us, the well-broken rubble of the road visible on my side.* That was to remain the case until Astrakhan, as the mild weather bringing a fair amount of snow had been followed by a bitterly cold spell. Despite −18 °C daytime temperatures, Anne left the window open on her side – because it steamed up otherwise and she could not see the countryside. When they had to slow to walking pace, she even opened the door. After a good four days and 280 miles, they arrived in Nizhny Novgorod (known from 1932 to 1992 as Gorky) at one in the morning, sleeping in their *usual night-things* for the first time, again at an inn.

Nizhny is *beautifully and picturesquely situated along the crest of the high ground and creeping down the slope, as it were in terraces, to the river,* the Oka, that flows into the Volga; *how fine the junction of these two noble rivers.* Thanks to a letter of recommendation from Countess Panina, the governor general invited them to dinner and provided them with the use of a calash carriage, with which Anne and Ann explored the town and the grounds of its famous fair. *2,635 shops in stone and, as was said later at the General Governor's, 2,600 in wood,* where goods from all over the world were sold for a month in summer, from raw materials to luxury items; *the length of the Dvor is just one English mile, and a person going into every shop, and not going out of his way, will have walked 40 English miles at the end of his journey! Extraordinary town of little shops!*[1]

From Nizhny, they continued along the frozen Volga, following its course almost to its mouth on the Caspian Sea. *Pass several large wooded islands in the river and drive close under the shipping of several little frozen-up ports.* The Volga was not yet controlled in 1840. Low hills ranged along its right bank. On its left bank, known as the meadow bank, prior to the construction of some two hundred reservoirs beginning in the 1930s, the Volga had no clearly defined bed in many places, sometimes flooding up to twelve miles during the spring thaw. Anne was not always certain whether they were travelling on ice or frozen earth. *Impossible to write while we are going on account of the motion and occasional big jolts. Could not write more than necessary at the station, too cold, my fingers began to ache.* Anne measured *Réaumur −14° (−17.5 °C) in the doorway of the kibitka at 3:17 pm.*[2] A day later, the thermometer fell to −37.5 °C and Anne broke two of the three windowpanes in their coach with her numb hands.

Travelling on the river had its dangers. On one occasion, *slumbering, and asleep till roused about 5 by a stoppage. Put my head out to ask if it was the station − nobody answered, all flat and snow, no house. But soon the plunging of the horses in water and the noise of the men and the breaking of ice shewed that our 'station' was on the bursting ice of the Volga! Luckily Ann was not apparently aware of danger. The servants' kibitka (always following ours) had avoided the bad place and was standing on firm ice twenty or thirty yards to the right and ahead of us. We were sufficiently near to the right bank, luckily, to be not over deep water. One of our horses sunk almost over his head − I think his feet were on the* <u>ground</u>. *Luckily the ice on which the carriage rested did not entirely give way so as to let water get inside. Gross came to us and advised our not getting out as he had got up to his knees in water. We took the servants' horses and were at last after ten minutes or more skewed round onto firm ice, and pushed our way without further upset.*[3]

They arrived in Kazan on 15 February, ten days after leaving Moscow. Then as now, most of the city's population were *Tatars with*

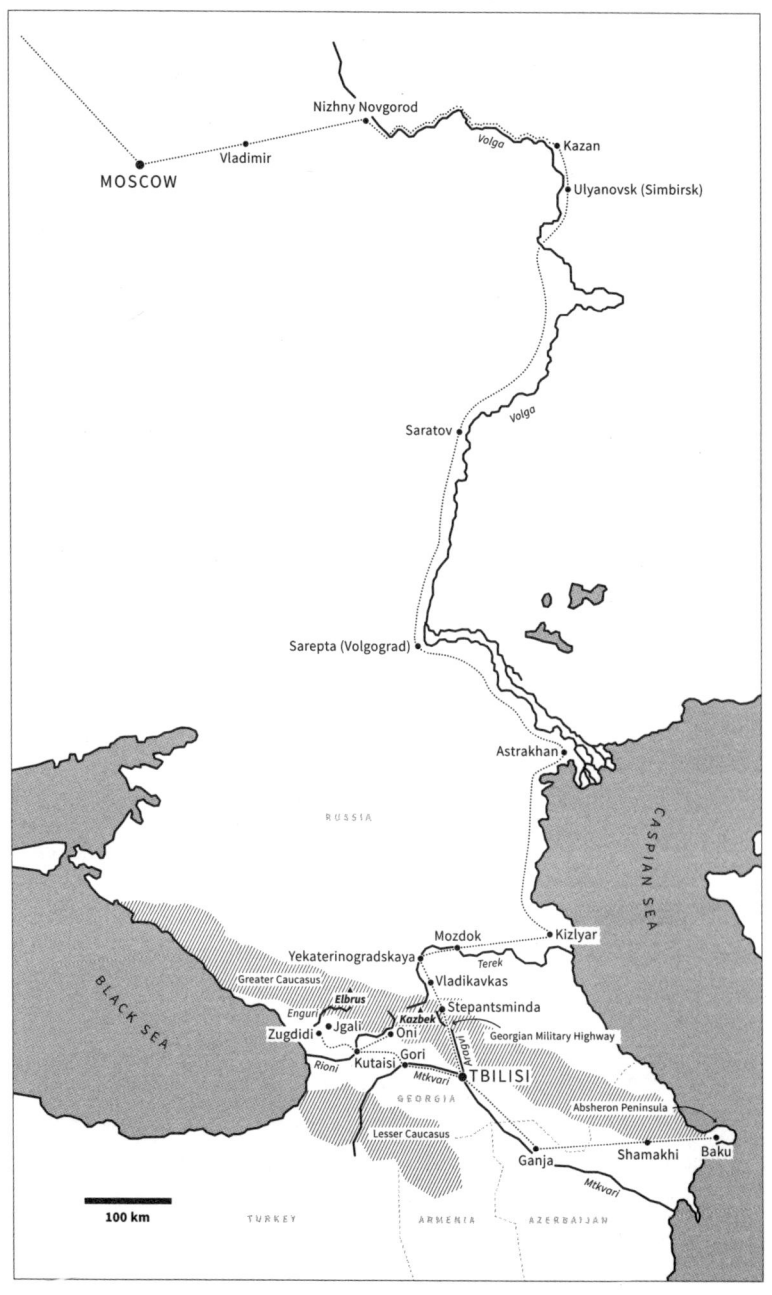

19 Anne Lister's and Anne Walker's journey through tsarist Russia in 1839–40, by Laura Fronterré.

*small dark eyes and a sharpish-looking countenance and dark complex-
ion, quite different from Russians.*[4] Here too, high society took care
of the two Englishwomen, who were invited to dinner, taken to the
theatre and shown around the university. The Orientalist Alexander
Kasimovich Kazembek, who was to number a young Leo Tolstoy
among his students four years later, obtained a very special invitation for Anne and Ann. They first visited a mosque, then *adjourned
to the house of the Tatar honey-merchant Arsayeff, not the richest here,
but very good and much respected and rich – 4 wives. Only saw one son, a
nice enough boy of 7 or 8. Three tables groaned under different species of
pastry and confectionery, then a regular Tatar dinner. A pilaff of rice and
little bits of meat, roast mutton, roast turkey in pieces (though the Tatars
never cut anything up, eat with their fingers), cold fish, etc. After this the
ladies were shown into the harem – the 4 wives and a daughter and niece
or two and 2 or 3 women servants, about 12 altogether. Richly dressed
in brocade and ornamented with pearls, turquoises, even diamonds. The
youngest wife rather pretty, rouged cheeks and blackened teeth. At first
the women were all for running away but they were soon reassured. Poor
things! So many human beings human animals! Except an asylum for
insanes I have never seen any sight so melancholy and so humiliating
as this harem. They are not admitted or capable of being admitted into
society – how terrible the degradation of one half mankind!*[5]

Their next main stop was Saratov, almost 430 miles away. It
became more difficult to get good horses at the postal relay stations
and their accommodation grew more and more basic. The windows
were made of ox gut and the beds – as Count Panin had warned
them in Moscow – were full of bedbugs and fleas. It was no more
comfortable in their coach, however. Several attempts to replace the
broken windows failed. *Cold wind, today the most winterly we have
had. Till the courier put the mat he sat upon against our front window
(still unglazed) we were covered with the flying snow – not snow falling
from the heavens, but the snow from the ground, a regular blizzard by a*

strong south-westerly wind sweeping over this high plain. Can't see 20 yards before us, the atmosphere so obscured by the driving snow. They passed the barrier to Saratov at 1:11 in the afternoon of 28 February 1840. Despite their six-day journey through the cold, they felt no inclination to warm up in their *good-looking* inn. *Impatient to look about us,* they went straight out to explore. The lively market in the busy trading town kept them *well amused, too much so for Ann to complain of being cold or tired.*[6]

They reached their next stop on the Volga, Sarepta, some 250 miles distant, within forty-eight hours. There, they came across Kalmyks, nomadic Mongolians of Tibetan Buddhist faith. Anne and Ann visited a family in their yurt. *The floor was literally a <u>ground</u> floor, the little fire in the centre, the smoke escaping through the circular opening of perhaps 2 ft. in diameter.* [...] *The people in dirty shubes* [wool caftans], *women, too, the latter only distinguished by their gold ear-rings and long black hair in two long tresses reaching down to the hips.* [...] *The faces of the people resembling all the drawings I have seen of the Mongolian – small, dark, rather sunk eyes, highish cheekbones and rather tapering chins, smoke-brown complexions, good white teeth. I thought the people, dirty as they were, so much less ugly than I had expected that I asked our cicerone to tell one of the women I thought her handsome – she grinned her satisfaction.*[7]

The people Anne scrutinised with such abandon stared back with no less curiosity. The less familiar the surroundings were to the Englishwomen, the more they themselves stood out. *The people coming in to look at us as if we were some strange animals such as they had not seen the like before.* They came across people *more Finn-like, and broader faces and stupider looking. 20 or more men and boys and as many women and girls about us in a few minutes, quite a throng, all trying to get a peep at us.*[8] Some Kalmyks became so intrusive that Anne and Ann had to block the door to their room with a table and suitcase; at the window, they *made a screen of two chairs piled with our clothes.* The next morning, though, *just beginning to dress when their curiosity could hold out no longer and they gently opened our folding doors and peeped in at these and the windows till we sat down to breakfast at 8:55. In fact children or grown people stood looking at us all the time we stayed.*[9]

Thanks to a letter of recommendation from Professor Kazembek, the Kalmyk monarch Prince Cerbedjab received the two women at his winter residence in Tumen. *Remarkably good countenance, an agreeable, good-looking, stoutish, gentlemanly man, his manner easy and prepossessing. Moderately Mongol as to features, but the ladies decidedly the very type of Mongolian.* One of these was *a celebrated Calmuck beauty.* They sat in the salon, furnished in European style with oil paintings of the tsar and tsarina above the sofa. George translated from Russian. The prince talked about the Kalmyks and his family, clearly *proud of his descent from Ghenghiz Khan.* His only obligations were to recognise the sovereignty of the tsar and to provide military service in times of war. Prince Cerbedjab had *headed a regiment of his Calmucks at the siege of Leipzig* and been in Paris with Tsar Alexander. One of his cooks had trained there too, and prepared a feast for Anne and Ann complete with French wines, just like *chez un prince Européen.* To finish off, they had *two excellent cups of tea, the best I have tasted in Russia.*

In Tumen, Anne and Ann visited a school and a temple built by Prince Cerbedjab. *A nice lively Russian woman* took care of Anne. *The lady took me by the arm and seated herself by me in the smaller sledge. She put her arm round me to hold me safe if there was any little jolt, I covered her gloveless hands with my cloak and we were very good speechless friends.* The village consisted of tents and huts. *They are Russianising.* What Anne considered the only Buddhist temple in Russia received them with its square tower over four tapering storeys, *very Chinese.* [...] *The thundering music, the din of drum and trumpet, commenced as we reached the steps.* For the two exotic guests, twenty-one priests *in yellow with shaved heads* performed a ceremony, accompanied by eighteen musicians, *all in long gowns, silk-embroidered flowered rich silk, but much worn, and a cap of black silk flowing halfway down the back.* As a parting gift, Prince Cerbedjab gave them a Mongolian grammar book; Anne was surprised *that such a man could still be pagan – could still revere Budda* [sic] *as his prophet, and the grand lama of Tibet as a divine incarnation!* [10]

The Lower Volga was home not only to Kalmyks, but also to Germans. Catherine the Great had invited them to colonise the fertile but sparsely populated territory some eighty years previously. Anne felt almost at home and was pleased to see many a *good tidy German village.* In *the neat little comfortable, well-built, partly stone, partly board town of Sarepta,* their servant Gross asked a fellow German to show them around. *People are not rich here, but live very well. They have no taxes to pay, are free of everything. The clock-and-watch-maker here gains a very good living – the coppersmith, the baker, the everybody. Plenty of work.* They bought nightcaps from weavers, their innkeeper explained the clever system behind his cooling room, and they denigrated the backward methods of the Russian farmers compared with those of their German counterparts. Anne regretted *my own German is not yet beyond a few words of speaking and about twice as many of understanding.* They enjoyed the German food as well; *good cinnamoned soup with tender chicken in it, pigeons cut in two and nicely done – they passed for game with Ann – and potatoes browned in the dish with the birds. And a salad, very pretty and good, dressed with vinegar and sugar, red and white cabbage cut in very fine shreds and well mixed half and half. Think of this for a pretty salad at home. And an excellent little dish of rice browned and cinnamoned over. Preserved plums and apples to eat with the birds, of which we had three – ate two and put one away in our casserole.* The only thing they were not impressed by was the German windows – *very cold last night* – because instead of the *good Russian fashion of double windows, these single concerns let in an air that would turn a mill!* [11]

A month of icy wind at the open coach window had brought Anne a bad cold and a case of conjunctivitis. After a day's bed rest with the Germans in Sarepta, she braced herself against the wind for another five days for the last stage of their journey on the Volga, *seldom out of foot's pace, the snow thickish,* [...] *the most terrible crawl we have had.* Where the wind had blown the snow away, they discovered *a wide expanse of bare red sandy ground.* They had reached the steppe. Approaching vehicles of goods from the Caspian Sea were the only distraction. *The large fish filling a sledge is the balouga, the tail sticking out behind.*[12] They arrived in Astrakhan on the evening of 12 March 1840.

There was not a single inn there. Anne turned to the chief of police, who *offered us his house for the night. He spoke a little French — thankful!*[13] The next day, George Tchaikin found them accommodation with a Belgian tailor who had taken part in Napoleon's Russian campaign, been taken prisoner and ended up marrying a Volga German woman. Although *the town and neighbourhood boast not of beauty,*[14] they stayed ten days, exhausted as they were by crossing 1,500 miles in exactly five debilitatingly cold weeks. *A W tired and out of temper.*[15] Anne, still very ill with her cold, had to stay in bed. Asked about her impressions of travelling in Russia, she answered: *Everything interests me — everywhere is good — no disparagements for me. Sleep well on the floor and care not about the floors, whether this or that, so far. Ann finds them dirty, and compared them at a discount with the Inns of England. Unfair. I neither do this to the Russians or to myself. Considering the real state of civilisation among the various peoples of Russia and how little the higher orders travel in their country or know it, it is more wonderful to have the comforts, the facilities we have than that any should be wanting.*[16] Their servant Gross did not agree. He asked for his dismissal and Anne and Ann had to let him go.

Eventually, their coach was repaired and put on wheels. George and Domna Tchaikin got a new kibitka. They replenished their supplies and paid for the pass to Tbilisi – 125 roubles for 550 miles. The tsar made good money out of permission to travel: six people could stay in an inn for eight roubles a night, but the travel pass didn't cover accommodation. That had to be paid for separately, along with the expense of the horses and coachmen. They set out on 22 March. *All sandy mud and steppe. We soon after leaving Astrakhan left the Volga, to see it no more.*[17] They spent fourteen days struggling across boggy ground against the still strong wind and came across *a new and worse kind* of postal station, where not even a samovar simmered away. *Well, we have our spirit lamp so we have had English tea very comfortably. No cream here, not much water – nothing but the room.*[18] From Kizlyar, a *dirty, muddy place* with *low shabby unpainted houses,*[19] they followed the course of the Terek River for the next 370 miles or so to the main ridge of the Greater Caucasus. Aside from military men, they saw no more Russians. In completely mud-ridden Mozdok, they received their first armed escort. *Our 2 Cossacks very picturesque, very dexterous. Threw down their caps and picked them up at a gallop, as also sticks. Played in this way till their poor sorry-looking horses were quite in a heat.* When they were initially refused an escort at the next station because a *paper* was missing, Anne *charged one of my pistols and we drove off with 5 horses each.*[20]

In Yekaterinogradskaya – *mud worse even than at Mozdok* – there was no escort to be had; attacks by Cherkess further south meant all the military forces were occupied, so the local commander simply forbade Anne and Ann from travelling any further. That gave Anne a day of rest on her forty-ninth birthday. She and Ann drove out before the town's gates and enjoyed their first view of the Greater Caucasus. *At 2:10 how fine! Magnificent snow-covered granite? range. Rugged, peaky, raviney.*[21]

While Anne could hardly wait to get there, her partner felt less anticipation. The postal courier did not want to go with them, *shammed illness, and would have left us at Ekaterinograd if I would have given him his passport.* But Anne needed every one of her men to cross the mountains, and the courier had to stay. *George, tho' he shared the servile fear, never breathed a wish or thought to leave us; and, considering his coward-company, this did him great credit.* Domna, the *little femme de chambre began gradually to recover itself,*[22] and Ann was not asked her opinion. Anne put together a private escort of four armed Yekaterinogradskaya men on horseback, and they set off.

Only a few miles along, they passed a quarantine station for those travelling in the other direction, where *if one has not a bill of health from the Governor further south one has to pass 14 days.* In Alexandrovskaya, the Englishwomen met a Russian officer travelling alone, who *was going to Tiflis and will be glad to travel in our train!* The next morning they received an escort from four Cossacks. Along the way, the coachman suddenly shouted *Tcherkess!* and brought the coach to an abrupt halt. Anne and Ann spotted numerous horsemen out of their windows. *Our Cossacks prepared for fight. I got out and reprimed my one loaded pistol. The Tcherkess, all apparently well mounted, wheeled round (I counted about 20) to the back of us and drew up on the rising ground behind us to the right. I concluded they were preparing for a regular cavalry charge down upon us – their halt was to me a moment of anxiety.* But the horsemen hesitated. *We drove on foot's pace, faster, nothing beyond a bit of trot now and then, we could not go. Both our doors were open. I mentally counted our strength – 4 Cossacks, 4 drivers, a Russian officer and his servant and drivers who had come along with us, a teleaga with a man or two, the courier and George and ourselves. I thought we could make a tolerable fight. I felt not the least afraid, nor did Ann.* After tense minutes, Anne noted, *they hesitated – they rode off.*[23] The party reached Vladikavkaz a day later, on 6 April.

Now the capital city of North Ossetia, the town was originally founded by the Russian government as a fortress against the people of the Caucasus. Since antiquity, a bridle path had led from here across the Greater Caucasus, which was eventually improved by the Russian army for its campaigns; it was called the Georgian Military Road from then on. Anne asked the military for directions to the postal stations so as to find accommodation, horses and escorts along the way. They also got hold of brake shoes for the kibitkas and exchanged their banknotes, which would be of no value any further south, for hard silver roubles. Snowfall delayed their departure. Anne used the time to write her journal, noticing she had forgotten it was a leap year. Instead of correcting all the dates, starting with 29 February 1840, she inserted a second 6 April.

They began the strenuous ascent into the mountains on the foggy morning of 8 April; each *kibitka* was pulled by six horses rather than the usual two or three. They reached Lars (1,122 m) at midday and the famous eight-mile Darial Gorge. *Cliffs stand on both sides like parallel walls*,[24] wrote a very impressed Alexander Pushkin, who had visited eleven years previously. Anne found *it is like a 'Chaos', sublimely wild and desolate.*[25] These days, heavy Russian, Turkish and Georgian trucks thunder along the gorge on the relatively well-maintained Georgian Military Road. By the evening, the group reached Stepantsminda (1,750 m) at the foot of the 5,047-metre Kazbek,[26] the mountain to which Prometheus was chained as punishment for bringing men fire, according to Greek mythology. As with Pushkin before her, the weather did not grant Anne a view of the famous peak. *Stood gazing till I could see nothing and my eyes ached towards Mt Kasbek. The monastery full in view for some minutes then clouded over again.* No modern-day Georgian tourist brochure would be complete without a photo of the Tsminda Sameba Church against the backdrop of Mount Kazbek's snow-covered volcanic rock.

On the second day, the road became steep and dangerous; *the courier wanted us to alight.* [...] *No guard, we might easily slip off the side of the narrow road into the river,* [...] *little frozen small snow flying about as we toil up to higher ground.* After a night in the *nice little whitewashed inn*[27] in Kobi (1,981 m), the next morning they took an extra sledge and *17 men to help us over the mountains,* the Cross Pass, the highest elevation on the Georgian Military Road; *a very useful precaution as it turned out, and 3 mounted Cossacks to take care of us. [...] All our men formed a very picturesque group over the snowy mountains.* The snow was so deep that Anne and Ann soon had to leave their *kibitka* on wheels for the sledge. *Very cold, cold wind in our faces.* [...] *At 7:55 we were at the difficulties, steep narrow pitches up hill that almost set fast the 5 horses to each kibitka. At 8:50 on the narrow road along precipitous mountain-side. All deep snow here.* They reached the Cross Pass (2,379 m) at nine. *At 9:20 steep narrow descent with tremendous precipice close right. Worst part of the road and here meet traineaux and laden horses and Tcherkess peasants.* [...] The *terrible road* led them to a *long very steep descent at an awful perpendicular height above the Aragna. I alight at 2:35 and walk to the bottom of this part (Ann was crying and would not alight).* Once they arrived in the *beautiful valley,* the worst was behind them. They reached the inn in Passanauri (1,050 m) at 4:50 that afternoon, and bade farewell to their many helpers. Despite the hard day, Ann Walker found a place to sketch while Anne went for a walk; *the white, rapidy river, the fine forms of the mountains – beautiful scene.*[28]

Via Ananuri (712 m), they reached Mtskheta two days later, *one of the most ancient cities of Asia,* the *ancient capital of Georgia* prior to Tbilisi and the country's spiritual centre to this day. Now a UNESCO World Heritage Site, the city disappointed Anne, who saw at first glance only rubble and a neglected village. At second glance, though, she discovered traces of the past in the people, their clothing and customs. *How this savours of remote antiquity!* [...] *The houses, ovens sunk in the floor, cattle-skin bottles of wine let out at one of the legs, boats scooped out of the trunks of trees, are surely the same as in the days of Homer.*[29] They continued to Tbilisi that same evening. It was 12

April 1840. Since leaving Moscow, they had been on the road for two months and one week.

They planned to stay a while and recover their strength in the Oriental-style city with its fifty thousand inhabitants, including more Armenians than Georgians, many Cherkessians and Persians, Pietists from Württemberg and a handful of Russians, mainly military men and civil servants. However, the rooms at their inn were unheated and damp; they had six windows *with cold airs blowing about in all six directions.*[30] They sent back the food they were brought from a cook-shop. Ann Walker improvised soups, eggs and rice on their spirit cooker. Cold and rain kept them inside for the first week. Ann was physically and mentally exhausted. Anne was too tired to write her diary, only reporting their arrival in Tbilisi to Princess Sophia Radzivill. *All is rose-coloured for us here, but nothing can make me forget the very happy hours I spent with you. [...] Did you receive my little farewell note? It at least has the merit of being true. I have only a single little letter with me – that from Saint Sophia.* That was a lie, as was all the rest. *Adieu!*[31]

A letter of recommendation from Countess Panina to her cousin, the wife of the Russian governor general, improved their situation. Mme Golovina took up the two women's cause, had a working stove installed in their accommodation, sent them meals and showed them around town in her coach. The Russian rulers had declared Tbilisi capital of the newly conquered territories in the Caucasus, which also included large parts of Azerbaijan and Armenia. The *full and busy* bazaar next to the bridge across the Mtkvari instantly became *our favourite place.*[32] They went on through the sulphuric baths district of Abanotubani to the picturesque gorge, at the foot of the ancient Narikala fortress, which was at that time being converted into the Botanical Garden, which still exists today. *25 minutes sauntering to the top and then the door opened and what a panorama! It is a long narrow ridge or promontory of rock on which the old castle and fortifications stand, dividing the town from the ravine of the garden – Magnificent! Gazed in mute admiration – the river, the circular opening-out for the German colony, the town throttled at the bridge, and the range of snow-covered mountains and Kasbek. How fine! How new and Asiatic to us.*[33] In a letter to Mariana, Anne made a first summary of their crossing of the Caucasus. *At the Pyrenees the transition from France to Spain is sufficiently striking; but here it is from Europe to Asia.* [...] *My expectations are exceeded.*

Thanks to Mme Golovina, Anne and Ann were invited to the homes of the Russian military and Georgian aristocracy. *We everywhere find an agreeable and polished society. A ball given by the commander in chief here (a very viceroy) is like a ball in London, or Paris, with the additional interest of Georgian beauty, and a picturesque mixture of Georgian costume with the <u>dernièrs modes de Paris</u>.*[34] Anne and Ann were particularly impressed by two sisters, still legendary in Georgia today, *a perfectly Europeanised specimen of Georgian ladies, très comme il faut,*[35] Nino Chavchavadze and her sister, Princess Ekaterina Dadiani, *jeune, jolie, et très gracieuse.*[36] The latter invited Anne and Ann to visit her palace in Zugdidi.

But Anne wanted to continue to Tehran and Baghdad. Everyone they met declared such a journey impossible. They might get as far as Tabriz in their *kibitkas* but they would have to switch to mules after that, for which the ladies would have to wear men's clothing. Persian servants and interpreters would be essential. The only way to travel from Tehran to Baghdad was by caravan, and they would have to wait up to a year for an opportunity to return. None of this shocked Anne. [37] Phyllis Ramsden sums up the situation as: *A W very put out – accuses AL of selfishness abt travel programme.*[37] In the end, Anne had to admit defeat for financial reasons, especially as the trip had already gone over budget. *No Persia for the present.*[38] As it was, they had to contact their banker in Moscow and ask him to tap into their emergency fund in Hamburg.

To make up for missing out on Persia, Anne at least wanted to see the Caspian Sea. The regular Russian post road went as far as Baku and she was determined to get that far. This led to a *disagreement with AW, who doesn't want to go further afield,*[39] but Anne got her way as usual. Only Domna was granted leave, being pregnant. With reduced luggage, they set off for Azerbaijan on 13 May, a month after their arrival in Tbilisi. George Tchaikin was with them, as well as four mounted Cossacks and an officer for their protection. For a time, they also had to add four Tartars to their escort, as the road ran through contested territories.

It took them five days to get to Baku. There were as few bridges as in Hanover; they used ferries to cross the rivers, swollen with melted snow. On the way, they visited homes dug deep into the earth. *5 women, their chemises open so as to show their flabby pendant breasts and great part of the stomach. Curiously examined our clothes, admired Ann's green silk wadded bonnet lined with pink.* They spent a night with a caravan of forty camels, *a delightful tranquil scene. I stood some minutes with the camels, a few browsing, some chewing their cud, some sleeping, their faces on the ground, doglike, and their hind legs curiously bent under them in the oriental sitting fashion.*[40] At the bazaar in Shemakhi, Anne Lister – who was beginning to go grey – was interested in henna, a *yellow-green powder with which they dye their beards black.* They tried the local specialities with curiosity, a *veritable plum cake. i.e. of plums dried* and *a dish of eggs poached in oil and eaten with cake. Half dozen men at one dish – dipped in the cake and took out the egg with their finger and one of the men held out a bit for me to taste. I ate it off his finger and found it very eatable.*[41]

Baku, located on a steep hill, was surrounded at that time by a double wall. The Russian city commandant, Colonel Tchekmarev, allocated the two women accommodation in *a house lowish in the town, not far from the sea. 1 large, 1 small room and a balcony looking over the sea. Close to the principal mosque and very near the Commandant's house,* *well-situated and quiet.* Mme Tchekmareva took care of the unexpected guests of the smallest and most remote military post in the Russian Empire. She sent them *cream and bread and a marinade of fowl* *(Ann never enjoyed any meat so much in Russia),*[42] to which Ann added rice, eggs and vegetables cooked on her spirit cooker, as in Tbilisi.

Ann Walker became particularly friendly with Mme Tchekmareva. She admired her loose Turkish-style doublet, which was more suitable for the increasingly hot season than the English ladies' fashion Anne Lister felt obliged to wear. *I could not stand this climate unclothed!*[43] Ann, however, bought Persian silk and sewed airy dresses for herself with Mme Tchekmareva's aid. She also got along well with a naval adjutant who sketched like her and had interesting things to say about the shells of the Caspian Sea. Despite her reluctance to come along in the first place, she was more cheerful and relaxed in Baku than usual. Anne Lister, too, found much to enjoy. For the second time on their trip, she visited a harem, this time that of the Persian jeweller Hadji Baba; *were so much amused among the women that there we sat till after* *8, about an hour I should think. We found the floor covered with hand-* *some carpetting and 3 chairs placed at the head of the room for us, and* *women standing all round the room, perhaps about 20, enough to quite* *fill the room. Hadji's son (a youth with sprouting beard) and a woman* *servant handed tea and sweetmeats and pistachios.* [...] *Two or three of* *the women were handsome, the rest not at all. Wide silk trousers hardly* *distinguishable from petticoats (generally red or crimson) and belaced* *or bejewelled jackets and veils. Necklaces and bracelets, and head orna-* *ments, and large Chinese-looking earrings, and 3-inch-diameter round* *brooches stuck on the middle of the chest in front, full of rubies, emer-* *alds, etc. mounted in enamel and gold.* [...] *They danced at our request* *the Georgian dance danced at Tiflis, but* <u>much</u> *better, much more natu-* *rally – especially one rather older girl (perhaps aged 20) who was quite* *taken with us. She hugged and embraced Mme Tchekmarev for 2 or 3 minutes, and me for half as long, at parting, and promised to come and see us in spite of their Prophet! How she managed the bonny wriggle-and-lifting petticoat I know not, but it was well done, and the animated eye and strong cracking of thumbs bespoke the interest she evidently felt. All cracked or struck their hands together in cadence with the dance, and so did I, and to their apparently great delight I made as much 'handy' noise as any of them. On leaving, just went up to Hadji and the Commandant and one or 2 more men. They had had sweetmeats, but had probably been less amused than we.*[44]

After Anne and Ann had viewed the ruins of the Shirvanshahs' Palace and the Maiden Tower, their new friends took them on an excursion to the oil-rich Absheron peninsula. A few decades before the oil boom, the crude oil near the surface was still being drawn by hand from eighty-five wells and used as naphtha for lamps, lubricant for wheels or a sealant for boats. Natural gas, which was *abundant here, one only has to dig for it,*[45] burned as an eternal flame in Zoroastrian temples. As the region was converted to Islam, their places of worship were converted to mosques; the Ateshgah temple, close to the oil and gas field, was the last one remaining. *Singular place, like a fortress-foundry.* A low entrance gate led to a courtyard, surrounded on all four sides by twenty-one windowless chambers. There were (and still are) *4 fire chimneys in the square open tower temple,* where gas was burned. In the middle of the building was a *square well about 5 ft x 3 ft and 3 ft deep with strong flame forever burning, but one of the Indians extinguished it with cold water and then immediately lighted it again for our amusement.* Because the temple also attracted Hindus, it was *put into good repair by an Indian in 1825* – and recently made even 'better' by the Azerbaijani government. Anne and Ann also saw a ceremony being performed. *The high priest was signed on his forehead with a red tongue between 2 yellow lines (the sign of fire), but called himself a worshipper more especially of Krishna. He and 2 others did the duty, very serious and pious-looking.* In a *neat little carpeted and divanned room for strangers* with two small flames of its own, they were served dinner, *cold meat and quass and wine.* They were back at their accommodation by eleven in the evening. *Tea, and sat whistling until 1 1/2 am.*[46]

A week after their arrival, they departed *in gratitude and regret,* equipped by Mme Tchekmarev with a giant meat pie, *a bottle of white naphta, bag of rice (best kind) containing 10 or 12 lbs at least, 18 hard-boiled eggs, fowl, cake of bread and 2 bottles of Baku white wine.*[47] Anne had actually wanted to return via Armenia for a spot of *gazing on the berceau of mankind, the sacred Ararat.*[48] None of the high-ranking military men of her acquaintance would issue a pass for the conquered but by no means pacified region, however, so they had to return to Tbilisi the way they had come. In *very picturesque* Ganja – now the second-largest city in Azerbaijan – *the caravanserai must have been handsome in its day, now a heap of ruins inside, all the rooms but 6 or 7 roofless and more or less filled with rubbish. [...] Could not sleep for heat and fleas.* The next day, too, they were *much bit even during the day. Have not had such a flea-hunt since Italy in 1827 when I frequently caught at night 30 or more. Poor Ann's legs were absolutely in blisters – got her to take her over-stockings off and leave her boots unbuttoned at the top.*[49] On 1 June they were back in Tbilisi, *back at our old quarters (same room, same price).*[50]

They found the banknotes from Moscow on arrival and their acquaintances exchanged them for silver coins. *Talking over journey and money matters and as usual this latter subject never ends happily. We have had in foreign money six hundred and fifty of the thousand pounds in circulars,* and they had also tapped into the Hamburg emergency fund to the tune of £85. After this financial stocktaking, Ann Walker urged that they return home immediately. Anne Lister, however, thought that they had enough money left and that the season was good for travelling. She wanted to see more of the Caucasus and the Black Sea and only then go *quickly home.*[51] For their return journey, Anne ordered another £200 to be taken out of their emergency fund in Hamburg via Moscow.

It took Anne three hot summer weeks to organize the next leg of their journey. As well as George and Domna, the Cossack officer who had accompanied them to Baku was to travel with them again. He spoke Turk, which *is indispensable here, almost all the Georgians speak Tatar as well as their own ancient language.*[52] They had an escort of three mounted Cossacks. Anne took directions from her new travel bible, Frédéric Dubois de Montpéreux's *Voyage autour du Caucase* (1839). They headed west along the Mtkvari valley. The vegetation grew more and more lush, and two days after they set out, on the dot *at 12:40 beauty begins. Wood on our right, good green valley about a mile wide, hills wooded left.*[53] They stayed in Gori for three nights; from there, they rode to the Ateni Sioni Church with its impressive frescoes and to the ancient town of Uplistsikhe, carved out of the rock high above the Mtkvari River, boasting pillars and Roman coffered ceilings. Ann Walker instantly whipped out her sketchbook and even Anne Lister made a few of her rare sketches in her diary.

The post road then left the Mtkvari River and wound upwards to the Surami Pass (949 m), past the mountain of the same name, which connects the Greater and the Lesser Caucasus and divides Georgia into eastern and western halves. Anne and Ann noticed that the mountain range was a watershed and climatic divide. *One of the most beautiful drives I have ever taken in my life – deep rock gorge, the road often a corniche cut out of the rock, and the narrow river filling the whole of the bottom. All sides beautifully wooded – beech, aspens, a few pinus sylvestris on tops of hills. The road lined with the white-cluster flowering red berried maple-leaved shrub I know not at home and with rhododendrum ponticum, the first time I have seen it in these parts. And with oak and beech and hornbeam in abundance, very beautiful. And elm and honeysuckle (and wild pear and apricot trees) and hazels and luxuriant common laurel (first time) and privet. The last 2 and the rhodo., honeysuckle and hazel forming a beautiful thick underwood fringe on each side the road.*[54]

On 28 June they reached Kutaisi, now the second largest city in Georgia, for Anne Lister the capital of ancient Colchis and *le séjour de Medée*.[55] According to Greek myth, it was the home of King Aeëtes, from whom Jason stole the Golden Fleece. In Kutaisi, Anne and Ann were welcomed by the *very amiable* Mme Boujourova, the wife of the local Cossack commandant. They stayed in the regional government's guesthouse for ten days, though it had to be furnished in haste on their arrival. *Ann said the other morning she had not felt so well for years. The climate not too hot for her, she likes Koutaisi very much.* Kutaisi is located on the Rioni River – the ancient Phasis, which Jason and the Argonauts rowed up – where it flows from the mountains into the wide plain of Colchis, its swamps not drained until the twentieth century. *I can't say I like the climate – too hot and moist – too thickly wooded. But very beautiful and interesting in the highest degree to the traveller.*[56] As eager to learn as ever, they viewed the sights: Bagrati Cathedral, a ruin at the time but now rebuilt, and the monasteries at Gelati and Motsameta.

In Kutaisi, the main road with regular posting houses came to an end. The only way on from there was on horseback. The route to the Black Sea would be hard work across the swampy, humid, mosquito-plagued plains, so Anne and Ann decided on a tour of the Greater Caucasus mountain range. Their excursion to the province of Racha-Lechkhumi lasted several weeks and outshone everywhere they had ventured on their trip. Anne and Ann hired a local guide, Adam, who got hold of the necessary equipment and supplies for a region without inns, shops or food stalls. He had a horse of his own for riding and they rented the others from Moshe, a Jewish horse breeder who came along to take care of the animals. There were six travellers in the party: Anne and Ann, George Tchaikin from Moscow, the Cossack from Tbilisi and Adam and Moshe from Kutaisi. They left the large part of their luggage, including books and fur boots, with the pregnant maid Domna at the Boujourovs' home. Their journey began on 9 July 1840, heading northeast. *At 11:25 we stopped at a shady grassy spot close to the highroad and the river. Breakfasted very well on cold tea, 2 cold boiled eggs, a piece of bread and butter and half a cucumber. Breakfast over at 12:25. I sat on my English saddle-bags and wrote till 1 1/2, Ann asleep on the grass (on her cloaks).* Anne considered their resting group extremely *picturesque – our horses grazing beside us, our suite talking at a little distance behind us. Adam wears a Circassian cap, black wool fringe and yellow top. Our Jew a black lamb's wool Persian cap, otherwise clad à la Georgienne. Our Cossack in uniform, blue light short jacket, blue trousers and white casquette. George in white trousers and short yellowish-green coat with courier's belt and kindjal* [a dagger]. *Ann in her habit and I in my pelisse and black tawny cloak and dark blue cloth (Jupp, London) casquette, and Ann and I men's Moscow boots.* [...] *A nice breath of air now and then. F 82°* [27.8 C] *at 2 pm in my bag in the shade and 90°* [32.2 °C] *where I am sitting reading at 3:20. In another hour the heat will be abating and we can be off.*[57] The path led along a river through the Colchis forest, blessed with such abundant vegetation that it seemed almost tropical. An amazed Anne recorded the circumference of particularly magnificent trees using her measuring tape.

Their documents from the authorities entitled them to demand free accommodation from every local administrator. Anne had anticipated empty barns or huts, but Adam always went directly to the best house in each village, which might be a *good wood house* or indeed *a very poor little place.*[58] They often got a room to themselves, but they sometimes had to share the house's one room with an entire family. On one occasion there was *no possibility of staying there – full of people ill in 'the hot fever', the 2 or 3 that came to the door pale as ghosts.*[59] Food had to be bought from the locals, often enough forced out of them – even silver coins were only of limited value to these mountain peasants. In their quarters, they were usually given the best people had, sometimes even treated to feasts with several courses and a choice of wines. They were also entertained in unusual ways. *We had a tame bear-cub in that ate out of our hand.*[60]

Via Satsire, the Nakerala Pass (1,217 m) and Khotevi, they reached Nikortsminda, where they admired the stonemasonry on the church, *the richest and best done we have seen.*[61] Anne and Ann probably exchanged amused glances when they discovered the curious fresco of Adam and Eve to the left of the entrance, both naked, androgynous and barely distinguishable from one another. Five days after setting out, they arrived in Oni (800 m) on the River Rioni. Various factors, including decent guestrooms in the so-called palace, a house made of stone, and a market – *some of the women were afraid when we touched their things*[62] – made the town the perfect base camp for expeditions to the mountains.

Their first destination was the source of the Rioni, on the main crest of the Greater Caucasus, surrounded by majestic mountains. They rode through deciduous forest clogged with azalea bushes to Utsera (950 m), where they were given an escort of four armed men the next morning as their route took them into the border region to Ossetia – a war zone then, as now. Via Ghebi (1,337 m) they reached a simple military camp high in the mountains, after nightfall. It was the first time they had had to sleep outdoors on the whole trip. *A few long thin poles set up meeting in a point and a few small branches thrown over them to the north and a fire in front – and this our bivouac for the night. I kept my thoughts to myself, set the Cossack to bring 3 pieces of wood and arranged Ann's bed very fairly. No wood convenient for me so spread my burca* [a shepherd's coat] *and saddle cloth on the ground, put on my light cloak and wrapped myself up in my mackintosh for the night. Ann had an egg and I my flat cake from Rebi and a bit of cheese and supped very well.*

The next morning, they set out at four with twenty-one armed peasants, heading for the source of the Rioni. By six, the path was too difficult even for the horses, and they had to fight their way through the underbrush on foot. It took them an hour to get there. *The source is from under a glacier, and 2 picturesque high falls of water, the one double or more the other.* [...] *A 'cirque' formed by 2 mountains, having the glacier on the col between them.* [...] *Left Ann almost immediately and actually at the source at 7:55.* [...] *Very rapid fall from the glacier all the way down to where Ann is sketching.* They were back at base by 10:10 and paid the men two silver roubles, *with which they seemed well satisfied.* [...] *Good honest mountaineers – I would go all the Caucasus over with them.* They returned to Ghebi that evening, sleeping in an open barn and receiving plentiful attention, with crowds of *people to look at us.*[63] Back in Oni the next day and without a maid, Anne was forced to wash her own laundry. *First time in my life*[64] – at the age of forty-nine.

A second major excursion from Oni took them to Sachkhere on the Kvirila, which they followed upstream; *crossed today Kvirila 29 times and Djouroudja 19 times.* [...] *My boots wet though I held up my feet as high as I could.*[65] Although Anne discovered beautifully located monasteries, archaic cavern homes and countless natural phenomena on this trekking tour – sights hardly any western Europeans had ever seen, let alone women – she never wanted to stay long in one place. She cursed the four-hour siesta that her men insisted on for themselves and the horses, feeling she was being robbed of valuable daylight hours; the only thing she could do during this long rest was write her diary. She ate little, complained a great deal and eventually went out walking on her own in the hot midday weather. On one occasion she tried to climb into an overgrown castle. *Scrambled up with difficulty, but the hole did not furnish means of getting into the castle. Scrambling down again took me 20 minutes – I had had 50 minutes of toil for nothing. Back to Ann at 2. A man with a ladder waiting to go with us into the castle. Broiling walk up along the traverses to the west end and in*

10 minutes in the castle. Five old pieces of cannon, one with an inscription in Georgian. [...] Very interesting old castle. Off at 3, back to the tree at 3:18, soaked through, my mouth quite parched. The 2 men (George and Adam) ½ undressed, <u>smoking</u> with heat. We had full sun upon us the latter part of the way, the heat near our walnut tree at 3:35 was F. 104 ½ [40.3 °C].[66] And yet Anne was surprised that *Ann bears the heat with much less thirst and much better than I, but I am improving. Left off my woollen undersleeves this morning.*[67]

In general Ann Walker coped better with life in the wilderness than Anne Lister. She liked to set out in the cool early morning, ate well at midday, took a nap and then found a shady spot to sketch and was refreshed and ready to ride on in the late afternoon. Unlike Anne, she was a good horsewoman, knew how to deal with horses and enjoyed their company. The two of them seem to have got on better in the remote mountain world, especially as Ann Walker now experienced her partner as caring, perhaps for the first time. On more than one occasion, they lost their way and rode through the pitch-black night. Anne *called every now and then to make sure Ann was close behind me.* Being a gentleman, Anne always insisted on giving Ann the better place to sleep – *1 divan (carpeted) for Ann and a long low table for me*[68] – and gave her the best pickings of their meals.

Back at Oni, two of their horses went lame. They hoped to find replacements in Lailashi, thirty-five miles to the west, but could only buy one horse in the *poor little place.*[69] Adam, George and Moshe refused to set out for Svanetia. Anne Lister had to concede defeat and they returned to Kutaisi along the beautiful Rioni valley after twenty-six days in the mountains.

Kutaisi was boiling in the summer heat and Anne Lister was in a rush to get away again. They bought four new horses and took their leave from Moshe and also from George, who was allowed to stay and recover with his pregnant wife Domna until they all planned to return to Moscow together in a few weeks' time. Only Adam, their guide from Kutaisi, and the Cossack officer from Tbilisi stayed with Anne and Ann, although they had no common language. They rode to Zugdidi to visit Davit and Ekaterina Dadiani. Along the way, they took a detour to the Martvili monastery, not finding it until late at night in pouring rain, and to Nokalakevi, equally difficult to reach along wild paths the next day. There, the aged Prince Bijan Dadiani showed them a very overgrown but spectacular *acropolis*, which has since been identified as the ancient town of Archaeopolis. They spent the evening chatting with the princess, who was so fascinated by Anne that the next morning she *watched me dressing through the little lattice close above where I slept. Hung up my cloak against her pretending not to see her.*[70] Anne was not interested in the women of rural Georgia, of whom even some Christians *wore the white thing that when pulled up covers the mouth.*[71] *These Georgian Mingrelian ladies sit squat all day on their carpets doing nothing, and are queer dowdy-looking figures. Crimson or white chemise under their long trailing gowns. Their breasts wobbling about like a couple of bladders.*[72]

To prevent them from losing their way again, Prince Bijan sent his servant Davit along with the Englishwomen to Zugdidi, where they arrived on the evening of 8 August. At the Dadianis' palace, the rather unkempt travellers had an opportunity to make themselves presentable. *Our room carpetted with Persian carpets. Several menservants in waiting and 2 nice little chambermaids arranging our 2 comfortable sofas to perfection – pillows, coverlets.* After five weeks in the wilderness, they were astounded by their room. *Silver ewer and pitcher. Large table, little round toilet-table and good looking-glass standing on it, 4 chairs, and 2 armchairs, luxurious, and 2 waxlights burning.* Plus *soap, combs and brushes, dressing-gowns and nightcaps (very pretty), pomatum and eau-de-cologne. Luxurious wash and flea-hunt (brought with us in our clothes) last night, and not bit at all.* Ravenous, they pounced upon the delicious bread and fresh butter provided as an appetiser and then could not eat the unexpected supper that came next. *Have not had so comfortable a bed and room since leaving Moscow.* They stayed in bed the next morning. *Ann had her hair done and then I had mine done very nicely. Our boots cleaned and pelisses brushed.* Then they could finally greet their hosts.

However, the young Ekaterina Dadiani was *looking pale and emaciated.*[73] Her firstborn daughter was so sick that the Dadianis had sent for a German doctor from Kutaisi. Anne and Ann met him over a Russian lunch at two, along with two more Dadiani ladies, the wife of a Russian officer and the French agriculturalist Joseph Liétaud, who was to modernise the young prince's estate. Another guest, an unnamed German botanist, was ill in bed and could not join them for the meal. The company exchanged political news in French, snapped up avidly by Davit Dadiani, whose principality, Mingrelia, was under threat from Russia's territorial claims. Afterwards, Anne and Ann strolled around the large botanical garden that the Dadianis were having planted.

The princess sent her apologies at tea. Anne and Ann had landed in a place as unhealthy as it was luxurious. Zugdidi is located on a plain – which was still swamps at that time – only 18 miles from the Black Sea. *It is the climate that so disagrees with the little Dadiani daughter, a fine little child. I advised the princess to change air – go up to Lailashi.*[74] Anne could barely stand Zugdidi; *hot and muggy, while sitting in my pelisse from 4 to 7 pm, in a profuse perspiration, not a dry stitch on me.*[75] As Ann Walker, too, was *off colour,* the two agreed to break off their journey to the Black Sea and instead ride into the mountains again, trying to find a way back to Kutaisi. They set out at five the next afternoon. Ekaterina Dadiani gave them *6 salted cucumbers and a large fresh cheese and 8 or 10 rolls or more and 2 bottles red wine for myself and 2 white for Ann and 6 or 8 wax candles and fresh cucumbers and apples.*[76]

They rode northeast, making do a few hours later with very modest accommodation at a farm in Lia. There too, *the children*

20 Anne Lister's last journal page, 11 August 1840; West Yorkshire
Archive Service, Calderdale, SH: 7/ML/E/24.

especially, and the men and women, look pale and yellow and unhealthy in this moist hot bottom valley. As they had to share the room with the family, *A— awoke me before six, anxious to be off.*[77] Less than an hour later, they reached the Enguri River and rode along *its broad, bouldery bedded, islandy, streamy course* up the valley. They stayed in Jvari, at that time a dispersed village, from nine to two, breakfasted in an empty hut and had *a tolerably comfortable wash* — perhaps fearing contagion. Today, Europe's highest dam wall rises behind Jvari, holding back the Enguri in its narrow ravine to form a long lake. We do not know whether that ravine was impassable at the time or whether Anne and Ann got lost, as they so often did. They left the river course and arrived in the village of Satchino. Rain set in at five that afternoon, *not heavy, but likely to continue,* and *all our 3 men have left us to seek somebody or something. Adam came back in 1/2 hour. Ann had had an egg beaten up, and I had the things off my horse and done up my mackintosh. David does not know the road — get a man to go with us to the village. An hour lost here. Off to the village, Djakali* [Jgali], *at 6:05 and arrived at 6 3/4. 2 cottages. Arrange ourselves in the Indian corn barn (a little wicker place perhaps 4 1/2 by 3 yards). Spread our burcas on straw and now, 8:25, I have just writ the last 19 lines. High hills north, and, within, ridges of wooded hill rising every now and then into little wooded conical summits. The sides of the hills furrowed, and little conical summits on the ridges of the sides. Tea etc. now at 8:25. Lay down at 9 1/2.*[78]

Those were the last words Anne Lister wrote in her diary. It was 11 August 1840. Six weeks later, she was dead. What happened between these dates is unknown. Did she feel faint and unable to continue writing? According to Muriel Green, they reached Lailashi in Lechkhumi again on 31 August. From there, they returned to Kutaisi by the same route as four weeks previously. George and Domna were waiting there and the German doctor summoned to Zugdidi by Ekaterina Dadiani practised there. But the doctor could have helped neither the child nor

Anne Lister, should he have met her. Her obituary notice dates her death to *Tuesday September 22, at Koutais, of 'La fièvre chaude'.*[79]

Fever was a blanket term for various diseases at the time. The illness lasting several weeks might suggest typhus, but Anne Lister may also have contracted severe malaria in the swampy Colchis region. She had demanded a great deal of her body on the journey. As persistent and tough as she was, she had always tended to overestimate herself. In the Lake District, at the Great Saint Bernhard Pass, on Monte Perdido, on Vignemale, and most recently on the frozen Volga, Anne Lister had challenged fate. Mr Duffin had been proved right: her mind wore her body out.

THE WIDOW

We are informed that the remains of this distinguished lady have been embalmed, and that her friend and companion, Miss Walker, is bringing them home by way of Constantinople, for interment in the family vault,[1] the *Halifax Guardian* wrote on 31 October 1840 in its notice of Anne Lister's death, reported back by Ann Walker. Ann was presumably fulfilling Anne's last wish; otherwise she would hardly have submitted to the long torture of transferring a corpse from Kutaisi to Halifax over several months. Once the body had been embalmed – an art practised in the region since ancient times – it was most likely bedded on sawdust in a zinc coffin, and then soldered shut.

The ship's passage as announced by the *Halifax Guardian* did not come about. Ann Walker returned to England by land. Did she hire a vehicle especially for the coffin? Or did it have to be loaded with the rest of the baggage? George Tchaikin probably took charge of the return journey; he and the heavily pregnant Domna wanted to be back in Moscow before winter set in. Ann Walker will have found the money for the trip waiting in Tbilisi, ordered by Anne Lister. Governor Golovin issued passes for Ann, her servants and the coffin, so that they could avoid the two-week quarantine after crossing the Caucasus.

21 *Anne Lister*, posthumous *c.*1841, oil painting by Joshua Horner (assumed); Calderdale Leisure Services, Shibden Hall, Halifax.

The outbound journey along the Georgian Military Road was incredibly strenuous; it is hard to imagine how it must have been with a heavy zinc coffin on the return leg. The time of year was at least more favourable, as the Cross Pass was snow-free in October. In Yekaterinogradskaya, George may well have suggested not taking the road via Astrakhan but the shorter route via Voronesh. They presumably arrived in Moscow at the end of November or in mid-December – having travelled 1,273 miles from Kutaisi. Ann went back to Mrs Howard's hotel, where the travelling carriage with the rest of the luggage was still in storage. Needing to wait for the end of winter before continuing her journey, Ann had Anne's coffin buried temporarily, according to Phyllis Ramsden. Did Count and Countess Panin or Princess Sophia Radzivill find words of consolation for Ann? She set off for home at the end of winter 1841. Did the travelling carriage pull the coffin after it on a trailer? We have no record of the route Ann Walker took across the almost two thousand miles from Moscow to Halifax, nor of whether Mr and Mrs Gross accompanied her.

Ann arrived in Halifax on 24 April 1841, moving back into Shibden Hall, for which she had a life tenancy resulting from Anne Lister's will. Five days after her arrival, she buried Anne Lister in the family crypt in the Parish Church on 29 April. It is impossible to tell where that place was. Anne's half-destroyed slab now leans against the wall in the church entrance. Marian Lister will no doubt have come over from Market Weighton for her sister's burial. Her relations with Ann Walker may have been rather frosty, now that the latter owned what Anne had kept from her sister. Marian lived another forty-one years in poverty, dying in 1882. Isabella Norcliffe and Mariana Lawton probably also paid visits to Ann Walker to find out more about Anne's death. Isabella died five years later in 1846, at the age of sixty-one. Mariana Lawton lived until 1868, passing away before her husband Charles, whose death had once been the stuff of dreams for her and Anne.

The renovations and extensions at Shibden Hall were almost finished. To this day, the house remains as Anne Lister envisaged it, though she never saw the work completed. The painter Joshua Horner delivered a posthumous portrait of James Lister, commissioned by Anne before her departure. Ann Walker, who had known Anne's uncle, seems to have been happy with the painting, as she then ordered a portrait of Anne in the same format. Joshua Horner had met Anne Lister on several occasions but she never posed for him. Ann helped him recall her, discussing her posture, clothing and hair with him and giving him an amateurish miniature (see p. 45) as a model, which Horner made into a handsome oil painting. It is not certain how accurately he portrayed Anne Lister. The lady of Shibden Hall surely bore more signs of ageing on her death at forty-nine than the idealised thirty-year-old in the painting. Her upper lip is suspiciously fuzz-free.

Only from the modest yields that Anne Lister's assets brought in did Ann Walker find out how much her wife had actually owned. There was now only £4,000 left, much less than Anne had claimed to possess. Ann Walker must have realised that she herself had funded most of Anne Lister's failed investments. Had Anne ever loved her? Or had she been lying to her from the very beginning? Ann sought answers to these questions in her wife's diaries and letters. There are some indications that it was she who consigned the correspondence between Anne Lister and Mariana Lawton to the flames.[2] Had she been able to decipher Anne Lister's secret code and read about the early days of their own relationship, she might well have thrown the journals on the fire as well.

Even after Anne Lister's death, Ann Walker did not make up with her relatives in Halifax and Scotland. What would she have told the Priestleys and the Sutherlands? That they had been right all along to warn her about Anne Lister? George Sutherland considered Ann Walker easy prey. He began by convincing his wife Elizabeth that her sister needed Stephen Belcombe's medical assistance again. He then hired the lawyer Robert Parker for the necessary legal proceedings to get Ann into the York mental asylum against her will. On 9 September 1843, the Sutherlands, the doctor and the lawyer broke into Shibden Hall along with the constable of Halifax. Ann fled to the Red Room on the top floor, locking the door behind her. Stephen Belcombe and Robert Parker told the constable *to open it which he did by taking it off the Hinges – the Room was in a most filthy condition, and on the side of the Bed were a Brace of loaded Pistols.* The lawyer described the situation, possibly dramatising to justify their behaviour. *The Shutters were closed – an old dirty candle stick near the Bed was covered with Tallow, as if the Candle had melted away on it –* Parker wrote, suggesting that Ann was no longer in control of fire and had to be protected from herself. *Papers were strewn about in complete confusion. In the Red Room were a* [great] *many Handkerchiefs shatted* [splattered] *all over with Blood.*[3] With Ann requiring urgent medical attention, as he allegedly saw it, she was put straight into Stephen Belcombe's asylum. We can assume Ann Walker was indeed suffering mentally after her traumatic journey across Europe with her wife's corpse. Whether she really needed monitoring in a clinic is questionable. Ann must have come across Eliza Raine in the asylum, as she lived there until her death in 1860. Anne Lister's first and last lovers were both declared insane.

The moment Ann was out of the way, Captain Sutherland came up against a strong competitor for his sister-in-law's income: Dr John Lister senior of Swansea. The latter disproved heartily of the life tenancy Anne Lister had granted her wife in her will, which Sutherland wanted to secure for himself. He tied Sutherland up in legal disputes over Ann Walker's claim to Shibden Hall for years. Sutherland claimed to have not only legal rights on his side but moral ones too, emphasising *how perfectly simple a matter it was for any designing or unprincipled person to deceive and dupe her; and I unhesitatingly say that*

Mrs Lister did so to an enormous extent. Step by step, I have traced the proceedings. She first instils into Miss Walker's Mind a Mistrust and hatred of her closest relatives; when this is accomplished, she prevails on Miss Walker to leave her her estate, and, as if this was not sufficient injustice to her Family, she persuades her to direct that the proceeds of her Estate should be placed to her (Mrs Lister's) credit during their absence abroad. Whether Miss Lister intended that Miss Walker should ever return, God only knows!! It was not Ann Walker who was Anne Lister's victim, he claimed, but he himself: *The injury Mrs Lister has done me, my wife and* [son] *I sincerely feel and who would not?*[4]

Although Sutherland managed to keep John Lister senior at bay, he could not enjoy the fruit of his success. In the same year in which he had Ann Walker locked away, he lost his oldest son, twelve-year-old George Sackville. His wife, Ann's sister Elizabeth, died the next year, 1844, at only forty-three. Only two years later, the widower married the very young Mary Elizabeth Haigh. He moved into Shibden Hall with her, his two young daughters and nine-year-old Evan Charles. He did not have long to savour the victory of becoming lord of the old country pile. George Sutherland died a year later, aged only forty-nine. He left a fortune of some £30,000 to his son.

By that point, Ann Walker had returned to live at Lightcliffe. After two years in the York asylum, her eighty-eight-year-old aunt took pity on her and fetched her to Cliffe Hill in 1845. Ann Walker senior died two years later, in the same year as Captain Sutherland. Now forty-four, Ann Walker inherited from him the legal wrangles with John Lister senior, who was unable to dispute Ann's legal claims to the property. However, she remained at Cliffe Hill, living with an Irish nurse until her death at the age of fifty-one in 1854. She left to her nephew what Anne Lister and George Sutherland had left to her, about £2,000 – a fraction of what she had once had.

Evan Charles Sutherland dissolved the Walkers' entire estate and moved back to Scotland. He sold the Walker family seat Crow Nest in Lightcliffe to Titus Salt, the founder of the Salt Mill and the Saltaire model workers' village in Bradford. Ann Walker's parental home no longer exists; its grounds have been converted to a golf course. The spacious Cliffe Hill has been divided up into flats. Lidgate, where Ann was living when she met Anne, is now surrounded by new houses. Only the old estate wall remains from the days when Anne Lister was such a frequent visitor.

John, Muriel, Vivien, Phyllis, Helena, Jill & Angela

A year after Ann Walker's death, Dr John Lister senior took over Shibden Hall in 1855. From then on, the doctor divided his time between his practice on the Isle of Wight and the new family home in Halifax, where his wife, Louisa Anna Lister (née Grant), raised their three children, John junior, Charles and Anne. In 1856, Dr Lister sold Northgate House, which remained a hotel, just as Anne Lister had planned, until its demolition in 1961. Her *casino* was used as a theatre and cinema hall.

John junior (1847–1933) became lord of Shibden Hall in 1867. As described in the Prologue, it was John who began researching Anne Lister with his 'Social and Political Life in Halifax Fifty Years Ago' series (1887–1892) in the *Halifax Guardian*. Unlike his Tory aunt, he was a founding member and treasurer of the Independent Labour Party, supporting workers' rights, organising soup kitchens for strikers and standing as the first ever Labour candidate in Halifax in the 1893 general election, though he lost against the Liberal candidate. The founding president of the Halifax Antiquarian Society, he spent decades investing more money in voluntary activities on behalf of cultural institutions and schools than Shibden Hall brought in. He was close to bankrupt by 1923. In view of his great accomplishments,

the town of Halifax purchased Shibden Hall from him and granted
him life tenancy. Edward, Prince of Wales, the uncle of Queen
Elizabeth II, opened Anne Lister's landscape garden to the public in
1926. Sadly, her *moss hut* is no longer standing, probably sacrificed to
railway works.

Shibden Hall was converted into a museum in 1934; visitors can
now view Anne Lister's writing materials and her false curls. After
visiting the house and gardens, those in need of a bite to eat or something stronger can walk the path she laid out, inaugurated in 1837 to
commemorate Queen Victoria's coronation, to Anne's Stump Cross
Inn on Godley Lane. These days, anyone can drink there, regardless
of their politics.

After John Lister died in 1933, the trainee librarian Muriel Green
(1909–1997) viewed Shibden Hall. *The books overflowed from the shelves
onto the chairs and tables and even onto the floor. There were numerous
large and dusty trunks containing leases, wills, accounts, recipes, funeral
notes, diaries, letters etc. and from time to time another trunk or box of man-
uscripts would turn up from beneath a pile of lumber from some other part
of the house.*[1] Over several years, Green compiled an inventory of the
Shibden Hall Papers, dividing them into sections. As her dissertation
project, Green transcribed 395 of Anne Lister's 1,850 surviving letters
and added editorial notes. She used the diaries found in John Lister's
'closet' for dating purposes and to clear up tricky details. Thanks to
Arthur Burrell's key to Anne Lister's code, Green realised who she
was dealing with – and decided not to mention Anne's love of women
in her letter collection *A Spirited Yorkshirewoman: The Letters of Anne
Lister of Shibden Hall b. 1791 d. 1840* (1938). She later commented *it
would have cast a slur on the good name of the Lister family.*[2]

The historian Vivien Ingham (*c.*1918–1969) was the next researcher
to work on Anne Lister. She looked into the diaries in the 1940s for

a work *about dress fashions in the period*. Not until 1958, though, did she find *time and opportunity to begin any real study of this vast quantity of material. This time I was joined, greatly to our mutual benefit and enjoyment, by my friend and our fellow-member, Mrs Phyllis M. Ramsden, BA, PhD. It appeared likely to us that the Journals had never before been read in their entirety, and this we decided to do.*³ Dr Phyllis M. Ramsden (née Crowther) was married to the editor of the *Halifax Courier* and hoped to find *material of more general interest.*⁴ Vivien and Phyllis spent eleven years poring over the journals together, reading each of the twenty-four volumes twice over. Using the key to Anne's secret code, the two jointly spelled their way through a great deal of lesbian sex. Did their elbows touch? Did their hands cross? Did Ramsden have reason to suspect anything of the unmarried Vivien Ingham?

The two friends did not agree on how to deal with Anne Lister's love life in any future publications. Ingham began a dissertation on 'The Life of Anne Lister' at the University of London in 1967; according to her adviser, Olive Anderson, she planned to cover Anne's *lesbianism (which there was no question of excluding).*⁵ Ingham sketched out several chapters on Anne Lister's travels and published an article about her ascent of the Vignemale in *Alpine Journal* in 1968 – the first publication on Anne Lister since John Lister's series in the *Halifax Guardian*. Ingham described Anne as *a forceful woman of great energy and masculine tendencies.*⁶ In a longer version of this article for the Halifax Antiquarian Society, she varied her insinuation. *She was tall by the standards of her time and in her long black coat and stout leather boots she could easily be mistaken for a man.*⁷ By the time this second piece appeared in April 1969, Vivien Ingham had died. Her unfinished dissertation went to Phyllis Ramsden.

After Ingham's death, Ramsden attempted to establish her own interpretation of the coded passages in Anne Lister's journals. Whereas Ingham had discovered *many details of general interest* in them, writing that *no one with pretensions to serious study of the Journal can entirely ignore them,* [8] Phyllis Ramsden vehemently opposed this view. *Her affection found her outlet among her own sex,* Ramsden did concede in her article 'Anne Lister's Journal' (1970); *she was naturally drawn to the prettiest, gayest, most good-natured and most accomplished in domestic arts.* However, *there are long accounts in crypt-writing of her sentimental exchanges with her friends, excruciatingly tedious to the modern mind.* All that Vivien Ingham had hoped to reveal, Phyllis Ramsden set about covering up again. *It is natural to assume that these secret passages are of some special significance and must be deciphered at all costs. Fortunately this is not at all the case. With very few exceptions the passages in 'crypt'-alphabet are of no historical interest whatever.* Instead, they covered merely *family and financial matters, but these passages can usually be identified by their context and are generally short enough to be quickly deciphered. Apart from this the 'crypt' passages tend to be purely personal, and it can be taken for granted that the longer the passage the less it is worth the tedium of decoding.* [9]

Despite her many years of research, Ramsden published only a single article on Anne Lister. Olive Anderson assumes the collection at the West Yorkshire Archive Service by the name of the Ramsden Papers might just as well be called the Ingham Papers. The collection contains long texts on Anne Lister's travels, chronologies and dated excerpts from the encrypted passages.

Ramsden died in 1985, sparing her the embarrassment of the first published edition of Anne Lister's journals, including detailed citations from the coded passages. Helena Whitbread (born 1931), a mature student and mother of four, came across Anne Lister by chance. In 1984, she was looking for a research project in the Calderdale District Archive in her home town of Halifax. *Did you know she kept a journal?* [10] the archivist asked her, and showed Whitbread a discouraging coded page on microfilm. Helena Whitbread was instantly fascinated. With the key by her side, she transcribed fifty pages of Lister's diaries, week after week. In 1988 she published *I Know My Own Heart: The Diaries of Anne Lister 1791–1840*, featuring extracts from the years 1817–1824. In 1992 came *No Priest But Love: The Journals of Anne Lister 1824–1826*. Parts of the British public reacted with shock. There were cries of forgery, which soon fell silent. Anne Lister's diaries debunked the idea of chaste 'romantic friendships' between women put forth by Elizabeth Mavor (1971) and Lillian Faderman (1981). When the BBC broadcast the sugar-coated TV drama *The Secret Diaries of Miss Anne Lister* in 2010, a new edition of Whitbread's first book was issued under the same title, with added extracts from 1816.

After Helena Whitbread's pioneering editions, eighty-three-year-old Muriel Green edited her 541 typed pages down to less than half the length and in 1992 published *Miss Lister of Shibden Hall: Selected Letters (1800 –1840)*.

At that point, the social historian Jill Liddington (born 1946) undertook to transcribe and digitalise the entirety of Anne Lister's journal. In preparation for a funding application she tallied up the amount to be transcribed, *arriving to my horror*[11] at four million words. Liddington estimated that a complete transcription of Anne Lister's diaries would take nine years. She therefore limited her project to the previously almost unknown partnership with Ann Walker. *In Female Fortune: Land, Gender and Authority. The Anne Lister Diaries and Other Writings, 1833–36* (1998), *Nature's Domain: Anne Lister and the Landscape of Love* (2003) and numerous articles, Liddington also examines Anne Lister's political and entrepreneurial activities.

I have had a similar experience with Anne Lister to all the women in her life – first she seduced me, then she betrayed me. What I liked even more than Anne Lister's astoundingly open way of speaking about her desire was her certainty of herself: her desire was an expression of her nature, and that was that. She knew about her *oddities* and made sure everyone in Halifax and York knew of them too, more or less. Most of her lovers, however, did not consider themselves odd. In what we think of as the prudish pre-Victorian age, there seems to have been no great risk or consequence to women loving women and it was not thought wrong. They simply did not talk about it, and went on to marry apparently unsullied. Ann Walker proved just as brave as Anne Lister by moving in with her and sitting in the front pew with her at church. Despite anonymous marriage announcements ridiculing Captain Tom Lister and Ann Walker, the two women laid the foundation stone for the Northgate Hotel together, clearly a couple – an emancipatory milestone in the history of women loving women.

Despite all this, Anne Lister was a beast of a woman. Like all her lovers, I could not escape this conclusion, and yet nor could I let go of her. All the sex in old-fashioned language was just too delightful. *Then the thing was over.*

Epilogue:
Reading Anne Lister's writing

In Italia seicento e quaranta;
In Alemagna duecento e trentuna;
Cento in Francia, in Turchia novantuna;
Ma in Ispagna son già mille e tre.

In Mozart and da Ponte's tragedy *Don Giovanni*, the womanising hero's servant, Leporello, explains with delightful comedy to poor Elvira that she is not alone in her suffering: *Madamina, il catalogo è questo.* Don Giovanni simply loves all women, tall and short, fat and thin, blonde and brunette, young and old, pretty and ugly, countesses and farmers' daughters. And he, Leporello, keeps a loyal catalogue of his master's conquests. Anne Lister resembled both Don Giovanni and, with her journal, Leporello.

Anne Lister began her journal as a list of letters from and to Eliza Raine and, like Leporello, Anne wrote to preserve her memories. *Volume three, that part containing an account of my intrigue with Anne* [Nantz] *Belcombe, I read over attentively, exclaiming to myself, 'Oh, women, women!' I thought, too, of Miss Vallance who, by the way, is by no means worse than Anne, who took me on my own terms even more de-cidedly. The account, too, as merely noted in the index, of Miss Browne, amuses me. I am always taken up with some girl or other. When shall I amend?*[1] Whereas Leporello merely listed the women, Anne Lister told stories – and yet believed she was noting things down *exactly as they are, thus leaving them to the operations of my cooler judgement hereafter.*[2] With no distrust of language and writing, she considered her style neutral and objective.

Nor did Anne ever doubt herself. *I am not at this moment conscious of having ever done a heartless thing in my life,* she wrote, believing *I had been more sinned against, than sinning.*[3] *Tho' bad, the best.*[4] All her life, she longed for *someone whom I can respect & dote on, always at my elbow.* Yet none of the women prepared to marry her ever seemed good enough, not Eliza Raine, nor Isabella Norcliffe nor Maria Barlow, certainly not Ann Walker or Mariana Lawton. Anne Lister's great love was herself.

She lavished her entire attention on her ego, her being, her body and her world. That ego was the reason she wrote. *'Tis just before 6:05 as I am writing at this moment & in the last 2 ½ hours, I have gradually written myself from moody melancholy to contented cheerfulness.*[5] She did not need another woman by her side for that purpose; *it seems made over to a friend that hears it patiently, keeps it faithfully, and by never forgetting anything, is always ready to compare the past & present & thus to cheer & edify the future.*[6] Her lovers knew that too. Every one of them was jealous of her journal, her great love letter to herself.

Obsessed with recording minute details of her life, Anne Lister worked incredibly hard on her journal, to the point of compulsion. She wrote before she got to her desk, she wrote as she was living life – *I was beginning to make pencil notes as usual*[7] – experiencing reality with pen in hand. In her daily notes, she included not only extracts from her reading material, but also long excerpts from letters she had received; she put printed material or things handwritten by others into her own writing and incorporated it into her journal. Only what she dealt with in writing became true and significant to her. Her journal is a grand-scale attempt to compile her life in the form of text, thus doubling it. *The looking over & filling up my journal to my mind always gives me pleasure. I seem to live my life over again.*[8]

Unabbreviated, her notes are of questionable value, as far as the information in them is concerned, and far from entertaining. In their egocentric indiscrimination, they foreshadow the banal uniquity of the selfie. Anne Lister's journal is anything but an opera libretto, it is not literature – it is a socio-historical occurrence in textual form, describing everything and anything. She had a particular interest in her own female body, focusing on it as no writer had done before, fascinated by its every stirring and considering it all worth writing down. This at a time when women's bodies were becoming increasingly taboo, referred to in male-dominated discourse as an object for inspiring men's lust but not thought to feel such a thing themselves. The German philosopher Johann Gottlieb Fichte put it in a nutshell: *No sexual drive is expressed in the unspoiled woman, and no sexual drive resides within her, but only love; and this love is the natural drive of woman to satisfy a man. It is, however, a drive that strives urgently for its satisfaction: yet its satisfaction is not the sensual satisfaction of the woman, but that of the man; for the woman, it is only satisfaction of the heart.*[9]

Anne Lister would have laughed out loud at her contemporary's claim. On the eve of the Victorian era, she created an audacious work of female corporeity. The joys of her desires and the hardships of satisfying them shaped her life and thus also her journal. Writing took the place of, and extended or renewed, her desire. The pleasure of sex was repeated in the act of writing. Sexuality becomes textuality in her diaries; the body and life become script. As a desiring woman and a writing woman, Anne Lister literally created herself in her journal, her body in writing, the novel of her life.

Acknowledgements

I want to express again my gratitude and thanks to all the scholars who have brought Anne Lister's world so vividly to light. Helena Whitbread and Jill Liddington deserve particular thanks. This book would not be possible without their work.

My research for this book began in Halifax at the West Yorkshire Archive Service, Calderdale, which at that time was housed on the site of Anne Lister's hotel in the Northgate building. John Patchett presented me with hundreds of papers and documents – including an original volume of Anne Lister's journal – unforgettably singing arias from Richard Wagner's music dramas as he did so. I would like to thank Dan Sudron for the reproductions and rights.

The Robert Bosch Foundation bestowed me on me 'border-crossers grant' that enabled me to travel in Anne Lister's footsteps in Russia, Georgia and Azerbaijan. In Tbilisi, I was able to give my first public presentation of my research on Anne Lister. Many thanks to Etuna Nogaideli from the Heinrich Böll Foundation, Natia Mikeladse Bachsoliani from the Goethe-Institut and Ekaterine Gejadze from the Women's Fund in Georgia for that opportunity. The writer Tamta Melashvili and Nino Gamisonia from the Rural Communities Development Agency in Tbilisi answered my questions on Georgian history and geography.

My English publisher Serpent's Tail has shown both courage and humour in publishing the biography of an Englishwoman by a German. Working together with Katy Derbyshire and reading her translation of this book has been a great delight.

I could not have written this book without Susette Pia Schuster. She rode a tandem through Yorkshire with me, she hiked through the Pyrenees with me, ate sweet bread in Sweden, arranged for a boat (though not a sledge) trip on the Volga, and fought tooth and nail for tickets for the right sleeping carriage to Baku at Tbilisi station. *Surely no one ever doted on another as I do on her.*

Timeline

1791   Anne Lister born in Halifax on 3 April to Jeremy and Rebecca Lister, the eldest surviving child of six.

1793   Family moves to Skelfler House in Market Weighton.

1798–1800   Attends a girls' school in Ripon.

1801–1805   Divides her time between Market Weighton and Shibden Hall with Uncle James and Aunt Anne Lister senior. — Private tuition in Latin and mathematics.

1805   Attends Manor House School in York. — Love affair with Eliza Raine (1791–1860) until 1811.

1806   Moves to Halifax with her family. — Learns Greek. — 11 August 1806 to 22 February 1810: diary on loose sheets of paper.

1808   Develops secret code. — Affair with Maria Alexander until 1809.

1809   Stays with Eliza Raine at the Duffins' home in York. — Further long stays there until 1815.

1811   Love affair with Isabella Norcliffe, 'Tib' (1785–1846) until c.1826.

1812   December: love affair with Mariana Belcombe (1790–1868) until c.1829.

1813   February to May: visits Bath with the Norcliffes. One loose diary sheet on the holiday in Bath. — June: Anne's favourite brother Samuel dies. The only living siblings are now Anne and her younger sister Marian.

1814   Eliza Raine put into Clifton Asylum in York.

1815   Anne moves permanently into Shibden Hall.

1816 Mariana Belcombe marries Charles Lawton on 9 March; Anne and
Nantz Belcombe accompany the couple until August. — From
14 August: journal has survived without gaps until Anne Lister's
death, initially as exercise books 2 and 3. — Charles intercepts a
letter from Anne and forbids his wife from seeing her. — Up to
1820, only brief encounters with Mariana. — November: affair
with Nantz Belcombe.

1817 21 March: first of 24 bound journal volumes. — 2 September:
visit to the Walkers, wearing all black for the first time. — 8
November: Uncle Joseph Lister dies. — 14 November: mother
Rebecca Lister dies.

1818 Unrequited infatuation with Elizabeth Browne, up to 1819 —
September to November: Isabella Norcliffe stays with Anne; they
exchange visits lasting several months every year until 1824.

1819 May/June: trip to Paris and London with Aunt Anne.

1820 Meets Sibella Maclean (1785–1830). — Affair with Miss Vallance
and flirt with Harriet Milne née Belcombe.

1821 January: new affair with Nantz Belcombe. — 12 June: flirt with
Ann Walker. — July: renews her vows with Mariana Belcombe;
Anne contracts a sexually transmitted disease from her.

1822 4 February: Aunt Mary Lister dies; Northgate House falls to
Anne's uncle, James Lister; Anne receives £50 p.a. from him. —
March: sale of Skelfler House falls through. — July: trip to Wales
with Aunt Anne, visit to the Ladies of Llangollen. — September/
October: trip to Paris with father and sister; the two of them move
into Northgate House. — Anne infects Isabella Norcliffe.

1823 February/March: Francis Pickford. — June: trip to the Yorkshire
Dales with Aunt Anne. — August to October: unhappy reunion
with Mariana Lawton.

1824 July/August: trip to the Lake District with Aunt Anne. — Late
August to late March 1825: Paris — November: love affair with
Maria Barlow, until 1827.

1825 January: moves into shared apartment with Maria Barlow. —
August/September: trip to Buxton with Aunt Anne; renews her
vows with Mariana Lawton. — December: flirts with Harriet
Milne, Miss Duffin and Lou Belcombe.

1826 26 January: Uncle James Lister dies, Anne inherits Shibden

Hall. — May: Anne sends Mariana back to Charles Lawton.
— June to August: trip to Liverpool, Dublin and Lawton Hall
with the Lawtons. — September: trip to Paris with Mariana and
Aunt Anne. — Jeremy and Marian move into Shibden Hall. —
October: after Mariana's departure, Anne continues her love affair
with Maria Barlow.

1827 June to October: tour of Switzerland and northern Italy with
Maria Barlow. — End of the year: affair with Mme de Rosny.

1828 17 March: leaves Paris. — May to July: tour of Scotland with
Sibella Maclean. — Winter in Yorkshire with Mariana Lawton;
she infects Anne again.

1829 March: London; Sibella Maclean leaves Anne. — April: trip to
Paris with Vere Hobart. — August to October: tour of Belgium,
Aix-la-Chapelle and northern France with Vere Hobart and Lady
Stuart. — September: trip along the Rhine with Lady Caroline
Duff Gordon.

1830 Studies anatomy and other subjects in Paris. — August to
October: tour of southern France with Lady Stuart de Rothesay;
misses the July Revolution in Paris, climbs Monte Perdido. — 16
November: Sibella Maclean dies.

1831 23 May: return to Shibden Hall with Aunt Anne. — August:
tour of the Netherlands with Mariana Lawton. — September:
first train ride, from Manchester to Liverpool; tour of southern
England. — From November: lives in Hastings with Vere
Hobart.

1832 15 April: Vere accepts Donald Cameron's marriage proposal.
— May: Anne returns to Shibden Hall; constructs a landscape
garden. — August to January: affair with Ann Walker (1803–
1854).

1833 February to end of year: Ann Walker in Scotland. — July to
November: Anne Lister travels from Paris to Copenhagen via
Germany.

1834 4 January: reunited with Ann Walker, who is treated by Stephen
Belcombe in York until June. — 10 February: 'wedding day' with
Ann Walker. — May: tour of the Yorkshire Dales with Ann. —
June to August: with Ann to Paris, around France and to the Alps.
— September: Ann Walker moves into Shibden Hall.

1835 January to April: 'marriage announcements' and threatening letters. — August: London, Buxton. — 26 September: foundation laid for the extension to Northgate House. — November: Walker Pit dug.

1836 26 March: *Halifax Guardian* accuses Ann Walker over Caddy Fields. — 3 April: Jeremy Lister dies. — Marian moves to Market Weighton. — May: Anne and Ann grant each other life tenancy in their wills. — Start of construction work at Shibden Hall. — 10 October: Aunt Anne dies.

1837 January: mortgage on Northgate Hotel.

1838 April: Listerwick Colliery dug. — May to November: tour of Belgium and France with Ann. — 7 August: climbs the Vignemale.

1839 Conversion work at Shibden Hall. — 20 June: departure for London. — July to September: Copenhagen, Gothenburg, Oslo; tour of Norway and central Sweden; Uppsala, Falun, ship's passage from Stockholm to Åbo, tour of southern Finland, Helsinki. — 17 September to 7 October: St Petersburg. — 12 October to 5 February: Moscow.

1840 February/March: via Nizhny Novgorod, Kazan, Saratov, Astrakhan to Vladikavkas, Georgian Military Road. — April to June: Tbilisi; in May to Azerbaijan, Baku. — July/August: Kutaisi; tour of Racha-Lechkhumi; Zugdidi. — 11 August: last journal entry, written in Jgali. — 22 September: Anne Lister dies in or near Kutaisi. — Ann Walker transports the coffin to Halifax via Moscow.

1841 29 April: burial in Halifax Parish Church. — Ann Walker lives in Shibden Hall.

1843–1845 Ann Walker put into Clifton Asylum in York against her will.

1845–1854 Ann Walker lives a withdrawn life at Cliffe Hill, Lightcliffe.

Bibliography

Anderson, Olive 1995: 'The Anne Lister Papers'. In: *History Workshop Journal* no. 40 (Autumn), 190–192.

Bayle, Pierre 1826: *A Historical and Critical Dictionary in 4 Volumes*. London: Hunt & Clarke, vol. III, p. 176.

Brothers, Hazel 1997: 'A New Portrait of Anne Lister'. In: *Halifax Antiquarian Society*, Newsletter 48.

Bull, Malcolm: *Calderdale Companion* (website), http:/freepages.history.roots web.ancestry.com/~calderdalecompanion/index.html

Castle, Terry 1993: 'The Diaries of Anne Lister'. In: *The Apparitional Lesbian. Female Homosexuality and Modern Culture*. New York: Columbia University Press, 92–106.

Choma, Anne 1994: 'Anne Lister and the Split Self (1791–1840). A Critical Study of her Diaries.' MA thesis in English Literature, University of Leeds.

Clark, Anna 2002: 'Anne Lister's Construction of Lesbian Identity'. In: Kim A. Phillips and Barry Reay (eds.): *Sexualities in History. A Reader*. London and New York: Routledge, 247–270.

Colclough, Stephen 2010: 'Do You Not Know the Quotation? Reading Anne Lister, Anne Lister Reading'. In: John C. Beynon and Caroline Gonda (eds.): *Lesbian Dames. Sapphism in the Long Eighteenth Century*. Farnham: Ashgate, 159–172.

Davies, Stevie 1994: *Emily Brontë: Heretic*. London: Women's Press.

Defoe, Daniel 1927: *A Tour through England and Wales. Divided into Circuits and Journies*. London: J. M. Dent.

Donoghue, Emma 1995: 'Liberty in Chains: The Diaries of Anne Lister (1817–24)'. In: Kevin Lano and Claire Parry (eds.): *Breaking the Barriers to Desire: Polyamory, Polyfidelity and Non-monogamy: New Approaches to Multiple Relationships.* Nottingham: Five Leaves, 79–86.

Euler, Catherine Ann 1995: 'Moving between Worlds: Gender, Class, Politics, Sexuality and Women's Networks in the Diaries of Anne Lister of Shibden Hall, Halifax, Yorkshire, 1830–1840'. Unpublished PhD thesis, York University. URL: http://etheses.whiterose.ac.uk/2471/

Faderman, Lilian 1981: *Surpassing the Love of Men: Romantic Friendship and Love between Women from the Renaissance to the Present.* New York: William Morrow.

Fichte, Johann Gottlieb [1796] 1845: 'Grundriß des Familienrechts.' First addendum to: 'Grundlage des Naturrechts nach Principien der Wissenschaftslehre'. In: J. H. Fichte (ed.): *Johann Gottlieb Fichte's Sämmtliche Werke.* Vol.III. Berlin: Veit, 304–368.

Goethe, Johann Wolfgang von, ed. Christopher Middleton 1994: *Selected Poems.* Princeton, New Jersey: Princeton University Press, 105.

Green, Muriel 1938: 'A Spirited Yorkshirewoman: The Letters of Anne Lister of Shibden Hall, b. 1791 d. 1840'. Library Associations Honours Diploma. Typescripts in London, British Library, and Halifax, Central Library.

Green, Muriel 1992: *Miss Lister of Shibden Hall: Selected Letters (1800–1840).* Lewes: The Book Guild.

Hughes, Patricia 2009: *Anne Lister's Secret Diary for 1817.* Print on demand.

Hughes, Patricia 2010: *Miss Anne Lister's Early Life and the Curious Tale of Eliza Raine.* Print on demand.

Ingham, Vivien 1968: 'Anne Lister's Ascent of Vignemale'. In: *The Alpine Journal*, vol. 73, issues 316 and 317, 199–204.

Ingham, Vivien 1969: 'Anne Lister in the Pyrenees'. *Transactions of the Halifax Antiquarian Society*, 1 April 1969, 55–70.

Lanser, Susan S. 2010: 'Tory Lesbians: Economies of Intimacy and the Status of Desire'. In: John C. Beynon and Caroline Gonda (eds.): *Lesbian Dames. Sapphism in the Long Eighteenth Century.* Farnham: Ashgate, 173–189.

Liddington, Jill 1994: *Presenting the Past: Anne Lister of Halifax, 1791–1840.* Hebden Bridge: Pennine Pens.

Liddington, Jill 1995: 'Beating the Inheritance Bounds: Anne Lister

(1791–1840) and her Dynastic Identity'. In: *Gender & History* 7, no. 2, 260–274.

Liddington, Jill 1998: *Female Fortune. Land, Gender and Authority: The Anne Lister Diaries and Other Writings, 1833–36*. London: Rivers Oram Press.

Liddington, Jill 2001: 'Anne Lister and Emily Brontë 1838–39: Landscape with Figures'. In: *Brontë Society Transactions*, vol. 26, no. 1, Apr., 46–67.

Liddington, Jill 2003: *Nature's Domain. Anne Lister and the Landscape of Love*. Hebden Bridge: Pennine Pens.

Lister, John: 'Social and Political Life in Halifax Fifty Years Ago'. *Halifax Guardian*, May 1887–Oct. 1892, no. I–CXVIII.

Martial 2015: Translation by Gideon Nisbet, Oxford University Press, 503 (Liber VII, 67).

Orr, Danielle 2004: '"I tell myself to myself": Homosexual Agency in the Journals of Anne Lister (1791–1840)'. In: *Women's Writing*, vol. 11, no. 2, 201–222.

Orr, Danielle 2006: 'A Sojourn in Paris 1824–1825. Sex and Sociability in the Manuscript Writings of Anne Lister (1791–1840)'. Unpublished PhD thesis, Murdoch University Sydney.

Plas Newydd and the Ladies of Llangollen. A Guide Book. No place or year of publication given.

Pückler-Muskau, Hermann von 1991: *Briefe eines Verstorbenen. Ein fragmentarisches Tagebuch aus Deutschland, Holland, England, Wales, Irland und Frankreich, geschrieben in den Jahren 1826 bis 1829*, vol. II. Frankfurt: Insel.

Pushkin, Alexander 1919: 'A Journey to Arzrum at the Time of the 1829 Campaign', trans. Ronald Wilks. In: *Tales of Belkin and Other Prose Writings*, London: Penguin Classics.

Ramsden, Phyllis [and Vivien Ingham]: typescripts in the West Yorkshire Archives Service, Calderdale, Halifax.

Ramsden, Phyllis M. 1970: 'Anne Lister's Journal (1817–1840)'. In: *Transactions of the Halifax Antiquarian Society*, 6 January 1970, 1–13.

Rowanchild, Anira 2000a: '"Everything Done for Effect." Georgic, Gothic, and Picturesque in Anne Lister's Self-production'. In: *Women's Writing*, vol. 7, no. 1, 89–104.

Rowanchild, Anira 2000b: '"My Mind on Paper." Anne Lister and the Construction of Lesbian Identity'. In: Alison Donnell and Pauline Polkey (eds.): *Representing Lives: Women and Auto/Biography*. London: Macmillan, 199–207.

Rowanchild, Anira 2000c: 'Skirting the Margins: Anne Lister and

Selfrepresentation in Early Nineteenth-Century Halifax'. In: David Shuttleworth and Diane Watts (eds.): *De-centering Sexualities: Politics and Representation beyond the Metropolis*. London: Routledge, 147–161.

Rowanchild, Anira 2006: '"Peeping behind the Curtain": The Significance of Classical Texts in the Sexual Self-Construction of Anne Lister'. In: Richard Pearson (ed.): *The Victorians and the Ancient World: Archaeology and Classicism in Nineteenth-Century Culture*. Newcastle upon Tyne: Cambridge Scholars, 139–151.

Shibden Hall. A Visitor's Guide. Calderdale Council 2010.

Steidele, Angela 2003: *'Als wenn Du mein Geliebter wärest.' Liebe und Begehren zwischen Frauen in der deutschsprachigen Literatur 1750–1850*. Stuttgart: Metzler.

Steidele, Angela 2004: *In Männerkleidern. Das verwegene Leben der Catharina Margaretha Linck alias Anastasius Lagrantinus Rosenstengel, hingerichtet 1721. Biographie und Dokumentation*. Cologne: Böhlau.

Steidele, Angela 2010: *Geschichte einer Liebe. Adele Schopenhauer und Sibylle Mertens*. Berlin: Insel.

Tuite, Clara 2002: 'The Byronic Woman: Anne Lister's Style, Sociability and Sexuality'. In: Gillian Russel (ed.): *Romantic Sociability. Social Networks and Literary Culture in Britain, 1770–1840*. Cambridge University Press, 186–210.

Vicinus, Martha 2004: *Intimate Friends: Women Who Loved Women, 1778–1928*. University of Chicago Press.

Whitbread, Helena 2010: *The Secret Diaries of Miss Anne Lister*. London: Virago. Slightly revised edition of: *I Know My Own Heart: The Diaries of Anne Lister 1791–1840*. London: Virago, 1988.

Whitbread, Helena 1992 and 1993: *No Priest But Love: The Journals of Anne Lister from 1824–26*. Smith Settle Ltd and New York University Press.

Whitbread, Helena 2010: 'The "Journals" of Anne Lister'. In: Liliana Sikorska (ed.): *Counterfeited Our Names We Haue, Craftily All Thyngs Vprright to Saue: Self-fashioning and Self-representation in Literature in English*. Frankfurt: Lang, 27–44.

Notes

ABBREVIATIONS IN NOTES

G1	Green, Muriel 1938: 'A Spirited Yorkshirewoman: The Letters of Anne Lister of Shibden Hall, b. 1791 d. 1840'. Library Associations Honours Diploma. Typescripts in London, British Library, and Halifax, Central Library.
G2	Green, Muriel 1992: *Miss Lister of Shibden Hall: Selected Letters (1800 – 1840)*. Lewes: The Book Guild.
L1	Liddington, Jill 1998: *Female Fortune. Land, Gender and Authority: The Anne Lister Diaries and Other Writings, 1833–36*. London: Rivers Oram Press.
L2	Liddington, Jill 2003: *Nature's Domain. Anne Lister and the Landscape of Love*. Hebden Bridge: Pennine Pens.
HG	Lister, John: 'Social and Political Life in Halifax Fifty Years Ago'. *Halifax Guardian*, May 1887–Oct. 1892, no. I–CXVIII.
RAM	Ramsden, Phyllis [and Vivien Ingham]: typescripts in the West Yorkshire Archives Service, Calderdale, Halifax.
RAM: 6–25	Anne Lister's last journey: a tour in Russia, 1840.
RAM: 26–28	Anne Lister in France.
RAM: 29	Summer holiday with political overtones, 1830.
RAM: 30	Anne Lister's first visit to Copenhagen, 1833.
RAM: 31	A terrible journey home, 1833.
RAM: 32–35	Travelling for pleasure: three tours taken from the journal of Miss Anne Lister of Shibden Hall.
RAM: 36–42	Miss Lister sees for herself; a series of short anecdotes taken from the journal of Miss Anne Lister.
RAM: 43–44	Three journeys: from the journal of Miss Anne Lister of Shibden Hall, Halifax.
RAM: 52–76	Chronologies with list of code passages.
RAM: 78	Code used in Anne Lister's journals.

W 1   Whitbread, Helena 2010: *The Secret Diaries of Miss Anne Lister*.
        London: Virago. Slightly revised edition of: *I Know My Own
        Heart: The Diaries of Anne Lister 1791–1840*. London: Virago,
        1988.

W 2   Whitbread, Helena 1992 and 1993: *No Priest But Love: The
        Journals of Anne Lister from 1824–26*. Smith Settle Ltd and New
        York University Press.

Anne Lister's papers are held by the West Yorkshire Archive Service, Calderdale, at the Central Library of Halifax (call number SH:7/ML with various sub-sections; the journals: SH: 7/ML/E/ 1–24; 26).

Quotes from Anne Lister's journals are listed with date and place of publication. Letters *from* Anne Lister are listed with their respective recipient, i.e. 'To Isabella Norcliffe', letters *to* Anne Lister with the name of the sender, i.e. 'From Ann Walker'. Quotes in the text without their own endnote are referenced in the following note.

Motto: 13 Nov. 1816, W1, 5.

PROLOGUE: DECIPHERING ANNE LISTER'S DIARIES

1 Inventory from 1850, item 206, Liddington 1994, 12.   2 Liddington 1994, 15.   3 W1, xiv.   4 Liddington 1994, 15.   5 Liddington 1994, 17.   6 Liddington 1994, 20.   7 Müller 1891.

ELIZA 1791–1810

1 27 Nov. 1806, Hughes 2010, 33.   2 To Maria Barlow, 26 May 1825, G2, 84.   3 To Sibella Maclean [undated], HG, lxiv.   4 To Anne Lister senior, 3 Feb. 1803, G2, 28.   5 17 Nov. 1824, W2, 53.   6 G2, 7.   7 13 Nov. 1824, W2, 49.   8 10 Nov. 1819, W1, 402.   9 19 Nov. 1822, W1, 247.   10 10 Mar. 1819, W1, 97.   11 19 Nov. 1822, W1, 247.   12 Rebecca to Anne Lister senior, 3 Feb. 1803, G2, 29, 30.   13 Defoe 1927.   14 11 July 1822, HG xliv.   15 To Anne Lister senior, 3 Feb. 1803, G2, 28.   16 To Anne Lister senior, 5 May 1800, G2, 27.   17 Anne Lister's school timetable, 19 Jan. 1804, G1, 7.   18 To Eliza Raine, 19 Nov. 1809, G1, 87.   19 To Anne Lister senior, 13 June 1834, G1, 471.   20 17 Sep. 1823, W1, 320.   21 13 Nov. 1816, W1, 5.   22 To James Lister, 20 Sep. 1804, G1, 11.   23 [Aug. 1806], Liddington 1994, 26.   24 From Samuel Lister, 23 Dec. 1812, G1, 63 f.   25 [Autumn 1806], Rowanchild 2006, 142.   26 Extracts from Readings, Clark 2002, 252.   27 Bayle 1826, vol. III, 176.   28 16 Mar. 1820, Clark 2002, 253.   29 Martial 2013, 96 (Liber I, 90).   30 Rowanchild 2006, 148.   31 Martial 2013, 503 (Liber VII, 67).   32 On several occasions while reading Juvenal, Rowanchild 2006, 148.   33 5 Sep. 1832,

NOTES

L2, 56. 34 To Eliza Raine, 21 Feb. 1808, G1, 80 f. 35 To Eliza Raine, 21 Mar. 1808, G1, 83. 36 From Samuel Lister, spring 1810, G1, 16. 37 Rowanchild 2006, 142. 38 Rowanchild 2006, 142. 39 16 Aug. 1819, W1, 111. 40 28 Oct. 1808, Liddington 1994, 28. 41 9 Apr. 1819, W1, 102. 42 To Eliza Raine, 30 Jan. 1809, Hughes, 2010, 55f. 43 To Eliza Raine, 12 Dec. 1808. From Eliza Raine [before 24 Dec. 1808], Hughes 2010, 41–43. 44 23 Nov. 1808, Liddington 1994, 26 f. 45 To Eliza Raine, 19 Nov. 1809, G1, 87, 86. 46 From Eliza Raine, 24 Apr. 1810, Hughes 2010, 88. 47 From Eliza Raine, 15 Apr. 1810, Hughes 2010, 78, 77. 48 From Eliza Raine, 21 Apr. 1810, Hughes 2010, 79. 49 From Eliza Raine, 24 Apr. 1810, Hughes 2010, 91. 50 1 May 1823, Whitbread 2010, 37. 51 From Eliza Raine, 10 and 18 May 1810, Hughes 2010, 110. 52 Diary of Eliza Raine, 10 May 1810, Hughes 2010, 108.

<h2 style="text-align:center">ISABELLA 1810–1813</h2>

1 From Eliza Raine, 21 Apr. 1810, Hughes 2010, 80. 2 12 Oct. 1818, W1, 80. 3 17 Sep. 1819, W1, 114. 4 From Isabella Norcliffe, 15 Oct. 1810, G1, 37. 5 To Isabella Norcliffe, 26 Nov. 1810, G1, 41. 6 From Eliza Raine, 18 May 1810, Hughes 2010, 116. 7 From Eliza Raine, 15 Apr. 1810, Hughes 2010, 77. 8 From Eliza Raine, 10 May 1810, Hughes 2010, 111 f. 9 From Eliza Raine, 18 May 1810, Hughes 2010, 113. 10 To Eliza Raine, 19 Nov. 1809, G1, 85. 11 Comment in the margin by Anne Lister, 15 Oct. 1817, on a letter from Isabella Norcliffe, 1 Sep. 1810, G1, 32. 12 From Isabella Norcliffe, 29 July 1810, G1, 23 f. 13 To Isabella Norcliffe, 3 Aug. 1810, G1, 26, 27. 14 From Isabella Norcliffe, 29 July 1810, G1, 23. 15 To Isabella Norcliffe, 3 Aug. 1810, G1, 24, 25. 16 Diary of Eliza Raine, 14/16/17 Aug. 1810, Liddington 1994, 28. 17 To Samuel Lister, 24 Apr. 1813, G1, 72. 18 From Samuel Lister, 5 Apr. 1813, G1, 68. 19 To Isabella Norcliffe, 30 Aug. 1810, G1, 30. 20 To Isabella Norcliffe, 26 Nov. 1810, G1, 40. 21 To Samuel Lister, 13 Apr. 1811, G1, 51. 22 To Miss Marsh, 9 Nov. 1810, G1, 41. 23 To Eliza Raine, 21 Mar. 1808, G1, 83. 24 To Isabella Norcliffe, 25 Dec. 1810, G1, 46. 25 From Eliza Raine, 2 May 1811, Choma 1994, 33. 26 To Isabella Norcliffe, 25 Dec. 1810, G1, 44. 27 From Eliza Raine, 2 May 1811, Choma 1994, 33. 28 To Miss Marsh, 9 Nov. 1810, G1, 41. 29 From Eliza Raine, [May 1811], Hughes 2010, 132. 30 From Eliza Raine, 15 May 1811, G1, 88. 31 From Samuel Lister, 15 Oct. 1812, G1, 60. 32 From Eliza Raine, 15 May 1811, G1, 88. 33 To Samuel Lister, 13 Apr. 1811, G1, 50. 34 To Samuel Lister, 24 Apr. 1813, G1, 72. 35 To Samuel Lister, 9 Sep. 1812, G1, 56. 36 To Samuel Lister, Feb. 1813, G2, 36, 35. 37 From Samuel Lister, 23 Dec. 1812, G1, 64. 38 To Sibella Maclean, 19 Apr. 1825, G1, 242. 39 From Eliza Raine, [Dec. 1812], G1, 88. 40 To Samuel Lister, 24 Apr. 1813, G1, 72. 41 3 Sep. 1819, Liddington 1994, 31. 42 12 June 1817, Hughes 2009, 9f. 43 27 [Dec.] [1816], Rowanchild 2000a, 93. 44 To Samuel Lister, 24 Apr. 1813, G1, 72. 45 To Samuel Lister, Feb. 1813, G2, 37. 46 To Samuel Lister, Feb. 1813, G2, 37. 47 To Samuel Lister, 24 Apr. 1813, G1, 73. 48 To Samuel Lister, Feb. 1813, G2, 36.

MARIANA 1813–1817

1 From Isabella Norcliffe, 7 Aug. 1810, G1, 28. 2 From Isabella Norcliffe, 1 Sep. 1810, G1, 33. 3 To Samuel Lister, Feb. 1813, G2, 36. 4 To Isabella Norcliffe, 30 Aug. 1810, G1, 31. 5 Liddington 1994, 58. Anne Lister counted the letters in a list and also wrote a diary at the time, see: *Contents of my letter-Drawer*, including: *Papers concerning M[ariana]. P[ercy]. B[elcombe]. 1814 & 1815 My journal of our acquaintance.* Up until 1822, Mariana wrote Anne over 400 letters, almost none of which have survived; Anne Lister presumably burned them in the 1830s, or perhaps it was Ann Walker in the 1840s. 6 From Samuel Lister, 15 May 1813, G1, 75. 7 To Samuel Lister, Feb. 1813, G2, 38. 8 29 Jan. 1821, W1, 161. 9 18 Aug. 1817, W1, 21. 10 25 Dec. 1816, W1, 7. 11 Goethe 1994, 105. 12 7 Sep. 1825, W2, 125. This and the following quotes date from later years of the relationship; they stand here in place of the destroyed diary entries of 1814 and 1815 as an illustration of the first rush of love. Anne Lister sometimes abbreviated Mariana's name as 'M–', which the editors of her diaries sometimes took over and sometimes did not. 13 14 Sep. 1823, W1, 317. 14 22 July 1824, W1, 378. 15 18 Nov. 1819, W1, 120. 16 31 Mar. 1825, W2, 88. 17 11 Dec. 1822, W1, 250. 18 25 May 1826, W2, 173. 19 20 Aug. 1817, Hughes 2009, 16. 20 21 Oct. 1817, Hughes 2009 20. 21 27 July 1826, W2, 185. 22 20 Aug. 1823, W1, 305. 23 5 Mar. 1823, W1, 261. 24 22 Oct. 1817, Hughes 2009, 20. 25 12 Dec. 1824, W2, 63. 26 13 Sep. 1817, W1, 24. 27 30 June 1817, Hughes 2009, 11. 28 9/12 Dec. 1824, W2, 62, 63. 29 9 Dec. 1824, W2, 62. 30 20 Aug. 1823, W1, 305. 31 20 May 1825, W2, 104. 32 10/12 Dec. 1824, W2, 63. 33 14 Aug. 1816, W1, 1. Anne Lister called Anne Belcombe both 'Anne' and 'Nantz'. 34 15/16 Aug. 1816, W1, 2. 35 8 Nov. 1816, W1, 3 f. 36 8 Nov. 1816, Rowanchild 2000a, 93. 37 9/11 Nov. 1816, W1, 4. 38 13 Nov. 1816, W1, 5. 39 To Sibella Maclean, 10 July 1824, G1, 194. 40 8 Nov. 1816, Rowanchild 2000a, 93. 41 20 Nov. 1816, W1, 7. 42 29/30 Jan. 1817, HG iii. 43 9 Dec. 1824, W2, 62. 44 30 Jan. 1817, HG, iii. 45 22 May 1817, W1, 17. 46 28 May 1817, W1, 17 and Hughes 2009, 9. 47 22 May 1817, W1, 17. 48 13 May 1817, W1, 14. 49 Ramsden 1970, 1. 50 23 Dec. 1817, W1, 42. 51 30 July 1838, Ingham 1969, 62. 52 31 July 1817, Hughes 2009, 14. 53 Apr. 1832, L2, 16. 54 24 Aug. 1818, W1, 68. 55 20 Dec. 1817, W1, 41. 56 21 Apr. 1832, Shibden Hall visitor's guide 2010, 11. 57 Undated, Brothers 1997. 58 15 July 1821, W1, 173. 59 1 Jun. 1817, W1, 18. 60 2 Sep. 1817, W1, 24. 61 31 Oct. 1821, W1, 188. 62 22 Mar. 1820, W1, 134. 63 4 Oct. 1820, W1, 152. 64 2 Apr. 1817, W1, 9. 65 26 Apr. 1817, W1, 10. 66 19 May 1817, W1, 16. 67 28 May 1817, Hughes 2009, 9. 68 5 June 1817, Hughes 2009, 9. 69 30 June 1817, Hughes 2009, 11. 70 2 Aug. 1817, Hughes 2009, 14. 71 21 Sep. 1817, Hughes 2009, 19. 72 13 Sep. 1817, W1, 24. 73 12 Dec. 1824, W2, 63. 74 11 July 1817, W1, 19 f. 75 20 Aug. 1817, W1, 22. 76 12 July 1817, Hughes 2009, 13. 77 9 June 1817, Hughes 2009, 9. 78 6 Sep. 1817, HG, vi. 79 3 Nov. 1817, W1, 26. 80 16 Oct. 1817, W1, 26. 81 18/19 Oct. 1817, Hughes 2009, 20. 82 7 Nov. 1817, Hughes 2009, 22. 83 9 Nov. 1817, W1, 31. 84 12 Nov. 1817, Hughes 2009, 23. 85 To James Lister, 14 Nov. 1817 (draft), G1, 98. 86 To

NOTES

Miss Marsh, 20 Oct. 1814, G1, 77.   87 13 Nov. 1824, W2, 49.   88 To Miss Marsh, 20 Oct. 1814, G1, 77.   89 From Mr Duffin, 6 May/23 Aug. 1815, G1, 89.   90 7 Dec. 1817, Hughes 2009, 24.   91 10 Dec. 1817, Hughes 2009, 25.   92 18 Dec. 1817, Hughes 2009, 28.   93 6 Aug. 1821, W1, 178.   94 2 May 1817, W1, 11 f.   95 9 Dec. 1817, W1, 35.   96 Vicinus 2004, 64, 65.   97 9 Dec. 1817, W1, 35.   98 12 Dec. 1817, W1, 36.   99 17 Dec. 1817, W1, 38.   100 18 Dec. 1817, W1, 38 f.   101 18 Dec. 1817, Hughes 2009, 29.   102 19 Dec. 1817, Hughes 2009, 29.   103 28 Dec. 1817, Hughes 2009, 31.   104 28 Dec. 1817, W1, 43.

'KALLISTA' 1818–1819

1 8 Sep. 1818, W1, 71.   2 27/28 Aug. 1817, W1, 23. Anne Lister occasionally writes 'Brown', but more often 'Browne', as unified here.   3 29 Aug. 1817, Hughes 2009, 17.   4 7 May 1817, W1, 13.   5 28 Aug. 1818, W1, 69.   6 2 June 1818, W1, 56.   7 29 Apr. 1818, W1, 53.   8 28 Feb. 1823, W1, 259.   9 8 Sep. 1818, W1, 71.   10 29 Apr. 1818, W1, 53.   11 14 June 1818, W1, 58 f.   12 6/7 Sep. 1818, W1, 70 f.   13 7 July 1817, Hughes 2009, 12.   14 8 Sep. 1818, W1, 72.   15 13 Sep. 1818, W1, 73 f.   16 15 Sep. 1818, W1, 75.   17 5/27 July 1818, W1, 62, 63 f.   18 12 Feb. 1818, W1, 78.   19 18/19 Sep. 1818, W1, 79.   20 21 Sep. 1818, W1, 79 f.   21 4 Oct. 1818, Choma 1994, 40.   22 12 Feb. 1818, W1, 78.   23 29/30 Oct. 1818, Choma 1994, 40.   24 17 Dec. 1818, W1, 86.   25 23/25 Dec. 1818, W1, 86, 87.   26 8 Jan. 1819, W1, 88.   27 18 Feb. 1819,W1, 92–94.   28 30 Jan. 1819, W1, 90.   29 23 Dec. 1818, W1, 86.   30 20 Mar. 1819, W1, 98.   31 9 Apr. 1819, W1, 101 f.   32 31 Jan., 1818, HG, iv.   33 7 May 1817, W1, 13.   34 26 Dec. 1818, W1, 87.   35 3 Mar. 1819, W1, 96.   36 9 Nov. 1824, W2, 43.   37 To William Duffin, 22 Dec. 1819, G2, 42–54, also G1, 132.   38 7 June/12 May 1819, HG, xxvi and xxi.   39 To William Duffin, 22 Dec. 1819, G2, 49.   40 9 June 1819, HG, xxvi.

ISABELLA, MARIANA AND MISS VALLANCE 1819–1822

1 5/10 July 1819, W1, 106, 107 f.   2 1 Aug. 1819, W1, 110.   3 26 Aug. 1819, W1, 112.   4 29/12 Aug. 1819, W1, 113, 111.   5 27 Aug. 1819, Liddington 1994, 36.   6 26 June 1819, W1, 105.   7 17 Sep. 1819, W1, 114.   8 16 Aug. 1819, W1, 111.   9 13 Aug. 1819, Liddington 1994, 36.   10 3 Sep. 1819, W1, 113.   11 18 Aug. 1819, HG, xxviii.   12 3/26 Sep. 1819, W1, 113, 116.   13 19 June 1818, W1, 59.   14 30 Oct. 1819, W1, 117.   15 3 Mar. 1819, W1, 96.   16 30 Oct. 1819, W1, 117.   17 19 Apr. 1819, W1, 103 f.   18 31 Aug. 1818, W1, 69.   19 18 Nov. 1819, W1, 119 f.   20 10 Mar./22 Apr. 1819, W1, 97, 104.   21 2 July 1821, W1, 172.   22 2 Feb. 1819, W1, 91.   23 25 July 1819, W1, 107.   24 7 May 1821, W1, 167.   25 Rowanchild 2000b, 205.   26 28 June 1818, W1, 60 f.   27 17 Sep. 1818, W1, 77.   28 25 July 1819, W1, 107.   29 29 Nov. 1819, W1, 121 f.   30 1 Oct. 1819, W1, 116.   31 5/11/31/16 Jan. 1820, W1, 128, 129, 130, 129.   32 19 May 1823, W1, 275.   33 To William Duffin, 22 Dec. 1819, G2, 47.   34 21 Mar. 1820, HG, xxxiv.   35 5 May 1820, W1, 139.   36 18 Nov. 1819, W1, 121.   37 18 Mar. 1820, W1, 133.   38 6 Oct. 1823, W1, 328.   39

4 Apr. 1820, WI, 135. 40 3/5/10/13 Apr. 1820, WI, 135, 136 f. 41 7 June 1820, WI, 144
f. 42 30/31 Aug. 1820, WI, 148. 43 11 Oct. 1820, Choma 1994, 29 f. 44 17/18 Nov.
1820, WI, 154, 155. 45 9 Dec. 1820, WI, 156. 46 5 Dec. 1820, WI, 155 f. 47 22 Dec.
1820, WI, 157. 48 7 Jan. 1821, WI, 158. 49 8 Mar. 1821, WI, 406. 50 8 Jan. 1821, WI,
158. 51 12 Feb. 1821, WI, 162. 52 8 Feb. 1821, WI, 161 f. Anne calls Mariana 'Mary' in
this letter, as she does on occasion. 53 13 June 1821, WI, 170. 54 31 Aug. 1818, WI, 69
f. 55 6 Aug. 1821, WI, 178. 56 13 June 1821, WI, 170. 57 22/23/28 July 1821, WI, 175,
176. 58 23 July 1821, WI, 176. 59 10 Sep. 1821, WI, 182. 60 3 Aug. 1821, WI, 177. 61
23 July 1821, WI, 176. 62 4/6 Aug. 1821, WI, 177, 178. 63 11 Aug. 1821, WI, 180. 64
10 Aug. 1821, WI, 179. 65 20 Aug. 1821, WI, 181. 66 22/24/25/26 Oct. 1821, WI, 187,
188. 67 19 Dec. 1821, WI, 191. 68 Anne Lister senior, 5 Feb. 1822, G1, 160. 69 4 Dec.
1821, WI, 189. 70 3/6 Jan. 1822, WI, 194. 71 28/22/21 Jan. 1822, WI, 196, 195. 72
28 Jan. 1822, WI, 196. 73 15 Feb. 1821, WI, 197. 74 17 Mar. 1822, WI, 199. 75 18/19
Mar. 1822, WI, 199, 200.

THE LADIES OF LLANGOLLEN 1822

1 17 Jan. 1819, WI, 89. 2 20 Sep. 1824, W2, 19. 3 27 June 1822, WI, 207. 4 12/13 July
1822, WI, 212. 5 17 July 1822, WI, 216. 6 Mavor 1973, 74. 7 Pückler 1991, 35. 8 Plas
Newydd catalogue, 6. 9 23 July 1822, WI, 222. 10 13 July 1822, WI, 213. 11 14 July
1822, WI, 214 f. 12 15 July 1822, HG, xlv. 13 23 July 1822, WI, 219–223. 14 25/26
July 1822, WI, 225. 15 To Maria Lawton, [July] 1822, HG, xlvii. 16 3 Aug. 1822, WI,
229. 17 11 Aug. 1822, WI, 231. 18 16 Aug. 1822, WI, 232 f. 19 12 Sep. 1825, W2,
127. 20 25 Aug. 1822, WI, 233 f. 21 3/5 Sep. 1822, WI, 238 f., 240. 22 To Anne Lister
senior, 7 Sep. 1822, G2, 63. 23 11 Sep. 1822, WI, 242. 24 To Anne Lister senior, 22 Sep.
1822, G1, 172 f. 25 27/25 Nov. 1822, WI, 249. 26 10/14 Dec. 1822, WI, 250, 251. 27
27 Nov. 1822, WI, 249.

'FRANK' 1823

1 31 July 1823, WI, 293. 2 2 Dec. 1819, WI, 122. 3 19/17 Feb. 1823, WI, 256. 4 19/26
Feb. 1823, WI, 257. 5 15/19 Mar. 1823, WI, 263. 6 7 Mar. 1823, WI, 261. 7 28 Feb.
1823, WI, 259 f. 8 26 Apr. 1825, W2, 102. 9 28 Feb. 1823, WI, 258 f. 10 12 Mar. 1823,
WI, 262. 11 11 July 1823, WI, 285. 12 4 June 1823, WI, 278. 13 30 Aug. 1823, WI,
314. 14 1 Sep. 1823, WI, 315. 15 31 July 1823, WI, 292. 16 1 Aug. 1823, WI, 293. 17 5
Aug. 1823, WI, 296. 18 30 Aug. 1823, WI, 313 f. 19 5 Aug. 1823, WI, 296. 20 1 Sep.
1823, WI, 315.

MARIANA AND ISABELLA 1823–1824

1 Apr. 1823, WI, 272. 2 15 Feb. 1823, WI, 255. 3 20 July 1823, WI, 288. 4 19 Aug.
1823, WI, 301–305. 5 20 Aug. 1823, WI, 304 f. 6 23 Aug. 1823, WI, 308. 7 20 Aug.
1823, WI, 306. 8 29 Aug. 1823, WI, 312. 9 22 Aug. 1823, WI, 307. 10 25 Aug. 1823,

W1, 310. 11 12/15 Sep. 1823, W1, 316, 317. 12 16 Sep. 1823, W1, 319. 13 17 Sep. 1823, W1, 320, 321 f. 14 15 Sep. 1823, W1, 317. 15 22/24 Sep. 1823, W1, 323, 325. 16 28 Sep. 1823, W1, 327. 17 15 Oct. 1823, W1, 329. 18 2 Nov. 1823, W1, 334. 19 15 Jan. 1824, W1, 350. 20 21 Feb. 1824, W1, 354. 21 16 Mar. 1824, W1, 357 f. 22 24 Mar. 1824, W1, 358 f. 23 27 July 1824, W1, 382. 24 29 July 1824, W1, 385. 25 27/28 Aug. 1823, W1, 310, 311. 26 21 Nov. 1823, W1, 339. 27 8 Dec. 1823, W1, 342. 28 23 Aug. 1823, W1, 309.

MARIA 1824–1825

1 To Anne Lister senior, 27 Aug. 1824, G2, 67, 69 f. 2 To Sibella Maclean, 12 Sep. 1824, G1, 214. 3 To Anne Lister senior, 28 Sep. 1824, G1, 219. 4 13 Oct. 1824, W2, 27. 5 10/14 Nov. 1824, W2, 43 and 50. 6 To Anne Lister senior, 31 Oct. 1824, G1, 223. 7 9 Oct. 1824, W2, 25. 8 To Anne Lister senior, 12 Sep. 1824, G1, 213. 9 26 Oct. 1824, W2, 37. 10 To Sibella Maclean, [Sep.] 1824, G1, 214. 11 5 Sep. 1824, W2, 14. 12 20 Sep. 1824, W2, 19 f. 13 30 Sep. 1824, W2, 24. 14 1 Oct. 1824, W2, 24. 15 8/10 Oct. 1824, W2, 25. 16 12 Oct. 1824, W2, 26. 17 13 Oct. 1824, W2, 27. 18 14 Oct. 1824, W2, 31 f. 19 15 Oct. 1824, W2, 33. 20 21 Oct. 1824, W2, 35. 21 22/25 Oct. 1824, W2, 36. 22 15 Nov. 1824, W2, 52. 23 5/7 Nov. 1824, W2, 41, 42. 24 13/14 Nov. 1824, W2, 49, 50. 25 25 Oct. 1824, W2, 36. 26 12 Nov. 1824, W2, 48. 27 3/10 Nov. 1824, W2, 40, 43. 28 11 Nov. 1824, W2, 47 f. 29 22 Dec. 1824, W2, 64 f. 30 14 Nov. 1824, W2, 50–52. 31 15 Nov. 1824, W2, 52. 32 20 Oct. 1824, W2, 34. 33 15/12 Nov. 1824, W2, 53, 48. 34 23 Nov. 1824, W2, 55. 35 26/28 Nov. 1824, W2, 57, 58. 36 29 Nov. 1824, W2, 59 f. 37 7 Dec. 1824, W2, 61. 38 15 Dec. 1824, W2, 64. 39 3 Jan. 1825, W2, 68. 40 8 May 1826, W2, 172. 41 3 Jan. 1825, W2, 69. 42 To Anne Lister senior, 17 Jan. 1825, G1, 233. 43 To Anne Lister senior, 5 Jan. 1825, G1, 231. 44 To Anne Lister senior, 17 Jan. 1825, G1, 233. 45 3 Jan. 1825, W2, 68. 46 16/23 Jan. 1825, W2, 75, 76 f. 47 8/24. Jan. 1825, W2, 71, 77. 48 19 March 1825, W2, 85. 49 W2, 55. 50 20 Aug. 1821, W1, 181. 51 19 Mar. 1825, W2, 85. 52 29 Nov. 1824, W2, 60. 53 12 Feb. 1818, W1, 78. 54 23 Sep. 1825, W2, 133. 55 22/31 Mar. 1825, W2, 85, 88. 56 19 Mar. 1825, W2, 85. 57 16 Jan. 1825, W2, 75. 58 8 Jan. 1825, W2, 71. 59 3 Feb. 1825, W2, 78. 60 29 Jan. 1825, W2, 78. 61 24 Feb. 1825, W2, 81. 62 20 Feb. 1825, W2, 80. 63 17 Mar. 1825, W1, 84 f. 64 23 Jan. 1825, W2, 76 f. 65 3 Jan. 1825, W2, 68. 66 24 Jan. 1825, W2, 77. 67 31 Mar. 1825, W2, 88 f. 68 12/14 Apr. 1825, W2, 98. 69 To Maria Barlow, 16 June 1825, G1, 254. 70 23 Apr. 1825, W2, 101. 71 From Maria Barlow, Apr. 1825, W2, 99. 72 23 Apr. 1825, W2, 100f. 73 26 May 1825, W2, 105. 74 16 June 1825, W2, 106. 75 20 May 1825, W2, 104. 76 16 June 1825, W2, 106. 77 To Maria Barlow, 16 June 1825, G1, 252. 78 19 June 1825, W2, 106.

MARIANA 1825–1826

1 16/8 Aug. 1825, W2, 116, 114. 2 11 Aug. 1825, W2, 115. 3 18 Aug. 1825, W2, 112. 4

16 Aug. 1825, W2, 116. 5 31 Aug. 1825, W2, 123. 6 28 Nov. 1824, W2, 58 f. 7 1/2. Sep. 1825, W2, 123, 124. 8 4 Sep. 1825, W2, 125. 9 9 Sep. 1825, W2, 126. 10 14 Sep. 1825, W2, 129. 11 12 Sep. 1825, W2, 127. 12 21 Sep. 1825, W2, 131. 13 23 Sep. 1825, W2, 132 f. 14 4 Oct. 1825, W2, 136 f. 15 13 Dec. 1825, W2, 143. 16 8 Apr. 1823, W1, 266. 17 23 Dec. 1825, W2, 148. 18 25/26 Dec. 1825, W2, 149. 19 26 Dec. 1825, W2, 150. 20 28 Dec. 1825, W2, 151 f. 21 31 Dec. 1825, W2, 152 f. 22 5 Jan. 1826, W2, 154. 23 From Maria Barlow, 15 Jan. 1826, W2, 154. 24 26 Jan. 1826, W2, 155 f. 25 L1, 3. 26 14 Feb. 1826, W2, 159. 27 22/27 Feb. 1826, W2, 160, 161. 28 28 Feb. 1826, W2, 161. 29 15/16 Mar. 1826, W2, 163. 30 2. Apr. 1826, W2, 168. 31 16 Mar. 1826, W2, 163. 32 17 Mar. 1826, W2, 164. 33 18 Mar. 1826, W2, 164. 34 6 Feb. 1826, W2, 159. 35 22 Feb. 1826, W2, 160. 36 18 Mar. 1826, W2, 164. 37 27 Mar. 1826, W2, 167. 38 31 Mar. 1826, W2, 167. 39 2 Apr. 1826, W2, 168. 40 27 Mar. 1826, W2, 167. 41 4 May 1826, W2, 171. 42 20 July 1817, Hughes 2009, 14. 43 10 Mar. 1826, W2, 162. 44 5 May 1826, W2, 171. 45 25 May 1826, W2, 173. 46 5 July 1826, W2, 181. 47 17/18 June 1826, W2, 176, 177. 48 20 June 1826, W2, 177. 49 15/16 July 1826, W2, 183. 50 5/7 Aug. 1826, W2, 188 f.

MARIA 1826–1827

1 5 Apr. 1826, W2, 169. 2 21 June 1826, W2, 177. 3 2 Sep. 1826, W2, 190. 4 4/5 Sep. 1826, W2, 190, 191. 5 6 Sep. 1826, W2, 192. 6 8/18 Sep. 1826, W2, 194, 196. 7 29/25 Sep. 1826, W2, 198 197. 8 1 Oct. 1826, W2, 198. 9 10 Oct. 1826, W2, 200. 10 13 Oct. 1826, W2, 202. 11 6 Sep. 1826, W2, 192. 12 To Anne Lister senior, 25 June 1827, G2, 97–99. 13 To Anne Lister senior, 2 July 1827, G2, 102–106. 14 To Anne Lister senior, 11 Sep. 1827, G2, 111. 15 [Sep.] 1827, RAM: 27, 9. 16 15 Apr. 1819, W1, 103. 17 23 Mar. 1828, W2, 205.

SIBELLA 1828–1829

1 To Sibella Maclean, 15 Aug. 1824, G1, 199. 2 To Sibella Maclean, 10 July 1824, G1, 195. 3 To Anne Lister senior, 28 Sep. 1824, G1, 218. 4 10 Aug. 1822, HG, xlvii. 5 To Sibella Maclean, 18 Jan. 1824, G1, 183 f. 6 To Sibella Maclean, [23 Feb. 1824], G1, 185. 7 To Sibella Maclean, 10 July 1824, G1, 195. 8 To Sibella Maclean, 21 June 1824, G1, 190–192. 9 To Sibella Maclean, 18 Jan. 1824, G1, 182f. 10 To Sibella Maclean, 10 July 1824, G1, 194. 11 To William Duffin, 23 July 1828, G1, 316. 12 To Anne Lister senior, 24 May 1828, G1, 310. 13 RAM: 52 –76. 14 Ramsden 1970, 10, 4. 15 3 Sep. 1828, HG lxvii. 16 To Anne Lister senior, 12 Jan./21 Feb. 1829, G1, 330, 334. 17 22 Mar. 1829, HG, lxx.

VERE 1829–1832

1 To Mariana Lawton, [May] 1829, G2, 115. 2 To Lady Stuart, 26 Feb. 1830, G1, 368. 3 To Mariana Lawton, [May] 1829, G2, 115. 4 May to Sep. 1829, RAM: 52–76. 5 To Anne Lister senior, 23 Aug. 1829, G2, 119. 6 To Anne Lister senior, 25 Sep. 1829, G2,

122. 7 To Anne Lister senior, 5 Oct. 1829, G1, 352. 8 From Lady Gordon, [26 Aug. 1831], G2, 158. 9 To Lady Gordon, 16 May 1830, G1, 373. 10 To Anne Lister senior, 25 Sep. 1829, G2, 122f. 11 To Anne Lister senior, 5 Oct. 1829, G1, 352. 12 Sep/Oct 1829, RAM: 52–76. 13 Ramsden's paraphrase, 12 Feb. 1830, RAM: 52–76. 14 24 Dec. 1829, RAM: 28, 7. 15 [Early 1830], RAM: 28, 8. 16 16 Apr. 1830, RAM: 28, 9. 17 [May 1830], RAM: 28, 12. 18 [July 1830], RAM: 29, 3. 19 [Early Aug. 1830], RAM: 29, 5. 20 To Lady Stuart de Rothesay, 21 Feb. 1839, G1, 509. 21 23 July 1838, Ingham 1969, 59, referring to this excursion in 1830. 22 To William Duffin, 20 Dec. 1830, G2, 145. 23 To Anne Lister senior, 13 Sep. 1830, G2, 134. 24 26 Aug. 1830, RAM: 29, 7. 25 To Lady Stuart de Rothesay, 21 Feb. 1839, G1, 509. 26 27 Aug. 1830, RAM: 29, 7. 27 To Anne Lister senior, 13 Sep. 1830, G2, 134 f. 28 [28 Aug. 1830], RAM: 29, 8. 29 To Anne Lister senior, 10 Oct. 1830, G2, 137. 30 To Anne Lister senior, 13 Sep. 1830, G2, 134. 31 [Late Sep. 1830], RAM: 29, 9. 32 To William Duffin, 20 Dec. 1830, G2, 147. 33 16 Nov. 1830, HG, lxxv. 34 17 Dec. 1830, HG lxxv. 35 From Marian Lister, 11 Apr. 1831, G1, 402. 36 To Vere Hobart, 18 Jan. 1830, G1, 365. 37 From Vere Hobart, 8 June 1831, G2, 150. 38 To Anne Lister senior, 9 Aug. 1831, G2, 156. 39 To Mariana Lawton, 5 Oct. 1834, Liddington 1994, 61. 40 To Anne Lister senior, 20 Aug. 1831, G2, 157 f. 41 To Anne Lister senior, 15 Sep. 1831, G2, 159. 42 12 Sep. 1831, HG, lxxviii. 43 To Anne Lister senior, 15 Sep. 1831, G2, 159. 44 20 Sep. 1831, RAM: 52–76. 45 To Anne Lister senior, 15 Oct. 1831, G2, 163. 46 To Anne Lister senior, 10 Nov. 1831, G1, 416. 47 To Anne Lister senior, 23 Aug. 1829, G2, 120. 48 Nov. 1831 to Apr. 1832, RAM: 52–76. 49 3/15 Apr. 1832, Euler 1995, 293, 294. 50 15 Apr. 1832, L2, 13 f. 51 16 Apr. 1832, L2, 14. 52 16–22 Apr. 1832, RAM: 52–76. 53 18 Apr. 1832, L2, 14 f. 54 To Mrs Hamilton, 9 Apr. 1832, G1, 427. 55 To Vere Hobart, 31 May 1830, G1, 375. 56 From and to Lady Gordon, 24/30 June 1830, G1, 382. 57 29 Apr. 1832, L2, 15. 58 To Anne Lister senior, 29 Apr. 1832, G1, 428.

ANN 1832–1840

Neighbours

1 23 Mar. 1832, L2, 10. 2 8 May 1832, L2, 21. 3 12 Aug. 1832, L2, 48. 4 17 May 1832, L2, 25. 5 8 May 1832, L2, 21. 6 19/30 May 1832, L2, 29, 32. 7 23/30 May 1832, L2, 31, 32. 8 6 Jan. 1831, RAM: 52–76. 9 18 May 1832, L2, 28. 10 12 June 1821, W1, 169 f. 11 Euler 1995, 296. 12 18 June 1822, W1, 206 f. 13 John Walker's will, L1, 34. 14 To Anne Lister senior, 13 Aug. 1828, G1, 317. 15 Henry Edwards to Elizabeth Sutherland, 30 Aug. 1831, L1, 37. 16 3 Sep. 1831, L1, 37. 17 30 Aug. 1828, L1, 35. 18 10/17 Aug. 1832, L2, 46, 49. 19 28 Sep. 1832, L2, 66. 20 31 Aug. 1832, L2, 53. 21 1 Oct. 1832, L2, 70. 22 3/5 Sep. 1832, L2, 55, 56. 23 12 Aug. 1832, L2, 48. 24 1 Oct. 1832, L2, 70. 25 11 Mar. 1824, W1, 356. 26 29 Sep. 1832, L2, 67. 27 27 Sep. 1832, L2, 63 f. 28 28 Sep. 1832, L2, 65. 29 29 Sep. 1832, L2, 67. 30 28 Sep. 1832, L2, 65 f. 31 29 Sep. 1832, L2, 67. 32

1 Oct. 1832, L2, 69 f. 33 1 Oct. 1832, L2, 70. 34 4 Oct. 1832, L2, 71 f. 35 4 Oct. 1832, L2, 72. 36 5 Oct. 1832, L2, 73. 37 5 Oct. 1832, L2, 73 f. 38 7 Oct. 1832, L2, 75. 39 8 Oct. 1832, L2, 76. 40 19 June 1824, W1, 374. 41 8 Oct. 1832, L2, 76. 42 11 Oct. 1832, L2, 78. 43 14 May 1821, W1, 168. 44 5/11 Oct. 1832, L2, 74, 78. 45 5 Oct. 1832, L2, 74. 46 11 Oct. 1832, L2, 77. 47 [Oct.] 1832, L2, 80. 48 15/16 Oct. 1832, L2, 78 f. 49 26 Oct. 1832, L2, 82. 50 1 Nov. 1832, L2, 84. 51 2 Nov. 1832, L2, 85. 52 5 Nov. 1832, L2, 86. 53 7 Nov. 1832, L2, 88. 54 From Ann Walker, 9 Nov. 1832, L2, 88. 55 27 Nov. 1832, L2, 91. 56 4 Oct. 1832, L2, 73. 57 25 Nov. 1832, L1, 68. 58 6 Dec. 1832, L2, 94 f. 59 25 Nov. 1832, L2, 90. 60 8 Dec. 1832, L2, 96. 61 19 Dec. 1832, L2, 101. 62 11 Dec. 1832, L2, 97. 63 14 Dec. 1832, L2, 99. 64 22 Dec. 1832, L2, 102. 65 26/25 Dec. 1832, L2, 103, 102. 66 31 Dec. 1832, L2, 103 f. 67 8 Jan. 1833, L1, 70. 68 25 Dec. 1828, HG, lxviii. 69 16/18 Feb. 1833, L1, 71 f.

Separation

1 To Anne Lister senior, 26 June 1831, G2, 150 f. 2 To Lady Stuart, 2 Dec. 1838, G1, 506. 3 19 May 1832, HG, lxxx. 4 11 Dec. 1832, HG, lxxxii. 5 11 May 1832, L2, 23. 6 17 Aug. 1833, RAM: 52–76. 7 To Mariana Lawton, 18 Nov. 1839, G1, 514. 8 To Anne Lister senior, 15 Sep. 1833, G1, 451–455. 9 21 Oct. 1833, HG lxxxvi. 10 To Anne Lister senior, 15 Oct. 1833, G1, 457. 11 To Mariana Lawton, 26 Oct. 1833, HG, lxxxvi. 12 To Anne Lister senior, 9 Nov. 1833, G1, 459. 13 To Anne Lister senior, 21 Sep. 1833, G1, 454. 14 To Anne Lister senior, 9 Nov. 1833, G1, 458. 15 15/21 Dec. 1833, RAM: 30, 7. 16 23 Dec. 1833, L1, 83.

Marriage

1 From Ann Walker, 27/30 Dec. 1833, L1, 84. 2 23 Oct. 1832, L2, 80. 3 4/5 Jan. 1834, L1, 85. 4 8 Jan. 1834, L1, 86. 5 11/7 Jan. 1834, L1, 86f. 6 8 May 1833, L1, 73. 7 13 May 1834, L1, 104. 8 4 Mar. 1834, L1, 96. 9 4 Feb. 1834, L1, 90. 10 10 Feb. 1834, L1, 92 f. 11 12/9 Feb. 1834, L1, 93, 92. 12 27/28 Feb. 1834, L1, 95. 13 17 Apr. 1834, L1, 102. 14 30 May 1834, L1, 107. 15 3/4 Apr. 1834, L1, 100 f. 16 22 Mar. 1834, L1, 99. 17 To Mariana Lawton, 27 Jan. 1834, G1, 466. 18 17 Apr. 1834, L1, 102. 19 23 Feb. 1834, L1, 94 f. 20 7 Mar. 1834, L1, 97. 21 8 Mar. 1834, L1, 98. 22 26 Aug. 1832, L2, 51. 23 17 Apr. 1834, L1, 102. 24 15 Mar. 1834, L1, 99. 25 30 May 1834, L1, 107. 26 21/22 May 1834, L1, 106, 107.

Honeymoon

1 Ann Walker to Anne Lister senior, 20 June 1834, G1, 472. 2 To Anne Lister senior, 13 June 1834, G1, 470. 3 To Anne Lister senior, 1 July 1834, G1, 473 f. 4 To Anne Lister senior, 22 July 1834, G2, 182 f. 5 From Anne Lister senior, 9 July 1834, G1, 475. 6 Ann Walker to Anne Lister senior, 22 July 1834, G2, 183 f. 7 Ann Walker to Anne Lister senior, 16 Aug. 1834, G2, 186. 8 To Isabella Norcliffe, 14 Oct. 1834, HG, xc.

NOTES

At Shibden Hall

1 1 Dec. 1834, L1, 131. 2 16 Oct. 1834, L1, 121. 3 20 Feb. 1836, L1, 149. 4 8 Sep. 1834,
L1, 111. 5 2 Oct. 1834, L1, 115 f. 6 Ann Walker to Elizabeth Sutherland, 15 Oct. 1834,
L1, 121 f. 7 7/8 Oct. 1834, L1, 116, 117. 8 [July 1835], L1, 182. 9 23 Dec. 1834, L1,
136. 10 23/25 Dec. 1834, L1, 136. 11 26/27 Dec. 1834, L1, 137. 12 26 Feb. 1835, L1,
151. 13 6/7/8 Jan. 1835, L1, 140–142, cf. HG, xc [2]. 14 10/12 Jan. 1835, L1, 143 f. 15
To Mariana Lawton, 31 Mar. 1835, L1, 158. 16 8 Apr. 1835, L1, 161. 17 11 Feb. 1835, L1,
148. 18 15 Mar. 1835, L1, 156. 19 13 Mar. 1835, L1, 155. 20 8 Apr. 1835, L1, 160. 21 28
Oct. 1834, L1, 122. 22 21 Apr. 1835, L1, 166. 23 George Sutherland to Robert Parker,
20 July 1835, L1, 185. 24 17/19 Sep. 1835, L1, 189, 190. 25 28/19 Sep. 1835, L1, 193,
190. 26 17 Oct. 1834, L1, 121 f. 27 To Mariana Lawton, 29 Nov. 1835, HG, xcv. 28
28 Aug. 1835, L1, 188. 29 26/28 Sep. 1835, HG, XCV and L1, 190, 192 f. 30 To Lady
Stuart, 2 Dec. 1838, G1, 506. 31 17 Aug. 1832, L2, 49. 32 HG, xiii. 33 27 Nov. 1835,
L1, 199. 34 24 Aug. 1835, L1, 187. 35 4 Oct. 1835, L1, 195. 36 26 Nov. 1835, L1,
196. 37 1 Aug. 1835, L1, 185 f. 38 8 Aug. 1835, L1, 186. 39 20 Apr. 1834, HG, xc. 40
[Early] Aug. 1835, HG, xciv. 41 [Aug.] 1835, L1, 186. 42 2 Oct. 1834, L1, 116. 43 14
Aug. 1835, L1, 187. 44 14/17 Oct. 1834, L1, 118, 121. 45 25 Feb. 1835, L1, 150. 46 23
Mar. 1835, L1, 157. 47 14 Aug. 1835, L1, 187. 48 29 Aug. 1835, L1, 188. 49 23 Aug.
1835, L1, 187. 50 23 Nov. 1835, L1, 198. 51 12 Dec. 1835, L1, 202. 52 11 Mar. 1836,
L1, 211. 53 24 Nov. 1822, W1, 249. 54 23 June 1822, W1, 207. 55 Liddington 2001,
49, calculated for 1838. In the 1830s, the coded passages make up only about a tenth of
her diaries. 56 11 Nov. 1834, L1, 126. 57 8 Aug. 1835, L1, 186. 58 23 Nov. 1835, L1,
198. 59 10 Feb. 1836, L1, 206. 60 10 Mar. 1836, L1, 210. 61 16/13 Mar. 1836, L1, 213,
212. 62 23 Mar. 1836, L1, 217. 63 27 Mar. 1836, L1, 221. 64 3 Apr. 1836, L1, 226 f. 65
11 Apr. 1836, L1, 228 f. 66 11 Mar. 1836, L1, 211. 67 26 Apr. 1836, L1, 231. 68 4/8
May 1836, L1, 233, 233 f. 69 16 Apr. 1836, L1, 230. 70 7 Mar. 1838, RAM: 52–76. 71
24 Dec. 1836, 2/3/7 Mar., 29 Apr., 12 May 1837, RAM: 52–76. 72 12 May 1837, L1,
235. 73 15/24/29/30 June, 3/4/16 July 1837, RAM: 52 –76. 74 16/17/28 Aug. 1837,
RAM: 52 –76. 75 8 Apr. 1835, L1, 161. 76 19 Sep., 7 Oct. 1837, RAM: 52–76. 77 13
Feb. 1838, RAM: 52–76.

France

1 To Vere Cameron, 3 June 1838, G1, 503. 2 8 June 1838, RAM: 52–76. 3 To Lady
Stuart de Rothesay, 21 Feb. 1839, G1, 508. 4 5 July/19 Aug/9 July 1838, RAM: 52–
76. 5 To Lady Stuart de Rothesay, 21 Feb. 1839, G1, 508. 6 24 July 1838, Ingham 1969,
59–61. 7 25 July 1838, Ingham 1969, 62. 8 To Mariana Lawton, 1 Nov. 1838, G1, 505. 9
6 Aug. 1838, Ingham 1969, 63–65. 10 To Mariana Lawton, 1 Nov. 1838, G1, 505. 11 6
Aug. 1838, Ingham 1969, 65. 12 7 Aug. 1838, Ingham 1969, 64–66. 13 To Lady Stuart
de Rothesay, 21 Feb. 1839, G1, 509. 14 14/15 Aug. 1838, Ingham 1969, 66, 67. 15 16
Aug. 1838, Ingham 1969, 68. 16 17/18 Aug. 1838, Ingham 1969, 69. 17 21/27 Aug.

1838, Ingham 1969, 69. 18 [Aug.] 1838, Ingham 1968, 203. 19 14 Sep./18/25 Aug. 1838, RAM: 52–76.

The Brontës

1 7 Jan. 1839, HG, cviii. 2 Davies 1994, 197 f. 3 George Nussey, the brother of Charlotte Brontë's best friend Ellen Nussey, was also treated in Belcombe's asylum from 1845, and it served as the basis for the psychiatric hospital 'The Retreat'. Charlotte was shocked by Belcombe's treatment methods. 4 [July 1835], L1, 278. 5 To Anne Lister senior, 17 June 1833, G1, 441. 6 To Lady Stuart, 2 Dec. 1838, G1, 506. 7 3/4 Dec. 1838, RAM: 52–76. 8 Ramsden 1970, 8. Setting up the Walker Pit had cost around £250, see L1, 201; in the second half of 1836 Anne mined coal from it at a value of £13. 9 3 Dec. 1838, Liddington 2001, 58. 10 5 Jan. 1839, RAM: 52–76. 11 3 May 1839, RAM: 52–76. 12 25 Apr. 1839, RAM: 52 –76. 13 25 Apr. 1839, Liddington 1995, 271. 14 To Vere Cameron, 3 Apr. 1837, G1, 494. 15 To Vere Cameron, 9 Sep. 1832, HG, lxxxiii (2). 16 25 Sep. 1832, HG, lxxxiii (2). 17 7 May 1839, HG, cix. 18 To Vere Cameron, 23 Dec. 1837, G1, 498–499. 19 To Lady Stuart, 26 May 1835, G1, 481. 20 To Sophie Ferrall, 19 Dec. 1838, G1, 507.

From Halifax to Moscow

1 To Messrs Hammersleys & Co., 28 Apr. 1836, G1, 488. 2 To Vere Cameron, 13 Jan. 1840, G2, 192. 3 Ca. 7/12 July 1839, RAM: 10, 9. 4 To Mariana Lawton, 18 Nov. 1839, G1, 512 f. 5 21 July 1839, RAM: 10, 5. 6 To Mariana Lawton, 18 Nov. 1839, G1, 513. 7 14 Aug. 1839, RAM: 10, 8. 8 To Mariana Lawton, 18 Nov. 1839, G1, 513. 9 To Vere Cameron, 13 Jan. 1840, G2, 193 f. 10 To Mariana Lawton, 18 Nov. 1839, G1, 513. 11 To Vere Cameron, 13 Jan. 1840, G2, 194. 12 To Mariana Lawton, 18 Nov. 1839, G1, 513 f. 13 To Marian Lister, 3 Feb. 1840, G1, 524. 14 To Mariana Lawton, 18 Nov. 1839, G1, 513. 15 16 Sep. 1839, RAM: 10, 12. 16 8–17 Sep. 1839, RAM: 10, 11 f. 17 To Vere Cameron, 13 Jan. 1840, G2, 194. 18 To Mariana Lawton, 18 Nov. 1839, G1, 514. 19 12 Oct. 1839, RAM: 11, 2. 20 20 Oct. 1839, RAM: 11, 6. 21 To Vere Cameron, 13 Jan. 1840, G2, 196. 22 [Oct.] 1839, RAM: 11, 4. 23 [Late Nov.] 1839, RAM: 11, 7. 24 31 Oct. 1839, RAM: 52–76. 25 [Nov. 1839], RAM: 11, 14. 26 28 Jan. 1840, RAM: 11, 14. 27 To Vere Cameron, 13 Jan. 1840, G2, 197. 28 3 Nov. 1839, RAM: 11, 13. 29 11/16/19 Nov., 8 Dec. 1839, RAM: 52–76. 30 16/18 Dec. 1839, RAM: 52–76. 31 20/21 Dec. 1839, RAM: 52–76. 32 [Dec.] 1839, RAM: 12, 3. 33 23 Jan. 1840, RAM: 12, 5. 34 16/17 Jan. 1840, RAM: 12, 9, 10 f. 35 23 Jan. 1840, RAM: 52–76. 36 26/27 Dec. 1839, 24 Jan. 1840, RAM: 52–76. 37 [2 Feb. 1840], RAM: 11, 14.

From Moscow to the Caucasus

1 9–11 Feb. 1840, RAM: 13, 2–5. 2 12 Feb. 1840, RAM: 13, 6. 3 5 Mar. 1840, RAM: 14, 7. 4 24 Feb. 1840, RAM: 13, 13. 5 21 Feb. 1840, RAM: 15, 3. 6 28 Feb. 1840, RAM: 13,

16 f. 7 5 Mar. 1840, RAM: 15, 6. 8 24 Feb. 1840, RAM: 13, 13. 9 11 Mar. 1840, RAM: 14, 14. 10 11 Mar. 1840, RAM: 15, 7-8 and letter to Mariana Lawton, 4 May 1840, G2, 202. 11 4–6 Mar. 1840, RAM: 14, 6, 8–10. 12 9 Mar. 1840, RAM: 14, 6, 12. 13 12 Mar. 1840, RAM: 14, 15. 14 To Mariana Lawton, 4 May 1840, G2, 202. 15 17 Mar. 1840, RAM: 52–76. 16 [Mid] Mar. 1840 RAM: 16, 3. 17 22 Mar. 1840, RAM: 16, 7. 18 30/26 Mar. 1840, RAM: 16, 14, 9. 19 28 Mar. 1840, RAM: 16, 12. 20 1 Apr. 1840, RAM: 16, 16 f. 21 3 Apr. 1840, RAM: 16, 17, 19. 22 To Alexandrine Panina, 23 Apr. 1840, G1, 532. 23 4/5 Apr. 1840, RAM: 17, 1, 2. 24 Pushkin, 1919. 25 8 Apr. 1840, RAM: 17, 8. 26 Georgian names are given in modern English transliteration. 27 9 Apr. 1840, RAM: 17, 9 f. 28 10 Apr. 1840, RAM: 17, 11 f. 29 12 Apr. 1840, RAM: 17, 16. 30 12 Apr. 1840, RAM: 18, 2. 31 To Sophia Radzivill, 29 Apr. 1840, G1, 537. 32 22 June 1840, RAM: 18, 15. 33 20 Apr. 1840, RAM: 18, 5 f. 34 To Mariana Lawton, 4 May 1840, G2, 203. 35 [April or May] 1840, RAM: 25, 1. 36 To Sophia Radzivill, 11 May 1840, G1, 537. 37 1 May 1840, RAM:52–76. 38 24 Apr. 1840, RAM: 18, 5. 39 12 May 1840, RAM: 52–76. 40 3 May 1840, RAM: 19, 2 f. 41 16 May 1840, RAM: 19, 5. 42 18 May 1840, RAM: 19, 7, 8. 43 3 June 1840, RAM: 18, 10. 44 [May] 1840, RAM: 15, 4. 45 23 May 1840, RAM: 19, 11. 46 23 May 1840, RAM: 15, 13. 47 [Late May] 1840, RAM: 19, 12. 48 To Mariana Lawton, 4 May 1840, G2, 203. 49 14/31 May 1840, RAM: 19, 4, 14. 50 1 June 1840, RAM: 19, 14. 51 12 June 1840, RAM: 18, 13. 52 2 May 1840, RAM: 15, 12. 53 24 June 1840, RAM: 20, 2. 54 27 June 1840, RAM: 20, 5. 55 To Sophia Radzivill, 29 Apr. 1840, G1, 537. 56 8 July 1840, RAM: 20, 12. 57 9 July 1940, RAM: 22, 1. 58 8/10 July 1840, RAM: 24, 6, 9. 59 2 Aug. 1840, RAM: 24, 5. 60 19 July 1840, RAM: 24, 6. 61 11 July 1840, RAM: 23, 4. 62 17 July 1840, RAM: 24, 3. 63 18/19 July 1840, RAM: 22, 11–13. 64 [21] July 1840, RAM: 21, 2. 65 24 July 1840, RAM: 23, 6. 66 13 July 1840, RAM: 23, 2f. 67 Late July 1840, RAM: 24, 2. 68 27 July 1840, RAM: 24, 12. 69 30 July 1840, RAM: 24, 3. 70 8 Aug. 1840, RAM: 25, 4. 71 28 July 1840, RAM: 24, 13. 72 7 Aug. 1840, RAM: 24, 8 f. 73 8/9 Aug. 1840, RAM: 25, 5 f. 74 9 Aug. 1840, RAM: 25, 9. 75 [9] Aug. 1840, RAM: 21, 7. 76 10 Aug. 1840, RAM: 25, 6, 9. 77 11 Aug. 1840, G2, 205. 78 11 Aug. 1840, RAM: 25, 10. 79 *Halifax Guardian*, 31 Oct. 1840, G2, 206.

The Widow

1 *Halifax Guardian*, 31 Oct. 1840, G2, 206. 2 Liddington 1994, 60. 3 Memorandum by Robert Parker, 9 Sep. 1843, Liddington 1994, 11. 4 George Sutherland to John Lister senior, 27 Sep. 1844, L1, 238 f.

JOHN, MURIEL, VIVIEN, PHYLLIS, HELENA, JILL & ANGELA

1 *Shibden Hall. A Visitor's Guide*, 2010, 5. 2 Liddington 1994, 17. Green suppressed, for instance, the notes with which Ann Walker and Anne Lister arranged to meet in the autumn of 1832. 3 Ingham 1969, 55. 4 Ramsden 1970, 1. 5 Anderson 1995, 191. 6

Ingham 1968, 199. 7 Ingham 1969, 56. 8 Ingham 1969, 55. 9 Ramsden 1970, 4, 10 f. 10 W1, xvii. 11 Liddington 1994, 24.

EPILOGUE: READING ANNE LISTER'S WRITING

1 18 June 1824, W1, 373. 2 To Sibella Maclean, 3 June 1824, G1, 190. 3 To Sibella Maclean, 21 June 1824, G1, 192. 4 28 Nov. 1824, W2, 58. 5 31 May 1824, W1, 371. 6 22 June 1821, W1, 171. 7 16 Oct. 1831, RAM: 38. 8 24 Aug. 1822, W1, 233. 9 Fichte [1796] 1845, 311.

Illustrations and Maps

While every effort has been made to contact copyright holders of illustrations, the author and publishers would be grateful for information about any illustrations where credit has not been found. Amendments would be made in any further editions.

1   Map of northern England, Laura Fronterré.
2   Manor House School, York, 1822, copperplate by Henry Cave.
3   First page of Anne Lister's diary. West Yorkshire Archive Service, Calderdale, SH: 7/ML/E/26.
4   Letter from Anne Lister to Eliza Raine, 21 February 1808. West Yorkshire Archive Service, Calderdale, SH: 7/ML/A/8.
5   *Mrs Duffin in York*, watercolour by Mary Ellen Best from: *The World of Mary Ellen Best* by Caroline Davidson (Chatto & Windus, 1986).
6   *Isabella Norcliffe (far left) and her family in Langton Hall*, watercolour by Mary Ellen Best from: *The World of Mary Ellen Best* by Caroline Davidson (Chatto & Windus, 1986).
7   *Bootham Bar, York*. Copperplate by W. H. Bartlett.
8   *Anne Lister*, miniature portrait. Calderdale Leisure Services, Shibden Hall, Halifax.
9   *Anne Lister*, 1817 or later.
10 *Anne Lister senior*, oil painting by Thomas Binns; Calderdale Leisure Services, Shibden Hall, Halifax.
11 *The 'Ladies of Llangollen'* Miss Sarah Ponsonby (left) and Lady Eleanor Butler (right), lithograph by an unknown artist.
12 Anne Lister's diary, 15 September 1822. West Yorkshire Archive Service, Calderdale, SH: 7/ML/E/6.

13 *James Lister*, oil painting by Joshua Horner (assumed); Calderdale Leisure Services, Shibden Hall, Halifax.

14 Map of Halifax and Lightcliffe, Laura Fronterré.

15 Halifax, 1836. Copperplate by N. Whittock in: *Concise History of the Parish and Vicarage of Halifax* by John Crabtree, 1836; Calderdale Leisure Services, Shibden Hall, Halifax.

16 Letter from Ann Walker to Anne Lister, 24 December 1832; West Yorkshire Archive Service, Calderdale, SH: 7/ML/644/1.

17 Shibden Hall before Anne Lister's alterations, *c.*1835, lithograph by John Horner, from: *Buildings in the Town and Parish of Halifax. Drawn from Nature and on Stone by John Horner*, 1835; Calderdale Leisure Services, Libraries Division.

18 Shibden Hall, draft for an extension by John Harper, 1836. West Yorkshire Archive Service, Calderdale, SH: 2/M/2/7.

19 Anne Lister's and Ann Walker's journey through tsarist Russia in 1839–40, Laura Fronterré.

20 Anne Lister's last journal page, 11 August 1840; West Yorkshire Archive Service, Calderdale, SH: 7/ML/E/24.

21 *Anne Lister*, posthumous *c.*1841, oil painting by Joshua Horner (assumed); Calderdale Leisure Services, Shibden Hall, Halifax.